DEAD FLESH

The police dog brought back a human bone with decayed flesh hanging from it. Investigators followed the trail and discovered a human spine and bits of teeth covered with maggots.

Then the bodies surfaced.

The first body was male, badly decomposed from months in a shallow grave. His feet had been gnawed off by wild animals.

Diggers found two more bodies, wrapped in sleeping bags, buried together. Both victims were bound hand and foot, a hard ball S&M device jammed into the mouth, head bagged with a plastic sheath. Cause of death: bullet wounds to the head.

As the grisly excavation continued, evidence of dozens of murder victims surfaced: eyeglasses, bloody clothing, wallets, checkbooks and handcuffs.

Three more bodies added to the terrible results. One body was even encased in lime to speed up the decomposition.

Evidence of human cremation and dismemberment added to the horrific discoveries of the police investigators.

After weeks of digging, authorities found six full corpses, various organ parts and a total of 45 pounds of human bone fragments from victims ranging in age from two to forty.

Enough for at least twenty-five more victims.

BOOK YOUR PLACE ON OUR WEBSITE AND MAKE THE READING CONNECTION!

We've created a customized website just for our very special readers, where you can get the inside scoop on everything that's going on with Zebra, Pinnacle and Kensington books.

When you come online, you'll have the exciting opportunity to:

- View covers of upcoming books
- Read sample chapters
- Learn about our future publishing schedule (listed by publication month *and author*)
- Find out when your favorite authors will be visiting a city near you
- Search for and order backlist books from our online catalog
- Check out author bios and background information
- Send e-mail to your favorite authors
- Meet the Kensington staff online
- Join us in weekly chats with authors, readers and other guests
- Get writing guidelines
- AND MUCH MORE!

**Visit our website at
http://www.pinnaclebooks.com**

DIE FOR ME

The Terrifying True Story of the Charles Ng & Leonard Lake Torture Murders

Don Lasseter

Pinnacle Books
Kensington Publishing Corp.

http://www.pinnaclebooks.com

PINNACLE BOOKS are published by

Kensington Publishing Corp.
850 Third Avenue
New York, NY 10022

First Pinnacle Printing: May, 2000
10 9 8 7 6 5

Printed in the United States of America

Chapter 1

October 1983
Wilseyville California

Settling into a well-worn brown fabric recliner chair, Leonard Lake turned his placid green eyes toward a tripod-mounted video camera and spoke in a calm, soft voice with no trace of any emotion. "Good evening. It's Sunday, October . . . twenty-second, twenty-third, something like that. Very close to my thirty-eighth birthday, and I'm starting this tape without script or without any real organization of what I want to say. But I do feel I need to explain."

Apparently alone in the room, occasionally leaning his head back to gaze toward the ceiling, then once more facing the camera lens, and crossing his ankles on the footrest, the burly, balding speaker continued. "This tape, which you're hearing now, is going to be the lead-in of the various phases of construction of a building which, hopefully, will be the first of a series of underground buildings.'' As if to rationalize the purpose, he described plans to erect what he called a tool and storage room. With no change in his quiescent tone, Lake gradually admitted a much more sinister intention for the planned structure. "But the main emphasis of the building, the whole justification for its expense and its effort, will be a hidden portion . . . a secret room, if we can call it that, that will house a cell . . . a jail cell, if you will.''

Dressed in a long-sleeved black-and-white patterned shirt, faded jeans, and brown boots, Lake clasped his hands in his lap. Still exhibiting no signs of excitement, he explained, "The purpose of that cell . . . will be the imprisonment of a young lady who probably, at this moment, is unknown to me.''

Drifting away from the chilling hint of capturing a woman, Lake turned to a rambling narration of his personal philosophy. "These are troubled times. There are wars and rumors of wars going on. Today, one hundred thirty-five Marines were killed in Lebanon. . . .'' Lake misstated the casualty count in his reference to a stunning tragedy that took place earlier that same Sunday, October 23, 1983, in Beirut. A terrorist had crashed a truckload of explosives into the U.S. Marine Corps headquarters building, taking the lives of at least 216 Marines in the massive explosion. Lake, having served with the Corps in Vietnam, identified closely with the fallen leathernecks. After mustering out, he had concluded that an imminent holocaust would wipe out most of humanity. The only survivors, Lake theorized, were those who possessed the foresight to build bunkers in the mountains and stock them with food, weapons, and money. His personal bunker, though, would also provide a place to live out his dark sexual fantasies.

Lake's soliloquy continued, describing the concrete and steel bunker he visualized. It would be ". . . designed not around the cell, but ultimately around the concept of a secret, secure living place for myself and perhaps for friends.'' But, he admitted, ". . . it would be a lie to say it was for anything other than primarily emphasizing the cell."

Leonard Lake's favorite book, *The Collector*, by John Fowles, told the tale of a butterfly collector who carried out his fantasy of capturing and enslaving a young woman. It meshed perfectly with Lake's own hidden desire. The idea of having complete control over a female slave formed the most erotic thrill he could imagine.

Wondering aloud about recording his most intimate thoughts on video, Lake said, "Posterity may care less about this tape, care less about what I have to say. To be honest, I'm not too sure who I want to show this tape to, or if I will ever show it to anyone. But, for anyone that is interested, anyone who needs my justification and my rationalizations as to why I would want to imprison, and, in fact, enslave [a woman] they have only to look closely at me. I'm a realist. I'm thirty-eight years old, a bit chubby, not much hair and losing what I have, not particularly attracted to women." Realizing his mistake, Lake corrected it. "Or, I should say, particularly *attracting* to women. All of the traditional magnets, the money, position, power, I don't have. And yet, I'm still very sexually active, and I'm still very much attracted to a particular type of woman who, almost by definition, is totally uninterested in me. Dirty, old man. Pervert." His hand gestures became momentarily animated.

"I'm attracted to young women. Sometimes even as young as twelve, although to be fair, certainly up to eighteen to twenty-two is a pretty much ideal range as far as my interests go. I like very slim women, very pretty, of course petite, small-breasted, long hair. [But] such a woman, by virtue of her youth, her attractiveness, her desirability to . . . the majority of mankind, simply has better options. There's no particular reason why such a woman should be interested in me. But there's more to it than that. It's difficult to explain my personality in twenty-five words or less, but I am, in fact, a loner. I enjoy peace. The quiet, the solitude. I enjoy being by myself, and while my relationships with women in the past have been sexually successful, socially they've been almost always a failure. I've gone through two divorces, innumerable women, fifty to fifty-five, I forget exactly the count.''

Pausing for a moment to stare at the ceiling, and again folding his hands in his lap, Lake sighed and sounded almost bored. ''I'm afraid the bottom-line statement is the simple fact that I'm a sexist slob. I enjoy using women and, of course, women aren't particularly interested in being used. I certainly enjoy sex. I certainly enjoy the dominance of climbing on a woman and using her body. But I'm not particularly interested in the id, the ego, all the things that a man should be interested in to complement a woman's needs. Now I can fake these emotions, and I can fake them very well. And in the past I've been very successful with attracting interesting and attractive women, simply because I did fake fairly well an interest in their needs and their requirements. So, momentarily, I had what I wanted, and they thought they had what they wanted. But, in the long term, I don't want to bother. What I want is an off-the-shelf sex partner. I want to be able to use a woman whenever and however I want. And when I'm tired or satiated or bored or not interested, I simply want to put her away. Lock her up in a little room, get her out of my sight, out of my life, and thus avoid what heretofore has always been the obligation to entertain or amuse or satisfy a particular woman or girlfriend's whims of emotional whatevers.''

Recognizing the shortcomings of his views, Lake acknowledged certain problems. ''Such an arrangement,'' he confessed, ''is not only blatantly sexist, but highly illegal, there's no doubt about that it. It violates all of the human rights and blah, blah, blah, blah, blah, and I'm going to spare posterity *my* concepts of other people's morality. I'm explaining *my* morality, what *I* feel, what *I* want, and as of this moment, I'm going to try to get. The advantages of such a situation are, of course, obvious and, even beyond sexual, such a woman, totally enslaved, would be useful for the mundane chores I have to do, but am not particularly interested in doing: clean house, washing dishes, et cetera. A slave. There's no way around it. Primarily a sexual slave, but nonetheless a physical slave, as well.''

Still expressionless, with his voice modulated not much louder than a husky whisper, Lake said, ''And I believe that if I can construct a holding cell, a place where I can put such a woman, where I can walk off and feel secure that she can't escape, that I can create a facility that is so stark, and so empty, so cold, so quiet, so totally removed from the world, that fairly quickly, by a combination of painful punishments when I'm displeased, and minor rewards such as music or magazines or some such stuff, that I can quickly condition—this is my belief—that I can quickly condition a young woman to cooperate with me fully, and in fact, even look forward to cooperating with me, simply for no other reason than such cooperation would be a relief from boredom.''

Taking a breath, and pausing no more that a few seconds, Lake added, ''Whether I can do this or not will remain to be seen. Obviously, I've never done such a thing before, and it may not work. However, I want to try. I want to try.'' Costs and logistics of constructing the bunker occupied Lake's monologue for a minute before his electric green eyes bored into the camera lens again. ''Life, as I am living it, is boring. The challenge of this project, the excitement, the thrill of it will be an exciting experience even if it fails. As long as I don't get caught, it's very attractive. It's something that I've fantasized daily about. We'll see. I don't think there's much more to say on the subject. This, hopefully, will be a mystery.''

Within a few days, Lake aimed his video camera at a churning yellow backhoe taking huge bites of earth from a hillside near the mountain house in which he had dictated what would one day be known as ''the philosophy tape.'' Pine and cedar trees surrounded the idyllic mountain site near Wilseyville, California, where miners had swarmed the cascading streams and tunneled the rich earth 135 years earlier in search of gold. Lake's videography recorded a growling chain saw ripping away trees, and a dark-coated German shepherd warily observing the backhoe as it dug a foundation for the sex-slave bunker. As the animal's interest changed, Lake noted, "Uh-oh. Little dog chasing a butterfly." In John Fowles's novel, the protagonist chases butterflies. In Leonard Lake's fantasy, he would leave flying insects to the dog. More erotic prey occupied his mind.

Panting into the video camera's microphone, he said, "I can hardly wait."

Chapter 2

April 1985
Milpitas, California

At the age of eighteen, Kathleen Elizabeth Allen felt pretty good about her life. Long dark hair tumbling past her shoulders, with full lips and exotically tilted brown eyes that she sometimes overdecorated with makeup, Kathi created a package most men found attractive despite her ongoing battle to keep her weight down. She always wore her favorite piece of jewelry, a gold chain from which a floating heart dangled.

Kathi spent as much time as possible with her younger sister, Dian, and her Japanese mother, Sumiko, in their San Jose, California, home at the lower tip of San Francisco Bay. Dian thought Kathi was "strong and intelligent." Of course, with an age gap of over two years, the siblings sometimes had misunderstandings. But, recalled Dian, "Kathi could always make me laugh, and if I had problems, she always had an answer for me. She had a knack for being everyone's friend.'' Dian recalled an evening near the end of March 1985, when she had needed to talk about some problems. In any emergency, Dian knew where to turn, so she had telephoned her sister. Without any hesitation, Kathi had driven from her workplace to pick up Dian so they could chat about it. Kathi's presence worked its usual magic.

Because their mother, Sumiko, struggled with the English language, Kathi frequently came to the rescue by volunteering to act as interpreter. Sumiko's live-in mate also expressed fondness for Kathi, characterizing her as ''loving and tolerant.''

A full-time job at the Safeway supermarket in nearby Milpitas, where she had worked for most of a year, allowed Kathi Allen to support herself. Her boyfriend, Michael Sean Carroll, twenty-three, contributed to their entertainment expenses with his earnings from a pizza restaurant, and provided most of their transportation with his 1974 yellow Mercury Capri. Because he'd served time on federal drug charges at Leavenworth Prison in Kansas, he'd had difficulty finding employment. Standing an inch less than six feet, and trim at 178 pounds, Mike sported dark hair parted in the middle, arched eyebrows, large brown eyes, and a youthful, alert face that caught the attention of most young women. He tried to look more mature by nurturing his light whiskers and mustache, but only managed to blur a well-formed chin.

Mike Carroll lived with a foster brother, who also acted as a father to him. The two men had exchanged letters often during Mike's absence for a hitch in the U.S. Marine Corps, where he ran afoul of the law. The correspondence continued during Mike's imprisonment in Leavenworth, Kansas. The brother met Kathi Allen on several occasions and could see that she loved Mike deeply.

The love Kathi felt was mixed with concern about his violent temper, which sometimes manifested itself in physical abuse of her. She found it easy to forgive those transgressions, but worried even more about his tendency to become discouraged. She didn't want him to fall back into the easy-money trap associated with selling drugs.

In early spring 1985, Mike Carroll moved out of his foster brother's home and convinced Kathi to share a rented motel room with him until they could find a more permanent residence. To her, it seemed to be a sign of his willingness to settle down and plan their future together. So, on April 12, when he failed to show up one night, the old worries reeled through her mind again. On Sunday, April 14, she parked his car in the Safeway lot, only a block from the motel, and struggled through her work duties trying not to think about her missing mate. Late in the afternoon, she received a telephone call at the store, a call that sent her fears about Mike Carroll skyrocketing through the roof.

One of Kathi's friends later divulged that the worried young woman had confided in her about receiving a mysterious message from Mike Carroll. According to Kathi, Mike had told her that he'd experienced some serious problems in San Francisco and had sought refuge near Lake Tahoe, about 140 miles northeast of the Bay area. Mike reportedly asked Kathi to meet him in Tahoe. If she could get time off and make the trip, he'd reportedly said, he would send someone to pick her up at the supermarket.

A coworker at Safeway stated that the message about Kathi's boyfriend actually came from someone, other than Mike, who made it sound even more ominous. The colleague reported that Kathi said, "Mike had been shot and might be dead."

Another Safeway employee, supervisor Monique Bobbitt, recalled that Kathi received the telephone call at the store. Shortly afterward, the worried girl had called the Safeway manager and asked for time off, explaining that she wanted to go to Lake Tahoe, where her boyfriend needed her. As soon as she received permission for a leave, Kathi told Monique

Bobbitt about it. Bobbitt later spoke of the conversation. "Kathi said her boyfriend had been shot and hurt, and that she was going to go to Tahoe to be with him." The supervisor remembered unlocking the supermarket's doors to let Kathi out of the store, which had been closed at 7 P.M. after customer hours. Concerned about the young employee, Bobbitt gave Kathi her home phone number to call if she needed anything, then watched as Kathi walked across the parking lot and entered the passenger side of a car parked near the yellow Capri. It was "a Honda, copperish color like a penny, with a luggage rack on the trunk." As Bobbitt hazily recalled, she thought she saw a Caucasian male, perhaps about forty years old, behind the steering wheel.

That same Sunday evening, James Baio, who described himself as a "very good friend" of Kathi Allen, answered his phone and could barely make out her worried voice. Kathi told Baio about the troublesome call at the store, but whispered that she couldn't talk much at that moment because there was someone in the room with her at The Best Inn in Milpitas. "She sounded like she was in a hurry and she said she couldn't talk to me," Baio explained. Probing his memory about the mysterious conversation, Baio could still hear Kathi's words about a man who had arrived to pick her up and take her to Mike, but the guy was "kind of weird," and he talked about wanting to take pictures of her.

James Baio asked Kathi to call when she arrived at her destination, and Kathi promised she would.

A few hours later, though, Kathleen Allen found herself in terrifying circumstances, unable to telephone anyone in the outside world. A video camera recorded segments of her nightmarish predicament.

As the tiny red light on the camcorder blinked, Kathi sat in a well-worn brown fabric recliner chair, her legs crossed. She wore a white jersey with red short sleeves, dark pants, and black shoes. Handcuffs bound her wrists together behind her back. She sat perfectly still with a numb expression on her face, saying nothing, perhaps in a state of shock, or possibly unable to comprehend the extent of danger. At her right, a table lamp bathed the room in a soft amber glow, illuminating the wall behind her, covered with a photographic mural depicting the flaming colors of a forest in autumn.

From behind the camera, the voice of Leonard Lake filled the room. "Mike owes us," he said, a hint of threat in his words. "He can't pay. Now we're going to give you a choice, Kathi, and this is probably the last choice that we're going to give you. You can go along with us, you can cooperate, you can do everything we tell you to do willingly, and in approximately thirty days, if you want a date to write on your calender—the fifteenth of May—we will either drug you, blindfold you or in some way or other make sure you don't know where you are and where you're going, and take you back to the city and let you go. And what you say at that time, I don't care. My name you don't know. His name is Charlie, but screw it." Lake made reference to another man who emerged from shadows in the dimly lit room, a short, black-haired Asian dressed in dark colors. Lake, wearing a tan knit sweater, entered camera range, knelt to adjust the bonds on her ankles, and moved back out of sight.

Alternately threatening in firm tones, then softly cajoling, switching from bad guy to good guy, then back again, Lake said, "You don't know where you are. And what you say hopefully can't hurt us, and by then, hopefully, Mike will have disappeared gracefully. Obviously, I'm telling you this because we'll have no control over what you say or how you say it once you're gone. If you don't cooperate with us, if you don't agree this evening, right now, to cooperate with us, we'll probably put a round through your head and take you out and bury you in the same area we buried Mike." Kathi's facial expression remained frozen, even though she had just heard devastating news about her lover.

''We do this,'' Lake continued, ''just because we're, we admit it, scared, nervous. We—we never planned on fucking up, much less getting caught, and we're not intending to get caught. It's the old 'no witnesses.' It's a little crude, but, uh, that's where it's at. While you're here, you'll give us information on Mike in terms of his brother, bank accounts, who we need to write to make things correct. We'll probably have you write some letters to the guy . . . his foster brother, telling him some bullshit story about how you and Mike have, uh, moved off to Timbuktu, and he's got a job doing this and that and doing something else and, basically, we want to phase Mike off, just sort of move him over the horizon, and, uh, let people know that, yeah, Mike moved off to God-knows-where, and we never heard from him again.

''That's semiacceptable. If anyone wonders, no one's going to wonder too hard. While you're here, we'll keep you busy. You'll wash for us, you'll clean for us, cook for us, you'll fuck for us. That's your choice in a nutshell. It's not much of a choice, unless you've got a death wish.''

Still sitting perfectly still, Kathi tried to speak, but her vocal cords constricted, and her words failed. She could only manage, ''No, I don't particularly . . . do . . .''

The Asian man whom Lake had called Charlie muttered something unintelligible, but Lake smothered him out with another effort to put his captive at ease. ''Actually, Kathi, I like you. I, uh, didn't like lying to you. Whether you believe it or not, that's not important. The fairness of what you're doing is, uh, not up for debate. We're not worried about whether we're fair or whether we're good.'' Again, he shifted from Jekyll to Hyde. ''We're just worried about ourselves. Selfish bastards, maybe. You'll probably think of worse names for us in the next four weeks. But that's where it's at. In the last twenty-four hours we've been tired, nervous, a little high-strung, perhaps. We expect you to do something about that. Believe me, we both need it. If you go along with us, cooperate with us, we'll be as nice as we can to you within the limits of keeping you prisoner. If you don't go along with us, we'll probably take you into the bed, tie you down, rape you, shoot you, and bury you. Sorry, lady, time's up. Make your choice."

Motionless, Kathi forced words through her dry mouth, barely audible. "Well, I have to be available."

"Spell it out for us on tape," Lake demanded. "I want to hear it from your own lips."

"I can't spell it out," she whispered. "I'll go along with whatever you want."

"That's all we wanted to hear," said Lake. "Mike was an ass."

Kathi attempted to reply to the insult of Mike Carroll, but her voice failed again.

"I understand," Lake said in mock sympathy. "Either he lied to you or you lied to us. You can believe this or you don't have to believe it. It has nothing to do with anything. Mike was getting ready to drop you. . . . He said you were clinging on to him, you were asking things of him that he didn't want." Apparently directing his attention to his Asian cohort, Lake asked, "Today, was it today? Yesterday?" Returning to his taunting of the helpless woman, Lake continued, "He [Mike] had some woman in the motel giving him a blow job. Again, this is what he said. Whether it's true or not, I don't know. He could have been lying to us."

Struggling again to speak, Kathi could only gasp.

His voice betraying enjoyment of the verbal torture, Lake said, "Okay. Then maybe he just liked talking big. He thought he was impressing us. He wasn't. He was disgusting us." Addressing Charlie, Lake asked, "Do you have keys for her cuffs?"

"Uh-huh," affirmed the collaborator.

"Stand up Kathi," Lake ordered. "If we're a little clumsy at this, forgive us. Stay on your feet. Undress for us. We want to see what we bought."

"Undress for you?" Fear and disbelieving sounded in her throat.

"Take your blouse off. Take your bra off. They're not all that bad. Take your chains off." Accepting the inevitable, Kathi began to disrobe.

Charlie muttered, "Now, what do you think?" Addressing Lake, he asked, "Take her pants off?"

"Sure, we'll run her through the shower."

"Should I go, too?" Charlie asked.

"Oh, you want to take a shower with her?" Lake seemed amused. "If you want to. Sit down, Kathi." She complied.

The Asian observed, "This is, uh, surprisingly cooperative."

"Wisely cooperative, Charlie." To the captive, he said, "We're prepared to do practically anything to get you to agree with us. I'm glad you've, uh, made all of that unnecessary. But a few ground rules, Kathi. We're real serious about this. Do what you're told, cooperate with us, and there won't be any problems. If you create problems whatsoever, you could very well die. Keep undressing, please."

Alert to the threat of death, Charlie said, "The piece is on the table," apparently reminding Lake of a handgun lying nearby.

"I see it."

Charlie, seeming to be concentrating on the possibility of joining the captive in a shower, slurred his next few words. "You didn't get the shower . . . she . . . time limits."

Ignoring him, Lake focused on Kathi as she rose to continue removing her clothing. "Keep going," he commanded.

Barely able to speak, Kathi said, "You'll have to excuse me for being shy. Sorry."

"I can understand," soothed Lake. "But don't be shy. You're going to take a shower."

Now joining in the activity more audibly, Charlie commented, "This won't be the first time. It won't be the last time."

Patronizingly, Lake chided his partner. "Don't make it hard for her, Charlie." Watching Kathi as she stood only in her underpants, he urged her on. "Panties too. Kathi, I don't want to have to make an example of what we need to do to make you cooperate."

Completely vulnerable, standing naked after removing her last garment, Kathi said, "I realize that."

"Then, please, cooperate. . . . Go ahead, Charlie."

As all three left the camera's view, Leonard Lake spoke one last time. "When you get out, there'll be slippers outside of the—"

The camera stopped.

But the torture had not ended. The video camera would record two more devastating episodes in the final few days of Kathleen Allen's eighteen years of life.

Chapter 3

Muted fog horns echoed through heavy mist shrouding the Golden Gate Bridge. The blaring noise signaled the passage of troop ships slicing through cold, choppy waters under the world-famous span, returning weary veterans home from the South Pacific combat of World War II. The devastating war had been over only a few weeks and families waited breathlessly, ecstatically, at the Embarcadero on San Francisco's north shore for the disembarkation of lucky survivors. Jubilant reunions, and the advent of world peace, gave the city, and the world, a warm glow in October 1945. For twenty-one-year-old U.S. Navy sailor Elgin Lake, and his wife, Gloria, it seemed the right time for the birth of their first child. Leonard Thomas Lake made his arrival on October 29, 1945, at St. Francis

Hospital, just five hours after his groaning mother waddled through the entry doors.

Unfortunately, world peace and booming economic conditions in the United States had little effect on what should have been a happy time for the young couple. They frequently argued, and Elgin found solace in alcohol. If the disharmony extended to their marital bed, it prevented conception of additional children until 1950, when Gloria delivered a daughter, Sylvia. One year later, their second son, Donald, arrived.

Shortly after the birth of the newest child, Elgin Lake announced he could take no more of the marital discord, and left his wife and children, ostensibly to seek better times in Seattle, Washington. Abandoned, with three small children, Gloria barely managed to scrape by, living in cheap public housing called "the projects," plus worrying about inadequate food, medicine, and other necessities. Whether driven by economic needs, or smoldering embers of affection, Gloria decided a few months later to follow her husband in an attempt to repair the marriage.

Little Leonard had started kindergarten, and his mother didn't want to interrupt the beginning of his education. Also, she felt uncertain about successfully reestablishing the union with Elgin. What if it didn't work? So, she decided to leave her first son in San Francisco, under the care of his grandparents, until she could establish a better grip on the future. One of Leonard's sisters would later recall hearing family stories about the traumatic separation. According to her vague recollection of the event, Gloria had asked Leonard if he wanted to go with her to Seattle, and the six-year-old boy had said he didn't want to go. But, at the train station, he evidently changed his mind and tearfully begged not to be left behind. It was too late. Gloria had reserved space only for herself and Sylvia, planning to carry the infant, Donald, in her arms. Leonard pleaded hysterically, sobbing and screaming, clinging to his mother's skirt. But he had to remain with his grandparents. Many years later, it would be theorized that the experience permanently scarred Leonard, and planted a seed that would grow into emotional problems. In any case, Leonard Lake would never again live with either of his parents, even though his mother and siblings did return to San Francisco within a year.

The relationship between Leonard and his mother, wounded by separation, remained unstable for years. Even when she remarried in June 1956 and invited him to rejoin her, the boy refused. Gloria gave birth to two more daughters with whom Leonard interacted cordially. He would later tell one of them that he had suffered constant hunger when he lived with Gloria in ''the projects,'' and that he never owned any toys there. Life in the custody of his grandparents offered more stability. Even though they weren't wealthy, he never experienced hunger or poverty while living with them. He had his own room, plenty of food, fashionable clothing, and an allowance. They even sent him to summer camp to enjoy mountain hiking and swimming in clean lakes. The aroma of pine trees and fresh air in high altitudes would stay with Lake and repeatedly draw him back to that environment. Not wishing to return to the privation he'd experienced with his mother, he kept civil contact with her, but chose to remain in his grandparents' home.

Chester Richardson, a cousin nine years younger than Leonard, lived only two blocks away in the same middle-class Glen Park district. At age eight or nine, Richardson enjoyed spending time with Leonard in the afternoons when the older boy came home from high school. Leonard, he recalled, owned a small chemistry lab. Experiments with it included the use of acid to dissolve various materials. Once, according to Richardson, Leonard set part of the room on fire with chemicals. The boys managed to extinguish it with minimum damage. Young Chester also loved to watch the hoards of mice his cousin had collected. Richardson recalled that Leonard had started with just a few of the tiny rodents, but they had reproduced to ''more than a thousand.'' ''He had a little city for them, a regular little mouse world. There were tunnels and castles, mazes, and even a little train for them to ride on." Eventually, Richardson said, it came time to get rid of the mice. Leonard sold some of them and gave a few away. But he killed the majority of them. An especially gruesome image remained in Richardson's mind, long into his adult years. He recalled that Leonard used chemicals and acid in an attempt to dissolve the little dead bodies. "They turned into an ugly green liquid," said Richardson.

Leonard Lake's compatibility with his sisters and his cousin did not extend to his brother, Donald. The younger boy had been involved in a debilitating accident at the age of nine, suffering serious head injuries when a train struck him. According to half sister Janet, it left Donald a "little slow." Leonard, she said, had no use for incompetent people, and held anyone who collected welfare payments in low esteem. People who "took from the system" should be punished, he told anyone who would listen. As Janet recalled, Leonard once said that if he could poison the water supply of everyone on welfare, he would gladly do it. Lake regarded Donald as one of the welfare cheaters because the younger boy collected Social Security disability payments. "He was a leech. He'd be better off dead," Leonard allegedly said of his brother.

Chester Richardson, too, recalled Leonard's disapproval of Donald. "I thought Leonard was trying to put his brother on the right track, to straighten him out. But later, I realized that he thought Donald was a big burden on their mother." The two brothers, Richardson said, "were never very close."

It could be accurately said that Leonard Lake didn't follow the biblical precept to be "thy brother's keeper." Instead, he shrugged off any theological teachings and developed his own religious views. At one point, he decided he'd like to worship ancient Nordic gods, then he changed to an interest in Buddhism. Eventually he announced that he was an atheist.

As Lake neared eighteen, images from *The Collector*, by John Fowles, swirled in his mind. He kept the dark fantasies secret, allowing himself to privately feel erotic pleasure, mentally picturing a beautiful young woman enslaved, kept in a secret cell, subject to any sexual whim of his, available whenever he wanted her, and completely under his control.

Even though Lake seemed relatively satisfied living with his grandparents, a restlessness and an urge to strike out on his own took hold early, and the wanderlust grew as he matured. Soon after completing high school, Lake found the opportunity he needed. On January 27, 1964, three months after his eighteenth birthday, Leonard Lake enlisted in the U.S. Marine Corps.

The teenaged boot adapted quickly to the military regimen. The use of weapons fascinated him, including fire control techniques, and rifle tactics. He paid close attention during classes about the use of chemicals in combat, guerilla warfare, explosives and demolition. Marine Corps training gave Lake the opportunity to drive large and small vehicles, and provided instructions on how to expertly read maps. Field survival techniques lodged themselves in his memory for future use. He learned military jargon, and in the future would refer to any project as an "operation" or "ops." The camouflage work uniforms, called "cammies," especially appealed to Lake, and he would continue to wear them in later civilian life.

After graduation from basic training, he entered and completed specialized classes to become a radar technician. The Corps transferred him to Camp LeJeune, North Carolina, where he took advanced courses in aircraft radar work. On weekend passes and during leaves of absence, Lake often visited relatives at the home of an uncle who lived in South Carolina.

At one of the gatherings in April 1965, Lake was pleasantly surprised when another guest showed up. Karen Lee Meinersman, eighteen, the daughter of his uncle's friend, had traveled from Delaware, where she attended college, majoring in math.

Homesickness motivated her decision to spend spring break with her parents. During the holiday, she joined them in acceptance of an invitation to pay a social call on Lake's relatives. As soon as they met, both Karen and Leonard felt a certain attraction. Before he returned to the Marine base, they agreed to correspond by mail.

The couple exchanged affectionate letters during the following months, until President Lyndon Johnson escalated the conflagration in Vietnam by feeding thousands of young men into the unpopular and deadly war. Leonard Lake arrived in Southeast Asia not long before Christmas 1965 and spent most of the following year "in country." The exchange of letters with Karen Lee dwindled and eventually stopped.

In late 1966, Lake was reassigned to duty in California at the Point Mugu Naval Air Station. His thoughts returned to the willowy young woman in Delaware. When they began writing letters again in 1968, Karen confided in Lake about her loneliness. She would later reveal that she felt "not very worldly at age twenty" and hoped to find "someone to direct her." She thought Leonard might "fill the bill." In March 1969, Lake used his leave to seal the relationship by taking a flight to Delaware, where the fondness they'd felt earlier grew to a romance. When Lake proposed marriage, Karen accepted and accompanied him back to California. Before the month ended, she became his bride.

As Karen would later recall, life during those first few months with her new husband was "sort of average." But a couple of behavior patterns in Leonard worried her: First, he often jested with fellow Marines about selling her body to them. Karen tried to see the humor in his bawdy comments, but they still embarrassed her. She wondered if he disguised his lewd offers as lusty humor, but was actually hinting that he wanted her to become a prostitute. Lake's constant urging her to dress in revealing costumes and bare as much flesh as possible made her nervous about his "joking." The second problem concerned

Karen even more. Prior to the marriage, she had never detected
any tendency for him to be unusually dominant. But now, in
his role as her husband, he became especially controlling and
overbearing about everything she did. He became the master
and expected her to be the slave. Trying to humor him, Karen
submitted to his wishes, but didn't enjoy being a possession.
Lake seemed to feel he could do anything he wished with her.

Her concerns faded away, though, when Lake volunteered
midway through 1970 for a second tour of duty in Vietnam.
Lake's grandparents had moved from San Francisco to Galt, a
small town in central California. They agreed to let Karen live
with them during the long wait for her husband's return.

In the green hell of Vietnam, Lake would later say, he really
"enjoyed" the experience. He boasted of "killing a lot of
people" and said that the toughest thing he had to do was zip
up body bags. As a radar technician, Lake was stationed in Da
Nang, the coastal city of 200,000, where 3,500 Marines had
stormed ashore on March 8, 1965, to begin the escalation that
would eventually cost the United States more than 58,000 lives.
Lake's role at the huge Da Nang air base involved repairing
radar machinery, not assaulting villages or slogging through
humid jungles in search of "Charlie," the nickname grunts
(combat Marines) gave the Vietcong fighters. Lake worked
long hours at the air base during monsoon weather and drove
himself into a state of fatigue. Reportedly, he once ascended
a radar tower during a raging storm just to put himself above
the hectic activities below. If he dreamed about violent combat,
he later turned the fantasies into horrifying stories of confrontation with the enemy. While other warriors experienced post-
traumatic stress syndrome from actual battles, Lake's mind
tortured itself with imagined experiences.

Compounding his own mental torment, Lake convinced himself that his little wife—back in the States where hippies and
flower children demonstrated against the war and preached free
love—had not remained faithful to him. Other Marines who

had received "Dear John" letters, or who suffered agonizing suspicion, could arrange to discuss such worries with a chaplain. But having declared his atheism, Lake couldn't allow himself to talk to a "holy Joe." Instead, he asked to see a military mental-health expert. The doctor diagnosed a serious condition of "impending schizophrenia" along with "hysterical neurosis" and recommended that Lake return home to undergo treatment in a hospital. He was shipped back to California at the end of 1970.

A medical evaluation resulted in Lake being declared "a danger to himself and to others." He spent the better part of two months in the hospital's psychiatric ward. The diagnosis distressed Karen, who later recalled a bizarre incident during Lake's confinement. She reported that Lake invaded a storage area one night to steal government property. Karen couldn't recall exactly what he sought, but knew it seemed important to Lake. During the furtive "operation," Lake failed to find the object of his search, which sent him into a deep depression. He blamed the failure on an attack of diarrhea. So, he returned to his bed and began eating all the chocolate he could find. The reason, he said, was that chocolate caused constipation. If he became constipated, he could return to the storage area and carry out his original mission.

Such behavior not only alarmed Karen, it also concerned the attendant doctors. They performed extensive psychiatric examinations, and recommended that Leonard Lake be discharged from the Marine Corps for medical reasons. He left the service in January 1971.

Within a few days of his departure, Lake and his wife looked for a place to settle, and bought a home in San Jose, at the lower tip of San Francisco Bay. According to Karen, the first few weeks were "fairly normal." Both she and Leonard enrolled at West Valley Junior College to prepare for the future. Lake looked for employment, but could land only temporary and part-time assignments. For a while, he drove a truck for a veteran's organization. But the minimum-wage jobs created increasing financial strain for the couple. They had to do something, and soon. Leonard came up with the solution, an easy way to supplement their meager income. He suggested to Karen that she could make good money in tips by dancing at a local topless bar.

At first, Karen indignantly rejected the idea. Gradually, though, it started to make sense. The more she thought about it, the more logical it became, especially since she could think of no other way to earn the money they needed. Still reluctant, she auditioned, and was accepted. Soon she found herself spending forty-five to fifty hours each week at the club. Meanwhile, Leonard stayed home, living leisurely, puttering around with yard work, and growing an organic garden.

Not very happy with providing tawdry entertainment to endless droves of ogling men, Karen's disenchantment grew even worse when Lake resumed his dominating behavior. This time it became unbearable. He began administering "controlled" beatings. In her recollection, he would first strike her lightly to the face with his open hand, then later use his fist. All the while, Lake would ask her if she enjoyed the punishment.

The money she earned by displaying her body, including the tips, went directly to Leonard. He demanded to be in control of their income, all of their expenditures, and their social activities. The beatings, to Lake, were nothing but a prelude to sex, his version of foreplay.

Sex became a way of life for Lake. He ordered Karen to pose nude for his camera, and he filled an album with revealing photos of her. During sexually intimate moments, he made suggestions to Karen about his desire to meet another couple and swap partners. To convince her of the need for extracurricular sex, he claimed he could no longer reach orgasm with her alone. Years later, Karen reluctantly admitted that they had sought out and met several other couples, but had engaged in sexual swapping only one time.

Other bizarre behavior by her husband worried Karen. He claimed he hated telephones, but finally gave in to her request to install one in their home. It seemed odd to her that he insisted on giving the telephone company a phony name, even though Leonard rationalized that it would enable him to screen out nuisance phone solicitors. He patiently explained that if a caller asked for the nonexistent person under which he had registered the service, he would know that caller wasn't really a friend or even an acquaintance.

Karen also found it puzzling that Leonard pressured her to read only one book out of a small library he had accumulated. *The Collector*, he said, was different from any other book. Another problem vexed her, as well. The weapons he kept in the house made Karen nervous. She couldn't understand why he needed a .25 caliber automatic, a 9mm handgun, and a small pistol. When they mysteriously vanished one day, Lake accused Karen of stealing them.

Lake, Karen would recall, was the only person she ever knew who had a "God complex." She concluded that he actually thought of himself as some sort of deity. Whenever someone uttered the phrase, "Oh, God," Leonard would answer, "Yes." And, she added, he wasn't joking.

Strangely enough, despite Lake's appetite for kinky sex and for involving his wife with another couple, he became jealous if she paid any attention to other men on her own volition. She, on the other hand, said very little when she found a hidden collection of photographs he had apparently taken of other women, mostly nudes.

Karen's working hours left little time for anything other than Leonard's sexual predilections. Periodically they visited a family living on the same street. She wasn't particularly impressed with Charles Gunnar or his wife, but liked their two little daughters. Gunnar stood about six feet tall, and appeared to weigh nearly 300 pounds. A heavy black beard, with mustache, and equally dark hair surrounded his portly face, which featured a high, bulging forehead and squinty eyes. He looked like an opera singer or maybe a professional wrestler. Karen thought Gunnar didn't treat his wife and daughters very well. But Leonard seemed to like Charles, so Karen tried to be courteous to them.

As the strain between Karen and Leonard heated up, thoughts of leaving routinely entered Karen's mind. One evening in November 1971, she exited the bar where she danced, accompanied by a regular patron who had offered to walk her to her car. At that same moment, Leonard arrived in his pickup and flared into an outburst of anger. While he yelled and threatened to throw her out of their house, she calmly entered her car to drive home, and took her time since she dreaded the confrontation. When she reached the house, she recoiled in shock. He had rushed home ahead of her, and arrived in time to toss all of her clothing into the front yard. Since he had locked her out, she gathered up her possessions, loaded them into her car, and curled up to sleep in the auto.

The next day after work, she discovered that someone had broken into her vehicle and stolen most of the clothing. It didn't take long to discover her things in Leonard's possession.

Until she could find a place to stay, Karen lived in the camper they owned, parked in the yard. On her next payday, instead of turning the money over to her angry husband, she rented an apartment and moved into it. Lake did not attempt to persuade her to return, but chose to harass her in other ways. On several occasions she found that he had broken into her apartment and burned holes in her clothing with acid. Once she caught him inside, but felt helpless to do anything about it. He verbally abused her by reciting his knowledge of where she had been, what she'd been doing, with whom, and when. He made it clear that he, or a confederate, had been spying on her. She realized that he still wanted to be in control of her life, and that he hadn't given up regarding her as his possession.

Finally the miserable relationship tapered off. Karen divorced

Lake in 1972. His half sister Janet recalled that the only time she ever saw Leonard cry was when he told her that Karen had left him. Janet also believed that the divorce marked the beginning of Leonard's powerful hatred for all women. Starting with his own mother, Leonard saw women as a source of hurt and rejection his whole life.

Even though Karen had walked out of Leonard's life, she hadn't heard the last of him.

Chapter 4

After the divorce, Leonard Lake drifted aimlessly, taking various unskilled jobs, eking out a living, mostly staying with relatives in the San Francisco area. He missed Karen in some ways, but didn't regret throwing off the bonds of marriage. To seek a replacement for female companionship, Lake placed personal ads in "the *Berkeley Barb*." In late 1972, Jennifer Gordon responded. "I was twenty-eight at the time," she would recall. "I answered his ad and we developed a relationship in October 1972." Before long, a deep fondness for Lake grew in her heart, and it soon turned "intimate."

"The relationship metamorphosed," Gordon recalled. "At first, he was like someone you see in the movies. Sweet, gentle, caring. He seemed concerned, like someone you would really like to know." But within three months, the intimacy turned, in Jennifer's words, "kinky." "I was stupid. Not naive, stupid. Our sex became aberrant. There was bondage and swinging ...

he liked to tie me up. He wasn't mean or hard-hearted. It was kinda funny in a way." Jennifer emphasized that Lake never let her tie him up. He always needed to be in complete control.

Eventually Lake even convinced Jennifer to earn money for them through prostitution. She admitted that he didn't force her, she simply consented because she wanted to please him.

As he had with his wife, Lake took volumes of photographs. He filled three albums with nude and seminude pictures of Jennifer. She also helped convince a few of her girlfriends to pose for Leonard's camera, usually in suggestive and titillating poses rather than completely nude. While she slept one night— in the buff—he snapped several revealing pictures of her. Lake presented her with prints of the sleeping-beauty shots, but kept duplicates and the negatives for himself.

No matter how much Jennifer accepted Lake's need for prurient behavior, nothing seemed to satisfy him. The romance lost its bloom, transforming into nothing more than a convenient sharing of living quarters. Jennifer paid her half of the rent, still turning a few tricks to earn the money for her share of living costs. But when she decided to give up the prostitution, "Leonard became irate. We argued a lot."

Warning bells went off in Jennifer's mind when Lake started talking about "snuff" films. She had never heard the term and asked what it meant. "He told me that it involved two people having sex, and one kills the other during a climax." Lake, Jennifer said, wanted to make a snuff film, and thought it would be the "ultimate sexual high." She wondered if he would wind up in prison as a result of such ideas. But Lake told her that if he was ever arrested, he would escape the consequences by taking cyanide. "He said he had the poison in a hollow spot in one of his teeth, but I didn't believe him."

The arguments between them increased in frequency and volatility. One day she wound up on the floor, pinned down by Lake's foot. Jennifer moved out the next day, in June 1973.

* * *

Two obsessions occupied Lake's mind. Fantasies about capturing a young woman and holding her as a sex slave filled his erotic daydreams, while images of a nuclear holocaust, which he regarded as unpreventable, lodged in his psyche. He needed to escape the city, to relocate in a rural area where he could use his Marine Corps skills as a survivalist when the expected disaster hit. If he could find the right spot, in the foothills or in an isolated forest, Lake hoped to build the bunker he visualized, where he could store provisions to sit out the conflagration. So, Lake packed up his meager possessions, and drove north. He stopped in Ukiah, about 130 miles north of San Francisco.

Nestled in a valley between two mountain ridges, Ukiah is the seat of Mendocino County. Pear orchards and grape vineyards cover most of the arable land, and giant timbers are trucked out of the high country to be processed in sawmills. The name Ukiah, meaning "deep valley," came from the language of Pomo Indians who occupied the region before Italian farmers settled there. About 12,000 residents lived quiet lives in Ukiah during the early 1970s, and enjoyed the peace and contentment of a small-town environment, where only one theater, for instance, which opened in 1950, offered motion-picture entertainment within eighty miles.

Not long after Leonard Lake arrived, he found a job with a government-funded firm that built and renovated low-income housing. Gradually, he worked his way up to the duties of crew leader, overseeing the labor of younger men. He also enrolled at Mendocino College, taking classes in animal sciences and meat cutting. In the butchery sessions, Lake learned the use of ordinary tools, such as kitchen knives and carpentry saws, to expertly slice through bone and flesh. The energetic student impressed the college staff, convincing them to offer him a part-time teaching assignment, tutoring boys in a class on survival in the wilderness. At first, Lake lived in a cheap motel, then found

the perfect place to settle and begin work on living out his
greatest fantasy.

In the western rise of the Coast Range mountains that cast
shadows over Ukiah early each evening, a winding road ascends
just north of town. Ten miles of tortuous turns, which ascend
through lush forests, eventually lead to an unmarked branch
road. It is difficult to find, and the people who live in the hidden
hills and valleys prefer to keep it that way. They, and their
predecessors in 1970, found the ideal site to establish a rural,
ecological paradise for people who wished to escape pollution,
noise, traffic, and social restrictions. "The Ranch," consisting
of 5,000 acres, approximately nine square miles, was purchased
from the original homesteaders.

Soft breezes clear the air in the high country, rippling across
grassy slopes and sunny meadows, sweeping over round knolls,
and whispering through the leafy oaks and red-barked madrona
trees. Various shades of green color the uneven terrain, from
which jagged granite boulders thrust toward breathtakingly blue
sky. In the spring, buttercups, California poppies, and Indian
paintbrush decorate the slopes in yellow, orange, and red. Down
in the deep, shadowed canyons, cedars, pines, and coastal redwoods form green canopies over rushing brooks of clean, cascading water. Narrow bridges span the streams along six miles
of a dirt road twisting through The Ranch's hills and dales.
Every few hundred yards, private driveways branch off, leading
to hidden domiciles. Deer, wild turkeys, bushy-tailed squirrels,
and other creatures roam unmolested throughout the hills and
valleys.

Originally, 200 families bought parcels of The Ranch, vary-
ing from forty to 200 acres of the undeveloped, forested land.
Electric power for the scattered rustic houses, cabins, and
mobile homes was generated by solar- or hydro-powered
sources. Water came from wells, pumped by windmills, or from

creeks, shared by all. No telephone cables or other utilities marred the landscape. A common area of 400 acres included a large barn with a ranch house, a pond, and a school. Roads on the property were maintained through the labor of residents and funded by the community. The landowners' association drew up bylaws prohibiting the use of pesticides or firearms.

Generally, the people who chose to live on The Ranch respected Mother Earth, and resisted anything that might pollute the land, water, or air. Adopting nicknames such as "Otter," "Zephyr," "Beaver," "Morning Glory," or other symbols of flora and fauna, they celebrated the summer solstice by donning medieval costumes, dancing and singing, and then skinny-dipping in a creek.

The concept appealed to "Venus" Salem, a single woman in her thirties, who still admired the freedom of the 1960s flower children. Venus bought a parcel on the ranch in 1970, and worked to improve it while she continued to live in Ukiah, earning her living as an occupational therapist. By 1974, though, the tiny woman had nearly exhausted her energy and money. She wanted to upgrade the cabin she'd built and plant an orchard, but needed help.

Her need appeared to be answered when she met Leonard Lake at a festival. She heard him talking about alternate energy sources, and his knowledge of it interested her. They chatted and she told him of her cabin and her wishes to improve it.

Lake immediately warmed up to the idea of providing assistance to Venus. He offered to do all of the work for six months in exchange for living on the property. "I was naive," Venus later declared, and vulnerable to exploitation. Leonard Lake, though, knew an opportunity when he saw one.

At first, the arrangement seemed pleasant. Venus saw Leonard as "charming and helpful," so she allowed their friendship to become a "personal relationship for a time." She didn't particularly like it when Lake tried to entertain her with his photo albums. "He showed me pictures of his past girlfriends and many nude young women." When he suggesting adding revealing photos of Venus to his collection, she adamantly refused.

As they became more intimate, Lake told Venus of the bitterness left over from his childhood. He complained that his mother hadn't been able to take care of both him and his brother, Donald. So while Donald stayed with the family, Lake muttered, he had been sent to an orphanage. Donald, Lake said, had always "mooched from their mom," and would be better off dead. Venus shuddered when Leonard "voiced an interest in killing his own brother."

Wondering if Lake was serious, Venus worried when she discovered that he kept a pair of handguns and a rifle in the cabin. He also spoke of survivalism to her, and admitted that he'd buried supplies on the property. She suspected that he might be growing marijuana there, as well, but had no proof. When he spoke of his "Miranda" project, she thought it meant building a shelter to provide refuge for people who would be driven from the city during a coming environmental collapse. Seeing the ugly excavation Lake dug, Venus assumed that he had fashioned a root cellar in which to store food.

When Lake introduced her to his visiting friend, Charles Gunnar, Venus thought Charles seemed nice enough, but terribly overweight. Lake's treatment of his old buddy surprised her. It seemed strange to her that Leonard "tortured" Gunnar by deliberately choosing especially steep trails during a hike, and insisting that the weary visitor walk up and down them at a fast pace. The out-of-shape guest struggled for breath and sweated profusely. Lake's cruelty puzzled Venus, and his attitude about a man he had called his friend seemed incongruous. Lake confided in Venus that he felt deep disgust at Gunnar for gaining so much weight. A sense of relief swept over her when the portly man and his wife departed for their home in Morgan Hill, near San Francisco.

"Pretty soon," said Venus, "things started to get strange"

in her dealings with Lake. "I had bad feelings about signing with him." Despite her premonitions, she tried to rationalize his actions, and avoided the thought of evicting the partner-tenant, choosing instead to delay any confrontation with him. But the troubling signs grew worse. "He started alienating the other people." Everything she did or said, Venus later revealed, resulted in Lake criticizing her. "He was mind-fucking me." Lake openly criticized her friends, too, finding fault with all of them. When Venus fully realized that she'd been manipulated, she challenged Lake. For the first time, he reacted physically by pushing her off a ladder. Frightened and disillusioned, she decided she wanted out. Lake offered to buy her interest in the property, and Venus reluctantly accepted his offer.

A woman living not far from Lake's cabin spoke often with the new property owner. Periodically, when she invited him to dinner, she listened to the same odd stories Venus had heard. She recalled, after meeting Lake's visiting brother, Donald, that "Leonard didn't like his brother. Said he was a stupid person." Lake also boasted of his combat experience in Vietnam, and asserted that he'd learned to be a survivalist there. The neighbor felt uncomfortable when Lake fired weapons during target practice. "He knew the bylaws . . . but he ignored them." It upset her when Lake brought in a bulldozer to move a large amount of dirt, which also violated the association rules.

Lake flirted with the woman, and frequently hinted that he'd like to take some photos of her, possibly even some glamour shots with little or no clothing. Even more offensive to her was when Lake suggested that her ten-year-old daughter might pose for him in the nude. "Of course, I refused."

Operation Miranda, the woman thought, referred to some legal issues against which Lake fought. She thought it particularly bizarre that he often joked about never being taken alive, and that if a nuclear holocaust came, he wouldn't suffer because he kept cyanide pills concealed. "I carry death in my pocket," Lake said to the alarmed neighbor.

The unwelcome proposals by Lake to take nude photos extended not only to female acquaintances, but also to women he barely knew. He suggested to a young man who worked on his housing maintenance crew that the youth and his girlfriend might like to pose for some intimate shots. The youth declined. Lake liked to talk about women, the employee recalled. "He was perverted about women . . . had this fascination with sexual things." The older man seemed to enjoy sharing his albums with laborers on his crew. A few of the men attended a party at The Ranch, invited by Lake. A teenage member of the group said, "Everybody got naked. It was eat, drink, and be merry." The event marked the first time the youth had seen such revelry. "It was really exciting being around naked women," he later admitted.

Leonard Lake, he said, needed lumber for something he was building on The Ranch. To obtain it, he would arrange for excessive purchases of supplies on the job, and steal the extra material to take home.

Another employee working with Lake, Bobby Barnes, eighteen, needed a place to live. His crew chief, Lake, offered the use of a small one-room cabin on his property at The Ranch. Barnes quickly accepted and moved into the dwelling next to Lake's cabin. In return, the youth agreed to help Lake excavate dirt, and take care of animals, chickens, and fruit trees. Because Lake's house contained the only kitchen, Barnes sometimes spent evenings with his boss to share cooking chores. He soon learned of Lake's interest in guns, weapons, and various magazines about survivalism, including *Soldier of Fortune,* which Lake studied hours on end. In discussions, Barnes heard Lake complain about his mother and brother, saying he didn't like either one of them. Speaking of Vietnam, Lake claimed that he'd had a "great time" in combat, and didn't want to leave.

To entertain Barnes, Lake would open a shoe box filled with photographs of women "in various stages of undress." It seemed odd to the youth that a man in his early thirties would be so interested in young girls, and peculiar that Lake didn't seem to get along very well with neighbors his own age. Barnes heard Lake complain of a disagreeable neighbor, and threaten that if any of the family ever trespassed on his property, he would shoot them and bury them in pits he had dug.

Barnes, just like his coworker, had observed Lake stealing supplies from job sites.

Not long after Barnes moved in, his eighteen-year-old girlfriend came to dinner, and stayed for several weeks. Lake, of course, welcomed the full-time presence of a young woman. And his pleasure was doubled when another woman, Gina Travers, nineteen, a friend of the young couple, visited on four different weekends. Turning on the charm, Lake escorted Gina on personal tours of The Ranch, astride a three-wheel motorcycle. The local people fascinated her with their beards, casual dress, and friendly manner. She loved the informal atmosphere, the windmills, and the community hot tubs. She met a couple named Otter and Morning Glory, whom Lake described as the high priest and priestess of The Ranch's "black magic cult." But Gina grimaced in horror when they took her inside their mobile home, and showed her a huge snake that had died in their closet. It had coiled itself so tightly in the small enclosure that it became necessary to cut the snake into pieces in order to remove it.

Gina's host, apparently thinking that she wanted to hear of his personal needs, told her that he wanted a woman who would be submissive to him. He also complained about his brother, and mentioned that he kept cyanide pills concealed to use in case of serious emergency. Back at his cabin, Gina asked Lake about an adjacent foundation under construction, partly underground. He explained his plan to use it for survival in case of a nuclear war. Certainly, Lake assured her, she would be welcome to join him there and be safe from the world catastrophe.

On the third visit by Gina, Lake made her an offer she instantly refused. He spoke of his dear friend, Charles Gunnar, who desperately needed to have sex. Would Gina accommodate his pal for $100 in cash? Trying not to sound offended, she said no. She didn't admit that she'd heard Bobby's girlfriend, who had met Gunnar, describe him by saying "he was fat and ugly."

Unfazed, Lake suggested that Gina might like to pose for him, maybe in the nude. She unequivocally refused, but he continued to "pester" her about it. Gina did, however, have fun on a day Lake took her and Bobby to a nudist camp, where they frolicked in a hot tub, swam, and ate their fill at a community dinner.

Although Lake preached rabidly against the use of drugs, he freely supplied his young guests with plenty of marijuana, telling them that he raised it in a hidden patch, and that many of the local residents also cultivated the plants. Gina liked smoking the cannabis, but felt uncomfortable when Lake constantly pressured her, along with Bobby and his girlfriend, to roam around The Ranch naked, as some of the other residents did. She finally did, however, succumb to his persuasive skills very briefly, removing her clothes "but only for a few hours one day."

The Ranch resident named Otter caught Leonard Lake's undivided interest. After a few meetings, Otter Zell revealed to Lake the existence of a remarkable animal, unlike any other in the world. And he owned it. Otter's beard, ponytail, and intense eyes under sharply arched brows gave him the look of a man who just might possess insight into the mysteries of life.

A researcher of rare books on myths and legends, Otter had long been interested in unicorns. "I rediscovered a lost process for creating a unicorn," he later said. By a simple surgical procedure in the first few hours after a male goat's birth, Otter produced a white goat with a single horn sprouting from the middle of its forehead. He named it "Sir Lancelot."

The unique possession fascinated Lake, especially in its potential for attracting young women.

As Otter spent more time with Lake, he thought Leonard somewhat odd in his exaggerated views about a pending holocaust. Neither Otter nor the other ranch occupants appreciated Lake's gouging a huge notch out of the slope near his cabin to construct the so-called refuge from disaster. Nor could the peace lovers on The Ranch attune themselves to the military jargon Lake used. They disliked his keeping guns and blatantly violating the rules against firing them. His references to Operation Miranda, some said, "freaked us out."

Lake, though, expressed a deep interest in the unicorn, and filed in the back of his mind a note to exploit it. He excitedly told Gina about the remarkable goat, and asked her to pose nude with it. He informed her that white unicorns symbolized virgins, thus she should be photographed with Sir Lancelot. Gina thought the suggestion ridiculous, since she wasn't a virgin, as Lake well knew. She had surrendered her chastity even before she, and Bobby's girlfriend, had given themselves sexually to Lake.

But for Lake, Gina's refusal to pose nude with the little goat didn't matter. One strikeout certainly didn't end the ball game. He could see unlimited potential for the seductive use of Sir Lancelot.

James Hendwood, a long-term resident of The Ranch, acted as a caretaker and general handyman at the barn located in the common area. The handyman held a low opinion of Leonard

Lake. "He was a sleazy dirtbag," Hendwood snarled, citing the use of firearms as deeply offensive. On one occasion he'd heard forty or fifty shots echoing across the quiet landscape, and rushed to the source. Seeing Lake with a gun, he "berated" the shooter, reminded him of the bylaws, and left. The next day, Lake approached Hendwood, acting as if nothing had happened, and boldly tried to sell him a gun. "Nobody liked him," said Hendwood.

Robert Tognoli agreed with that assessment. Lake often cut across Tognoli's property as a shortcut to his own place. Trying to ingratiate himself, Lake talked incessantly about the need for a bunker to survive the collapse of civilization, and the necessity of storing food, weapons, ammunition, water, and other provisions. "He was kind of a creepy guy," said Tognoli. "You really needed to be on your guard around him."

Chapter 5

While Lake offended neighboring property owners and took advantage of vulnerable women, he simultaneously sought to feed his lust for young girls. Zell's unicorn goat provided the perfect bait.

Recognizing the potential for selfish use of the charming, single-horned white goat, Lake suggested a deal with Otter to show the animal at various festivals. They could set up a booth to display Sir Lancelot. Lake would photograph customers posing with the unique animal, and they could split the profits. Lake, of course, realized that few women, especially very young ones, can resist the mystical attraction of unicorns.

In the spring of 1979, the ruse worked when Cindy Morgan, sixteen, talked to the balding photographer about the sweet, wonderful little goat. She sighed when Lake chanted, "Through the power of the wizard, we have created the unicorn." Cindy's mother, wanting portraits of her daughter with Sir Lancelot, accepted Lake's proposal to schedule the photography sessions in the "natural" environment surrounding his home at The Ranch.

Within a few days, Cindy and her mom met Lake in Ukiah and followed him to his residence. During the ensuing photo shoot, Cindy sensed a distinct feeling that Lake wanted to separate her from her mother. She was right. When he managed to get her alone for a few moments, he asked if she would be interested in posing for "other types of photos." Carefully wording his suggestions, he hinted that she would make a beautiful model for artistic shots in which she should shave her body, apply green paint, and he would attach wings to give her the appearance of a fairy. Cindy giggled and declined. But the romantic idea interested her enough to avoid telling her mother of the whispered conversation.

Lake took another approach within a week. An annual event held in the spring in both Central and Southern California was called "The Renaissance Pleasure Faire." The organizers and patrons dressed in medieval costumes to attend the celebrations, which were usually held in pristine rural hillside settings amid streams surrounded by trees. Tents, colorful banners, and costumed crowds created a festive atmosphere reminiscent of Olde England. Jesters and singers entertained, and an actress portraying the English queen made a grand entrance into the grounds accompanied by a gala procession. The ancient carnival, Lake correctly figured, would be the perfect place to seek out his fantasies by using Sir Lancelot. He telephoned Cindy and asked her to accompany him to the Los Angeles renaissance fair to help promote the unicorn.

Unable to obtain parental permission, Cindy told Lake she couldn't go. But her refusal didn't discourage him.

Determined to achieve his goals with Cindy after returning from Los Angeles, Lake "coincidentally" turned up with unprecedented frequency at the Ukiah spots where she hung out. Using all the charm he could muster, he invited her to festivals at The Ranch, and repeated the proposals for her to become a model. He even dropped by her home one day, and offered her a bundle of silver dollars if she would pose for him in the nude. "You can make all sorts of money," he promised. With a coy smile, Cindy said she didn't need any money. But the persistence and power of suggestion finally worked. Without her mother's knowledge, Cindy agreed to meet Lake and pose for him. She would later say she gave in "just to get him off my back." But she also acknowledged that she'd always been a "thrill seeker" and that "part of her wanted to experiment."

On a warm afternoon, they met at an isolated spot by the winding Russian River. With a backdrop of water rippling noisily over stones and swirling in pools near a trestle bridge, Lake posed the teenager and exposed several rolls of film. Feeling the excitement of being a model, Cindy agreed to remove her blouse and bra for more intimate pictures. As she lay on a smooth boulder, Lake moved in close, and zoomed in for tight shots of her breasts. Putting his camera aside, Lake reached into a bag and pulled out a tube of scarlet lipstick. He daubed her nipples and areolae with it, then took more shots, in extreme close-up. Pushing for even more erotic poses, Lake asked her to remove her jeans and underwear, but Cindy drew the line and refused. The strange thing, Cindy later explained, was that during the entire photo shoot, Lake kept lecturing her against premarital sex, emphasizing the importance of remaining a virgin. For some reason, she felt compelled to tell him she had already lost her virginity. He smiled and continued to snap photographs.

Afterward, Cindy felt certain that Lake would pursue her for more photo sessions, and probably for sex. It astonished her that he never again tried to find her or contact her. Maybe he felt guilty for not offering any payment for the single session by the river.

It is more likely that Lake had cultivated a more exciting

substitute for Cindy Morgan in a teenager he'd met several
years earlier.

The Davis family home occupied property adjacent to The
Ranch, with only a low wire fence separating their driveway
from the community's main entry road. They had moved to
the house in 1972. Their pubescent daughter, Darlene Davis,
met and befriended several of the free-spirited Ranch residents
as she grew into her early teen years.

During a particularly wet storm in 1977, thirty-one-year-old
Leonard Lake, burly and balding, with a dark fringe of hair
and piercing green eyes, stepped out of his big pickup truck
and trotted to the front door of the Davis home. When they
answered his knock, he asked permission to park next to their
driveway, explaining that the heavy rain had made the road
into his property impassable. He carried a motorcycle in the
truck bed, and could ride it alongside the muddy ruts that led
to his house.

Rural people are usually more neighborly than suspicious
city dwellers, so the Davises invited him inside, and courteously
gave the permission he requested. Young Darlene, now thirteen,
slim with shoulder-length dark hair and shining eyes, silently
watched the powerful-looking man, and felt a certain admiration, maybe even the inner tugging of adolescent sexual attraction. He wore Marine-style cammies, seemed nice, and
bristled with machismo energy. When he exited, she watched
him through a rain-streaked window as he unloaded a three-
wheeled vehicle from his truck bed, and sped away in the
soaking downpour.

Before long, Lake found reasons to visit the Davises more
often, volunteering to assist them with various jobs. Darlene
pitched in to help when Lake and her father built a greenhouse
and a new fence. During the next couple of years, she grew
fond of Lake and considered him her good friend. After school

and on weekends, she accepted Lake's offer to take her riding on what she would call his motorized "tricycle." Darlene loved the feel of wind in her hair and the excitement of bouncing along the foothills and forests with her arms around the big driver. Of course, she carefully kept the meetings secret from her parents. He asked her if she had boyfriends and expressed curiosity about her experiences with them. She felt a warm rush of emotion when he first kissed her.

The first time Darlene saw the inside of Lake's house, it was during a visit with her parents, and she noted that it was extraordinarily neat and clean. The second time, she and her younger sister made a visit, and Lake showed her photographs of dogs. It would be much later that he would allow her to view his albums of nude women.

In the summer of 1979, Lake invited Darlene to accompany him on a drive nearly 200 miles down to Morgan Hill, south of San Jose, to visit Charles Gunnar. "He's my best pal," Lake said, insisting that she must meet him. Lake wanted Darlene to go, but knew it could not happen unless her mother came along. He wound up taking both of them, as well as Darlene's younger sister. During the few nights they stayed there, Darlene didn't understand why Lake spoke of Gunnar so negatively. The big man, he said, was an employee of the postal service, but an injury prevented him from working, so he collected disability insurance payments from the government. Cynically referring to him as "Fat Charles," Lake seemed to be constantly irritated at his portly pal and was sharply critical of his use of "welfare." At the same time, Lake treated Gunnar's wife, Vicky, whom Charles had married the previous March, and Gunnar's two young daughters by a previous marriage, with respect and courtesy. In private whispers to Darlene, Lake spoke affectionately of his friend's first wife, lamenting her death due to cancer, and criticized Gunnar's cruel treatment of the woman during her long illness. Darlene decided that Lake must have been secretly in love with the late Mrs. Gunnar. Charles, she found out, also kept a secret lover, whose picture Darlene saw in an album of provocatively posed women.

Darlene didn't mind leaving behind the tangle of sex and secrets when it came time for Leonard to take her home.

Two weeks before Darlene turned sixteen in early December, she surreptitiously joined Lake at his cabin, and surrendered her virginity in his bed. She confessed to Leonard that she loved him. Years later she would admit that Leonard was the best lover she'd ever had: "He was extremely gentle and sensual." The notion that he might be involved in sadism or masochism surprised Darlene. "He wasn't into that stuff at all with me." He did, however, frequently bring up the subject of inviting another woman to join them for sexual fun. Because she gasped that the idea was repugnant to her, he didn't pursue it. But he did show her his collection of erotic pictures and convinced her to pose in the nude for a series of photos.

Now that he regarded Darlene as a woman, Lake shared his plans to prepare for Armageddon, and told her she would survive with him. Revealing his aversion to confinement, Lake declared his intent to take cyanide if that ever happened. He also offered to conceal one of the deadly capsules in a necklace for her to use in case of serious emergency, but Darlene nervously told him that the idea scared her, and she wouldn't want to wear such a necklace. He spoke very little to her of his Vietnam experiences, except to say that he had killed people.

Midway through 1980, Lake asked Darlene to marry him, promising that they would travel the country together. Although she loved him, Darlene realized that at sixteen she was still too young to leap into marriage. She wanted to wait until after her eighteenth birthday. Lake pouted and said he would probably run away to become a mercenary soldier. He confessed that he'd seen a program on *60 Minutes* about such adventures, and if he couldn't have her, he'd join up. Then, changing his tack, Lake simply said that he needed a wife now, and couldn't wait two more years. But Darlene convinced him that it would be better to wait.

The sexual contacts continued. Realizing the dangers of being caught, or getting pregnant, Darlene refused to enter his home anymore, but succumbed again in a hidden spot near her residence, and once more in a motel. Her parents grew suspicious and issued orders to never be alone with the older bachelor. Still, Darlene managed to meet him whenever she could. The young woman knew that she would always love him.

At last, the worried parents decided to assure the safety of their vulnerable daughter and sent Darlene away to a boarding school. The move interrupted the relationship, but did not end it.

Lake didn't devote all of his time and energy to the pursuit of young women. He studied books and magazines for information related to survivalism, and corresponded with other men sharing his interest. He found most of his contacts through *Soldier of Fortune* magazine, and even placed a personal ad to meet other survivalists. To maintain his anonymity, Lake used the name "Tom Meyers." A twenty-one-year-old U.S. Army soldier in Fort Lewis, Washington, saw the ad and wrote Meyers a letter. Mark Novak had already heard of Meyers through another soldier who had corresponded with the survivalist. Leonard replied to Novak and eventually invited him to come to The Ranch for a visit. When Novak received orders to report to Schofield Barracks in Hawaii, he decided to visit Meyers on the trip down to San Francisco, where he would catch transportation to the islands. Novak took a bus to Ukiah, where Lake met him, still using the pseudonym. En route to The Ranch, Lake asked Novak if he was open-minded, explaining that some of the residents walked around naked. The soldier said it didn't matter to him. The pair chatted about common interests, and Lake showed him around the property. On the subject of religion, Lake told his guest that he was into a "Viking" cult, and claimed to be an "Odinist." The former Marine also hinted of dark experiences in Vietnam combat.

During his stay, Novak helped "Tom Meyers" work on a water line to a goat pen, and listened to Meyers talk about building a bunker for survival. The older man also spoke of his interest in a completely free society, various cults, and astrology.

Something didn't seem quite right to Novak about his host's claim to being an authentic survivalist, and it was odd that several people called him Leonard, not Tom. Later, the soldier would characterize Lake as a "shit talker." As far as Novak could discern, his host hadn't really prepared adequately for any kind of an emergency. Still, he enjoyed talking to Lake, and made a mental note to refer other interes   ddies to him. Novak's stay lasted three days.

Lake seldom suffered from loneliness at Th his frequent liaisons with various women, he visitors. Charles Gunnar and Vicky stopped during which he managed to get her away taking her on tours of the community abo motorcycle. He explained his plans to surviv showed her where he'd buried supplies. Whi he sometimes hinted that Gunnar might be his "clandestine" activities. Vicky didn't because she knew that Charles spent most of lounging on a couch and watching televisior

When the visitors had left, Lake resume seduction targets. Long before the term stalker b mon, Lake fit the definition perfectly, as recalled by shop owner. Pamela, who resembled actress Doris Day, oper ated a consignment store on State Street, Ukiah's main thoroughfare. She met Lake one night at a local bar, and he subsequently started dropping by her store, never buying anything, just hanging around to chat with her. "You look like a model," he said, and started a campaign to convince her to pose for him. Pam had noticed Lake taking pictures at a public barbeque held in Ukiah's main park, near a municipal swimming pool where kids splashed and screamed in noisy fun. She accepted the idea that he might be an accomplished photographer, but had no reason to pose for him, until he suggested that she might want to do some glamour shots as a present for her boyfriend.

When Pamela mentioned it to her mate, he strenuously objected in a manner that angered her. "I'm twenty-seven, I'll do what I want," she retorted. So she met Lake for Mexican food and beer, then accompanied him to the office of the firm where he worked to pick up his camera. There he showed her an album of photos he had taken. The first few portraits pleased Pam, but as she turned pages, her face reddened. "I was shocked to see girls, no more than ten or twelve years old, seminude. There was one picture of a young boy and girl, partially unclothed, hugging each other." As they left for her apartment, where he wanted her to pose, she wondered about the advisability of allowing Lake to know where she lived. Now concerned, she hesitantly permitted him to follow her. Inside her residence, he suggested that she pose nude. Her adamant refusal ended the session, but not Lake's determination.

More visits to Pam's shop followed, during which Lake began harassing her younger sister, Traci, who worked there. Lake had previously met the sister at The Ranch during an outdoor party. Most of the residents were skinny-dipping in the creek, but Traci kept her clothing on, despite Lake's clumsy attempts at persuading her to disrobe. He continued his unwelcome solicitations at every opportunity in the store, and Pam saw Lake several times following Traci in his pickup as she walked in town. Lake's operation finally came to an end when Traci's boyfriend, a member of the local Sheriff's Posse, made it clear that Lake's behavior would cause more trouble than he wanted.

During Lake's extended residency on The Ranch, other members of the community suffered a mysterious rash of burglaries. A number of power tools disappeared, including chain saws. In Ukiah, and throughout Mendocino County, the burglars seemed particularly interested in stealing rifles, handguns, and ammunition. A demolition firm lost several boxes of dynamite.

In the late summer of 1980, Lake again took Sir Lancelot to the renaissance fair, this one in Marin County, north of the Golden Gate Bridge. Wearing a hooded sweatshirt to ward off the chilly fog, Lake zeroed his wandering gaze on a woman who lingered in admiration of the unicorn. Something in her manner, and certainly her appearance, electrified Lake. Standing about five seven, with dark hair, blue eyes, and a quick smile, she wore a virginal white lacey dress and had flowers in her hair. It excited Lake when she responded to his opening comments with a special sauciness that made him want more. He learned that she worked as a teacher's aide in the Bay area, and sensed that she was ready for adventure. She matched him quip for quip in sensual, yet earthy language. He asked to see Claralyn "Cricket" Balazs again.

In the next few weeks, Lake drove frequently down to San Francisco to spend time with Cricket. She introduced him to her parents, and Lake felt comfortable talking to her chain-smoking father, a retired carpenter. Each meeting drew Leonard and Cricket closer. They dropped in on Charles Gunnar in Morgan Hill, and the huge pal approved of Lake's new love.

Sexually, Lake had met his match. Cricket seemed open to experimentation with a variety of erotic thrills. She had no qualms about fantasies of sharing their bed with another woman, using sex toys, and participating in bondage and domination. Willingly and brazenly she posed for his cameras. Lake couldn't have found a better partner. When he took her to his house at The Ranch, she liked the isolation and natural setting.

While Lake declared his love for Cricket, he continued to

write long letters to Darlene Davis at the boarding school where her parents had tried to place her out of his reach. According to Davis, he also sent "tons and tons" of photographs, including a myriad of nude pictures of his new girlfriend, Cricket. When the teenager's responses contained no objection to the erotic shots, Lake spiced up his correspondence by sending more explicit photos of him and Cricket having sex, and reported that she had moved in with him at The Ranch. Cricket, Lake told the teenager, was "extremely jealous" of Darlene. He also informed Darlene that "Cricket is a bisexual, and wants a female partner, as well as a woman to have three-ways with."

Lake introduced his new love-mate to neighbors on The Ranch, who accepted her but had grown to distrust and dislike him. Several residents suspected him of stealing from them, and one felt quite sure he had burglarized her home. Another, who grew marijuana on his parcel, growled that Lake had raided his property and stolen a good portion of his crop. Despite the ban on guns in the community, Lake openly flaunted the rule. Fed up, one member challenged him about engaging in target practice, pointing out that a stray bullet could kill someone. Lake responded by shouting, "I could kill everyone on the ranch, one by one ... I could go to every house with an automatic weapon and no one would ever know."

A storage shed on Lake's property erupted in flames one afternoon, and local volunteers rushed to help him put out the fire. When the heat enveloped his hidden ammunition, it exploded with loud hissing and popping. The firefighters leaped for cover behind trees to avoid flying bullets and shrapnel.

As unrest and suspicion grew among the population, Lake at last gave them a reason to ask him to leave. His employers at the housing rehabilitation firm caught Lake stealing building material, so they called the police. Lake spent several days in jail before he could rake up enough money to be released on bond. He swore he would never again allow himself to be incarcerated. Fortunately for him, a lenient judge sentenced him to a year on probation rather than a lengthy jail term. When a committee from The Ranch heard of his arrest, they asked Lake to sell his property and move out. Recognizing the futility of resisting, he agreed. Within a few days, he and Cricket packed up and left the area.

Chapter 6

Philo is a tiny hamlet situated in the verdant rolling foothills of California's Trinity Alps, approximately twenty miles west of Ukiah. Black oaks, manzanita and a few Jeffrey pines border the region's fertile grape vineyards that once were cattle pastures. No more than 150 citizens live in Philo, several of them employed by a lumber company that occupies the southeast quadrant. A sweeping S-shaped curve of two-lane State Highway 128 divides the dozen buildings that make up Philo, about twenty-two miles from the coast where picturesque artist colonies such as Mendocino attract swarms of tourists in the summer. But Philo is generally only a stop along the way for gas or snacks, or maybe to look over the wares in an antiques store. The only overnight accommodations located there in 1981— a single-story structure with eight units, built in the 1940s— aptly bore the name Philo Motel.

When Lake and Cricket hurriedly left The Ranch, they drove

toward the coast, and stopped in Philo. Leonard may have been interested in the area from reading a magazine article that promoted Anderson Valley as an ideal haven from a nuclear holocaust. The motel owner, Lake learned, needed someone to occupy and manage the place, so Leonard and Cricket decided to stay. She landed a part-time job at the Anderson Valley Elementary School as a teacher's aide.

Settling into a routine at Philo, Lake met Robert Glover, captain of the Anderson Valley Fire Department. The two men hit it off, and Lake became one of forty unpaid volunteer firemen in the county. To further ingratiate himself, he took on duties as the organization's recording secretary and wrote their bylaws. Lake's knowledge about fire fighting impressed Glover, and the chief expressed his gratitude for a bundle of books Lake donated, several of which included instructions for the handling of incendiary devices and fire starting. One of the books had been published by the U.S. Central Intelligence Agency.

Outwardly Lake appeared to be an ordinary citizen trying to live a responsible life. But his obsessive sex drive, encouraged by Cricket's willingness to experiment, fueled his secret lust for thrills. So he placed an ad in *The Bay Guardian,* a San Francisco publication. It looked innocent enough, nothing more than an offer of employment for someone willing to relocate to a rural town to help operate and maintain a small motel.

Meanwhile in the city, Connie Richards, eighteen, needed a job. At the end of August, the attractive, young woman wrote a letter to Lake outlining her skills, and he quickly responded with an invitation to meet him in Philo. She rode a Greyhound bus 120 miles north and stepped off in the tiny burg, impressed by the welcoming embrace of Leonard and Cricket. They explained that she would receive room and board in exchange for helping with the motel chores. It didn't take long for Connie to recognize that the couple really wanted a sex partner. She realized "it was mainly for Cricket, not Leonard."

"I wasn't really into what Cricket wanted," recalled Richards, but she chose to stay with them anyway, somewhat curious about the arrangement. "I saw sado-masochistic paraphernalia, just the basic stuff, nothing extreme. There were eye hooks [for securing ropes] at each corner of the bed Cricket and Leonard shared, along with a mask and whip." The couple explained that Lake liked to tie Cricket up and whip her, but Connie never witnessed the act.

"I was really young," she rationalized in revealing that she experimented one time in a ménage à trois with the lusty couple. That experience ended any bisexual activity, but Connie did have sex with Leonard "a few times" with Cricket's knowledge and approval. She thought it interesting that Cricket expressed no jealousy about the trysts. Asked about Lake's treatment of her, she said that he was not "kinky" in any way. On the contrary, he was "actually very gentle and caring." Lake, she said, told her that Cricket was really the "kinky" one in her desire for S&M and sex toys.

In the intimate moments between Connie and Leonard, he told her of his sexual fantasies, and revealed that he had wanted to sleep with his sister Janet. He never laid claim to actually doing it, but spoke of it as a fantasy.

When Leonard asked Connie to pose in the nude, she refused, but did allow him to photograph her with her shirt unbuttoned, exposing her breasts.

Lake was still writing steamy letters to Darlene Davis at the boarding school. He mailed photos of Connie. "We have started making porno videotapes," he said. "Cricket is really into doing porn tapes and selling them. A friend told her that we could make a lot of money doing it." Regarding Connie's presence in Philo, Lake said that she had been recruited for the primary purpose of having three-way sex, and, if she was willing, to satisfy Cricket's bisexual needs.

Connie, unaware that Lake revealed such personal matters about her, performed her chores at the motel. Her work took

her into all of the rooms and storage areas. She noticed a
collection of guns, but having no interest in weapons, ignored
them. Lake never mentioned the arsenal, but did confide to
Connie that he carried cyanide pills with him at all times to
prevent ever being locked up in prison.

On September 13, 1981, Lake, Cricket, and Connie drove
to Morgan Hill, where Lake and Cricket took the vows of
marriage. Charles Gunnar acted as Lake's best man, returning
the favor for Lake who had been best man at Gunnar's wedding.
Connie met Lake's half sister Janet at the ceremony, and
couldn't help but think about Lake's incestuous feelings toward
her. Gunnar tried to "make a move" on Connie, but she turned
him down. When she informed Leonard about it, he criticized
Gunnar and told Connie that the hefty fellow had propositioned
Cricket, too. Gunnar, Lake complained, abused his own wife
and children. And speaking of people who made him angry,
Lake told Connie that he disliked his own brother, Donald. She
paid little attention, never having met the brother.

Back in Philo, Connie resumed her duties and her periodic
sessions with Leonard. The couple didn't seem very wealthy
to her, but Lake bragged to Connie that he had buried $30,000
in silver near Ukiah. He planned to use the money, he said, to
buy property. Later, she heard that Lake had moved the money
to Cricket's house in the Bay area.

Connie's stay in Philo lasted three months. Feeling that she
served no real purpose other than her role as a sex object, she
said good-bye to Leonard and Cricket fourteen days before
Christmas. She also bid farewell to a short, quiet Asian man
named Charlie who had arrived two weeks earlier.

Prior to Charlie's arrival, Lake had heard from Mark Novak,
the soldier who had spent a few days with him on The Ranch.
From Hawaii, Novak had kept in touch through Lake's secret
post office box. Having finally learned Lake's real name, Novak

gave it to Charles Ng (pronounced eeng), a Marine who had gotten into some trouble. Ng, facing a court-martial in Kaneohe Bay, had slipped away from custody and needed a safe place to hide out.

When Charlie Ng showed up in Philo, Lake realized that Connie Richards had already made a decision to leave, so he figured the newcomer could take over the chores she'd been doing. Because the Marine was a fugitive, he would be grateful for a place to stay, and would work for room and board. Standing only five seven and weighing 145 pounds, the wiry young man looked agile and powerful, despite his need for thick glasses. He proved a willing laborer and his interest in survivalism fit right into Lake's lifestyle.

As would later be revealed in trial testimony, according to a police report in Milbrae, near the San Francisco International Airport, Charles Ng may have shared something else in common with Lake. A woman who worked for an escort service in the city stated that a man calling himself Tom Meyers had arranged to use her services. After paying in advance, he asked to photograph her. He first took her out to dinner, then to a motel where she posed for him. When she emerged from the bathroom, a short Chinese man lunged at her with a knife, and forced her to lie down on the bed. While repeatedly stabbing at the mattress, within inches of her head, the woman told police, the Asian brutally raped her while Meyers watched. During the sexual assault, she said, Meyers commented, "This is something we do all the time, but we usually kill the girls we've been with. But I like you, so we're not going to kill you."

The victim later identified Tom Meyers as Leonard Lake, and the rapist as Charles Ng.

Within a very short time after Ng's arrival at Philo, Lake and Cricket gave up the motel management job. Along with Charlie, they moved out. A woman who lived nearby, on property called Indian Creek Ranch, wanted to start a youth camp.

She owned a secluded cluster of one-story wooden buildings, including a white house trimmed in red, detached guest quarters, and a barnlike structure used as a workshop, located near a meandering stream 300 yards off the highway. When she learned about Lake's military background and interest in survivalism, she decided he and his teachers' aide wife would be well qualified to manage the camp. Lake ended his arrangement at the motel, and happily accepted the youth camp offer. The motel owner also breathed a sigh of relief. He had heard complaints from customers that Lake practiced voyeurism while they sat nude in an enclosed hot tub. Once, the owner had dropped in to check on Lake's work, and saw several hand grenades on a table. "Are those live?" he asked.

"Go ahead and pull the pin and find out," Lake shot back.

The owner felt happy to be rid of the strange fellow who ceaselessly talked about military operations and holocaust survival, to the exclusion of nearly everything else.

Ernie Pardini lived in a mobile home fifty yards from the Indian Creek main house with his wife and two young daughters. He labored part-time maintaining the owner's property in addition to working a regular job in the logging business. The landowner, after introducing Pardini to Lake, Cricket, and Ng, asked him if he would use his truck to help the trio move. Pardini graciously concurred. The chance of any meaningful friendship nearly ended within the first few hours when Lake saw a piece of furniture slip from the grasp of Pardini and Ng. Lake barked furiously at them. "He reprimanded both of us," Pardini recalled, "and I felt like walking away right then." Instead, he shot a dark glance at Lake and kept his cool. Tempers calmed, and the men finished the moving job.

Pardini wondered why Lake and Ng always wore military cammies, but didn't bother to ask. He found Lake sociable enough after the initial flare-up, but perceived Charlie as silent and solemn, albeit respectful. As Christmas approached, Ng didn't even mention that December 24, 1981, was his twenty-first birthday.

The loquacious Lake told Pardini of his need to find an ideal spot for constructing a bunker that would survive Armageddon. He drew diagrams and plans for his secure retreat. The site, said Lake, must be on a hillside that could be excavated to allow a portion of the building to be underground. Lake's conversations with Pardini also extended to his interest in women. In a tool storage shed, he showed Pardini a photographic collection of scantily clad females, many of them totally nude. Lake explained that some of them were his ex-girlfriends. When Lake commented that Pardini's two young daughters were beautiful, and offered to take pictures of them, Pardini instantly and firmly declined. He didn't yet know that Lake had already secretly snapped several shots of Pardini's wife while she worked in her garden.

Gradually Pardini grew wary of Lake. He would later say that his neighbor's sexual innuendos around Pardini's wife made them both uncomfortable. Several times, while Pardini worked, Lake invited Mrs. Pardini to join him and Cricket in watching video movies. The offers weren't accepted because she assumed he meant porno movies. Although Lake's off-color comments usually took place within Cricket's hearing, she didn't seem to notice. One evening, Pardini returned from a short trip to find his wife in tears. She explained that Lake had been harassing her all day long, telling her that she was doing everything wrong. Furious, Pardini marched over to Lake's house and ordered him to stay away from his wife. His eyes and clenching jaw muscles sent an unequivocal message that if Lake responded negatively, there would be a fight. Standing about five eight and 150 pounds, Pardini could certainly take care of himself, as some of the local bar patrons had learned.

Calmly Lake said, "I would never fight you. I'm a coward." But he added a warning. Although he wouldn't slug it out with anyone, he might come back and shoot them. Pardini bluntly told Lake that such threats didn't scare him. He had some guns of his own.

Guns turned out to be the catalyst that ended the residency of Lake, Cricket, and Ng at Indian Creek Ranch. The FBI, working closely with the Mendocino County Sheriff's Office, had received a tip that Charles Ng, a fugitive wanted by the U.S. Marine Corps, was hiding out in Philo. Spearheaded by Sheriff's Investigator Steven Satterwhite, a dead ringer for actor Montgomery Clift in his young days, the team finalized plans for a raid on the Philo Motel, where they thought Ng still resided. They had information that Ng might be armed and dangerous, and probably carried a .357 caliber revolver. Also, the reports on the fugitive pointed out his expertise in martial arts and his skill with the use of nunchaku sticks (two cylindrical handles connected by a cord, a martial arts weapon). Furthermore, a search of his locker at the Kaneohe Bay Marine Base in Hawaii had revealed remnants of dynamite and timer devices, so investigators prepared for the possibility that Ng might be in possession of bombs or booby traps.

On April 29, 1982, the task force, consisting of nine FBI men, a half dozen sheriff's deputies, and Satterwhite—deployed in unmarked cars, a helicopter, and a fixed-wing aircraft—prepared to move in on the Philo Motel. At the last minute, men in the airplane observed the targeted men's car leave the motel. It crossed the bridge across Indian Creek, turned into a long driveway, drove through a grove of giant redwood trees, and halted in the ranch compound. Hurriedly altering the attack plan, Satterwhite redirected the team to the cluster of buildings off Ray Road.

They launched the operation at 9:15 in the morning, springing from the noisy chopper and several vehicles. As the officers surrounded the central camp area, one of them spotted Charles Ng vaulting from a bedroom window. The fugitive trotted toward an open field in the direction of an adjacent lumber company. Just as he attempted to hurdle a fence, Satterwhite and a sheriff's sergeant grabbed him, patted him down for weapons, and snapped cuffs on his wrists. They hustled him into the helicopter for a quick flight to Ukiah's county jail.

Satterwhite caught sight of Leonard Lake walking along a fenced area behind the living quarters, moving toward the workshop building. The officer barked a command for Lake to halt and stand still. Instead, Lake reversed his direction, sprinted toward the house Ng had left, and disappeared inside. With members of the FBI SWAT team, Satterwhite entered Ng's room and saw a pair of rifles, nunchaku sticks, and a billy club on the rumpled bed.

Other agents caught Lake in a room containing a small arsenal of weapons. Satterwhite introduced himself, and asked Lake who owned all of the rifles, handguns, and ammunition. In what Satterwhite described as a "calm and reasonable attitude," Lake said a few of the guns were his, but he knew nothing about any of the contraband material.

Asked about Charles Ng, Lake said he was "a guest who helped with odd chores." Lake also granted written permission for the officers to search the compound. They turned up six handguns and six rifles, several of them fully automatic, along with hand grenades, TNT, a silencer, tear gas, and several boxes of ammunition. Lake stood by, observing each discovery, and acknowledged that he knew the weapons were illegal contraband. He also volunteered that Ng had brought in a MAC 10 (Military Armament Corporation) assault weapon with a sound suppressor, converted to fully automatic operation, which would make it illegal. But, Lake claimed, he didn't know where Ng had hidden it. A few other stolen guns were found in Ng's room, along with martial arts weapons.

From the beginning of the raid, an officer had located and detained Lake's wife. But Lake insisted that she knew nothing of the weapons cache and had not participated in anything illegal. Most of the guns, Lake said, had been purchased by Ng through mail order. The dynamite, according to Lake, had been sent by Ng from Hawaii prior to his arrival in Philo. At each new discovery of hidden armaments, Lake claimed that Ng must have hidden the guns. Apparently, the old "Semper Fi" tradition of protecting your Marine buddy meant nothing to Lake.

Determined to find the MAC 10 weapon, Satterwhite telephoned the county jail and spoke to Ng, who said that he had disassembled it. He had left the parts on a table in his bedroom when he fled. A second search of the room turned up nothing. Finally Lake beckoned Satterwhite and led him to a laundry hamper. On his knees, Lake reached into the dirty clothing and retrieved several of the missing parts. Outside, at a junk pile behind the workshop, he moved a stack of logs and recovered the remaining components. Hanging his head, Lake said, "The gun is registered to me. I knew Ng had converted it to fully automatic, so I didn't want it found." He admitted rushing to Ng's room while the officers had been busy capturing the fugitive, grabbing up the dismantled rifle parts, and quickly concealing them.

Satterwhite placed Lake under arrest and sent him with a deputy to the county jail in Ukiah. They left Cricket at the compound. She immediately drove to the county seat and helped Lake post bail. They returned to Indian Creek Ranch the following morning.

Follow-up investigation by Satterwhite revealed that several of the weapons had been stolen in recent Mendocino County burglaries, but a few recently heisted guns had not been found. He obtained a search warrant, and drove once again to Philo, along with a deputy and two ATF agents. Lake and Cricket, irritated at the persistent cops, watched another search. Satterwhite asked Lake to explain his whereabouts a few days earlier when a burglary had taken place in Ukiah. Lake claimed he had been working, but volunteered that Charles Ng had not been in his room that night. Cricket corroborated the information about Ng's absence.

Describing the specific guns he sought, Satterwhite asked Lake if he had ever seen them. No, Lake answered, but said he might know where Ng could have hidden them. A woman living in a nearby trailer house, Lake said, had seen Ng climbing out of the workshop attic. Lake led the investigator to the attic, where Satterwhite found a bundle wrapped in plastic, containing the weapons described in his search warrant.

Someone had removed the serial number from a recovered rifle. Lake confessed to Satterwhite that he had used a grinder to obliterate the number, then used a welding torch to fill in the groove.

Charged with seventeen felony counts, including firearms violations, and the violations of probation from the previous burglary and theft in Ukiah, Lake faced a probable prison term. The prospect of being confined behind bars filled Lake with abject horror. He had often made the claim that he would take his own life with cyanide rather than accept imprisonment. But he wasn't ready for that yet. No, he decided, he would neither kill himself, nor go to jail. He would simply flee and use his wits to avoid ever being caught again. He still had a mission in life: to build his bunker for survival of a holocaust, and to carry out his fantasy of capturing and enslaving a young woman. The ideas of using his survival skills and of owning a sex slave would sustain him.

Lake took the plunge, stepping into his new role by failing to show up at his scheduled court hearing. From that point on, Leonard Lake would live as a fugitive.

Cricket, too, understood that her husband's choice to run from the law meant radical changes in the way she would live. She had a choice to make: life on the run, always looking over her shoulder, or returning to her parents in San Bruno and beginning anew.

Charles Ng, under close guard, found himself on a military plane, headed toward Kaneohe Bay, Hawaii, the site of an earlier decision that changed his life forever.

Chapter 7

In 1960, more than 4 million people lived and worked in bustling, noisy Hong Kong, the United Kingdom colony packed into a little over 400 square miles. Among those citizens were Kenneth Ng and his family, who squeezed themselves into a small apartment in a towering high-rise. Against nearly insurmountable odds, Ng had carved a niche for himself in the middle-class world by working as a camera salesman for the German firm Leica. Through self-sacrifice, long hours of hard work, and extensive travel, Ng provided comfort for his wife, children, and four relatives, assuring they wouldn't be subjected to pain and hunger as he had been during his childhood.

At the age of twelve, Kenneth Ng and his family had fled from the city to escape Japanese invaders during WWII. They returned at war's end, and faced a tough struggle just to survive. With no formal education, Ng helped earn a living by selling trinkets to the English soldiers who had pushed out the Japanese conquerors. Through his frequent contact with army personnel, Ng learned how to speak the English language. This made him realize the importance of education, so he enrolled in night school and took classes for two years. When he landed the sales job, and started his family, Kenneth Ng vowed that his children would go to the best schools. Through applied study, he hoped, they could ascend the social and professional ladder. Nothing would make Ng happier than to see his children succeed.

After marrying his sweetheart, Oi Ping, Kenneth wanted a son. Two attempts produced a pair of daughters, but they decided to try once more. In his charmingly broken English, Kenneth explained, "Because I came up with a family of ten, that is too much. So I thought, 'Well, if lucky enough, I have a boy and a girl. That is enough for me.' My first one, Alice, is a girl; second one, Betty, is also a girl. So I try one more time. I thought, 'Well, if it is a girl again, no more.' Because I know . . . you got too many children, you couldn't really educate them."

On Christmas Eve of 1960, Kenneth Ng and his wife received the gift they wanted more than anything else. Charles Chitat (pronounced Cheetah) Ng rounded out their family.

Kenneth Ng's dream of providing an uncrowded dwelling for his wife and kids didn't work out quite as well. Because family ties are extremely important in the Chinese culture, he felt obligated to help relatives in need. In the two-bedroom apartment, Kenneth made room for not only his wife and three children, but also two grandmothers and two aunts.

As his children grew, Kenneth worked even harder to produce respectable living conditions. He even bought an automobile, a true luxury among Hong Kong residents, leading many people to think the Ngs were wealthy. He also furnished the apartment with a piano so his children could take lessons. Outings in the car, picnics, and good food became an important part of the Ng family routine.

Betty, the second daughter, recalled some fond memories of home life, as related to her brother. "Charles would always prepare snacks for me to come home to after school. Many hot and humid nights he slept on the top level of the bunk bed and I below. He would fan me to sleep before himself." With a soft giggle, she remembered Charlie's pet, a chicken. "He always looked after his chicken very well, always feeding it with goodies like cheddar cheese."

Early in his life, Charles discovered his martial arts guru, movie star Bruce Lee, and tried to copy the actor. Of course, his parents wouldn't allow him to have real martial arts weapons, such as nunchaku sticks, so young Charlie made his own. He packed tightly twisted paper into a pair of cardboard tubes from paper towel rolls, and connected them with twine. To harden his small fists, he filled a cloth sack with sand, attached it to a wall, and repeatedly punched it with all the strength he could muster. His mother, fearing that such activity would encourage him to fight with other boys, did all she could to discourage the Bruce Lee imitations.

Both parents attempted to prevent any interference with the all-important goal of a fine education. Kenneth Ng said, "I feel education is very important . . . you know, schooling in Hong Kong was quite tough because good school is hard to get in. But I tried so hard. My eldest daughter, Alice, she get the good school, the missionary school called Mary Knoll. That is hard to get in." In the opinion of Kenneth Ng, Catholic schools provided the best teaching services. So, determined to secure enrollment in outstanding schools for his second daughter and his son, Ng made personal calls on the headmasters to plead his case. He understood that wealthy professionals, such as lawyers and doctors, would probably receive preferential treatment. Nevertheless, he doggedly sought admission for his children into the parochial schools.

"I have to try a few schools," Kenneth recalled, " because I don't have social position. I also am a Christian, but not a

Catholic." His intense campaign finally convinced administrators to accept both of his younger children. Betty went to St. Paul convent school, and Charles was accepted by St. Joseph's. To Kenneth, this could be counted as a major victory. So, he expected all three offspring to honor him by working hard to achieve superior grades.

Alice and Betty generally met Ng's expectations, but young Charles faltered. The father worried. "They have very good teachers and you have to pass. I mean, if your study is no good, they just kick you out." Kenneth Ng couldn't allow all of his efforts to be wasted. He desperately wanted his son to succeed. When Kenneth came home late from work, exhausted, and heard that Charles had failed to complete his homework, or had been given a poor grade, the father turned to the only method of discipline he understood. He punished his son, sometimes using a cane or the handle of a feather duster to beat him.

Many years later, with Western society frowning on the parental use of corporal punishment, and social behaviorists labeling the spanking of children as primitive child abuse, it might be easy to look with a critical eye at the methods used by Hong Kong parents in the 1960s to discipline their children. In retrospect, even Kenneth Ng wondered if he had erred in his child-rearing methods. "I [was] very angry. Because I want him good . . . I beat him with a stick. But I didn't know . . . and now they are teaching the different way than the old way what we do."

Asked if he restrained the boy in order to prevent his attempts at escaping punishment, Kenneth answered, "Yes. I beat him very hard. And I not permit him to run away. And even my wife tried to stop me. I feel very bad and angry if he doesn't have a good result. . . ." Tears welled in the little man's eyes. "Now I look back, well, maybe this is not the way to teaching the children. Now I know." But, said Kenneth, "I did it because I love him. I want my children to be good."

Young Charles Ng reacted to the punishment by withdrawing. He interacted with few people, mainly his sister Betty and a male cousin, Benny Chung. Five years older than Charlie, Benny sometimes took on the role of surrogate brother to his cousin at family picnics in the mountains surrounding Hong Kong and at a community pool, where they splashed in the water together and took swimming lessons. Regarding the discipline, Chung recalled, "We all got spankings that way."

To Charles, the physical punishment hurt, but other traumatic events may have wounded him even more deeply. His mother, Oi Ping, later recalled two such incidents. Speaking through an interpreter, she said, "Charlie loved pets. He used to have a chicken, which he raised from very small to over a pound. Our mother thought that [the] chicken is . . . very smelly. She suggested to kill it." When his pet chicken wound up in a cooking pot, Charles burst into tears and retreated to his bed, brokenhearted. "And then later on he had a turtle, and he would not let us lock it up, so the turtle was all over the place in the house. Every day, he would buy fish to feed the turtle." Unfortunately, said Oi Ping, the small reptile relieved itself in the house. "It was very smelly. So [we] wanted to bring it to a pond very far away where Charlie could release it himself." The loss of his second pet again distressed the boy. "Then, there was the dog. I am afraid of dog. But he brought a dog home, and I told him he cannot keep it. So he release it [where] there are some other dogs, so the dog can have some companion."

Thus, Charles faced life without the companionship of any pets, and with few friends. He spent hours in his room, alone and reading. Early on, it became apparent that Charles was nearsighted, which required him to wear strong corrective eyeglasses.

Young Charles appeared to have a talent for art, and a teacher even exhibited his work. Oi Ping recalled a related event that hurt the boy. "One time he was waiting on the street for me to pick him up. He left his art supply there, and I did not let him go back to pick it up, and he stop his lessons." The loss of his pencils, brushes, and paint temporarily ended Charlie's artistic endeavors, but his skill at drawing, painting, and origami (folding paper into various forms, such as animals) would emerge again years later, in a much different context.

Another influence from Charlie's father may have had a big effect on his future. Kenneth Ng joined the army reserve which required him to don a crisp, pressed uniform and attend training sessions. His son seemed impressed by the apparel and the associated military trappings. It would later be speculated that the sight of his father instilled in Charles a desire to emulate him and seek a military career.

As Charles grew into his teen years, another cousin, several years younger, enjoyed bonding with him. "He always bought me presents, and gave me ice cream."

In an article for *Penthouse* magazine, journalist Rick Mofina revealed that Ng's family sought psychiatric treatment for Charles by the time he reached age ten after he stole a photograph from a friend's home. According to Mofina's research, Charles found trouble in several ways. He would seek out Western children in parks to assault them, would hurl Molotov cocktails from rooftops, and would engage in destructive vandalism such as arson, which resulted in his being arrested. At school he allegedly wrote obscene letters to a teacher. Once, Charlie's mixing of chemicals in a classroom caused a fire, which was quickly extinguished. Mofina reported that Ng was expelled at age fifteen.

Perhaps, thought the embarrassed father, it would be better to send his son away from Hong Kong, where he might concentrate harder on school. One of Kenneth Ng's brothers, Rufus, had also ascended from their poverty-stricken childhood to become a teacher. He had relocated to Preston, England, on the western coast north of Liverpool. The uncle had already accepted Ng's daughter Betty, allowing her to live in his home while attending an English school. Kenneth Ng asked if his son, Charles, could also be allowed to reside, part-time, with the relatives while attending a boys prep school. During most weekdays, the boy would live in a campus dormitory.

Charles Ng, pleased to rejoin his sister, journeyed to England and enrolled in High Bentham Grammar School. But after a few months, the reticent youth felt that his uncle Rufus really didn't want him. Charlie's mother, Oi Ping, made a trip to the home of Rufus to personally evaluate the situation, and agreed with her son. She later said, "I felt that his uncle's temper is very funny. There [was] not enough food for Charles, either. Once, when Charlie came back from the school dormitory, I noticed that his room has no heat and bed was icy cold. I was wondering why he doesn't even have a warm place to stay. At meal time, I told him to eat more, but he said, 'Oh, I have enough.' Actually I noticed that he was afraid and he did not eat enough."

According to Oi Ping, she spoke to Uncle Rufus about what she perceived as unfair treatment of her son. "He did not like it. He said he no longer wishes to be Charlie's guardian."

The *Penthouse* article alleged that Ng's problems in England also involved the theft of $40 from a schoolmate as an act of revenge for ignoring Charles while paying more attention to a different pal.

Oi Ping took both of her offspring back to Hong Kong.

Still determined that Charles would receive an education, the parents consulted his aunt Alice who had moved to San Leandro, on the east side of the San Francisco Bay. She agreed to let Ng live with her and attend Notre Dame College, a small parochial school on the bay's west side, not far from the San Francisco airport. With a student visa, he arrived in the United

States in early 1979. While waiting for the fall semester to start, he worked and commuted by bus. His aunt taught him to drive that summer, and Ng bought his first car, a big cumbersome station wagon. Ng turned out to be a terrible driver. On the first day, he backed the car into a utility pole. Not long afterward, once again trying to back out of the driveway, he slammed into a neighbor's car. According to his aunt, he apologized, paid for the damage, and sold the station wagon. Thereafter, Ng depended on being chauffeured by his aunt or on the use of public transportation. When he enrolled in Notre Dame College, he moved into a campus dormitory.

The college routine of work and study did not appeal to Charles Ng. He'd barely started when he made one of the most important decisions of his life. Without informing any of his relatives, he marched into a U.S. Marine Corps recruiting station in October 1979, before his nineteenth birthday, and enlisted. Noncitizens were ineligible for membership in the Corps, but somehow Ng managed to sidestep that problem. His military records indicate that he was born in Bloomington, Indiana! Ng would one day claim that the recruiting sergeant helped him fake documents needed to prove citizenship.

Adapting quickly to the hardships of boot camp at the Marine Corps Recruit Depot in San Diego, Ng easily completed the rigorous preparation for combat. Advanced infantry training at Camp Pendleton, north of San Diego, gave him expertise in the use and care of weapons, especially with a variety of guns. The whole process ignited in Ng an interest in the ability to survive nearly any challenge or hardship. He began to read publications on the subject of survivalism and to seek out other men with the same interest.

Not counting the few barrack mates who shared his fascination with survivalism, Ng generally behaved as a loner. A fellow Marine, Ray Guzman, recalled that Ng often kept to himself, making few friends during his six months at Camp Pendleton. Guzman accompanied Ng to town a few times where the two men ate in a Chinese restaurant and attended 'Bruce Lee and kung-fu type" movies. "Charlie liked to practice martial arts," recalled Guzman. Ng would show off by asking someone to hold a pencil at face level, and then he would kick the pencil from the person's grasp.

During on-duty drills, according to Guzman, the Marines learned macho chants such as "No gun, no fun," or "No kill, no thrill." While marching, double time, the men would shout, "Bravo Company, kill-kill-kill."

Ng also learned the meaning of "Semper Fi," the traditional verbalization of the Marine Corps motto, Semper Fidelis, meaning "always faithful." Those who have served in the Corps generally agree that there is no such thing as an "ex-Marine." Even after completing their tours of duty and leaving the service, Marines are always faithful to the Corps. Veterans claim there is an allegiance, a camaraderie that lasts a lifetime. And a Marine's conduct, on active duty or even on leave, involves backing up the members of his unit. This reliability, according to statements from men from Ng's Company, was essential to the all-important cohesion necessary in peace or in combat.

In the life of Charles Ng, "Semper Fi" would be severely tested.

Upon completion of his training at the sprawling base in Southern California, Lance Corporal Ng was assigned to the 1st Battalion, 3rd Marine Regiment, Weapons Company, at the Marine Corps Air Station, Kanehoe Bay, Hawaii. Located on Mokapu peninsula, the base was the home of 5,000 Marines. Ng received training as an "A gunner," meaning that his duties were to help the lead gunner in the team operation of an antitank missile device. Intensive practice sessions, designed to prepare the team for combat, involved carrying the ammunition, helping to set up the weapon, and assuring the lead gunner's safety during his vulnerable process of zeroing in on the target. According to Hugh Daugherty, who was Ng's team leader, the bespectacled, quiet lance corporal met all the requirements of his military operational specialty, and "did what he was told."

David Burns, a slim, articulate sergeant during Ng's tour of duty in Hawaii, saw him almost daily, and rated Ng as an "outstanding" weapons handler, who was a Marine "of the best order." Said Burns, "Lance Corporal Ng corrected errors without question."

As Hugh Daugherty remembered, Ng was a "quiet loner," who sometimes practiced martial arts in the barracks. "I never saw him drink, use drugs, or chase women," said Daugherty. "He was usually alone, even when I bumped into him on leave."

Leave for the Marines at Kaneohe, or "K-bay" as many of them referred to the base, often meant a twenty-mile trip via bus or private cars across the lush Koolau mountains to Honolulu. Charles Ng generally avoided the more hedonistic pursuits available in the city in favor of an occasional movie or simply staying at the base. Sometimes, he participated in platoon parties for families of men in the Weapons Company. A few of them later recalled that Ng was never boisterous, loud, or outspoken. However, some of his barrack mates thought of him as a lonely man who desperately wanted to be accepted by them, but didn't know how to gain their friendship. A few of the men noticed that Ng was sometimes subjected to racial insults and became the butt of crude jokes.

The men close to Ng, though, saw something else in him. They detected a certain toughness and interest in adventure. Lance Corporal James Williamson and Corporal Vic Mowry associated with him after duty hours, as did Corporal Dan Mitchum. Williamson trusted Ng enough to confide in him about an extramarital affair. Ng impressed Williamson with his proficiency in martial arts, and agreed to become his instructor. They practiced together frequently. Williamson enjoyed Ng's company, and invited the loner to join him and his wife at his off-base apartment for dinner, after which the two men spent hours practicing martial arts. To Ng, Williamson and a few other men were his "Semper Fi" buddies on whom he could rely, and who would back him up in the face of danger.

The strong interest in survivalism led to an acquaintanceship with a man from a different branch of the service, a young Army corporal stationed in the center of Oahu at Schofield Barracks. While browsing through a military surplus store, Mark Novak happened to notice that another shopper, a Marine, wore a scuba-diving watch similar to his own. The two men, chatting about the watches and merchandise in the store, found they had some interests in common. Charles Ng enjoyed Mark Novak's conversation about weapons, tactics, and methods of staying alive in the wild. Over soft drinks, Novak learned he shared with Ng a distaste for drinking, smoking, using drugs, and hanging out in bars. As a married man, Novak wished to avoid a lifestyle that might get him into trouble and cause problems with his wife. Ng, he thought, might be the type of a buddy he needed, a man who also wished to avoid temptation. During the next few weeks, the alliance grew. Novak told Ng of an interesting survivalist he'd met in Northern California, at a place called "The Ranch." He'd known the man as Tom Meyers, but later learned his real name, Leonard Lake. Lake, he said, may have been a "shit talker" who didn't appear to be fully prepared for a disaster, but he did know a lot about weapons and also had a great collection of pictures he'd taken of young women.

Most young military men sooner or later get around to discussing women. It seemed a little strange to Novak that Ng showed little interest in the topic. Novak even entertained the idea that Ng might be bisexual. The quiet Chinese man seemed far more interested in weapons, martial arts, and proving himself as a perfect Marine.

Chapter 8

As in most military organizations, all of the weapons assigned to Charles Ng's Marine company were stored in a locked armory when not in use. Armed guards were posted at the secured entry to the facility twenty-four hours a day. In early September 1981, Ng drew guard duty at the armory.

During his watch, an idea formed in Ng's mind. What if he could steal some of the more valuable rifles, grenades, handguns, and other arms, and sell them? It would be a highly profitable enterprise, and would demonstrate his ability to pull off a dangerous operation. As he stood his post, and marched around the armory, he observed a metal grating covering a window that might easily be breached with a pair of bolt cutters. Even better, tall bushes obscured the grating. A successful entry would require complicity by the guard on duty, who would deliberately avoid checking the window, or fail to look closely at the breached grate. If carried out correctly, it could be made to appear that the guard was innocent of any involvement. The more Ng thought about it, the more attractive his idea became.

After mulling it over a couple of weeks, Ng suggested the raid to Vic Mowry, who could see the possibilities. Just after midnight on October 10, minutes before Ng's pal Lance Corporal Williamson began his watch as guard of the armory, Ng approached him. Ng later said, "I asked him if he would do anything if something happened at the armory, and he said he did not care as long as he wasn't involved, or something like that. I asked him if he would say anything if he saw me inside the armory during his watch. I guess he thought I was joking, and he said he wouldn't say anything. He asked me what I was planning on doing, and I told him that I was going to steal weapons ... and gave him some details of my plan. He said he didn't know if he wanted to get involved and would have to think about it."

Even when Ng offered his pal a share of the stolen weapons, Williamson didn't take the bait. Ng walked away to find Mowry, and firmly stated that the raid would have to be carried out right then, because they would need cooperation from the duty guard whom they knew. Ng recalled, "I felt confident that Williamson would go along with my plan because he seemed like a weak-willed individual and I could exert control over him ... he seemed reliable and he disliked the Marine Corps." Ng admitted that he had befriended Williamson primarily with the idea in mind of using him at some time in the future. Williamson's off-base apartment could be a perfect place to store some of the weapons, and he owned a car they could use.

Having successfully recruited Mowry, Ng returned to Williamson, still on guard duty, and asked him to participate in the break-in. The nervous lance corporal said he couldn't, because he didn't want to disappoint his wife. Perhaps Ng could do it another time, Williamson suggested, when someone else was guarding the building. Impatient, Ng informed the reluctant pal that he'd been planning the raid for that night, and furthermore, he needed Williamson's car to haul the loot away. He and Mowry could make it appear that Williamson was innocent of any involvement, Ng promised.

The soft sell didn't appear to be working, so Ng turned up the heat. "I told him that if he didn't assist us as I had asked, I would tell his wife about the affair he'd had. . . . I also told him I would kick his ass. He knew of my martial arts ability since I had demonstrated for him several times while instructing him." Williamson caved in and agreed to cooperate.

Ng told Williamson that he and Mowry would enter through the grated window. If anyone approached while they were inside, Williamson's duty would be to signal by knocking on the front door with his rifle butt. Ng also demanded that the accomplice leave his car keys in the ignition, with the window down. That way, if the car was ever connected to the raid, Williamson could claim his vehicle had been stolen.

In the wee, quiet hours, with the only sound being made by the caress of warm trade winds rustling palm fronds, Ng and Mowry found the car, with keys inside as instructed, and moved it into dark shadows behind the weapons company armory. Ng recalled, "I posted Mowry as a watch while I cut a one-foot hole in through the screen covering the window. I entered the armory through the hole." As he crawled inside, the jagged, razor-sharp ends of the metal grate he had cut ripped into his right thigh, drawing blood, but not causing a serious injury. "I started gathering weapons. While I was attempting to obtain a sniper rifle by cutting the lock off the cage, I made noise because the bolt cutters were too small to cut the lock."

Williamson heard the metallic clanking inside, pounded on the door with his rifle butt, then opened it a crack to peer inside. In a hoarse whisper, he told Ng to stop rattling around in there. Ng snapped at him, "Get back to your post."

After shoving the cache of stolen weapons through the window where he'd entered, Ng crawled outside. He and Mowry hurriedly began loading them into the car when the headlights of a military "liberty" bus startled them. They hid until several passengers stepping off the vehicle disappeared into the darkness. As soon as they'd jammed the heavy plunder into the backseat, they drove to a prearranged spot, still on the base, within walking distance from Ng's barracks. Pulling up on Makaha Road, near a gully adjacent to an old railroad-track crossing, they loaded the munitions into two seabags, concealed them in heavy brush, and returned the car to its original parking spot.

As the sun rose Ng slipped into the barracks and shook Corporal Dan Mitchum awake. Mitchum had previously helped Ng purchase an illegal weapon, so Ng knew his buddy would help remove the stolen munitions from the air station, and assist in selling them. Yawning, Mitchum listened, grinned, and told Ng he had a friend who would hide the loot for them. Mitchum made a telephone call, and reported to Ng that his cohort would conceal the guns in exchange for an M-203 grenade launcher. The remaining weapons would be heavily greased, said Mitchum, and packed inside large diameter PVC tubes, so they could be safely buried. Satisfied, Ng returned to his barracks for some sleep.

When he woke in the afternoon, he met Mitchum again, who handed him a walkie-talkie. It would be used, Mitchum said, to communicate with the man who'd agreed to hide the weapons. While Mitchum sped away in "a green Duster," Ng walked to the concealed loot, tried to carry both seabags, but found them too heavy. He used the two-way radio to request help, and within minutes, Mitchum, even though annoyed, arrived in the green Duster to transport Ng and the loaded seabags. In an off-base shopping center in the town of Kialua, they met the accomplice, who called himself "Slick." The weapons, said Slick, would be buried in a secret place, and even Ng wouldn't know where, just in case he was interrogated. Ng insisted on making an inventory so he wouldn't be shorted on the deal. Afterward, Mitchum dropped him off at the base.

Vic Mowry listened as Ng described the arrangements, and didn't like them. He wanted to send his share of the weapons to his hometown on the mainland. With Mitchum, they drove to Waikiki Beach and met Slick on the fifth floor of the Coral Reef hotel. Grumbling about the requested change in plans, Slick talked Mowry out of it, saying the stuff was too hot. He also informed Ng that "the syndicate" would be in charge of the stolen weapons, and they would charge $500 for their services. Feeling he had no choice in the matter, Ng accepted the conditions. He later complained that he never saw the stolen weapons again, nor did he receive any money for them.

Three days later, officers of the Naval Investigative Service (NIS) arrested Charles Ng, and charged him with conspiracy to commit larceny of military weapons; theft of weapons including machine guns, grenade launchers, rifles, and pistols; and burglary to commit theft. The total value of the missing arms exceeded $11,000. Ng's plan hadn't been as foolproof as he thought it would be. Too many people had been involved, and someone had leaked vital information.

Convinced that one of his collaborators had betrayed him, Ng gave a full statement of his involvement in the armory break-in and theft. In return for his confession, the Marine Corps promised that, if convicted by a court-martial, Ng would serve a relatively short prison sentence of hard labor.

On the cool morning of Friday, November 13, 1981, two Marine guards, called "chasers" in military jargon, delivered Ng to the NIS office to be interrogated. The marathon session lasted until 2:30 the following morning. No transportation was available at that hour to return the prisoner to the brig, so the chasers escorted him into a squad bay. While one of the men sat down, allowing Ng to move about freely within the room, the other chaser stepped into the duty NCO's office to telephone transportation authorities with a request for a vehicle. Neither of the two chasers had been briefed about the possibility that Ng might be an escape risk. News of the armory raid had been widely broadcast, and both men knew that Ng was a suspect in the case, but he'd been quiet and cooperative, apparently demonstrating no desire to run. The man closest to Ng, exhausted and drowsy, let his head drop for a moment.

Ng later spoke of the incident. "I was interrogated by Special Agent Thomas LaFrenniere until the early morning hours." At the squad bay, he recalled, "One of the chasers was talking on the telephone and the other was sitting back, smoking. I was allowed to freely wander about the office with very little security precautions being taken. I noticed that a rear window was open. I was very concerned that the information I'd given the agent might put me in danger with the syndicate because [Slick's and Mitchum's] involvement, and that my testimony would get [Williamson] into trouble. So I decided to escape through the window.

"While the chasers weren't paying attention, I went through the back window and ran across the field by Mokapu School. I went directly to the residence of a Corpsman friend of mine. He came to the door and asked me what I was doing. I told him that I'd been framed for the weapons theft . . . and asked him to put me up for the night. He agreed and told me that he and his wife would take care of me as long as they could. I took a shower and went to sleep."

Ng's benefactor provided breakfast and civilian clothing for him the next morning. During the meal, the phone rang, and his pal spoke with an agent of the NIS who asked if he'd seen Charles Ng. The agent made it clear that anyone attempting to give assistance to the fugitive would be severely prosecuted. When he'd hung up the phone, the buddy told Ng that it would be too dangerous for him to stay there, so he would first equip Ng with food, water, and clothing, then drive him to a remote area where he could camp out.

Stuffed into the trunk of his helper's car, Ng rode for a long time, then crawled out at a place he recognized as "Junkyard Road," marked on maps as Quarry Road. Bidding his pal goodbye, Ng picked out a hidden spot as a campsite.

That night, the friend returned to inform Ng that the NIS had distributed a photo of the fugitive all over the base and offered a $500 reward. He asked Ng to turn himself in, but got a negative reply. Ng asked him to contact his other buddies and collect some money to help him get away. But the effort failed, so the helper coughed up $20 of his own, along with a few supplies purchased at a 7-Eleven store. Ng recalled, "Before he left, we shook hands and I knew that he wouldn't be able to help me anymore."

On the windward side of Oahu, the lush green landscape grows prodigiously for a good reason; there is a great deal of rain. For two days, Ng huddled with no tent, afraid to make a fire, soaked and miserable. "I developed diarrhea from being continually wet. I also couldn't sleep good at night because of the mosquitoes. I knew that I had to leave, so I dried some civilian clothes given to me, and decided to blatantly walk to a bus stop and get to a telephone."

Having nowhere else to turn, Ng called his Army pal, Sergeant Mark Novak at Schofield Barracks. Ng later said, "I stayed with him two days in the barracks, and kept out of sight. I even showered at oh-two-hundred in the morning so I wouldn't be detected. While I was with Novak, I contacted my parents, who sent me three hundred dollars." He used the money to buy clothing, a backpack, and a plane ticket to San Francisco. "Novak gave me the name and address of Leonard Lake, who managed a motel in Philo, California, and said he would help me out. He called Lake and made the arrangements."

Ng left Schofield Barracks before dawn on a November morning in 1981, walked to nearby Waihiwa, and caught a bus to the airport. Trying to avoid any military police who might be on the lookout for him, he hid in a rest room until the boarding of his flight was announced.

In San Francisco, Ng rode a bus to San Leandro to seek temporary refuge in the home of his aunt. There he telephoned Leonard Lake at Philo, and accepted the fellow survivalist's offer of a place to stay for a few months.

Chapter 9

Charles Ng's stay with Leonard Lake and Cricket at Philo lasted almost six months before the sudden police raid that took both men into custody. At the same time the government sent Ng back to Hawaii to face court-martial, Leonard Lake jumped bail and embarked on the life of a fugitive. But his wife, Cricket, could see only misery and pitfalls in being constantly on the move, and always trying to evade arrest. She still cared for Lake, and reveled in the sexual adventures they shared, but couldn't see her way clear to share his nomadic life as an outlaw. Could she have it both ways? It would be impossible to live with Lake, she decided, but she saw no reason to discontinue their relationship, or to reject money he provided for her. So the couple decided to live apart, but to meet frequently for fun and sex. Cricket moved back to San Bruno to stay with her parents. Perhaps, she thought, she might even spend some time in a remote mountain cabin her father had recently purchased, up in the Sierra Nevada foothills near a tiny village called Wilseyville.

Lake, moving from place to place, staying in various motels, lodging with friends, and sometimes rooming with relatives, financed his existence by committing petty thefts and by selling drugs, mostly marijuana. He referred to these activities as operations, or ops. By assuming various aliases, he managed to stay out of the law's grasp.

Early in his flight from the law, Lake often sought refuge with his longtime pal Charles Gunnar, in Morgan Hill. Gunnar welcomed him into the home he shared with his wife, Vicky, and two daughters from his previous marriage. Lake ridiculed Gunnar for his obesity, and Charles Gunnar agreed, calling himself "Orca" or a "beached whale." Lake sometimes called him "Moby Dick."

During Lake's stays with Gunnar, he grumbled to others about the harsh way Charles treated the two young daughters. It infuriated Lake when he witnessed the portly man striking the helpless girls for minor misdeeds. The government disability checks on which Gunnar subsided also grated on Lake, who regarded most welfare recipients as parasites. And Lake detected building friction between Charles and Vicky. He knew that his pal became sexually aroused by mentally picturing his wife in carnal contact with other men. But it surprised Lake when Vicky confided to him that her husband had suggested she have sex with Leonard. She said that Charles would pruriently want to hear all the details afterward. Years later, Vicky would tell an investigator about the incident, reporting that she had "a onetime sexual encounter with Lake after it was suggested by Gunnar." According to Vicky, "It was normal sex, and Lake was not violent or kinky." Neither did he ask her to pose for any nude photos or videos. Gunnar, she said, enjoyed a type of voyeurism in which he wanted her to have sex with other men, then come back and tell him all about it.

He never wanted to actually watch, but simply to hear the details.

Even though Lake may have been unhappy with the alienation from Cricket, he still felt an infatuation with young Darlene Davis, the underage girlfriend he'd courted while living at The Ranch. Their exchanges of mail had never ceased. In remarkably candid letters, Lake admitted to Darlene that he and Charles Ng had been arrested, and confessed to her that he "was not entirely innocent." He said that he'd kept various guns and knives in a storage shed, referring to the illicit arsenal as "things I shouldn't have had." Lake added that Cricket was involved in the crimes, as well, but that he had lied to the police to keep her out of jail. Expressing his ongoing affection for Darlene, he asked if they could meet somewhere. In her rapid reply, she assented.

The reunion took place in July 1982, three months after the raid in Philo. They met at Pacific Union College in Napa, the center of California's wine country, northeast of the Bay area. Lake told his young paramour that he was living on a remote ranch in the mountains, and that Cricket had left him to participate in a new bisexual relationship in San Francisco. But, said Lake, he couldn't stay in any one place too long, so in order to continue their correspondence, he asked Darlene to address her letters to his pseudonym "Ted White." He gave her a street number on Cabrillo Way, San Bruno, California, and said that a friend who lived there would forward his mail. After their brief intimate encounter, in which they renewed vows of mutual affection, he vanished again. The exchange of letters continued for another six months, then stopped, partly due to a new boyfriend in Darlene's life. She wouldn't hear from Lake again, or see him, for more than two years.

* * *

The obsessive sex drive haunting Lake kept him constantly on the move. He frequently drove around the Bay area not only to sell marijuana, but to visit women he knew, or to seek out new female companionship. Recalling the utopian days on The Ranch, when Bobby Barnes, his girlfriend, and Gina Travers had stayed with him, Lake decided to seek a déjà vu encounter. He discovered that both women now lived in Fremont, in the southeast sector of the Bay. As Gina recalled, the new episodes with Lake began when he just popped in by surprise. "He would visit us on the average of once every three months or so. He would just show up at our door. We'd usually feed him, have sex with him, and then he would leave. He never explained why he was in the area, or what he was doing, and we learned not to question him because he was so secretive about his life. That's just the way Leonard was."

Still adding to his collection of revealing photos of female friends and lovers, Lake asked Gina to pose for him. She modeled, but refused to disrobe. His face growing red and muscles twitching in his jaw, Lake demanded that she at least pull her bra straps down. She complied, and he explained that he could retouch the pictures to make it appear she was nude, which would enable him to sell them. She shook her head in disbelief, and shrugged off his foolishness.

Insatiable, Lake haunted San Francisco, where plenty of female prey lived, especially in the liberal Haight-Ashbury district. He resorted again to an old ploy, placing personal ads in newspapers to lure them. Rhonda Railey, a slim, comely brunette, twenty-six, who could pass for a teenager, answered an ad placed by Tom seeking an eighteen-year-old female to accompany him to Hawaii. She telephoned Tom at his mother's home and agreed to meet him for lunch. The husky, green-eyed man she met appealed to her, even though he had lost most of the hair on top of his head. His charm made the baldness unimportant. Rhonda characterized their first meeting as "wonderful." After lunch they chatted amiably during a long walk on the beach that took the remainder of the afternoon, then had dinner together. She felt comfortable enough to invite him to her apartment, where Tom impressed her by not pushing for a sexual encounter. Not wishing to start off with a lie, Rhonda confessed her true age, but it made no difference to him. A week later, he drove her to Morgan Hill to meet his pal Charles Gunnar, whom she later described as "a big guy with reddish hair," close to her companion's age.

Gunnar invited Tom and his companion to stay the night in his guest room. According to Rhonda, when they were alone in the bedroom, Tom stated that he needed to tell her some things. First he informed her of his real name, Leonard Lake, then confessed he was married but separated. Lake also admitted to being recently arrested for burglary and said he'd been released on his own recognizance pending a trial. Gaining Rhonda's confidence and her appreciation for his honesty, Lake told her that his wife, Cricket, had encouraged him to "do his time," instead of running away. But, Lake said, he didn't want to go to jail. So he had argued with his wife, and this issue had caused their separation.

As Rhonda recalled it, they talked for hours that night. She, too, suggested that it would be better for him to serve his jail term so he could make a fresh start. Lake alternately agreed with her, then backed off, saying he would rather commit suicide than be locked behind bars. His next comment sent a tremor of deep concern through her. Lake asserted that if he killed himself, it would be only after the elimination of certain people who "needed to be erased from the world." She asked who he meant, and Lake surprised her by naming his buddy Charles Gunnar. The big man, he said, deserved to die because of the terrible way he treated his wife and daughters.

Leaving such grim topics behind, Lake seemed to flip an internal switch that turned on his soothing charm. By telling

Rhonda of the "abandonment" he'd suffered as a child, he manipulated her sympathetic nature. The pity she felt, mixed with the intimacy of the conversations, drew her closer to Leonard. She didn't resist when the sexual foreplay started. But, she recalled, Leonard experienced difficulty. Finally, though, the catharsis of unburdening himself and confessing his problems while talking all night long, and only "after the birds started singing early in the morning," did the temporary impotence fade away, allowing him to make love to her.

Lake kept his promise of taking Rhonda to Hawaii for an idyllic week. They continued spending time together after the trip and he unveiled even more of his private life. About his experiences in Vietnam, Lake even admitted that he'd spent many of the days stationed aboard a ship, and had never really killed anyone in combat.

Once, as a passenger in Lake's vehicle, Rhonda inadvertently discovered a handgun in the glove compartment. He explained that he kept it only for self-protection.

Commenting years later about their sexual activities, Rhonda recalled that Leonard often talked about S&M and that she once had allowed him to tie her to the bed. He liked the idea of spanking a woman, so she submitted to his mild fetish, but only one time. Lake showed her his collection of nude and seminude photos of women, and persuaded her to pose for him, as well.

She had only one dark confession to share with Lake. She had worked for a "social club" in San Francisco for a month. She described the Vantage Club, and how the 200 male members paid for dates with female escorts. Rhonda didn't say whether or not she had engaged in sex with any of the clients.

Not long after their return from the Islands, Lake told Rhonda that he had discussed a reconciliation with Cricket and they'd reached an agreement to resume their marriage. But, Lake assured Rhonda, he didn't want to give up the relationship with her. He had always fantasized about a "group marriage," Lake said, and he hoped Rhonda would be the third member of a triad. He and Cricket had always had an "open marriage," he said. As a matter of fact, Cricket would probably continue to see a man with whom she was involved. Of course, if Rhonda accepted the proposal, Lake explained, it would involve sexual intimacy between her and Cricket. Rhonda, confused but also curious, admitted that she wasn't opposed to group marriages as long as everyone was willing and compatible. She wanted to meet Cricket, though, prior to making any commitments.

Before Rhonda could change her mind, Lake made immediate arrangements for the two women to meet. Over dinner at a restaurant, it didn't take long for the awkwardness to vanish, and both women chatted as if they'd known each other forever. They found a great deal in common, especially in their involvement with Leonard. Rhonda sensed that Cricket's way of lightly touching her signaled a willingness, perhaps even a desire to have sex. Still unsure, Rhonda deliberately failed to respond in the same way. Leonard told them his greatest fantasy was to get them both pregnant at the same time.

Two weeks later, Lake drove Rhonda and Cricket to the Wilseyville cabin, where they stayed five days. Less a vacation than a work party, the trio labored together refurbishing the interior, installing Sheetrock and painting. Rhonda observed that Leonard and Cricket "fought like a couple of kids," and she found herself frequently acting as mediator. Such "immature" behavior struck her as unpleasant and disturbing. Gradually she began to reconsider any willingness to enter into a group marriage. Near the end of the stay, Cricket asked Rhonda about her intentions, to which she replied, "Actually, I've just sort of been playing with Leonard. It's been fun, but I really don't want to break up your marriage to him." Rhonda's diplomatic answer hid her real feelings of not being sexually attracted to Cricket.

After returning from the Wilseyville trip, Rhonda continued to see Lake for several weeks, but the magic had dimmed. As the frequency of their dates tapered off, she realized that she'd made the right decision. A month apart didn't change her mind, even when Lake showed up at her house with a gift, a white negligee that he said was "a symbol of her purity and innocence." But Rhonda had made a decision. She informed him that she had joined a spiritual group that required her to change her lifestyle: to be a vegetarian, to stop using marijuana, and to cease all sexual activities.

Not to be outdone or rejected, Lake replied that he was "on the lam," anyway, for burglary charges, and wouldn't be seeing her again. He confided that he had adopted a new phony name, but didn't want to reveal it just in case the FBI came snooping around. Before he finally left, Lake asked Rhonda not to tell anything about him if the police contacted her. Rhonda could make no promises.

The brief experiment with a group marriage had no noticeable effect on the relationship between Lake and Cricket. They continued to date and cohabit periodically, but she stated unconditionally that she did not want to remain married to him. The divorce became final on November 30, 1982.

Just a couple of weeks later, Lake heard from Charles Gunnar that his wife, Vicky, had left him, too. But Gunnar's daughters remained with their father in the Morgan Hill home. Lake wasn't certain that Charles deserved custody of the young girls because of the harsh way he treated them.

As the year drew to a close, a remarkable event shocked, yet pleased Lake's mother and sisters. Leonard showed up at his mother's home in the Bay area, and appeared to be ready for a reconciliation with his brother, Donald.

Always before, when Lake spoke of Donald, it was in the most denigrating way, reaffirming his contempt for the partially handicapped sibling. Because Donald still lived with their mother, and drew Social Security payments, Leonard openly regarded him as a lazy parasite who took unfair advantage of his family. It didn't seem to matter to Leonard that his law-abiding brother, who had served a hitch in the Army, caused little trouble for anyone. The sisters felt sorry for Donald, and didn't appreciate Leonard's comment that people like his brother should be lined up and shot.

In view of Lake's record of disdain for Donald, it came as a pleasant surprise to the family when he suggested that his brother accompany him on a trip up north to fill a job opening as a house sitter. The surprised sibling readily accepted, and left with Leonard.

No one would ever see Donald Lake again.

Remarkably, though, just a few days later, a man walked into the Vantage Social Club in San Francisco and took out a membership under the name of Donald Lake. He even presented a driver's license to prove his identity. No one seemed to notice that the photo bore little resemblance to the applicant. The new member, a husky, green-eyed man in his late thirties, who wore an obvious hairpiece to mask his baldness, often asked the female escorts provided by the club to pose for his camera. Several of the women did so willingly, and even provided additional services. One of the Vantage women later told of being with Lake several times, and of his paying for her services by giving her drugs.

On New Year's Day, 1983, Lake made the first entry in a daily journal he would faithfully keep for the next two years. That same day, he rented a basement room on 19th Avenue in a San Francisco house occupied by several tenants. "I haven't met my house mates yet," he noted, "and probably won't for a few days." He'd been living with his sister, and hadn't yet completed the process of moving into his new quarters. His diary notation during the ensuing four days later reflected his undiminished interest in seducing young women. One notation read, "Returned [sister's] car today, bussed back. On the bus I saw a young girl (16?) Of uncommon beauty ... with long styled hair, clear complexion, petite figure ... and tasteful makeup." The thirty-seven-year-old Lake wrote, "Ah, if I were

only young and handsome.'' He also recorded having lunch at
''18th & Mission. Food is plentiful and cheap, and the place
is also a contact point with some dope-using whores.'' He
would hang out regularly at the restaurant, befriending the
hookers and peddling drugs to them.

Lake's entry for January 6 stated that he'd made a trip to
San Bruno, and stopped on the way back to visit a female
acquaintance who gave him oral sex. Not very appreciative, he
described her as ''a stupid, ugly woman'' and lamented, ''What
levels I have fallen to!''

A few days later, Lake's record reflected his ongoing relationship with Cricket during a trip to the mountain cabin at Wilseyville. ''Borrowed Mom's car and off to Calaveras [County].
Cricket and [her father] have turned the house into a piece of
crap. Country ticky-tacky. Sigh! What a worthless place . . .
empty vibes.'' Still mourning the end of his marriage to Cricket,
Lake wrote, ''It could have been so nice if she hadn't valued
money and security over love.''

In Lake's journal, he identified several women as potential
sex partners, including one he called Bev, age twenty-four.
''Angularly pretty, smokes, mucho drugs. Professional administrator, ambitious, part-time call girl . . . no doubt a heavy user
of men. Not really my type, but probably available.'' Cricket,
though, remained his primary focus. ''Very foolish lady,'' he
wrote. ''Why do I love her so? Wish I could turn it off.''

Frequent mention of his mother in Lake's written record
indicated that the long-standing emotional strain and hurt
between them seemed to have healed. He noted incidents of
helping her with work on her home, borrowing her car, and
dropping by just to spend time with her.

In his rented quarters, Lake mused about trying to seduce
women who were fellow tenants. He broadened his scope of
candidates by advertising in *The Bay Guardian* for female

photography models. His diary also expressed a desire to add homemade videotapes of women to his collection of still photos. In a list of items he planned to obtain, noted in late January, Lake included a wish to own a new video camera along with more sophisticated equipment for copying and editing his tapes. Itemizing the "Things I want to get," Lake listed an assault rifle, a 9mm Colt Commander, and an AR-7 .22 caliber rifle. In his carefully planned budget, he allowed $120 for a membership in a dating service.

Boredom set in after he'd lived one month in his basement room. Lake wrote, "I must leave this city. I have to return to the country not only for my own security and peace of mind, but even more for the privacy to create a true base of operations. The country, with an adjacent slope of suitable size for the construction of an underground base." A methodical and organized man, Lake registered the need for a truck to haul supplies, as well as a convenient place to live near the site of his bunker. Then, he noted, he would require the "establishment of a suitable line of females to help cohabitate same." The dating service, he hoped, might provide a source of these women. Lake ended the day's entry with a philosophical sentence: "We commit the rest to fortune."

Cricket did not make herself available to Lake as much as he wanted, so he wrote frequent letters to her, and made entries in his journal about each one. On Valentine's Day, his plaintive letter renewed his declarations of devotion. "I loved her beyond all reason." Directly addressing Cricket, he wrote, "I hate to sound like a broken record, but simply because you broke your vows, *mine* were to death. Neither you nor your mother will ever want for necessities as long as I am operational. Even beyond that, you are provided for." The claim of economic security may not have been quite valid, since Lake maintained a rather insubstantial financial position.

Along with his mundane recording of daily activities, including visits to his mother, sisters, and friends, ordinary chores, ops for profit, and a series of dates with women, Lake returned to his thoughts of a secret bunker. "Country living is required for [a] secure base. If it were only possible to establish such a base here in the city. The idea of a hidden base here intrigues me, but I can't really see it happening. Perhaps I'll find a way."

The dating service membership turned up a pair of women who inspired him to observe, "If I'm going to start womanizing [more], I'd better get out and get some ops under my pocketbook."

In many of Lake's journal entries regarding illegal activities, including burglaries, he used his own code words to disguise his ops. In late February, he wrote of a visit to a "stage area" that appeared to be The Ranch where he had lived several years. Of his late-night arrival, he wrote: "No moon, heavy clouds. Slept usual place. Awoke around 0900, stayed in bed till noon. Heavy rains on and off, then low fog. Checked out number of possible targets. All occupied, all buttoned up against weather. Disappointing. Picked up approximately $20 worth of loose goods. Barely covers expenses . . . Difficult, dirty, wet." Another failure in the life of Leonard Lake.

His diary entry for February 19 notes that he videotaped a motion picture version of *The Collector*. That night, he wrote:

"Ah, 'The Collector.' Has it really been near 20 years I've carried this fantasy? And Miranda . . . how fitting . . . my lovely little prisoner of the future. I suppose in my way I am the same wimp as 'the hero,' and in my way just as crazy. I have no doubt that we wimps have been compensating for our inabilities since the dawn of history. Sad, really. Still, how can we die if we never live? . . ."

Chapter 10

"There was a conspiracy in this case," a lawyer would one day write in a legal document, "but that conspiracy existed between Leonard Lake and his girlfriend, wife, ex-wife/girlfriend, Claralyn Balazs (aka Cricket) and no one else. . . . The existence of the conspiracy is evidenced in Lake's diary. . . . Cricket read the diary and knew of the *Miranda Project* as early as 1980. She also assisted Lake by recruiting potential female victims to be photographed under the ruse of portraying him as a professional photographer. Lake and Cricket created a homemade video of themselves in March, 1983. It featured them cavorting nude on a bed, giggling, engaging in various sexual antics, and interspersing erotic conversation with plans to lure women into Lake's web. They are shown looking at photographs of women during a break in a sado-masochistic sex episode, and joking about the women as potential victims of the *Miranda Project*. Cricket knew Lake was a fugitive from the 1982 arrest. She knew Lake assumed the names of other persons, and introduced him under a false name to numerous people.''

Routine activities occupied Lake's time in February and March 1983. His journal logged each lovemaking session with Cricket, movies he saw either in theaters or on television, family events with his mother and sisters, sexual conquests, photo sessions with women, and various ops to boost his meager bank account. He coldly entered a note, ''Changed Don's address,'' referring to a new post office box for the purpose of receiving his brother's SSDI checks.

With more frequency, Lake drove to Wilseyville, in Calaveras County, which took at least three hours each way from San Francisco. At the cabin, he worked feverishly on home-improvement projects. The property belonged to Cricket and her father, but new visions formed in Lake's mind for his personal use of it. Several times he invited Charles Gunnar to join him in the long trip, but his old buddy kept postponing it. Lake wrote, ''Called Charles. He turned me down for Calaveras. Offered bribe. We will see what happens there.''

On the last day of March, Lake made an unusually long, prophetic, and chilling entry in his journal: ''Once I had a wife. She was my connection to the world. Through her, I could love, trust, believe in things others are allowed to believe in. I could have died for her, killed for her, even gone to jail, give up my freedom in exchange for the security of her love. Once I had a wife.

''Now I have no ties to the world. I am both above it and removed from it. Oh, there are those I love, my sisters, even Cricket still. But none of these bind me to the order of existence. I am free to die, with no responsibility. All I love, I love alone. Freedom. An empty privilege [but] still one I must bear with determination.

"Amusing. Our 'land of the free' is not prepared to deal effectively with a truly free man. What can they do to one who carries cyanide pills in his pockets? When death holds no fears—when there are no responsibilities beyond the next meal? Society. You are being socked and you don't understand by who or why. And if you did, you are powerless against one who is not afraid to die."

Transactions for marijuana filled Lake's agenda during the first few days of April, along with a variety of failures and successes with women. Growing nervous about the use of his brother's SSDI income, he needed to earn more from drug deals. "Must close down Donald," he noted. Receiving and cashing the checks could turn into his worst nightmare, incarceration. He moved to the front burner an op he'd been formulating for months, one that might give him a new source of government checks. Thinking over possible code names for the plan, he rejected a short list, then hit upon the perfect name. He decided to call it "Operation Fish." Who could possibly connect the word fish with a "beached whale" or "Orca," as Charles Gunnar had once self-deprecatingly called himself? Whales aren't even fish, they are mammals. Lake allowed himself a smug smile, and made another call to Gunnar, inviting him to ride up to Wilseyville.

April 5, 1983: "Left early for Calaveras with Charles. Arrived, completed trench for gas line, installed water filter, insulated hot water pipes. Made video tape of Charles. Operation Fish failed. Charles is simply too heavy to move. Sigh."

Maybe, Lake thought, he should scrub Operation Fish. The problem, he noted, revolved around "the fact that I have to move the object, without help, to total security." But a few days later, he reconsidered, having thought of new options. "I believe I have found an acceptable plan for Fish . . . A new hole, a winch to move the weight. Also, acid. . . ."

Another failure occurred when Lake lured Gunnar again to Wilseyville. Charles declined an offer of snacks that had been laced with a powdered poison, and a mixture of gas vapors proved inadequate to knock him out.

At the end of April, Lake borrowed Gunnar's yellow Volkswagen van, loaded most of his belongings into it, and moved in with Charles at Morgan Hill. He paid a month's rent in advance, bought groceries for the household, and cooked dinner for Charles and his daughters. At night, he entered more plans in his journal for carrying out Operation Fish. In early May, he noted, ''I am a dangerous person. Society would worry if they knew I existed and what I was up to. But more than my victim, I am the most suitable of victims. I don't exist in the official world. No job, no taxes, no one to keep track of me day to day. If I were to disappear it might be months before anyone would even wonder, and then what could they do?''

The abuse Gunnar heaped on his daughters irritated Lake even more, now that he actually observed it. ''Charles whipped his oldest girl today. I've seen him hit his children before, but I'd never seen him actually tear into one . . . with a full force belt. I have fantasized about whipping a young woman before, but watching him whip a little girl was too much for me. He watches TV . . . has time to watch stupid comedy over and over, but nothing of any historical or educational worth. He has time to make a play for his favorite lady, time to yell at his children, time to sleep 12 to 14 hours a day, but no time at all to read (except comic books or the Sunday funnies). He lives in a clean house only by virtue of the fact that his girls must do the cleaning. He sows not, nor does he labor, oh but he reaps. Gold, in the form of government handouts.'' It might be interpreted that Lake's journal recorded a rationalization for planning to kill his old buddy.

To many neighbors, Charles Gunnar just seemed like an

overweight, good-natured, if somewhat oafish, ne'er-do-well. In a suburb of Chicago, a man named John Wayne Gacy gave the same impression ten years earlier before he turned out to be a notorious serial killer. Gacy entertained at children's events by dressing as a clown. So did Charles Gunnar. He presided over a local group of charitable clowns who met periodically to discuss types of makeup and to sharpen their skills in making kids laugh. Among the members was a young woman in her early twenties who thought the activity was enjoyable and worthwhile. Wendy Oatman grew to know Charles Gunnar, and periodically baby-sat his two daughters. On one of those evenings, she met Leonard Lake, who told her that he was a professional photographer.

Within the first hour of the meeting, Lake asked Wendy if she would consider posing for him. Reluctant at first, she gradually succumbed to his persuasive pressure. He provided garments he wanted her to wear, and insisted that she change clothes in the bedroom, and not the bathroom. She wasn't aware that he had a habit of secretly videotaping his models while they undressed. When she donned a white T-shirt, Lake requested that she first remove her bra. She posed for several pictures, but never completely nude. While Wendy reclined, Lake massaged her, to "help her relax," and confided that he usually massaged his partners before sex. Lake's bizarre suggestions disconcerted the young woman. She later reported that he wanted her to apply contrasting light and dark makeup and a long wig, giving her a deathly pale appearance, then pose nude as if she had died and lay "naked in a graveyard." She rejected the strange request, along with his proposal that they have sex.

Wendy recalled that Lake telephoned her one day and told her he wanted to see two women having sex together. At that moment, he stated, he had a girl with him who was ready, and he would be leaving shortly to pick Wendy up. In a demanding voice, he said, "Don't worry, I know where you live." Nervously, Wendy called a boyfriend, Steve, who rushed to her house, and waited until Lake and his female companion arrived. Wendy recalled the woman as having, "Dirty blond or brown hair, quite long, and wearing large glasses." She thought Leonard called the woman "Cricket."

Feeling safe with Steve along, Wendy accompanied Leonard and Cricket to a place that offered indoor hot tubs. All four cavorted in the steaming water, but according to Wendy, nothing else happened.

Operation Fish failed two more times during the following week. "The frustration of Fish has overwhelmed me these days." But at last, Lake recorded success on May 24, 1983. "Phase one of Fish complete, FINALLY."

A couple of days before Lake's triumphant journal entry, Wendy Oatman agreed to look after Gunnar's two daughters for two weeks. Lake remarked to her that Charles really needed to get away for some badly needed relaxation. The poor man's wife had left him, said Leonard, and he deserved all the help his friends could give him. Lake insinuated that he would take Gunnar to Las Vegas or Tahoe to help him recover.

When Lake returned a few days later, he told Wendy that Gunnar had met a girl, fallen in love, and "won't be coming back." Lake benevolently divulged that he would take responsibility for Gunnar's daughters, until their father sent for them. Surprised, Wendy shrugged her shoulders. Stranger things had happened, and after all, Lake and Gunnar had told her many times of their comradeship while serving in the Green Berets together. Surely, such men could take care of themselves. She never stopped to consider that Green Berets were part of the U.S. Army, not the Marine Corps. Wendy never saw Leonard Lake, or Charles Gunnar, again.

In Lake's journal, he disguised the end of a man's life by noting, "Charles stayed up north. I have the children for a while."

Perhaps considering the future of Gunnar's daughters, or concerned about the possibility of the disability payments becoming the property of Gunnar's estranged wife, Vicky, Lake arranged to meet her at a fast food restaurant, where he asked her to delay divorcing Charles. "The only way I would stop the proceedings," she said, "is if Charles was dead."

"You don't have to worry about him coming back," Lake assured her.

"How do you know?" she asked. Lake tried to avoid answering, but Vicky persisted.

At last he explained, "Well, I have something on him. I videotaped him beating one of his daughters. I gave it to my sister. If he ever shows his face around here again, it's going to get in the authorities' hands."

Vicky shook her head. She said that the ploy might keep Charles away for a little while, but he cared enough for the daughters that he would eventually come back.

Lake suggested that Vicky should take custody of them, but she refused by pointing out that she had her hands full with her own two sons.

Still determined to place Gunnar's daughters with Vicky, he showed up at her house again a few days later and once again appealed for her to take custody. To Vicky, Lake seemed even more certain that Charles would never return. But she still declined. He left in a huff. When he held a garage sale the next week to sell Gunnar's possessions, and some of the household furniture, Vicky showed up to collect items she regarded as hers. But Lake insisted that she pay for them.

Now using Gunnar's yellow Volkswagen van as his own, Lake ran his marijuana trade and tended to the daughters as if they belonged to him. He bought clothing for them, cooked, and even helped clean the house. Cricket spent time with them, as well.

Years earlier, when Gunnar had married Vicky, and Lake had acted as his best man, Leonard had met a friend of Gunnar's named George Wesley Blank, who was called "Wes" by most people. Blank and his wife, Norma, lived in Watsonville, near Monterey Bay. Gunnar had once asked Wes for a special favor. "If anything ever happens to me, would you make sure my daughters are taken care of?" Blank had assured him that he would.

With Gunnar now missing, Lake contacted Wes Blank, wondering if he would be willing to look after the two girls. It wasn't the only request Blank heard. Prior to Gunnar's disappearance, Vicky had approached Blank. He would one day recall the incident. "Victoria came to me and asked if I would take care of the children because she was afraid of Charles. She didn't want him at her house—where he would have to come back and pick them up. So, at that time, when they were living in the house with Leonard Lake, I told her we would. She contacted Lake. He contacted us, and asked us to come get them."

In the interim, Lake, buoyant at his success in Operation Fish—which allowed him to take over anything valuable belonging to Gunnar—kept a busy schedule. He managed to find time for women, too. On June 2, he noted, "Up early. Laundry, shopping, house cleaning, painted bunk beds. Moved girls to separate bedrooms. Had Tania over to help work. Took some slides of her and some keyhole nudes," meaning a videotape without her knowledge.

Gunnar's young daughters didn't seem to mind the absence of their abusive father, especially since Lake treated them so well. He took them on a boat to tour the vacated federal prison on Alcatraz Island, to nice restaurant dinners, to a water-slide park, and provided several other entertaining outings. On June 13, after the girls' school semester had ended, the final parting with them took place. George "Wes" Blank and his wife had agreed to provide foster care, at least until the girls' father returned, and perhaps permanently if legal arrangements could be made. The benevolent couple arrived, packed the children's things, and drove away to give them a new home.

Chapter 11

In the northeast corner of Kansas, the small town of Leavenworth is the site of several prisons, among them: one of the oldest and toughest federal penitentiaries, and the United States Disciplinary Barracks at Fort Leavenworth, the old military encampment. Convicted inmates from all branches of the services do time at this high-security prison.

Charles Ng arrived there in 1982, soon after his plea bargain at Kaneohe Bay, to serve eighteen months. During his incarceration, unmarred by any notable behavior problems, Ng made a few friends, inside and outside. A young Marine name Mike Carroll, serving three months on drug charges, allegedly met Ng and chatted with him periodically. They had several interests in common. Both of them had been in the Marine Corps and both had lived in San Francisco. It's quite possible that, before his release, Carroll gave Ng a phone number in the Bay area, and suggested they meet again after Ng regained his freedom.

Ng couldn't be certain that he would actually return to California. Since he was not a legal citizen, he could well have expected the U.S. government to deport him to Hong Kong immediately after he'd completed his sentence.

Correspondence with Leonard Lake filled large gaps in Ng's long, boring days of prison life. Lake wrote frequently, and sent photographs with most of his letters. He included pictures of himself, Cricket, other women, and the property at Wilseyville. Ng, in return, used his artistic skills to draw greeting cards for Lake and sometimes sent origami angels, animals, or other figures. He always sent his best regards to Cricket, too. Later, in the spring of 1984, Ng would receive several photos depicting Lake's progress in building a cinder block structure resembling a military bunker close to a mountain cabin.

Ng shared the letters and photographs with a new comrade inside the walls of the military prison. John Carty, twenty-nine, had been sentenced to serve three years for stealing his battalion commander's jeep. When Carty saw Ng practicing what appeared to be kung fu exercises, he admired the skillful execution. "We had common interests in guns and martial arts," Carty later reported. Ng's athletic moves, according to Carty, could be regarded as showboating, but "he was the best I've ever seen, doing spin kicks and that kind of stuff." As the two men established a mutual trust, Carty recalled, Ng revealed that he planned to assemble men to train as a paramilitary unit for the purpose of robbing banks and stealing valuable goods at military posts.

But as Ng's scheme expanded, Carty grew nervous about being part of it. "He went from simple bank jobs to talking about stealing military missiles and shooting down seven-forty-sevens." The grandiose ideas included mass murder, as well. "No pain, no gain," and "Kill, kill, kill," Ng reportedly chanted. In Carty's account of Ng's plans, Charlie wanted to bomb a bus station or cause the crash of a jetliner to kill a large number of people in a single blow. And, said Carty, Ng loved to talk about sexually torturing women. "He had a real imagination for it."

When Ng shared the photos sent by Lake, and described the bunker, Carty listened in awe. "It was going to have a torture room in it, and he was going to have video cameras. It was out in the woods somewhere." At that point, Carty decided he didn't want anything to do with Ng's future plans.

Another inmate, Ed Popovich, often walked with Charles Ng in the exercise yard. According to Popovich, the two men formed a friendship, and Ng fell into the habit of calling him "brother." Popovich's release date preceded Ng's. Charlie promised to call, and maybe visit as soon as he got out.

While Ng made a few other superficial buddies inside the Disciplinary Barracks, he established by mail an important, warm relationship with a woman who lived in Kentucky. Sally Jean Pyle, in her forties, needed someone to care about her. The soft-spoken blond-haired nurse's aide had lost a son to a murderer in early 1983, and the trauma devastated her. She had also been raped, which destroyed her self-esteem and trust of men. According to Sally, her husband couldn't cope with the sexual assault. "He said it was my fault, and he made me feel like I was useless, just a nothing." The insensitive reaction eroded the couple's ability to communicate. And it made matters worse when her husband abused their children. "I left him several times," she said. But she always returned.

Prior to marrying her husband, Sally, previously wed, had already given birth to four children and hoped not to have any more. Her fiancé, though, told her not to worry, that he was sterile. A few months after the honeymoon, she discovered that he had lied, and the result was another daughter.

Due to the murder of her son and the rape, followed by mistreatment from her husband, Sally Jean needed help. She turned to a church support group. As part of a therapy program, to convert hatred into compassion, they recommended to Sally Jean that she begin corresponding with prison inmates. She complied, finding solace, healing, and comfort in giving her time and sympathy to incarcerated men. Charles Ng, one of the prisoners with whom she exchanged mail, seemed different from the others.

She found Ng's letters refreshing in their absence of "smut and filth." Instead, he demonstrated a sensitivity and understanding of her problems, which she readily shared with him. "He was very giving," she explained, "and helped me cope with my sadness. His letters were good. He talked about his family and sent me pictures of them. No one had ever sent me gifts, but he gave me a little ceramic figurine of a nurse inscribed with my name. I developed a deep affection for him." She kept the gift prominently displayed in her living room, but couldn't reveal its source to her husband.

Ng even offered to pay her transportation costs if she would travel to Leavenworth to visit him, but she couldn't get away from her job and family. Instead, she suggested he drop by and call upon her when he completed his sentence.

As Leonard Lake prepared to move from Charles Gunnar's house in Morgan Hill on June 17, 1983, in his journal he ecstatically entered impressions of someone he'd met by chance.

Doris Kerns, a vivacious redhead who lived a few blocks away, had met the Gunnars through the friendship of her own girls with Charles's daughters. The kids occasionally slept over at each other's homes. One afternoon, Doris called the Gunnar residence and spoke to Leonard Lake.

"What a magical day," Lake wrote. "Your basic scrub and pack until a lady called to chat with Charles. Chatted with me instead and later came over to meet me, and then to her house, then out to the park, then dinner, then a warm and close moment on her living room floor.

"A woman is only a woman, but every now and then a lady comes into my life that I <u>know</u>. It matters not that I never met her before today, I know her, I can feel for her, can look into her mind and heart. Why on my last day here do I have to meet her? Why not the first? Like Cricket, like Rhonda, she is lovely, petite, warm, tender, easy to get to know, a person I feel comfortable with. If she gives me the slightest chance, I'll fall in love with her. Doris, good night."

Despite the new enchantment, the danger of potential capture pushed Lake into the realization that he needed to move on. He'd already been careless enough by lingering in one spot and using his real name. Seeking another rustic hideaway, he drove north to Meyers Flat, a rural community in Humboldt County, eighty miles north of Ukiah and The Ranch.

The town is surrounded by Humboldt Redwood State Park, where a magnificent forest of the towering conifers shades the lush, undulating land. Lake rented a small, secluded house, then began scouting the region. Roaming around, he stopped in a little village called Miranda, just south of the state park. Inwardly he chuckled at the name. It reminded him of his driving sexual fantasy, which he called Operation Miranda, involving the capturing of a woman to use as a sex slave. The cryptic name came from a female character in *The Collector*. Lake had no way of knowing that future investigators might argue over the source Lake had used to label his repulsive plan Operation Miranda.

It took several more round-trips over the next few days to move his things, during which he spent nights at Morgan Hill with Doris Kerns. Each departure tore at his emotions, driving home the point that a fugitive has no business falling in love.

As he headed north with the final load, Cricket accompanied him on the long drive, during which he informed her, in complete detail, of his encounters with Kerns. "It's so nice," he noted in his journal, "being open and honest with Cricket about Doris. Wish I could be same with Doris. Suspect she wouldn't like me going from one lady to next in 24 hours. Love Cricket very much, even if she wasn't much of a wife." After a few nights of sex and photography, Cricket boarded a bus for the return trip to San Francisco.

Lake hadn't been settled into his new digs long before Doris Kerns, along with one of her preteen daughters, traveled north to spend some time with him. The couple walked hand in hand in the cathedral-like forests, during which Leonard spoke of his goal to stockpile food, supplies, and guns for an inevitable catastrophe. He also admitted that he was a fugitive, and that he sold marijuana to survive. In only two years, he assured Doris, the statute of limitations would run out on his offense, and he would be free again.

In his bedroom Doris saw "piles" of weapons, including rifles, grenades, and handguns. In a closet she caught sight of nude and seminude photographs of women posted on the inside of the door. Lake explained they were "ex-girlfriends."

Doris's daughter asked to watch some videotapes one night, and pushed one into the player. It startled Doris when the amateurish onscreen picture depicted a woman inside a bathroom, removing her clothing, seemingly unaware that she was being photographed. Lake snatched it from the machine without explanation, and replaced it with a family-entertainment movie. At the end of her stay, Doris left with gnawing doubts regarding her relationship with Leonard.

Another visitor came to Meyers Flat in late summer: Lake's half sister Janet.

While preparing for bed on the first night, Janet also saw the photographic collage of scantily dressed women displayed on the interior closet wall. She sometimes wondered what motivated Leonard to possess such pictures, but worried more about his need to own several guns and to carry cyanide with him at all times. Janet suspected that he operated on the outer fringes of the law, and that part of his income came from the sale of marijuana. She had first learned of it from an incident that took place when he had lived briefly in her San Francisco home. She'd walked in one day and found a cluster of marijuana plants hanging on lines inside the house, like laundry hung up to dry. Angry, she objected, but Lake hastily explained that selling the drug supplied his only source of income at that time. To her questions about where he'd obtained the plants, he candidly explained he had stolen them from a ranch up in the mountains.

In another conversation during Janet's visit to Meyers Flat, Leonard said he'd had a falling-out with his pal Charles Gunnar. However, he gave no details.

Before she left for home, Janet received a packet of photos and maps from Leonard to be delivered to Cricket, and he explained that the documents recorded sites where he had buried valuables for his estranged wife's use in case of serious emergencies. Janet could see in his tender reference to Cricket that Leonard regretted their separation.

For Lake, scouting hillsides in search of a possible bunker site, and organizing his living quarters, occupied the next few days. Unable to resist seeing Kerns again, and needing to transact some marijuana business, he hurried back down to the Bay area. In Doris Kerns's bedroom one morning, he discovered that she had rummaged through his overnight bag in which she had found a handgun and phony identification papers. Lake later wrote, "Now she thinks I'm Jack the Ripper. I am compromised. What risks and foolishness I endure for women."

Doris apparently disregarded the clues. She and her daughter traveled to Oregon, but stopped in Humboldt County for an overnight stay with Lake, and again on the return trip. In mid-July, during another visit, she pumped him about his secretive activities. To her surprise, Lake opened up and divulged all. That night, he wrote, "Had to tell Doris everything. Again, I am compromised. Still, I must trust her not to betray me. Will probably never see Doris again."

But his pessimistic forecast was premature. Doris Kerns came north again, still hoping the romance could be rehabilitated. Yet, she couldn't shake the feeling of distress that clouded her views of Leonard after he'd confessed his outlaw status. They had exchanged letters in the interim, but his written words hadn't closed the wounds. At least, she noticed, he had moved the erotic photo collage from his bedroom onto a wall in the garage. But when she asked about his future plans, he avoided giving any satisfactory answers. Before returning to Morgan Hill, Doris told Lake she wanted to end the relationship. He said he hoped they could remain friends. She agreed. He would turn up in her life several months later, in disturbingly mysterious circumstances.

After her departure, Lake concentrated on preparing again for the holocaust. At various locations, he buried medicines, food, weapons, clothing, photographs, money, and personal effects, all sealed in drums. Suffering from breathing problems brought on by his allergy to cats, he located and killed a mother cat and her kittens. In the evenings, he updated his journal, wrote letters, many of them to Charles Ng, and watched videotapes. He interspersed the laborious daytime work with trips to San Francisco, where he acquired more supplies, had sex with Cricket, and sold drugs. Frequently Cricket rode with him back to Garberville to spend weekends.

Still obsessed with Operation Miranda, Lake began excavating an adjacent hillside to build his survival/sex-slave bunker. At lumber and hardware stores in the region, he bought material for the construction, and hired local teenagers to help with the digging. He wrote, "Met the cutest of blondes, named Jessica, who is 12 years old, and the worst of jail bait. May take her picture, but must not touch." Needing some company to fill the time between visits from Cricket and his sister, Lake bought a female German shepherd puppy that he named Wubon.

By August, growing doubts assailed Lake about his plan to build the bunker and implement Miranda in the site he had picked. He decided once again to relocate the operation. In late September, he loaded Charles Gunnar's yellow van and made four exhausting fourteen-hour round-trips moving to the house in Wilseyville, in Calaveras County. Cricket joined him there for the first weekend in October.

Calaveras County is shaped like a giant arrow point, aimed northeast toward Lake Tahoe, 135 miles away over the rugged peaks of the Sierra Nevada range. San Francisco is more than a three-hour drive due west, 133 miles over winding mountain roads and across the fertile central valley. Hordes of gold seekers in 1849 left the Bay area on horses and wagons to make the long trip.

Leonard Lake was not the first outlaw to find Calaveras County attractive. Joaquin Murrieta and Charles E. Boles, known as Black Bart, held up stagecoaches along the main north-south thoroughfare, Highway 49. Boles wound up serving time in a new prison on the shoreline of San Francisco bay, San Quentin. The jail that held him while he awaited trial still stands in San Andreas, which became the county seat.

It is a torturous journey of more than twenty miles along twisting two-lane roads from San Andreas to Wilseyville. The tiny hamlet sits a few yards off Railroad Canyon Road, and can be bypassed in the wink of an eye. It consists of a post office, a small general market, and a cluster of two or three other buildings. The residential section, perched on the other side of Railroad Canyon Road, consists of twelve identical homes arranged in a perfect circle. Two dozen additional modest houses line both sides of a rustic spur extending from the circle. Sawmill employees once occupied the community, but the mill has long since been demolished, replaced now by a fire-protection-services heliport. The entire area is shaded by towering ponderosa pines and a scattering of live oak trees. In the winter, snow often covers the rugged, hilly terrain.

Leonard Lake, in order to reach the property belonging to Cricket and her father, took a branch, about two miles below Wilseyville, called Blue Mountain Road, and turned from it onto an unpaved driveway. About 200 yards up the dirt road, he pulled into a clearing where the house stood. A one-story, rectangular, yellow wooden structure, topped by a low-angle light-green roof, stood at the top of a steep slope. On two sides, an expansive redwood deck projected over the hillside. A tall man could stand under the high point of the deck and never bump his head. Inside, two bedrooms, one bathroom, and a combination kitchen-dining room filled 1,100 square feet.

The presence of thick trees and low hills that provided a privacy screen around the property appealed to Lake. The only hindrance to complete seclusion came from the presence of another house, situated on an adjacent rise. The occupants of the higher elevation could not, though, see the Balazs house or the surrounding yard.

Law enforcement in Calaveras County was provided by the Sheriff's Department, consisting of Sheriff Claude Ballard and thirty-five deputies. Among them were Mitch Hrdlicka, a veteran since 1978, and Larry Copland, who had started in 1980. Both men would eventually hear a great deal about Leonard Lake, but would never meet him.

No sooner had Lake moved into the Balazs house, then he launched the usual search for female targets. In the morning entry of his diary, October 7, 1983, he wrote, "A lady named Jackie called in response to [an] ad I put on bulletin board in West Point. Wants to do photography with/for me. Age 19, 5'1", shoulder length brown hair. Arranged for her to call me back next Monday evening. Must pick up some cammies for her before then." Later the same day, Lake noted, "Interesting.

Jackie came over. Called as if she had nothing to do and wanted to visit. I guess she just wanted to check me out. Casually pretty, but uninterestingly so. Smokes, dark skin, short hair. Nothing special or useable. I'll take some shots of her but I can't see anything to come from this." A young woman named Jackie had the good fortune of being rejected by Leonard Lake.

The bulletin board drew another potential victim for Lake. Laurie, twenty-one, five seven, married, came to the house on October 11. "Very pretty, but equally useless. Smokes, two children. Took two rolls of pictures. May be able to use them in sex con. Tried to video her undressing, but layout here is poor and got nothing." He included pictures of Laurie in his next letter to Charles Ng.

Lake's life settled into a routine. Weekends with Cricket, cleaning, painting, burying the drums of supplies he'd exhumed from the sites in Humboldt County, and ordinary chores consumed most of his time. His journal for October reflected his boredom and need for something exciting to happen. He also worried about his diminishing finances, and even tried panning for gold. "Found three whole flakes of gold. Whoopie!

"This place has a lot of disadvantages," he noted. "It lacks a lot. Still, there is something about these mountains that is peaceful and free. Perhaps it is simply the smell of pine and granite dust, bringing back old memories of summer camp. Whatever, the air is clear and the night is quiet. . . . Maybe if I develop the place more and make it more secure, I'll be more comfortable here."

Once again, Lake decided to build his bunker. He rented a backhoe to scoop dirt out of a slope only fifteen yards from one corner of the house. Black clouds in the autumn sky signaled the need to hurry before the rainy season could delay construction.

*   *   *

On October 23, he attached his video camera to the top of a tripod, eased his body into a well-worn brown fabric recliner chair, faced the camcorder, and described his plans for the bunker. Later, he entered in his journal, "God, what times. 200+ Marines killed in Lebanon. . . . Hope I can get this building finished before the world ends." He also wrote of nightmares that had started plaguing him. "Weird ones last night. Being caught and not having my pill." The dreaded rain started the next day, and kept him from making construction progress for over four weeks.

In the first week of December, Lake noticed a sheriff's deputy in West Point watching him, twice. "Two encounters in a week has me nervous." Deputy Mitch Hrdlicka would later wonder if he was the officer that had sent chills through Leonard Lake.

The money he gained from cashing Charles Gunnar's checks, and selling his possessions, created a new strain on Lake. "Op Fish will terminate soon," he wrote. "Paperwork is arriving that I can not comply with. Must start scouting around for suitable replacement. Should have already been at this."

Two weeks before Christmas, needing help on the construction project, Lake placed an ad in the local newspaper. Randy Stuart, fifteen, responded and accepted an invitation to the house. Lake introduced himself as "Charles Gunnar" and hired the youth.

As Stuart recalled, he liked "Mr. Gunnar." His own father had moved away years earlier, and he saw Gunnar as a surrogate uncle. The man took him into the woods, where they used rifles and handguns for target practice near an old logging company. Randy was also allowed to use Gunnar's yellow dirt bike, since he had no transportation of his own. He met Cricket several times, and liked her, as well.

Lake appreciated Randy's hard work, but an incident on Christmas Eve infuriated him. Lake wrote, "Tore house apart looking for wallet. Could not find. Suspect theft. Planning on tossing Randy's bedroom [in the Stuart home] when he's not around." Two days later, Lake carried out his threat. He waited until Randy, his mother, and his sister left their house, then slipped inside. He found the wallet, but all of the cash, credit cards, and identification had been removed. He left the wallet precisely where he discovered it, and quietly exited.

The journal entry for December 27 reads, "Got Randy over here. Video taped interrogation. Full confession. Got wallet back and cards. He either destroyed or lost the ID (great). He'll work off stolen cash."

Stuart's version of the incident varied slightly. He said that Gunnar owed him $80 for work he'd completed, but hadn't paid him. When he saw the wallet lying in the open, and his employer not watching, Randy grabbed it and took it home. In his bedroom, he examined the contents, and was puzzled to find credit cards in three different names. But the cash caught his real interest. He pulled $800 out of the billfold, then tossed the empty wallet into his trash can. As Randy recalled it, Gunnar approached the boy's mother, without telling Randy, and said that he thought her son might have stolen his wallet. She let him into the bedroom, and he found the billfold among the trash.

Unaware of Gunnar's visit to his mother, Randy accepted the man's invitation into his home. There Gunnar interrogated him while videotaping the whole thing. Unfortunately, the money had all been spent on crank by Randy's mother. So his boss agreed to let him work until he had repaid the entire amount.

A couple of times during Randy's employment, he said, Cricket brought young girls, age sixteen or seventeen, to the cabin so that Lake could photograph them. Once, his boss showed him three videos of girls disrobing and putting on new garments. Randy realized, from the odd point of view, that the camera was hidden and the girls didn't know they were being recorded. Each video depicted at least three different women.

They also included sequences in which the women posed while Gunnar circled them, snapping photographs.

Videotapes also led to a misunderstanding between Randy and his boss. Gunnar showed him "rows and rows" of tapes stored on shelves along one wall inside the house, and told the youth that he could borrow any of them if he wished. Randy scanned the labels and saw familiar movie titles. But when he took a few of them home, and popped them into a tape player, he was shocked to see "a sex video of Gunnar with a woman." To Randy, it seemed that the woman didn't know that a camcorder recorded the sexual activity. Embarrassed, he immediately ejected the tape. When he returned the videos on the following day, Gunnar was furious. Randy tried to explain that he thought the tape was a movie, since it was so labeled. But the owner didn't seem to understand and remained angry. For the next full week, while Randy worked, Gunnar ignored him.

To celebrate New Year's Eve, Lake drove to San Francisco to meet a female friend of Cricket's and her boyfriend. He wrote, "Went hot tubbing with them. Later took them to dinner. Discussed new idea, 'Operation Scott.' Small time revenge. She left me with an IOU for a midnight orgasm. I may just collect. Happy New Year."

Chapter 12

On New Year's Day, 1984, Lake wrote in his journal, "I'm older, fatter, balder, and not much wiser. Interesting to see where I go from here."

With the help of Randy and another youth, Lake escalated efforts in January to actually build his fantasy bunker. The men worked vigorously in the chilly weather, scooping loads of earth from the hillside. Lake shopped for and purchased concrete, lumber, and other materials to begin the construction.

He carefully measured a space within the bunker perimeter, and laid a thick concrete slab over some recently turned earth.

One of Lake's former female conquests called, needing a place to stay. He wrote, "Took her to lunch and set her up in a motel for later 3-way with Cricket." That night, after taking his mother, sister, and Cricket to dinner, he and Cricket met the woman at the motel. But Lake's' diary entry reflected disappointment because the "3-way was a flop." The next day, attempting to recover something from his investment, Lake noted, "Brought her to my place for 2-way and to help with the work."

February saw real progress in construction of the bunker. With completion in sight, Lake's thoughts turned to his plan to enslave a female victim, which would change the need for other women in his life. He philosophized: "While I enjoy company, I don't want an independent guest or girlfriend around for too long or too often. I enjoy quiet, not having to entertain or clean up after others. People around seem to get in the way, get into things, attempt to change things. When Miranda arrives, she'll be on a strictly helpmate basis. She'll be around when I need help, do what she's told, and to go [to] her room when I'm finished with her.

"Lately, life seems to be too often a beauty contest. The prettiest girl gets the job, the most opportunities, the richest man. The best looking man gets the same. People help out the person with the best smile, nicest personality, etc. Completely understandable, but us not-so-great-looking types frequently take second, or third best at everything. I live to correct this."

Financial worries overtook Lake again in February. "I need money these days. Van, insurance, and most important, the building is taking everything out of me. I expect I'll be ending up at armed robbery next trip to Bay area." Indeed, when he drove to San Francisco on the 16th, he noted, "Departed Cricket's house around 1930 [7:30 P.M.] to AR prospect. No go—too many people around. But cased place. Very good prospects." Instead of conducting a holdup, he reported to Cricket's employer, called Pacific Research, where he sometimes worked part time driving a truck, and actually earned money for five days. Weary and depressed, Lake turned to Cricket for solace, but making matters even worse, they argued, leaving him in a bitter mood.

Back in Wilseyville, Lake set up a yard sale outside the little town store to unload various items he'd acquired, legally and illegally. His journal fattened with longer entries in which he recorded construction progress. His enthusiasm for the project soared so high that it didn't even bother him when Cricket called to describe her new boyfriend. Instead, he noted simply, "Hope he turns out to be someone special for a change, rather than just someone trying to use her."

At the end of February, Lake's love interest turned backward to Rhonda Railey, the woman he had taken to Hawaii. He wrote, "Thought a lot about Rhonda today. She might be a good candidate for Miranda."

Randy Stuart continued to work with the man he knew as Charles Gunnar. Lake asked him if he knew any girls who might pose for him, and Randy could think of no one other than his own sister. Lake wrote, "Met his (16 year old) sister. Cute, quiet, dumb looking. I believe the young, sweet, easy to take advantage of look will always attract me. Too close to home for me to do anything, however."

On his weekend trip to the Bay area, Lake worked again driving a truck and visited Cricket, but a temporary bout of illness kept her in bed. Frustrated, he picked up a tabloid newspaper, scanned the personals, and made a telephone call to a gay man named Phil wishing to find a partner who enjoys oral sex. "Went over to his house to case the place. Nothing of immediate grabable (sic) value, so I let him give me head. Surprisingly very good. Slow and deep as I like it. Still very strange having a man do it. No reciprocation of course. With a little work, I might be able to pass for him. Consider a Fish-like operation."

Cricket's illness disabled her, so Lake worked for wages again. "Spent most of the day thinking about the possibilities of 'Phil.' Decided to go ahead with op. Dubbed it SAMSON, since he fought the Philistines. Called him to invite to Calaveras County next weekend, but he couldn't make it. Invited for weekend of 16–18 March. Started planning."

Resuming the construction project, Lake picked up Randy

and his sister to help him. "She is a doll. Worked them both, he moving concrete blocks, she cleaning house."

On the day before the scheduled arrival of Lake's targeted gay victim, Phil, he received a phone call from the man, and dejectedly wrote, "He scrubbed. Plans, hopes and expectations down the drain. A week of waiting shot to hell. This operation was to provide a new car, new ID, credit cards, new furniture. Everything lost. Now what?"

Randy's sister finally agreed to model for Lake, but insisted on being completely clothed. While posing, she told him of her engagement to a local man. Lake had acquired a diamond ring, and offered to sell it to them. But when the boyfriend came to examine it, he backed out of the purchase. That night, Lake tried to contact an old girlfriend, only to hear from an angry landlord that she was broke, pregnant, and had skipped out on her rent. Growing desperate for a new female companion, Lake even joined a Bible-study group hoping to meet a woman he could target, but found none of them to his liking. Everything seemed to be turning sour for Lake except the bunker construction.

Already angry at the series of negative events, Lake lost his temper when he caught a neighbor's dog trying to mate with Wubon. In an angry fit, he shot the hapless animal, which he described as "one of the more mangy, pitiful dogs in the neighborhood."

Concerned about the possible consequences of his act, Lake wrote, "A stupid thing to do as it wasn't clean and the dog ran screaming home. Vengeance rarely makes sense. Event may cause me trouble. Took certain precautions against investigation. Moved dope plants, hid weapons. Nervous." As it turned out, he managed to charm the couple who owned the dog, and they invited him to a barbeque on the following Saturday. They even exchanged pornographic tapes with him.

Lake's relationship with Cricket, and the sexual satisfaction they achieved with each other, peaked again when she made her weekend visit. After she left, Lake felt regenerated. On May 13, he noted, "Picked up Randy's sister for two hours of photography. Got her into a cut down T-shirt which occasionally shows her tits. May be able to work her out of her clothes yet, although this is not sure."

As the bunker neared completion, Lake continually sprayed the wet concrete on hot days to prevent it from cracking. He arose early one morning and thoroughly flooded it. "Tried to avoid the heat of the day. Only today was cool! Whom the gods wish to destroy, they first drive mad."

Charles Ng walked out of the Fort Leavenworth Disciplinary Barracks on June 29, 1984, twenty-six months after he had been arrested at Philo. To his astonishment, the government simply set him free and never mentioned deportation to Hong Kong. The incredible bungle by officials would turn out to be a tremendous source of controversy. Perhaps they relied on the bogus birth certificate that had gained him entrance into the U.S. Marine Corps. Or, maybe they just overlooked the fact that a citizen of the British Commonwealth, who had committed felony crimes for which he'd served more than two years in a federal prison, should be deported. Certainly, there had been ample time to investigate Charles Ng's citizenship.

Before myopic officials could change their minds, Ng caught a bus to Shawnee, Oklahoma, where Ed Popovich, the inmate he'd befriended, now lived. They had been corresponding regularly, and Popovich had invited Ng to visit him upon release from prison.

During Ng's short stay with Popovich, he told his pal about his plans to reunite with Leonard Lake, the survivalist in California. Ng brought out a stack of photographs to show Popovich, pictures of the bunker under construction, of Lake, and of Cricket. They were his second family, Ng said, and he was anticipating the reunion with them. Maybe Popovich could come out to California and join them for some operations.

But someone else, other than Lake and Popovich, was also on Ng's mind. Ng called Leonard on July 4 to say he wouldn't arrive in the Bay area until Sunday or Monday.

Prior to leaving the prison, and making the trip to Shawnee, Ng had written a letter to his lonely pen pal, Sally Jean Pyle, to inform her of his release. Sally Jean, delighted at the news, had suggested they meet. She would travel with her sister to Oklahoma. About bringing her sister along, Sally later explained, "That made me feel safer, and put me at ease."

The first face-to-face meeting between Sally Jean and Charles Ng took place at the home of Ed Popovich. To Sally, Ng seemed as kind and considerate as he had in his letters. Both of them had trouble concealing the excitement at finally being able to hug one another, and they talked about their long months of friendship via the letters. Ng hadn't touched a woman for more than two years, and the magic of a female embrace stirred him deeply. The warmth he exuded filled Sally Jean with tenderness and joy. They hated for the moment to end, and parted reluctantly that evening.

Feeling unsatisfied with their short time together, Sally Jean called the next morning, and drove alone to pick Charles up. They rode around for a while, as the sexual tension and desire slowly built. By mutual agreement, she pulled the car into a motel lot, and they checked in. "We were both lonely and needed affection," she later explained. She also admitted that during the incident in the motel room, she kept thinking she shouldn't be there because of her marriage, the age difference, and the fact she had very little in common with Charles.

After the sexual encounter, a passionate two hours both of them would always remember, they talked. Acknowledging that she was old enough to be Ng's mother, Sally Jean realized that the future could hold nothing for them. "The closeness comforted me, and I needed it. And it was my way of saying

I really cared for him," she would recall. But both of them understood that they had no future together. She took Charles Ng back to his friend's home.

Shortly after the Independence Day celebration, Ng departed for California. On Monday, July 9, Cricket picked him up at the San Francisco airport.

Leonard Lake, growing excited at the possibility of Operation Miranda becoming a reality within the next few months, needed a base of operations in San Francisco to hunt for the first victims. In early July, he again rented an apartment in the same building where he'd lived a year earlier, on 19th Avenue, near Golden Gate Park. Other new tenants had moved in during Lake's absence. He looked them over, especially the females, but found only one of any interest to him: "Doper. Reasonably poor. Might attempt to put the make on her." A better possibility turned up in a postcard he received, a response to a personal ad he had placed. "Linda," Lake noted, "seems very eager to get together." A few days later, he noted, "Went over to meet Linda. Took her to Cliff House for drink, to her house afterwards. Age 35, short hair, not especially pretty, sort of dumpy figure. Still eager for a relationship. Expect we will be lovers soon."

It happened sooner than he expected, as reflected in his next day's entry. "Picked Linda up at 10 a.m., took her to beach. Basically, it was an excuse to get her out and spend some more time with her, without much cost. Took her to lunch in the city, dropped her off at 3:30 . . . back to her house at 8 p.m. Horny little chub. Made love until midnight. Spent the night."

Years later, social behavior experts would analyze the remarkable success Lake enjoyed with a variety of women. Certainly, Lake knew how to turn on the personal charm. Articulate, intelligent, and somewhat mysterious, he knew when to use humor, and when to speak seriously to his prey. But something else lured women to him. Some of the experts suggested that Lake exuded a sense of danger, and though most women won't admit it, a man who seems dangerous is often magnetic, irresistible, and exciting. Also, despite Lake's disparaging description of himself as not very attractive, he underestimated his own physical allure.

The reunion with Charles Ng took place on July 9 when Cricket gave him a ride from the airport to Lake's apartment on 19th Avenue. Ng helped with the moving-in chores at the new apartment, while the two men conversed about old times and Ng's prison experiences.

With Ng's arrival, remarkable changes were set in motion, affecting an untold number of human lives.

Lake had kept his diary faithfully, making entries every day since January 1, 1983. Now, eighteen months later, and only one day after the arrival of the man he hoped would help him carry out Operation Miranda, he stopped recording his activities. His last entry before the sixty-day hiatus in the chronicle of his daily life noted that he was teaching Charles Ng how to drive. Two months later, he would resume keeping the journal, with a cryptic explanation of the blank time frame. The missing entries, he said, were ''to allow a period of time to pass that was best left unrecorded.''

A few miles from Lake's apartment, a man named Donald Albert Giuletti, thirty-six, had no inkling that his life was about to end. Giuletti, a disc jockey at a small San Francisco radio station, openly admitted his homosexuality. He earned a comfortable income, enough to pay for an upscale apartment in the residential Castro district. He and a roommate, Richard Carrazza, thirty-one, shared the flat. Sexually adventurous, Giuletti placed an ad in an underground Bay area newspaper, *The*

Spectator, offering "oral sex for straight men." On July 11, a reader responded, and came to the residence. Carrazza discreetly stepped into a back room to allow his roommate and the guest privacy.

Moments later, Carrazza heard a popping noise and a scream. Alarmed, he ducked into a hiding spot, and waited until he heard the visitor leave. Moments later, he rushed into the study and found Giuletti sprawled on the floor, blood gushing from a bullet wound in his head, barely breathing.

Suddenly, the entry door creaked open, and the gun-wielding visitor reappeared. He lifted the weapon and squeezed off another shot, which slammed into Carrazza's chest. As the shooter sprinted away, Carrazza managed to grab the phone and dial 911. Although his wound was serious, it was not a mortal injury, and he was able to speak not only to the paramedics who arrived within minutes, but also to a police investigator. He described the gunman as a Chinese man wearing prescription glasses, about five eight and thin. Ballistics tests of shell casings found in the study proved the weapon to be a .22 caliber pistol.

Emergency medical technicians rushed Giuletti to a hospital, but he lost his struggle for life twenty-four hours later. Carrazza survived.

Not far away, another man who had placed an ad in a newspaper would attract disaster.

Harvey Dubs, twenty-nine, had worked for Petrov Graphics, a printing firm on Mission Street in San Francisco, for nearly eleven years. Stan Petrov, his boss, regarded Harvey as "extraordinarily conscientious" and loyal. So when Harvey failed to show up at work on Thursday, July 26, 1984, Petrov knew something must be wrong.

One day earlier, Harvey's wife, Deborah, had talked on the phone to her best friend at about 5:45 P.M. Karen Tuck and Deborah had grown up together in Hillsborough, California, about twelve miles down the peninsula from the Dubses' apartment on Yukon Street. They treated each other as if they were sisters, and any day that passed without a telephone conversation between them just wasn't complete. Karen and her husband, George, were the godparents of little Sean Dubs, sixteen months old. The two families often vacationed together, and the Tucks had helped Deborah and Harvey move into the apartment on Yukon Street.

In that final phone conversation, Deborah told Karen that her father had dropped by and had taken her and the toddler to Golden Gate Park. That evening, Deborah said, she was expecting someone who had responded to an ad Harvey had placed in a newspaper offering his services in using high-tech video equipment. In addition to working at Petrov Graphics, Harvey had started a business venture, Video Dubs, in which he would professionally make video recordings of weddings, christenings, and other events, or rent out the expensive equipment he owned. The phone chat had ended when Deborah told Karen that someone was at the door, probably the person who was interested in the video services.

Not long after Deborah Dubs hung up the phone, her neighbor Dorice Murphy saw something strange. Dorice had lived on the high end of the short, sloping cul-de-sac street for forty-five years, and knew everyone in the neighborhood. She felt comfortably safe in the prewar home and the countrylike atmosphere provided by thick trees and shrubbery on the hillside above her. She liked the young Dubs family, who lived diagonally across the small courtyard in the top floors of a three-story, gray-shingled house, just below the curving terrace of Upper Market Street.

A few minutes after 5:45 P.M., Dorice Murphy glanced out of her third-floor window, and noticed an Asian man walking down the exterior stairs of the Dubs apartment. He appeared to be straining under the weight of a black "oblong suitcase" he carried. She also saw that a Volkswagen Rabbit, which belonged to Harvey Dubs, had backed uphill on the narrow street, which was no longer than seventy-five yards, and no wider than an alley. A man with short, thick arms emerged from the driver's side, but she couldn't see his face. While Murphy watched, the Asian hoisted the load he carried into the car's open luggage compartment. As soon as they slammed the trunk, and jumped into the car, it sped away. Dorice Murphy's senses tingled with alarm.

After the telephone conversation between Deborah Dubs and Karen Tuck ended, a restlessness troubled Karen. She tried several times to call Deborah back, but no one answered. She couldn't shake the feeling of something being terribly wrong.

On Thursday morning, after repeated attempts during the night failed to reach her close friends, and Karen's nerves had tightened to the breaking point, she asked her husband, who worked in the city, to drop by and see if anything was wrong. During his lunch break, he drove to Yukon Street, climbed the four concrete steps to the landing, where he stopped for a moment, feeling a crawling sensation in his spine. Tentatively he ascended the remaining nine wooden steps and reached for the entry doorknob. George's heart skipped a beat when he spotted Deborah's key ring dangling from the key inserted in the lock.

Afraid of what he might find, George opened the door and entered. Nothing but silence greeted him. In the kitchen, he found dishes in the sink, submerged in cold soapy water. Deborah would not have willingly left them that way. First calling their names again to see if Harvey and Deborah might be asleep, he ascended interior stairs to the two bedrooms, one for the two adults, and one for little Sean. Inside the master bedroom, George instantly noticed empty spaces on the shelves where Harvey kept his video equipment and an assortment of tapes.

George Tuck left the ghostly quiet apartment and called Deborah's father. Neither he nor Karen would ever again see Harvey, Deborah, or little Sean Dubs.

In an apartment underneath the Dubs residence, in the same building, Barbara Speaker could often hear their baby, Sean, crying. Also, because the old structure had wooden floors, the sounds of footsteps above Speaker's living room creaked whenever Harvey or Deborah moved around.

Barbara shared her concern with her Yukon Street neighbors on Thursday evening when the news spread about the Dubs family mysteriously vanishing. On Friday, while getting ready to leave her apartment at 11:30 in the morning, Speaker heard the floor above her creaking with the weight of someone walking. It flashed through her mind that Harvey and Deborah might have returned home, but Speaker was running late and didn't have time to check on them. As she rushed outside, she heard the door to the Dubses' apartment close. She turned to wave, and jerked in surprise as a total stranger turned from the door to face her. The Asian man, who wore thick glasses, jumped as if startled, too, and moved down the steps toward her carrying a bulky, heavy duffel bag in one hand, and a stuffed flight bag in the other. Staring at him, Speaker halfway expected a greeting of some sort, but stepped out of his way as he hurried past without a word. She noted that he looked to be in his midtwenties, that his height approximately matched her own five seven, and that he weighed about 140 to 150 pounds.

As the stranger trotted down toward the intersection close to a row of hedges, Speaker followed and spoke to him. "Excuse me," she said twice, but he ignored her. Intending to ask if he was a friend of the Dubs family, she was cut short when a 1984 Volkswagen Rabbit screeched to a halt at the curb, and the stranger jumped into the passenger seat. The Caucasian driver, Speaker noted, wore a full beard. Dumbfounded, she watched as the car sped off into city traffic.

Bothered all day about the strange events, Speaker spoke of it to her husband and some friends when they dined out that night. At about 11:30 P.M., twelve hours after the first encounter, as she emerged from the friends' car in front of her residence,

Speaker thought she saw some movement in a window of the Dubs apartment. From inside their own rooms, they watched through their window blinds, and saw a bearded man carrying a bulky dark bundle from the apartment. She thought he resembled the person who'd been driving the Volkswagen earlier that day.

When they reported both events to the police, Speaker used her artistic skill to draw a picture of the Asian man she'd seen. The portrait bore a noticeable resemblance to Charles Ng.

Chapter 13

The Haight district of San Francisco, which became notorious during the 1960s as the center of hippie culture, attracted free-spirited wanderers, drug addicts, homeless souls, and throngs of young people who wanted to break the restraints of parental control, social restrictions, and middle-class morality. Centered at the intersection of Haight and Ashbury Streets, the district acted as a magnet for a broad spectrum of transients. Charles Manson thrived in Haight-Ashbury, where he gathered vulnerable teenagers, mostly women, and formed his "family" of killers. From all across the nation, curious and restless young people hitchhiked to San Francisco and landed in the district, seeking the uninhibited experiences of flower power, free love, psychedelic music, and plentiful drugs. Among them was a curious, somewhat rebellious fellow named William Kelley, who, nearly three decades later, would find himself linked with Charles Ng in a life-and-death struggle.

The heyday of hippies tapered off in the 1970s, but still hasn't died in Haight-Ashbury. A colorful array of street people still populate the sidewalks twenty-four hours a day. They find affordable rent in old hotels and apartments. Among the more popular buildings that denizens of the district called home in 1984 was a three-story structure on Carl Street, just one block from the southeast corner of the sprawling greenbelt named Golden Gate Park. Known as the "pink palace," the apartment complex had been called that for years, despite the fact that it really wasn't pink. It had been a drab earth color for many years. Some knowledgeable locals thought the name had been borrowed, somewhat tongue in cheek, from a large public housing project at Turk and Webster Streets. Pink or not, the residence on Carl Street offered thirty units, ten on each floor, most of which required the tenants to use bathrooms at the end of the hallways. Those halls were often filled with the sweetish odor of marijuana smoke. Because of the common usage of "weed," anyone who could supply it at reasonable prices was always welcome at the palace. Thus, a few of the occupants would come to know Leonard Lake, but thought his name was "Alan Drey."

Randy Jacobson, a 134-pound, five ten, wiry wanderer, age thirty-five, with wavy dark-brown hair reaching to his narrow shoulders, lived in the pink palace. His faded blue eyes seemed world-weary, yet mirthful. He wore the required beard and mustache of his subculture, along with a gaily patterned headband. His experiences in Vietnam had disillusioned Jacobson, and he'd been unable to settle down after leaving the military. Alcohol and drugs became a major part of his life. In 1980, he hitchhiked from Georgia to California, seeking relief from mental demons and a life that was "traumatized by the past," according to his wistful comments to anyone who would listen. He also spoke of a shotgun wedding in Iowa, in which he had "been made to marry a girl" he'd impregnated.

With Social Security Disability Income, Jacobson lived marginally in the pink palace among kindred spirits. One night at a place called the Shady Grove, he met an intelligent, young woman who also struggled with substance abuse. Maysha McLennan, testifying in court years later, told of her problems and spoke of Jacobson. She said she saw Jacobson as a "local Haight-Ashbury character, a street person who couldn't keep a job," and a "virtuous but spacey" person whose "only ambition was to smoke pot and play the guitar." Yet she couldn't resist strong feelings of attraction. "I was more interested in him than he was in me," she would say. Soon after their meeting, she moved in with him at the pink palace.

Relationships between people in the drug culture are often rocky, and theirs was no exception. Jacobson would occasionally vanish without notice and pop up later with no explanation. Maysha, in keeping with a perception of herself as nonjudgmental, and hesitant to question the behavior of others, kept her mouth shut. But eventually Jacobson's "lukewarm and inconsistent" interaction with her led to disillusionment for Maysha. A desire for something more substantial began to occupy her mind, and she decided to resume her education at San Francisco State University. The campus on 19th Avenue was over four miles away, so it became necessary for her to seek closer living quarters. She answered a classified ad for inexpensive rooms available in the 2400 block of 19th Avenue. In the spring of 1984, McLennan moved from the "raucous and ribald" pink palace. She continued her relationship, though, with Randy Jacobson.

Among the residents and people who hung out at the "rundown communal household," Maysha met a man who called himself Alan Drey.

Leonard Lake, using the Drey pseudonym, had moved from the 19th Avenue quarters, but kept a basement apartment there. He dropped by frequently to sell marijuana and to look for potential "models" and Miranda candidates.

The apartment manager told McLennan, "This guy Alan

Drey is a really strange dude, but kind of cool, and kind of not cool." He added, "He likes growing pot and he's a military-type person." The characterization frightened Maysha, who thought of herself as a pacifist. Explaining the antimilitary attitude, she said that her mother had "followed Joan Baez."

When she actually met Lake, as "Drey," Maysha said, "He didn't fit the description I'd heard. He was kinda heavy and he had short, dark hair . . . and he wore a beret. He reminded me of my uncle." Her initial impression soon gave way to a deep suspicion of Drey. She knew that he had moved out of the basement several months earlier, but wondered why he was "always moving equipment in and out through the downstairs door." She also noticed a short Asian man, who seemed to be hiding in the basement, perhaps living there on the sly. The silent stranger never joined in any of the communal discussions or meals.

Regarding Drey, Maysha said, "I found him weird . . . and friendly. But he was too friendly. Charming, but overly charming . . . he bothered me a lot." Drey represented himself as a professional photographer and wanted to take photos of McLennan. "He said he had done pictures for magazines, and he had all this equipment, tripods, lights, all this stuff."

In McLennan's memory, Drey had put the word out that he was looking for someone to handle the retail end of his marijuana enterprise. The apartment manager suggested that Randy Jacobson would be ideally suited for the job, considering his notoriety for pot consumption and his connections with the street people in Haight-Ashbury. When Randy came to visit Maysha, the manager introduced him to Drey, for two reasons. Firstly, Randy might be interested in selling Drey's goods, and secondly, the manager was trying send a message to Drey that Maysha was romantically involved, therefore off-limits. Perhaps that would discourage the insistent photographer.

But it didn't. Drey continued to pressure her until she gave in. "And I did it," said McLennan. "He took the pictures in my room, but the door was always open. I was in a velvet dress and I wore a hat and a shawl. It was like modeling, kind of fun, not risqué or anything. . . . The only thing was, he tried to put his arm around me. I tried to give him the message. I just lifted his arm off of me. I said I had a boyfriend. I reminded him of Randy."

Eventually, said McLennan, "Drey had more interest in Randy than [in] me. He got chummy and close to Randy and offered him opportunities." Jacobson didn't seem to realize what was happening. Said Maysha, "He was a naive farm boy from South Dakota, just learning from experience. And the whole atmosphere in the complex was one of trust." McLennan said that everyone was open and accepting of strangers. "People would filter through, getting high here, crashing there. No one was too uptight or suspicious of anyone else. . . . Everyone had the attitude that we are all friends." Drey, though, seemed too eager to fit in and too accommodating.

As part of Drey's attempts to endear himself, he constantly "made offers and talked about opportunities." During a visit to Jacobson's apartment, with Maysha present, Drey "talked about a marijuana farm he had up in the mountains in Humboldt or Mendocino County. He asked us if we wanted to move up there and be caretakers of the farm. We thought it might be interesting but it was too impractical. I didn't want to. I wasn't scared, I was just too repelled by Alan Drey. And I didn't want to get involved. Randy was so indecisive and passive. We discussed it and decided it wasn't a good idea." As McLennan recalled it, the marijuana enterprise never materialized, but Drey achieved his goal of insinuating himself into Jacobson's life, and became a regular habitué of the pink palace.

It struck McLennan odd, too, that while Drey seemed so fond of Jacobson, he would ask her out on dates, saying, "Forget about Randy. He's no good for you. He has no money for dates or dinners." She refused to go out with the man she knew as Alan Drey. After four months at the 19th Avenue rooming house, McLennan moved back to Carl Street, near the pink palace.

Maurice Rock, another resident of the pink palace, lived for music. The thirty-seven-year-old African American played the guitar and sang with enough gusto that other residents in the complex could hear him clearly through the walls. Six feet tall, Rock weighed a trim 160 pounds. He wore his hair in a two-inch bushy "Afro" style, and always had a big grin for everyone, which unfortunately flashed his bad teeth. He used marijuana prodigiously.

Maurice knew a wheelchair bound African American who lived on the ground floor of the pink palace with a woman named "Sheryl Okoro." The attractive, young woman had adopted the name Okoro as a street identity. Born Sheryl Lynn Porter, she stood an inch over five feet, had blue eyes, and nicely styled brown hair, giving her an out-of-place appearance in comparison to many of the strung-out, haggard women of the palace.

For Leonard Lake, the pink palace offered high potential for meeting women to pose for him, and to possibly accompany him to Wilseyville as Miranda candidates. One woman, who also happened to be a friend of Sheryl Okoro, met Lake in a hallway while he helped a tenant move a refrigerator. Lake later knocked on her door, told her she was beautiful, and suggested she should be a model. She consented to pose for him, and did so in nearby Golden Gate Park, but refused to take off her clothing. During the next few weeks, he badgered her with offers of free marijuana, showed up uninvited at the A&W Root Beer restaurant where she worked, and generally made a nuisance of himself. He nearly ruined her marriage when the woman's husband spotted her outside the restaurant talking to Lake, and assumed she was playing around. After she adamantly refused to model in revealing poses, he finally gave up. Within days, someone burglarized her apartment and took every bit of clothing she owned.

Lake's pursuit of another resident, Camera Bougher, who could double for actress Jamie Lee Curtis, followed the same pattern. Her neighbor Maurice Rock, for whom she sometimes cooked meals, introduced her to Alan Drey. Initiating a campaign to convince her to model for him, Drey even invited her husband to accompany them on a "photo shoot." Once, she almost caved in and agreed to pose, but a "funny feeling" caused her to change her mind. Drey sent her a letter and enclosed four marijuana joints as an inducement, promising all the pot she could use in exchange for her agreement to pose. Each new effort by Lake reinforced her determination to avoid him. He finally gave up. A short time later, her pal Maurice Rock mentioned that Alan had invited him to a ranch in the mountains, where they could pick all the marijuana they needed. Bougher had declined the same offer several times. But Rock seemed happy at the opportunity. Dressed in his favorite tan three-piece corduroy suit, Rock left. No one would ever hear Maurice Rock's music again.

Nor would anyone know what offer Leonard Lake made to Sheryl Okoro when she suddenly disappeared, never to be found.

Randy Jacobson and Maysha McLennan owned a broken-down van, which they kept parked nearby, close to a greenbelt. Alan Drey hinted that he would like to buy it. Said McLennan, "I liked the idea because it was getting a lot of parking tickets. Everything was a struggle then. Street people were crashing in the van." One morning in June 1984, Drey made an uninvited appearance at Jacobson's apartment, ostensibly to discuss buying the van. McLennan later recalled it. "It was real early. There he was. I was in a hurry. I was late to school and had to take the bus. I said to Alan, 'Go look at the van and see if you want to buy it.' Then he offered me a ride to school. With Jacobson's consent, she accepted.

"On the way," she recalled, "I started asking Alan about his personal life. He said he had a wife and that they were separated. He talked about his marijuana farm and his photography. When I got to school, I called Randy and let him know everything was all right. After school, I went to his room, but he didn't show up and I spent the night there."

She spent three more nights waiting for Jacobson, all in vain. On the third day, back in her own apartment, her roommate said, "You got a note in the mailbox from Randy. I don't remember when he left it." Worried, she grabbed the note and hurriedly read it. "It was four sentences on a small piece of yellow paper." She couldn't tell for sure whether or not the "shaky handwriting" belonged to Randy. Disappointed that it contained nothing "intimate or personal," McClennan recalled that it said Randy "had gone to San Jose to help a guy named Steve he had just met. It said he had a part-time job in San Jose with this big-time dope operation." The note informed her that Jacobson planned to return to pick up his clothing, and that he would contact her in about a week. It was signed, "Randy." A sick feeling of suspicion raced through Maysha. The words sounded nothing like the laid-back man she knew. But the fact that he'd disappeared on previous occasions kept her from being seriously alarmed.

When Jacobson failed to show up after a full week, McLennan canvassed the neighborhood to see if anyone had heard from him. As time passed, she even checked his bank account, and learned that his SSDI checks were being cashed, "So I figured he was okay." No one, including her friends, thought of seeking official help. McLennan explained, "It wouldn't be their way of doing things, like to call the police or anything."

Neither Maysha McLennan, nor anyone she knew, would ever see Randy Jacobson alive again.

Chapter 14

During his first few weeks back in San Francisco, Charles Ng moved around constantly, sometimes sleeping in Lake's 19th Avenue apartment and sometimes in his aunt's home. At some time during that period, he started introducing himself as "Mike Kimoto," using a driver's license and social security card to prove his identification. The real Michael Kimoto's wallet had been stolen while he was surfing near Watsonville, not far from Morgan Hill where Lake often visited his pal Charles Gunnar. In late July, Ng found a temporary job at China Bazaar in Chinatown.

At the beginning of August, Lake's sister Janet rented an apartment on 17th Street, but didn't need to move in until the first week of September. Lake introduced Ng to her, as Mike Kimoto, and asked if Mike could stay in the apartment temporarily. Janet generously consented, and Ng used one of the bedrooms for a full month. In September, he needed a new place to stay. After a short search, he located a converted garage room for rent in a private home on Lenox Way, an inclined residential street less than two blocks long. Only a half mile from Lake's apartment on 19th Avenue, Ng found his new residence convenient and within walking distance of everything he needed: food stores, a laundry, and public transportation.

The location also provided easy access to Portola Drive, which curves through the West Portal district, loops north, and becomes Upper Market Street. The thoroughfare traverses a hillside terrace before descending into the business district as San Francisco's well-known Market Street. Just below the terrace is a block-long lane that narrows into a rustic residential alley. At the end of Yukon Street, on the west curve of the cozy tree-lined cul de sac, Harvey Dubs, his wife, Deborah, and their toddler son, Sean, had lived in the upper floors of a gray-shingled home, where they felt secure from the world's ills.

When the Dubs family vanished on July 25, Harvey's father had called the police to file a report. A San Francisco Police Department commander had passed the report to a pair of experienced sleuths on the missing persons squad.

Irene Brunn never expected to become a cop when she worked as a carhop at Mel's drive-in restaurant in 1969, although she'd often fantasized about it. A native of San Francisco, the brown-eyed, medium-stature Irene married soon after graduating from Lincoln High School, and produced four children. After a divorce, she was dating a "bike cop," who suggested she "take the test." Much to her surprise, she passed and joined the force as a policewoman. In those days, women weren't regarded as officers. Instead, they were required to wear dresses and high heels to perform mostly desk work. But Irene's Aztec-Mexican heritage not only gave her multilingual skills, but also instilled in her a fiery drive to compete. She pressured her bosses until they finally allowed her to work the streets as an undercover narcotics officer in the tough Mission district. She later served in child abuse investigation, and moved to the missing persons bureau in 1978. The stress led to a heart attack in 1982, but by this time she had grown so deeply involved in her work she couldn't think of doing anything else. When she recovered, she dove right back into the thick of it.

In the Dubs case, Irene was teamed with Inspector Glenn Pamfiloff, a methodical detective in his early forties. Of Russian descent, but born in China, Pamfiloff had been with the SFPD nearly two decades. A skilled chess player, who used the game's logic in analyzing each move to make on a case, he joined Irene for the drive up into the hilly section where the Dubs family lived.

They met Deborah's father at the gray-shingled house, and hoped to make entry through the front door, where a key had been left dangling after Harvey, Deborah, and Sean vanished. But the key had also disappeared, so Pamfiloff hoisted his nearly six-foot frame through a side window. Inside, he and Irene listened as the father mentioned that Deborah never went away overnight without a black knit suit she loved, and that she always took along a medicine kit. The officers found both items still inside the apartment.

In the third-floor master bedroom, they made note of a severed telephone cord still lashed to a closet doorknob, where someone had apparently been bound. All of Harvey's shoes, as recognized by Deborah's father, also sat neatly aligned in their places on the closet floor. It appeared that Harvey had left the place barefoot. A peculiar arrangement of furniture in the child's room caught the attention of Brunn and Pamfiloff. Chairs had been pushed against the daybed Sean slept in, which had been jammed against one wall.

From her observations, Irene Brunn mentally sketched a rough theory. Considering the timing of the event, when combined with the report from Karen Tuck about her telephone conversation with Deborah, it seemed fairly certain that the perpetrator, or perpetrators, had arrived before Harvey came home from work. Brunn figured the intruder had either talked his way inside the apartment or forced his way in when Deborah opened the door, expecting someone who wanted to rent Harvey's video skills and equipment. Once inside, the suspect had grabbed the child and used force and threats to keep the mother quiet. When Harvey arrived home, he'd been forced, also by threatening harm to the little boy, to remove his shoes and submit to being tied with the telephone cord. It's even possible, Brunn figured, that the Asian man who was seen by two witnesses, and drawn by one, had taken the child out, gagged and tied, inside the black oblong suitcase or bag. Fear of never seeing Sean again would force the parents to comply with any demand made by the intruder.

Probably under cover of late-night darkness, both Harvey and Deborah had been kidnapped and taken away while neighbors slept. That way, the perps could return anytime and remove the valuable video equipment, which had sat in the vacant spaces noticed by George Tuck.

Now, the real challenge faced Irene Brunn and Glenn Pamfiloff. They hoped desperately that they could find the missing trio before any harm came to them. But it would be more than nine months before they would find any solid leads regarding the fate of the Dubs family.

Among the various people Charles Ng met while moving around the city was Cliff Peranteau, twenty-four, originally from Philadelphia, Pennsylvania. His quick smile and cordial attitude didn't reveal the hardships he'd suffered during a childhood about which he seldom spoke. Few people knew that he'd been one of twelve children and that he'd been seriously mistreated as a toddler. His father had vanished early, and a host of problems had forced the mother to release her children into foster homes. Cliff had been placed with an extremely strict family who punished him for the slightest infractions by isolating him in a small room. One of Cliff's siblings called it "solitary confinement." But in his early teens, Cliff maintained a fierce loyalty to his brothers and sisters, and would skip school in order to pay them surreptitious visits. He took any risk to help them however he could. When they cried on his shoulder, and criticized their mother, Cliff tried to offer solace by reminding them to consider what she might have suffered as a child.

Still in his teens, Cliff met Cynthia Tanner and fell in love. He could share his problems, as well as the joys of life, with Cynthia. They became inseparable. He even bought a personalized miniature Pennsylvania license plate on which capital letters spelled out "CINDY."

As a young adult, Cliff hated to leave the region where his siblings lived, but in the face of economic needs, he migrated to San Francisco in search of stability and to escape his tortured early years. Cynthia Tanner joined him in the move.

Having found a regular job with comfortable pay at a downtown moving-and-storage company, Cliff Peranteau rented an apartment in which he and Cynthia lived together. In commuting to his San Francisco workplace, he circumvented heavy traffic congestion by weaving through the jammed streets on his blue Suzuki motorcycle. Sometimes, though, he left the bike at home and rode public transportation. By spending evenings with Cynthia, and working full time, Cliff generally avoided much contact with the constant stream of noisy street people near his apartment and job. Charles Ng, one of the few neighborhood people he met, seemed decent enough, though. And upon discovering that Ng needed a job, Cliff even recommended that he apply at Dennis Moving Company, Peranteau's employer.

Ng, after living two months on minimum wages and with the help of relatives, had decided he needed a better paying job in order to pay his rent and to buy basic needs. On September 10, 1984, he and Lake entered the office of Dennis Moving Company on California Street, just a few blocks from the piers at the Embarcado, San Francisco's waterfront. The firm provided moving and storage services for business and industry. Twenty employees, including Cliff Peranteau, worked in the large warehouse, where they loaded, unloaded, and rearranged boxes, crates, furniture, and a variety of other items placed in the company's care.

A serious decision faced Ng and Lake. Should they use their real names on the application forms, or the false identifications they'd used for other activities? Ng entered his correct name, age, and address. In the space requesting military history, he wrote: "U.S. Marine Corps, entered October 1979, Honorably discharged July 1984."

More accustomed to keeping his true identity a secret, Lake decided to slightly alter his name, and applied as Leonard "Blake." In the space provided for work experience, Blake noted that he could operate a backhoe, a bulldozer, and could drive trucks up to five tons. Additional skills included competency with a typewriter and electronic test equipment.

After they'd completed the paperwork, they stepped into the business owner's office to be interviewed. Dennis Goza glanced at the short Asian man who wore neat slacks and a dress shirt and, with some surprise, his companion. Goza had expected only Charles Ng, who had called in advance. The other man, husky, medium height, sporting a dark beard, and a bushy fringe of black hair below his bald pate, wore an "infantry-type" jacket. To Goza, the man appeared somewhat "disheveled." The recent work experience entry on Blake's application indicated he'd been employed by a construction firm called Balazs Building Company, in Wilseyville, California, at the rate of $12 an hour. Ng introduced himself and Blake, saying they had been in the military together and were looking for employment.

Goza, needing only one man, chose Charles Ng. His employment started on September 28. That morning, Ng met several of his coworkers, and chatted with Peranteau, who introduced him to Jeff Gerald, twenty-five, a happy-go-lucky bachelor originally from Denver, Colorado. His streaked thatch of blond hair suggested endless afternoons on a surfboard, but he carried his share of the workload in the warehouse. Gerald kept people around him constantly laughing with his quick wit and infectious smile. It was rare to see him without his guitar. Anyone acquainted with Jeff knew of his driving ambition to be a musical entertainer. With a buddy he'd met in junior high school, Jeff had formed a band called Crash 'N Burn. His pal had helped him shop for and select the guitar at a music store. Jeff had good-humoredly decorated it with stickers used at Dennis Moving, such as "Shred" and "To be destroyed."

Gerald and Peranteau, Ng learned, liked talking about the San Francisco professional football team, the Forty-Niners, and their phenomenal quarterback, Joe Montana. Now and then, they participated in betting pools on various pro games.

Charles Gunnar's ex-wife, Vicky, left her place of work in Morgan Hill one afternoon, and was stunned to seen his old yellow Volkswagen van sitting at the curb. Nervous, she wondered if Charles had returned and was going to give her trouble. Then it occurred to her that the van might be booby-trapped. She called her boyfriend, who soon arrived to carefully inspect the vehicle. Nothing dangerous turned up. Vicky had been receiving notices from a finance company about delinquent payments, so she made a call and arranged for the van to be repossessed. It would be a long time before she knew that

Leonard Lake had been using the Volkswagen, and had returned it.

Having given up Gunnar's van, Leonard Lake needed another car. He began reading the classified section to see if he could obtain one through an "operation."

On the same day he and Ng applied for work at Dennis Moving, Lake resumed making entries in his daily journal. He wrote an observation that the previous two months were "best left unrecorded," then noted that he had learned "items of interesting personal value."

Now typing instead of scrawling words in his usual longhand, Lake wrote, "I have learned that my programming [in my] youth . . . that which is called morality, either was not given or was given poorly. To all purposes save a *very* few, I have no morality . . . accept it as fact. In terms of life or death, neither seems to move me.

"The past two months saw Miranda come to fruit. That taught me more. The perfect woman is one who is totally controlled, a woman who does exactly what she is told and nothing else. There are no sexual problems with a totally submissive woman. There are no frustrations. There [is] only pleasure and contentment. I have observed, I believe, one woman who found this not only acceptable but even desirable. I doubt this will be the norm and in this case the woman's low mentality probably affected the discovery. A whore, druggy, and fool. Still, I enjoyed using her and (seemingly) she enjoyed the use. I do hope I do better next time, however. . . . Pink Palace I and II helped with money and [sex]. Fish was formally closed with the return of the van. I am now city bound and living at my mother's." He mentioned the names of several young women, including Darlene Davis and Rhonda Railey, with whom he had spent time in recent days, and suggested some of them might be candidates for the next Miranda operation. As usual, he complained about being low on money.

"Again, I must act. . . . My thoughts turn to Pink Palace III."

In another side project, Lake took special pains to reinforce a fence around his chicken coop, to be certain his German shepherd, Wubon, couldn't dig underneath it and expose buried secrets.

In mid-September, Lake's entry recorded that he and "Charlie" had "pulled a raid" on The Ranch without being detected, and had stolen two garbage bags full of "low grade dope."

Another gap in his records marked the final week of September and the first nine days of October. "Part of this," Lake noted, "was because I was living with C [Cricket] most of the time. Finally her constant selfishness and ego problems (arguments over everything, she must always be right and must never be criticized) drove me away." Depressed and bored, Lake complained of low funds, not having a vehicle, and no immediate targets.

The ominous entry for Monday, October 15, shrouded in coded syntax, said simply, "Coordinated with III and completed op. Pulled off with no hitch. It is routine now. Sweat, dirt, but no regrets." Another life had ended, and the body buried. And Leonard Lake treated it as if he had rid himself of excess mice, disposing of their tiny bodies with acid. No remorse, no feelings.

"Charlie," as Lake referred to his pal in the journal, joined him for dinner. "He gave me two answering machines, one for mom and one to sell." It brought Lake a sorely needed $60. The diary made no mention of where Charlie obtained the machines. However, four days later, Lake recorded, "Charlie got busted for shoplifting. Sigh." A newspaper reported that Ng had been arrested for shoplifting in Daly City. On October 17, Lake complained that he "dealt with bail bondsman . . .

for Charlie. Much hassle getting the money together and getting him out. And he, of course, shows no appreciation. Problems, always more problems." Reportedly, Ng was bailed out when Claralyn Balazs posted $1,000 for his release. Freedom was gained for Ng, but when Lake heard that Charlie's citizenship was being questioned, he wondered if it would be necessary for "Charlie to jump bail and split."

The next weekend, Lake returned to the site of his latest op to steal the missing Randy Jacobson's van, but failed. It had been towed away. Lake's frustrated entry ended with "Sigh." But he did manage to change the victim's address so that Social Security checks would be forwarded to a post office box, where Lake, using Jacobson's stolen identification, could cash them.

By Halloween Day, Lake's need for a car had grown critical. That night, he wrote in his journal, "Spent day checking out potential ops." A newspaper ad had caught his eye a few days earlier. A San Francisco Man named Paul Cosner wanted to sell his car. Lake's simple entry read, "Honda Prelude (80) with owner that could pass for me."

Chapter 15

Paul Cosner lived the Norman Rockwell life in Reynoldsburg, Ohio, where everyone knew each other. His mother, Virginia, delivered him in June 1945, four weeks after the final bell rang on the European theater of WWII. As a schoolboy, Paul regularly walked with his feisty, green-eyed little sister, Sharon, to Livingstone Avenue Elementary School, holding her hand to be certain of her safety. In the summers, they took a bus to the community swimming pool, and he watched over her with the care of a lifeguard.

After temporarily living in another town, Virginia brought her two children back to Reynoldsburg in time for Paul to attend high school, where the handsome youth dazzled pony-tailed coeds with his quick smile and mirthful hazel eyes. Energetic and ambitious, Paul rode his bike in the mornings to deliver newspapers, then rushed each afternoon to work in the time-honored tradition as a soda jerk in the town's corner drug store. Bright and gregarious, he liked reading the humorous works of James Thurber, another Ohio native, and earned the job of editing the school paper. By the time he graduated, he'd reached his full height and weight, five nine, and a wiry 145 pounds. Following graduation, Paul attended Ohio State University and took a degree in American history, with a strong minor in journalism. For a while, he worked as an intern at a local newspaper, then resumed his education at Kent State University, where he earned a master's degree in vocational rehabilitation. He also found time to tinker with another major interest, cars and motorcycles. A brief tenure as a rehab specialist in a state juvenile facility made Paul realize that he really wanted to work as a writer, so he accepted a journalistic position with *Cycle News East.* His boss asked him if he would be interested in moving to Los Angeles to help with the publication's western edition. Always ready for new adventures, he accepted.

Meanwhile, Paul's sister, Sharon, graduated from Ohio University, at Athens, with a degree in fine arts. When her brother decided to move west in 1969, she also had a yearning to migrate, so they loaded their possessions in a Corvair Monza, and drove to Long Beach, in Los Angeles County. She sadly recalled that she couldn't bring her pet parrot, Atticus Finch, because she dreamed he would die in the Painted Desert. Both Paul and Sharon hoped to find their real father, who had left the family while they were infants. Unfortunately, the reunion never took place because he passed away before they could locate him.

When their mother, Virginia, remarried in 1967, she picked a WWII veteran of the U.S. Marine Corps, who had been wounded in the invasion of Saipan. She and Dave Nessley had known each other since high school.

Virginia missed her two offspring, so she traveled west for a visit. During her stay, Paul and Sharon drove her north to San Francisco. Paul instantly realized he'd found the place he wanted to live. He moved, and started investing in real estate. He also sold automobiles, and would eventually own a couple of dealerships, one in upscale Marin County, north of the Golden Gate Bridge.

Sharon stayed in the southland until a terrifying event in 1971. A hoodlum attacked her with a twelve-inch knife. Subsequently captured and tried, he received a thirty-year sentence, but was paroled in nine months. Shattered and frightened, Sharon followed Paul to the Bay area. From childhood she had been athletic and musically inclined, talents that helped her break into show business in 1973. She started by dancing on the stage in Lake Tahoe and Reno, Nevada. While visiting her brother in San Francisco, they attended the Ringling Brothers Circus. As a lark, Sharon auditioned and won a role as an aerial ballet artist. She stayed with the circus four years. At each performance, she twisted and twirled while hanging forty feet in the air from loops in the rigging, and followed it up by dancing on the back of a marching elephant.

Sharon would later speak of an incredible coincidence. The circus acquired as a side attraction a beautiful, little white goat named Sir Lancelot, with a single horn in the middle of its forehead. Sharon even remembered posing for pictures with the charming, little animal.

During a stay with the traveling show in Chicago, she met the "right man," accepted his proposal, and became Sharon Sellitto. The marriage lasted a little over two years. When, in tears over the breakup, she called Paul, he asked her to come back to San Francisco to "get herself together." She and Paul had always been able to talk over their problems, and she had never needed him more. She missed his sense of humor, which Sharon described as a cross between Woody Allen's and Peter Sellers', and longed to hear again "his hideous, cackling laugh." The laugh was so unique, she said, that during a funny scene in a movie theater, Paul had chortled loudly, and someone in the back row had yelled, "Cosner, is that you?"

For Sharon, nothing sounded better than being with Paul again, so she returned to San Francisco. Her brother lived in a house he owned, located in the Glen Park district, and Sharon happily moved in with him. As she expected, he provided the healing she needed.

At about the same time, Paul met, started dating, and fell in love with Marilyn Namba, a beautiful, young X-ray technician, who had descended from a member of the heroic all-Japanese U.S. Army group, the renowned 442nd Regimental Combat Team, the most decorated unit in WWII. Petite and slim, with shining black hair worn in a pageboy, the soft-spoken woman returned Paul's love. She lived in an apartment building on Filbert Street, not far from Fisherman's Wharf. Since Glen Park lay in the city's southern sector, a good half-hour drive from Filbert Street, longer in commuter traffic, Paul needed to be closer. Over a period of months, his sister, Sharon, regained her old spark and self-confidence, so Paul leased an apartment in the same four-story building as his girlfriend, Marilyn. They began to talk about tying the marital knot.

Being in the automobile sales business, Paul knew a good deal when he saw it. When, in the autumn of 1984, the opportunity to buy a bronze-colored 1980 Honda Prelude came, he grabbed it immediately. It would be perfect for the extensive driving he did around the city. Five chrome strips had been attached to the trunk lid to form a luggage rack, giving the vehicle a distinctive, racy appearance. The car's owner, Linda Moll, had recently had a baby, and needed less sporty transportation, so she offered to sell the Honda to Paul at an attractive price. Very candidly, she told him that she had damaged the front passenger seat. Being a smoker, she had burned a hole in it, and had also hit the driver's sun visor with a cigarette, leaving a gray stain. Other than those two minor flaws, the car was in pristine condition. Moll had liked the Honda, and would always recall the license plate number, 592ZWX.

Sharon Sellitto had befriended a man she called David.

Another eerie event took place through him. He took a job near the only motel in a small town 120 miles north of the city, called Philo. Marilyn and Paul visited him there and spent several days vacationing in one of the cabins.

Paul liked showing people around his favorite city, with the spectacular surrounding bay, mountains, and ocean. His mother, Virginia, would always remember that during her visits, Paul enthusiastically played the tour guide, driving her to the stately redwoods in Muir Woods National Monument, to Mount Tamalpais, and north to Mendocino, the charming artists' village, which sits on a bluff overlooking the crashing Pacific shoreline. He even hosted her on a boat to tour the notorious Alcatraz Federal Prison, closed since 1963 and converted to a tourist attraction.

Paul loved the city, but hadn't achieved the fulfillment he sought with his career. The old urge to write in the style of James Thurber stirred within him again, and he decided to liquidate all of his assets and use the money to pursue life as a literary humorist. By the end of October 1984, he'd sold his share of the Marin auto business to a partner, and placed a newspaper ad to sell the Honda. On Halloween Day, a man arrived at the Filbert Street apartment and asked to take a test drive. That evening, Paul described him to Marilyn as "a really weird guy," who didn't even shift gears while driving the famous block of Lombard Street, the brick-paved, twisting section known as the "crookedest street" anywhere. The prospective buyer said he would return later.

On November 1, Leonard Lake entered in his journal, "Meet Charlie tomorrow noon and make plan."

Sharon owned a pickup truck, sold to her by Paul, and intended to drive it 130 miles up to Mendocino. The spare tire for the vehicle was encased under the cab, but the jack was missing. When she talked to Paul on Friday, November 2,

Sharon mentioned that she didn't have the jack. He called her later and insisted that she drop by his apartment on Saturday morning and he would have it ready for her.

On that same Friday, Marilyn Namba also spoke to Paul by phone. She couldn't leave her work before seven o'clock that evening, but still planned to cook dinner using the groceries he had bought that day. They chatted about a Saturday date with another couple to attend a music program and she reminded him of an 8 P.M. television program they wanted to watch that Friday night. He laughed and said he was going to meet a couple of buddies for drinks first.

At about 7 P.M., Marilyn called Paul again to confirm their plans. She later said, "He was kind of rushed. He told me that he had to go out and deliver the car he was selling. He didn't tell me who he was selling it to, or where he was going."

Paul Cosner vanished that day, like the evening sun dropping into the cold Pacific.

When Marilyn arrived home, neither Paul nor his car was there. The dinner hour and the television program passed, and he still didn't show up. Maybe he had gone drinking with his pals, after all. Tired and disappointed, Marilyn went to bed.

By nine o'clock the following morning, she still hadn't heard from Paul. Feeling a sense of alarm, she called Sharon. Both women tried to fight down the rising panic. As the day dragged on into early afternoon, they could no longer rationalize his silent absence, and called the police.

The contact with the San Francisco Police Department left Sharon Sellitto dissatisfied and angry. As she later recalled it, "They wouldn't take the report on Paul. Marilyn and I took a photo of him to the station, along with the vehicle identification number and license number of the Honda. We had to wait until twenty-four hours had passed."

Undeterred, Sharon took another tack. "If they wouldn't listen to me about a missing person, they would have to take a stolen car report." So, back at the apartment, she called to complain about the missing Honda. A patrol car arrived within minutes and the officer took her statement. Sharon later complained, ''They would take a report on something with a dollar value, but not one on my missing brother.''

With their nerves on edge, both Sharon and Marilyn waited. Each minute seemed to drag by. When they returned to the police station to finally register the missing persons report, Sharon still felt frustrated by her perception of an apathetic attitude.

On November 2, Lake made another journal entry. ''Met Charlie. Performed op. Met resistance for the first time. Unsuccessful in obtaining credit cards or bank codes. Drove to country for completion. Canceled Charlie's running debt to me.''

Unable to sit and wait for news, Sharon Sellitto launched her own efforts at investigation. She looked at the ad Paul had placed to sell the Honda, then listed all similar ads. Recalling Paul's description of a ''weird guy'' who had taken the car for a test drive, she called each of the sellers and asked if they'd had any responses or calls that seemed unusual or weird. She made a flyer including a photo of Paul and the car, had reams of it duplicated, and placed them at strategic locations throughout the Bay area. Later describing her state of mind, she said she was ''irrational'' and ''crazed,'' unable to sleep, and obsessed with finding her brother.

Even hiring a private investigation firm to help with the search didn't satisfy her. She sought out any minuscule lead, and followed it through. But they all led to dead ends. To be certain the police didn't relax, she refiled the reports each month.

The quest for information, and eventually justice, would extend well beyond Sharon Sellitto's wildest imagination.

*   *   *

Leonard Lake entered in his journal on November 5 several mundane records of buying supplies for the bunker, progress on the work, and about writing letters to "C." He concluded by noting, "Final trip with the Honda until license problem is resolved."

On the evening of November 9, he made the last entries in the journal that had covered a little more than two years. He typed, "And so life goes on up here. On alternate days it has rained and I've done nothing." He mentioned the possible arrival of another woman he'd met. "She may come up this weekend. If she does come, I expect to screw her. Why else would a woman over 40 travel 100 miles to visit a man she doesn't know if she doesn't want to be screwed? Been playing with the vid equipment. Walking the dog. General stuff. As ever, reading a lot. Tonight, I retyped all my written journal notes. End here."

There would be no more record of Leonard Lake's daily life.

While the search for Paul Cosner tore apart the lives of his loved ones, they couldn't even think about the Thanksgiving holiday. But Leonard Lake and Charles Ng, who was still posing as Mike Kimoto, drove a bronze-colored Honda down to San Bruno, where Lake's mother, Gloria Ebeling, prepared turkey and all the trimmings for them. Leonard's sister Janet and her family also attended. Donald, of course, was still missing. But the fifteen people there ate heartily and enjoyed the festive atmosphere, discussing the recent reelection of President Ronald Reagan over Democratic challenger Walter Mondale.

If Ng seemed relaxed and complacent during the holiday, he was covering a festering anger stemming from a conflict he'd had on the job at Dennis Moving Company. He and Cliff Peranteau had argued over the distribution of the workload. Furious words had flown between them. Peranteau had yelled, "You goddamned Chinaman, I never should have gotten you this job." It wouldn't be the last argument between the two men.

Irritation at some of Ng's behavior bothered other employees, too. Several of them bristled in disgust when they periodically heard him chanting, "No gun, no fun," and "No kill, no thrill." The men were particularly disgusted at the expression "Daddy dies, mommy cries, baby fries." Someone, never identified, posted a picture of a Chinese man on the warehouse wall, and printed "No kill, no thrill" on it. Most recognized the implication, and openly chuckled about it.

A few of the coworkers, though, overlooked the strange words and tried to establish rapport with Ng. Some of them would later recall that Ng, in what appeared to be a sociable gesture, invited them at various times to join him for a weekend in the mountains at his friend's place, where they could go target shooting or just relax. None of them accepted. One co-worker, Perry McFarland, shared Ng's interest in martial arts. He and Ng ate dinner together occasionally and practiced the athletic spins and kicks of Asian defensive combat.

McFarland needed some help in refurbishing a bathroom at his house in Alameda. Ng mentioned that Leonard Lake, whom he called "Tom," had experience in home improvement and might be willing to work at a reasonable rate. In mid-December, Lake showed up at McFarland's house, carrying a duffel bag and leading his German shepherd, Wubon. He worked on the bathroom for two days. When he departed at the end of the first day, to stay the night in San Bruno, he asked permission to leave his duffel bag until the next morning. McFarland and his wife, curious and suspicious of the man, couldn't resist examining the contents after Tom left. They found a woman's negligee, videotapes, a book on the subject of bondage, and other odd items.

When Lake completed the job at the end of the second day, he asked if McFarland could give him a ride home, to Wilseyville, a three-hour drive. En route, Lake explained that he owned a car, a Honda Prelude, but that he couldn't drive it because the registration tags were expired.

Back at his home, McFarland discovered that someone had removed photographs of his wife from an album. Angry, he contacted Charles Ng, who apologized and guaranteed they would be returned. The very next day, Ng kept his promise and handed McFarland the pictures.

In that same week, Lake and Ng made a stop at the post office in Pioneer, a few miles above Wilseyville. They rented two post office boxes. Lake used the name and identification documents of Randy Jacobson, while Ng claimed to be Michael Kimoto.

As the Christmas holiday approached, San Francisco glowed with lights, ornaments, and music. Mobs of shoppers jammed the big department stores and tiny street shops throughout the city, from Market Street to Chinatown; from Union Square to Fisherman's Wharf. Charles Ng and Leonard Lake, though, paid little attention to the shopping crowds, carols, or spirit of the season. There is no record of them exchanging gifts, or buying presents for anyone else.

Ng's coworker Cliff Peranteau didn't feel much like celebrating, either. His girlfriend, Cynthia Tanner, after deciding to end the relationship, had moved out of their apartment in mid-December. Cliff's mood sank deeper just by looking at the things she left behind: her oak-framed mirrors, a carnival glass candlestick, a silly little ceramic fish, and a small Buddha. He needed to get out of the apartment and walk, and maybe buy a few gifts for his siblings back in Pennsylvania. As he strolled, looking in store windows, Cliff saw a record turntable he'd always wanted. On an impulse, he walked in and bought it for himself.

Cliff Peranteau had no way of knowing it would be the last Christmas he would ever see.

Chapter 16

Robin Scott Stapley valued his membership in the Guardian Angels, a group dedicated to protecting innocent people from criminals. When he joined, he'd never heard of Leonard Lake or Charles Ng, but his destiny would place him on a collision course with them.

Born in Lancaster, California, on August 16, 1958, Scott Stapley was the fourth child for Lola and Dwight Stapley, who already had two sons and a daughter. They worried about little Scott when he first learned to speak because he tended to twist his phrases. In his attempt to say he wanted to go back outside, the words came out, "I want out backside." He also told his parents he wanted to be "a fire engine so I can spray water on everyone." But he really didn't suffer from dyslexia and turned out to be an excellent student. That suited Dwight just fine, since he was a teacher who would go on to become a principal in several schools. He'd started in a tiny Arizona village between

Tombstone and Tucson, moved on to the south bay region of Los Angeles County, and relocated to Lancaster the year of Scott's birth.

Scott grew to a strapping five ten, weighed 170 pounds, and earned a place on the high school's wrestling team. His parents never had trouble finding him in a crowd, due to the color of his hair. In Lola's words, it was "bright orange. Not red, but orange hair. A real carrottop." As he matured, though, it turned brown. His eyes, said Lola, were "greenish brown, but seemed to change colors with his apparel." The fact that Dwight was principal of the school caused him to wonder if the other kids would give Scott a bad time, but the boy assured his dad that no one would pick on a member of the wrestling team.

Dwight taught his sons how to sail the twenty-five-foot boat he owned. The family used it nearly every weekend.

Lola worked for IBM, and her job took her to the city of Orange at about the time Scott graduated from high school. The assignment forced her to take an apartment nearby, and commute home to Lancaster only on weekends. But Scott came to live with her and attend Orange Coast Community College.

Eventually he transferred to San Diego State University to study law, but became disillusioned with the idea of being an attorney. He thought of teaching, but his father talked him out of it in the face of new California tax laws that would potentially undermine funds for education (which didn't happen), so Scott changed his major to political science and sociology. He earned his bachelor of science degree in 1983, and began working for a hospital-supply firm.

Still interested in law and the protection of innocent people, Scott joined a brand-new chapter of the Guardian Angels in San Diego and soon worked his way up to the chapter presidency. The original founder of the organization, Curtis Sliwa, planted the seeds for the organization in the late 1970s by assembling a multiracial group of thirteen young men. One of their first goals was to reduce the danger facing New York subway riders. Originally calling themselves the "Magnificent Thirteen" and wearing berets as identification, they patrolled the stations and passenger trains, where their very presence discouraged would-be muggers or thieves. As the movement grew, they focused on helping inner-city children by counseling them and providing alternatives to drug and crime cultures.

Sliwa took notice of Scott Stapley and promoted him to Southwest Area Director. Scott was instrumental in establishing new chapters in Las Vegas, Hollywood, Beverly Hills, San Francisco, and Oakland.

In 1983, now six feet tall, 190 pounds, Scott attended a chapter meeting in Las Vegas and found himself in a serious situation. Walking from a Casino to his hotel, he cut through a dark alley and came face-to-face with a knife-wielding thug, who demanded his wallet. Scott complied, handing the man his billfold. In a sudden rush of clarity, all the training he'd been through reeled through his mind. Instinctively he lashed out with a swift kick that broke the thief's knee, then caught him with a series of blows to the chest and ribs. Just at that moment, a patrol car screeched to a halt in the alley. The officer—having seen only the blows by Stapley, and the other man toppling to the pavement—pulled his weapon and demanded that the fight stop immediately. Scott realized that he appeared to be the assailant. Cautiously watching Stapley, the officer called for paramedics to help the downed man, and reached for his handcuffs to arrest Scott. But Scott noticed that the would-be robber had never dropped the wallet, and said to the officer, "Why don't you check what he has in his hand, and see who it belongs to?" It turned out that the thief was wanted for a long series of such robberies. Not only did the police release Stapley, but they expressed gratitude for his help in stopping the crime wave.

* * *

Even as an adult, Scott maintained a loyalty and deep affection for his family, and called his parents every Sunday just to check in. He always opened the conversation with his mother by saying, "Hi, Mama Jo, what's up?" She never did know how he'd picked that nickname for her.

Living in San Diego, and working for a home-health-care company, Scott shared an apartment with his girlfriend, Tori Doolin, and her baby daughter. Problems between Scott and Tori led to them splitting up several times, but always reuniting. Financial stress contributed to their disagreements.

Part of the glue that held Stapley and Doolin together were the friends they had in common. Scott had met one of his best pals, Lonnie Bond, twenty-seven, while backpacking in the Sierra Nevada. Stapley admired Bond for not allowing a physical deformity to get in his way. Several fingers on Bond's left hand were frozen into a claw shape and he couldn't straighten them out, but he blithely ignored the crippling defect. The two men became inseparable buddies.

Bond's girlfriend, Brenda O'Connor, nineteen, gave him a son on April 5, 1984, and named him Lonnie Bond Jr. Originally from Michigan, Brenda was the youngest of seven children. Her sister Sandra had married Lonnie Bond's younger brother, Art, so both families were tied together by more than one knot. Brenda's deep affection for her mother and siblings was reflected in the cards and letters she frequently sent.

Lonnie Bond wanted to take Brenda and the baby out of the bustling San Diego region. He'd heard about the rural isolation that could be found in Northern California, so he started looking around for the right spot during a trip to Calaveras County. A real estate manager showed him a cabin known as the "Carter House" just off Blue Mountain Road, near Wilseyville. A common driveway, actually a winding dirt road, served three houses: the one Bond liked, a second cabin that sat deeper in the ponderosa woods, and the third house, sitting downslope about 100 yards. Bond could see that someone had dug into the hillside close to the house, and appeared to be adding a concrete block building there. The environment pleased Bond, and he couldn't wait to sign the rental contract. He finalized it in mid-January 1985.

During the first two weeks of 1985, Super Bowl fever reverberated through San Francisco. The Forty-Niners had won the National Football Conference championship and earned the right to face the AFC champion Miami Dolphins on Sunday, January 20. Even more exciting to fans, the game would be played just a few miles down the peninsula at Stanford University stadium.

At Dennis Moving Company, Cliff Peranteau and his fellow employees eagerly contributed $5 each to a betting pool organized by the dispatcher, Richard Doedens. Several people who worked in the same building, at another company, also pitched in to fatten the pot. Whoever came closest to the winning score would become richer by more than $100.

Cliff Peranteau and his closest buddy at work, Hector Salcedo, left work on Friday evening, January 18, and stopped for a few beers in celebratory anticipation of the Super Bowl, only two days away. Cliff agreed to meet Hector at his home on Sunday for a pregame party and then to watch the game on television. Since both men were scheduled to work on Saturday, Salcedo dropped Cliff off at his residence on Waller Street at midnight. Cliff waved, said, ''I'll see you tomorrow,'' and disappeared into the building.

Salcedo couldn't believe it when Peranteau didn't show up on Saturday morning. Wondering what could have happened, he tried to call Cliff a number of times that day, but got no answer. As soon as he completed his shift, Salcedo drove to Cliff's residence. His knocking and ringing the doorbell raised nothing in return but silence. Something didn't seem right to Salcedo, especially when he saw Cliff's blue Suzuki sitting in its customary parking spot.

Two Super Bowl parties had been scheduled, one at Salcedo's home, and one hosted by another employee, Kenneth Bruce. Peranteau failed to show up at either celebration. His buddies yelled, drank beer, and cheered while watching quarterback Joe Montana complete twenty-four of thirty-five passes in crushing the Miami Dolphins 38 to 16. When they checked to see who won the pool, it turned out to be Cliff Peranteau. The enigma of his absence grew even more puzzling.

Peranteau's estranged girlfriend, Cynthia, heard that he was missing, and paid a visit to the apartment they had shared. It upset her to see that someone had removed some of their possessions, including her oak-framed mirrors, candlesticks, the Buddha, and the little ceramic fish.

Over the next week, Salcedo dropped by Cliff's place repeatedly, trying to discover where his pal might be. The mystery deepened when, on the sixth day, he found the motorcycle missing. Yet, no word came of what had happened to Peranteau.

Finally, at the end of January, an envelope arrived at Dennis Moving Company addressed to Richard Doedens, who had organized the pool. He opened it, and read a typed note:

Hey Bro,
I was hoping that Dennis would give you my address and you'd just mail along my winnings. Since I haven't heard from you yet, I'm sending along an addressed envelope to save you the trouble of spelling my name. Hey, how about them 'Niners, huh?

At the bottom, Doedens saw the scrawled signature, "Cliff." On the enclosed envelope, someone had printed, "Clifford R. Peranteau, Post Office Box 349, Mokelumne Hill, California."

The envelope in which the letter arrived contained the postmark: "Wilseyville, C. January 28, 1985, 95257."

The owner of the company also received a note that read:

> *Dennis,*
> *Sorry to leave on such short notice, but a new job, place to live and a honey came all at once. Please send my check for the last three days I worked and my W-2 to my new address below.*
>
> > *Thanks,*
> > *Cliff*

The address was the same as the one on the envelope sent to Richard Doedens.

Doedens dutifully sent the money Peranteau had won. Neither he, nor anyone else, would ever see or hear from Cliff Peranteau again.

By February 1, Lonnie Bond and Brenda O'Connor, with the baby, had moved most of their things into the cabin near Wilseyville, although she'd left some of her belongings stored in San Diego to be picked up later. They had also met the neighbor who lived down the slope from them, the fellow who was constructing a second building. He introduced himself as Charles Gunnar, and said that he was a professional photographer. As a gesture of goodwill, he took a series of photos of the trio.

That same week, Brenda flew back to Michigan so that her mother and the family could see how big Lonnie Bond Jr. was growing as he neared his first birthday, April 5. She returned on February 8.

Scott Stapley and Tori Doolin drove up to the cabin in early February to help Lonnie settle in during Brenda's absence. During their brief stay, they also met the man calling himself

Gunnar. Scott bought a Walther handgun from him, and obtained a signed receipt dated February 5.

When Scott and Tori made a second trip to Wilseyville on February 19, a snowstorm covered the area, making the roads impassable. They stayed with Bond and O'Connor a full five days, during which a photo shoot took place inside the cabin in front of a roaring fire. When Stapley and his girlfriend returned to San Diego, he showed the pictures to his coworker, Terijo Kohler, who had been a close friend for nearly six years. Kohler later spoke of the photos. She said they depicted Stapley in a leather vest and Doolin wearing leather pants while holding two guns in her hands. Other shots showed a party atmosphere, with the couples toasting each other.

At the time Kohler saw the snapshots, she examined one picture that showed someone she didn't recognize. She commented to Stapley, "He looks weird."

Scott answered, "He is weird." Kohler asked what he meant, and Scott answered, "You don't want to know, in case anything ever goes down."

Troubled by the comment, Kohler pressed for more. Scott explained that the man lived close by and shared a common driveway with Lonnie and Brenda. "He's a pain in the ass," Scott growled, adding that Charles Gunnar was always bothering them. It wouldn't be a good thing to have Gunnar as an enemy, Scott said.

Jeff Gerald, Ng's blond coworker whose musical talents had led him to form a band called Crash 'N Burn, spent nearly every weekend and most evenings practicing music with his buddy and fellow band member, Ray Houghton. The pair had met in junior high, about the same time Jeff had fallen for a cute little thirteen-year-old girl named Sandy. In their teen years, Jeff and Sandy dated exclusively, until she moved to New Jersey. Even after that, they kept in regular contact.

When Ray and Jeff first moved to San Francisco, they shared an apartment on O'Farrell Street. Both of them liked photography, and Ray gave Jeff one of his cameras. Jeff loaded it with black-and-white film, and took several test shots through the apartment window looking outside, one capturing a view of the adjacent buildings, and another of the Kaiser Hospital just across the street. Afterward, Jeff tossed the camera in a drawer and forgot about it.

The two men remained close, united by their band and by years of companionship, even after Jeff moved to another apartment on Geary Street. He shared the two-bedroom unit with a woman and her three-year-old daughter, on a strictly platonic basis.

At his job with Dennis Moving, Jeff had taken a week off for personal reasons. Ordinarily, such absence would cause him to lose seniority, but when he returned, his boss had generously granted him the unbroken seniority level. Only one person had complained. Charles Ng objected, saying that Gerald should have been forced to start at the bottom again.

The music career for Jeff and Ray took a positive move in late February 1985. Ray later recalled, "We had a show lined up. . . . We were going to be with some of the larger-named alternative bands and were really looking forward to it." On Saturday night, February 23, as Ray recalled, he dropped Jeff off at his apartment. "We had agreed to meet again on Sunday to . . . audition some bass players for another band we were hoping to put together."

On Saturday morning, Jeff's roommate answered the phone, twice, and recognized the voice of Charles Ng. She knew the sound of it from previous occasions when he'd called for Jeff, and she had answered. The third time the phone rang that morning, Jeff answered and spoke briefly. When he hung up, he told his roommate that he was going to the bus station to meet Charlie. The two men, Jeff said, were going to do a private moving job, not connected with their regular employment. "I'll be back by suppertime," Jeff said, with his usual big smile, "and bring some Chinese food."

Before leaving, Jeff made a call to New Jersey. In a conversation that lasted over an hour, he told Sandy that he was going to help a friend move, and would be paid $100 for the work. Most of the hour's talk centered on a discussion of Sandy possibly traveling to San Francisco so the couple could resume their romantic relationship.

When Jeff's roommate arrived home from work at 6 P.M., she frowned with deep concern. Jeff never left his bedroom door standing open, yet it was ajar. No one had picked up the evening newspaper. And even more strange, the covers from his bed had been removed, along with several items of his clothing. Specifically, she later said, "His guitar and amplifiers were missing, and some pictures, as well."

There would be no Chinese food with Jeff Gerald that Saturday night, nor ever again. He had vanished completely from his world of music, friends, and life.

Brenda O'Connor further solidified the residency in Calaveras County by obtaining PO Box 25 at the Wilseyville post office on Monday, February 25. That same day, Leonard Lake visited a doctor in Jackson, on Highway 49 about twenty miles from Wilseyville. One of Lake's fingers on his left hand had been wounded by a gunshot, within a day after Jeff Gerald met Charles Ng to "help someone move."

Prior to showing up unannounced at the doctor's office, Lake had sought help from his sister Janet in San Francisco. He called her at home at close to eleven o'clock Saturday night and told her he'd accidentally sustained an injury to his hand by gunshot. Since she had experience as a nurse, he wanted advice on how to treat it. Janet gave him instructions on cleaning and bandaging the wound. It startled her when he showed up at her door early the following morning, after a three-hour drive from Wilseyville, and asked her to give him treatment. As she worked on the injury, he told her how it had happened. He said he'd picked up a man who wanted to buy marijuana. But the customer had tried to "burn" him, and a struggle ensued in which the guy's gun discharged, sending a bullet into a finger of Lake's left hand. A piece of the bullet had lodged in his finger.

Janet did her best tending to the wound, but told her brother he needed to see a doctor.

On his way back to the mountain cabin, Lake stopped in Jackson to see a physician he'd previously met. The doctor had attended a Bible study class near Wilseyville, and had encountered Lake through mutual acquaintances. It surprised the medic, though, when Lake showed up, without previously calling. Lake told him a story about his .22 caliber handgun accidentally discharging while he showed it to a friend. After removing the lead slug and cleaning the raw tissue, the doctor suggested to Lake that he see an orthopedic surgeon to make certain no tendons had been damaged. Lake chose to ignore the advice, and let his hand heal by itself.

Lake's new neighbors up the hill, Lonnie and Brenda, were getting on his nerves. They didn't respond well when he offered to use Brenda as a model, and they frequently left the driveway gate unlocked. Also, when Scott Stapley, the fellow from San Diego, visited, he and Bond fired guns at targets in the yard, which angered Lake. Someone might get shot. He called the real estate agent who'd rented the place to Bond and complained heatedly. She contacted Lonnie Bond and advised him of Charles Gunnar's grievances.

One of Scott Stapley's hobbies involved photography. He didn't pursue it in the same way as Leonard Lake, but he liked to have his cameras available when an interesting event or landscape caught his attention. Back in San Diego, he discovered that his 35mm Ricoh KR5 was malfunctioning, so he took it along with a second camera to Dean's, a sales and repair shop in the Kearny-Mesa district, on March 12. The two cameras would be ready for him to pick up on April 8.

Chapter 17

Two people bought two guns in two cities within two days at the end of March 1985. Leonard Lake's sister Janet knew he'd been on the run, and living under assumed names due to the arrest in Philo. When Lake had shown up at her apartment with a wounded hand and a story of being shot by some thugs, she worried about him. So when he asked her to help him obtain a handgun for self-protection, she couldn't refuse. On Friday, March 29, she walked into a San Francisco gun store and bought a Ruger .22 caliber pistol to give her brother. California law requires a waiting period, so she wouldn't be able to pick up the weapon until mid-April.

One day later, in San Diego, Scott Stapley entered the Accuracy Gun Shop and spoke to Thomas Peck. Stapley selected a handgun almost identical to the one purchased by Lake's sister, a Sturm Ruger blue steel .22 caliber semiautomatic pistol, serial number 12-70329. Salesperson Peck filled out the legally required document, a "Firearm Transaction Record," to register the sale in the name of Robin Scott Stapley. After the necessary fifteen-day waiting period, the buyer would return on April 16 to pick up his gun.

Another sales transaction took place in early April involving Leonard Lake. On Monday, April 8, the same day Scott Stapley picked up his repaired Ricoh 35mm camera, a newspaper classified ad caught the attention of William R. Gross, a resident of West Point in Calaveras County. After calling the listed number for directions, Gross turned off Blue Mountain Road onto a curving dirt driveway, drove between walls of ponderosa pines and cedars, and stopped in front of a one-story house. The balding man, wearing a bushy beard and cammies, came outside to tell Gross about the blue Suzuki motorcycle he had offered for sale. He explained that he couldn't yet show the bike. "My friend Cliff Peranteau, over in San Francisco, wants me to sell it for him, but it's not here yet." The vehicle should be available in a couple of days, Lake explained. Gross said he'd return on Wednesday to buy it.

Two days later, Gross kept his word. He met Lake at the house again, examined the blue motorcycle and agreed on Lake's asking price. Lake went into the house, brought out a receipt book and the ownership title certificate. Gross examined it and saw that Clifford Peranteau had bought the bike in October 1983. Ordinarily, the owner should sign the document in the presence of the new buyer, but the certificate already contained the signature of Clifford R. Peranteau on the line to transfer ownership. Gross paid, pocketed the title document, and drove away happy with his purchase.

Having gained all he could from the operation involving Cliff Peranteau, Lake's thoughts again turned to Operation

Miranda, and his desire to capture another woman for sexual enslavement.

Kathleen Allen, eighteen, would be his next victim.

Mike Carroll, Kathi's boyfriend who had served time in Leavenworth at the same time as Charles Ng, often took her to the Milpitas home in which he lived with his foster brother, John Gouveia. The older man had acted over the years as Mike's surrogate father, trying to help him avoid the pitfalls of life. Mike had lived with John from 1974, at the time of John's divorce, until the spring of 1985, with the exception of Mike's years in the U.S. Marine Corps and the three months in Leavenworth.

Gouveia would later recall that Mike had received at least one phone call at the house from Charles Ng.

In March 1985, Carroll finally convinced his girlfriend, Kathi, to move into a motel room at the Milpitas Best Inn. In moving from Gouveia's home, Mike took only the necessary things, such as clothing and toiletries. He left behind most of his possessions, planning to retrieve them when he and Kathi could find more permanent living quarters.

Gouveia's son, Eric, supervised Mike at a Domino's pizza restaurant where they both worked. Mike had held the job eight months. After closing time one evening in April, Mike told Eric that he planned to drive up to San Francisco, approximately twenty-four miles, to see a friend about purchasing some video equipment.

Another employee at Domino's, Les Stuckey, knew both Mike Carroll and Kathi Allen, and frequently socialized with them. On April 12, Stuckey paid a visit to Mike and Kathi at their motel room. At ten o'clock that night, Mike announced that he had to leave, and that he'd return the following day. Stuckey also left. It was the last time he, or any other of Mike's acquaintances, ever saw him.

Two days later, on Sunday, April 14, Kathi Allen received a call at the Safeway store where she worked. She subsequently told her supervisor that she needed some time off to join her boyfriend, who may have been wounded by a gunshot. In the parking lot, she climbed into a copper-colored Honda Prelude, with a chrome luggage rack on the trunk lid. A witness said it was driven by a Caucasian male, about forty years old. Shortly afterward, Kathi telephoned from the motel room and talked to a male friend of hers. He recalled that she seemed to be in a hurry, that she was with a man who acted "kind of weird," and that the man wanted to take pictures of her. She promised to call back as soon as she arrived at her destination with the mysterious fellow.

Kathi couldn't call anyone from the bunker room at Wilseyville, where she was imprisoned for several days and nights. Not long after she arrived at the secluded place, she found herself being stripped naked while a video camera recorded the terrifying sequence of events. Leonard Lake's words to her hinted that her boyfriend, Mike Carroll, had been killed.

Back in the Milpitas Safeway, the store manager received an unexpected call from Kathi Allen on Monday. She asked for an extended leave of four weeks, explaining that she had a prospective job lined up in the Lake Tahoe area. The manager granted her request. He would subsequently receive a typed letter, under which appeared to be her signature, announcing that both she and her boyfriend, Mike Carroll, had found permanent jobs and would be staying in their new location. It also contained a request for the manager to clean out her locker and forward the contents, along with her W-2 form, to a post office box in Wilseyville, California.

Another letter from the same address came to John Gouveia, Mike Carroll's foster brother, with whom he had lived before moving into the motel with Kathi:

Dear John,
Mike and I have moved up to Tahoe where Mike got a
job with some friends. Our place doesn't have a phone
yet, so Mike asked me to drop you a line and let you
know the car is not working. And until we get some money
to fix it, we'll have some friends get our stuff. We'll send
you a phone number as soon as we get one.

Take care.
Kathi

In the remote Wilseyville cabin, a second videotaping session took place not long after the one that recorded Kathi Allen being forced to strip for Lake and Ng. In this one, Kathi, wearing only panty hose ruined by a rip in the crotch, hunched over a nude Charles Ng. She is giving him a back massage. As the camcorder ran, placed either on a tripod or being held by Lake, Ng lay facedown on a bed, while Kathi straddled his legs, and rubbed his lower back and buttocks. He could be heard saying, "Get my ass, too." His left leg moved upward so that his heel caressed her bottom and left hip.

In a third and final videotaping session with Kathi Allen, Leonard Lake placed the camcorder on a tripod, and moved around in the scene snapping still photos of her in various revealing lingerie. At the beginning of the tape, she lay face-down on a brown-and-white bedspread patterned in large diamond shapes, wearing nothing but cutoff jeans. Her wrists were handcuffed and her ankles bound. Lake walked into camera range, let his eyes roam over her body, and said, "Not bad. Anyway, uh, I very much intended to keep my promise, and I couldn't say that I have. I told you there's a lot of things I'd like to do with you that I know you wouldn't like." He removed the handcuffs but left the leather straps around her ankles.

Kathleen didn't answer. Lake moved about the green-walled

room, adjusting tripod-mounted lights. His German shepherd appeared in the doorway, and Kathi cast a nervous glance at the dog.

Holding his 35mm camera up, and adjusting a floodlight, he said, "Would you look over here please? And even though it shouldn't make any difference to me in terms of what you like and what you don't like, I've tried to . . . respect your feelings as best I can in these matters. On the other hand, when I tell you to do things, I tell you things that are very important to me that I want you to do." As Lake adjusted the lighting, causing his shadow to fall over her, Kathi followed his instruction precisely, her face an impassive mask.

Making another lighting adjustment, Lake spoke to her as if she were a paid model. "Can you, uh, turn your head . . . around? Yeah, that's it. Just lay on the bed if you want. I really want you, or expect you as a matter of fact, to do them. And, uh, you haven't."

In a tiny voice, Kathi asked, "What haven't I done?"

"I'm referring to, uh, me telling you not to beat on the doors and make noise."

"I didn't beat on it. It's just that . . . ," her words trailed off like a child, who is afraid to argue with a scolding parent. The German shepherd, standing in the doorway, stared innocently, unable to comprehend the terror. Kathi glanced again at the dog, a deep sadness in her eyes.

"I'm afraid you did beat on it. Those latches were especially picked. Well, I don't know if you beat or pushed . . . but that metal would never break." He accused her of putting "immense" pressure on the hinges of a door from the inside of a room in which she had been locked up. "This leaves me somewhat disturbed, and I realize no one heard you . . . I showed you those cyanide pills and I'm trying to tell you the truth . . . that they're never going to take me alive. Hopefully, no one's ever going to catch me at these weird things, but if someone ever did, I'd die. The fact that you'd die is immaterial right now. I don't want you to die, and I don't want to die, and the best way to accomplish that is for neither one of us to get caught. So, I suppose my question is, what do I do to prove to you that I'm serious about this?''

Kathi spoke timidly. ''Are you asking me if you can hit me?''

Kneeling close to the bed, his face inches from hers, Lake spoke calmly. ''No. I'm not asking you if I can hit you. I can very much hit you, very easily. . . . I don't want to hit you, Kathi. No, let me take that back. Erotically it would turn me on. I would get a great thrill out of it. But, let's say I'm still trying to keep a little bit of sanity, okay? I'm having a little war within myself, between what I want to do, and what I think I should do. Because I promised you, and that is what we might call the decent thing to do . . . I'm going to go hammer those hinges back flat again, and I don't want to find them bent again at all. I don't want to hear anything. Let me put this in the strongest possible terms. It was like the first night, when I told you I wanted you to drink me. It ever arises again, if there's any circumstance whatsoever that leads me to think that you're even attempting to make noise—it's immaterial as to whether I hear you or anyone else hears you—you'll be whipped very severely. Now, tell me you understand.''

Like a whimpering puppy, Kathi murmured, ''I understand.''

''Okay. Good. Some girls are into pain, Kathi, and I don't think you're one of them. If you were, I wouldn't feel so guilty about yielding to my lesser impulses. It's a fact that you're partially a stranger, that you don't know my name, and that you're going to go away, and I'm never going to have to deal with you again.'' Lake stopped to look for something he'd misplaced, then resumed his lecture. ''Rats! . . . that I can even talk to you like this. Needless to say, the, uh, common person on the street, I don't confess my sadistic tendencies to. I don't know if you're flattered or not. There's no reason you should be. But, uh, if nothing else, I'm being honest with you.'' He released her right arm from the shackles, fumbled with the other one for a moment, and growled, ''Oh, screw it. Can you, uh, take those straps off by yourself?''

''I think so, yeah.''

''Are they binding, tight?''

''That one's cutting off my circulation.'' She reached to unbind her left arm.

''Okay. Take off your jeans and panties and put these on.'' Without a word, she stood, slipped the cutoffs down over her full hips along with her underwear, and dropped them to the floor. Obeying his demands with an almost hypnotic calm, she donned transparent blue bikini panties and a matching filmy chemise, tied loosely between her exposed breasts. While appearing calm and compliant, Kathi's face, fully made up with mascara and lipstick, expressed a deep sadness. Lake casually chatted to her as if she were a willing model. Intermittent strobe flashes lit the room.

He wanted to know if the revealing apparel felt comfortable. Kathi said the waistband seemed large enough, but ''I have heavy hips and heavy legs.''

Lake seemed oblivious to her words and launched into another one of his rambling stories about his ''IRS girlfriend.'' He said, ''I actually met her when [she] was three years old. I was nineteen at the time and visiting her house. She got up at some ridiculous hour, and I took her out to play. But, of course, she was naked as a puppy when she came running into the room, so I put what I thought were her clothes on, and let her go outside.''

Kathi listened but didn't really hear. She examined another diaphanous garment in preparation for putting it on, and asked, ''Is this inside out?''

They didn't seem to be on the same conversation page. Lake snapped more photos as he continued his tale. "When she got back, though, her mother gave me this big lecture, and it seems that I had done everything wrong. I put her panties on backward. I didn't know they had a front and a back, and I put her shirt on backward. I thought her shirts were like my shirts that buttoned in the front. Hers buttoned in the back. I put trousers on her, which evidently is nothing to put on a three-year-old girl to let her go outside to play. In general, I blew it."

Checking the remaining film in his camera, he eyed Kathi again as she stood beside the bed adjusting her underwear, and said, "Okay, hop on the bed, please. And I didn't see her again for twenty years, and oh, my, what twenty years will do for a three-year-old. I know you're not trying to do anything foolish, like smile, but you have such a pretty face that even when you're not smiling, you have sort of a sultry look about you. The guys would find it very attractive. Okay, take that off. There's only two more pictures by the way . . . notice I haven't done any full nudes."

Nodding as if in a trance, Kathi said, "Uh-huh."

"Personally," Lake confided, "I don't find full nudes very attractive. I think a woman should always have . . ."

Kathi ungrammatically filled in the thought, "They don't leave nothing to the imagination."

"Right. Yes, I agree completely. Well, actually, I've done full nudes before, but . . ." He trailed off to tell Kathi to adjust her underpants. Handing her another slinky outfit, he said, "Here, try this on. It may actually fit you."

"It probably will," she muttered.

In Lake's journal, he had spoken of conditioning a female slave to the point that she would become accustomed to obeying his every command, and might actually learn to enjoy it. Kathi Allen had been under his control for several days. Her behavior in the tape almost seemed as if she had been brainwashed.

"There, that's okay." He tossed her yet more lingerie, a

white lace bra and a black slip. "Try to put this on. You told me awhile back that you were religious. Are you still so?"

"That's what you heard me say in the bathroom this morning when you walked in. Did you notice I was kind of mumbling?"

"Oh, yes. In fact, that's what I went in for, to check up on you. I thought you were working up for a kamikaze wrist slash, and I was going to tell you not to."

"No. I was saying my morning prayers."

"Jump in bed, please. Look at me." Lake grumbled about his unstable tripod. "Okay, stay there. Okay, take your bra off." She slipped out of the undergarment as if she'd been modeling for years. He asked, "Do you ever wear bras that fasten in the front?"

"Yeah, I used to. This one's kind of trippy, though."

Smirking, Lake asked, "Can I help?"

"Yeah, well, I don't know. It's got a little string that's stuck right now."

"Okay. Put your legs out in front of you. Sit on the bed rather than lean on the bed. There you go. That's it." He slipped into the role of a fashion-magazine photographer humoring a prima donna model. "That's it. Lean back slightly. I should have these photos . . . before you leave, whatever that's worth. You can see them. There you go. Okay. Get your clothes on, get warm, whatever you have to do to get ready to go outside, 'cause that's where we're going next. Tell me, Kathi, you've given up smoking for four days, or however long you've been here. Wouldn't this be a nice opportunity just to . . ."

"That's why I shake a lot," she said. "It's the nicotine that I want."

"Right. And that's what happens if you don't get it for a month or two. After a while, you'll stop shaking."

"Yeah, I'll just quit, but I don't want to quit. It's not something I want to do."

"Okay. I just want you to know that I'm giving this stuff to you under protest. Not that we care, mind you."

The taping session ended. Nothing would ever reveal how many more hours or days passed before Kathleen Allen's short life came to an end.

Chapter 18

A few days before Kathi Allen endured the last videotaping session, on the same day that she left the Milpitas Safeway, Sunday, April 14, a man in the same city received a strange phone call. It surprised Wes Blank, who had taken custody of Charles Gunnar's two daughters, to hear from Leonard Lake. Blank had seen Lake only once or twice since assuming responsibility for the girls, and had moved to San Jose. He had been in contact with Lake's ex-wife, Cricket, though. She sent him monthly money orders to help with expenses for Gunnar's daughters. He would later be asked, "Did Cricket indicate to you that she was receiving government checks for his children and then making money orders out and giving them to you?"

"Yes," Blank replied.

"Do you remember how much she was sending you?"

"I think it was about two hundred dollars."

"At some point, did you start directly receiving these checks yourself?"

"Yes." He explained that Social Security, after contacting him to ask if he had custody of the children, had subsequently started sending the checks to him.

"Were the amounts, once you started getting the direct checks, more than what Cricket was sending you?"

"Yes."

When Lake called, Wes Blank wondered if it had anything to do with the finances for Gunnar's daughters. But it didn't. Lake wanted to know if Wes would help him pick up a car that had been stranded. A 1974 yellow Mercury Capri, Lake said, that belonged to a friend of his had broken down in the Milpitas Safeway parking lot. Lake explained that he couldn't personally get to Milpitas, but would make other arrangements if Wes would be willing to help. Blank recalled, "He said that he would send another young man by the name of Charles down to the bus depot with keys to the car."

On Tuesday, Blank's daughter, Debra, twenty-eight, drove to the bus station, where she was met by Charles Ng, who introduced himself as "Charlie." He gave the woman an envelope containing the keys to Mike Carroll's yellow Capri along with a diagram pinpointing the location of the car.

Wes Blank and his son went to the Safeway lot, found the car, and Wes drove it back to his San Jose home. Over a week passed before Lake showed up to inspect the Capri. Unimpressed with its condition, he said, "This car is not worth fixing. Why don't we just go ahead and sell it?" Blank had already invested several hours repairing the Capri, and had bought parts for it. Lake still insisted on selling it, and would then allow Blank to reimburse himself from the proceeds. When Blank agreed, Lake removed everything of value from the interior and said he would mail the necessary paperwork related to the car. Within a few days, he sent Mike Carroll's ownership and insurance documents to Blank, along with a deposit slip for Kathleen Allen's checking account, and a typed note that read:

> Wes,
> *Just a short note. Enclosed are forms you should need. Also enclosed is a deposit slip. After you take your share, send whatever is left to this account. I don't think she'll need to endorse your check if it is for deposit. These people are screwballs, but they appreciate the help. Ever notice how youth is wasted on the young?*
>
> Leonard

Unaware that anything bad might have happened to Kathleen Allen and Mike Carroll, Blank disposed of the Capri according to Lake's wishes.

In San Diego, Scott Stapley had entered into a transaction for a handgun, as had Lake's sister in San Francisco. While Lake arranged to sell a vehicle in the Bay area, Stapley bought one in the southland. He already had a small car, but wanted to buy a pickup truck. When he found the right one, a 1979 blue-gray Chevrolet, he couldn't raise the cash, so he turned to a woman he'd known since 1980 as a coworker and friend. Terijo Kohler agreed to lend him $1,250 on a handshake basis and an agreement that he would pay it back whenever he could. Scott transferred his personalized license plates to the pickup. He had picked the letters "AHOYMTY" in honor of the sailing days with his father.

Stapley's friends Lonnie Bond and Brenda O'Connor grew increasingly restless about the man they knew as Charles Gunnar, their neighbor in the mountains of Wilseyville. While Bond conducted out-of-town business, Brenda endured Lake's unwelcome suggestions to pose in the nude, but these come-ons frightened her. Curtis Everett, Lonnie's pal and business associate, stayed overnight at the cabin and heard Bond say that it would be a good idea to "stay clear" of Gunnar, because he was a survivalist who had weapons, and because he dealt in marijuana. Bond told Everett that he'd been in Gunnar's house, and had seen all sorts of guns, grenades, and a grenade launcher. He'd even bought a MAC 10 from him, but soon rid himself of it because it fell apart while being fired.

Bond had noticed, in addition to the weapons, shelves in Gunnar's house jammed with videotapes, and he had heard the man "was into making smut movies." Gunnar, Everett later said, had the "hots" for Brenda and continually bothered her about modeling for him. He'd started by suggesting she pose in military clothing while holding weapons, and even wanted the baby to be in the photos with her. She'd been so unnerved by the insistent proposals that she feared staying there alone. On one occasion, Brenda fled to the town of Lodi, twenty-five miles away, where she stayed with colleagues of Bond, simply to put some distance between her and Gunnar. Much of Bond's anger stemmed from his suspicion that Gunnar had been entering the cabin and snooping around while he and Brenda were both away. Bond had even taped hairs in strategic places to see if windows or doors had been opened in their absence.

On Wednesday, April 17, Bond and Everett met in a valley town to work on a commercial enterprise, while Brenda and Lonnie Jr. stayed with acquaintances in San Diego. Bond told Everett that as soon as their business was completed, he was going to "take care of the problems in Wilseyville," with a gun. Everett would later say that he interpreted the comment to mean that Bond planned to "have it out with Gunnar and pay him back for messing with his woman."

Everett's wife, who was Lonnie Bond Jr.'s godmother, beseeched Bond not to go to Wilseyville in a confrontational mood. Years later, she would recall, "I begged him not to go.

I had a feeling something bad was going to happen there. I grabbed him and said, 'I'm afraid I'm never going to see you again.' ''

Bond replied, "I'll be okay. I have my twenty-two." He left on Thursday morning, promising to contact the Everetts the following week when they planned to return from a trip to Yuma, Arizona.

In San Diego, on Friday night, Scott Stapley backed his truck into a storage facility to load Brenda O'Connor's remaining clothing and possessions, in preparation for taking her and the baby to Wilseyville. The trip north would not only provide transportation to Brenda and Lonnie Jr., it would also give Scott a measure of relief from recent emotional stress related to his job at a home-health-care organization. He'd been involved in tending to several terminally ill geriatric patients and had seen two of them die within the last ten days. One elderly lady, of whom he'd grown particularly fond, had simply given up her hold on life while Scott stood at her bedside. He needed a breath of fresh air in the clean environment of the mountainous Sierra Nevada.

The previous Sunday night, Scott had made his usual weekend call to his parents. "Hi, Mama Jo, what's up?" he laughed. Lola Stapley, always glad to hear from him, listened as Scott explained that next week he would be up north, where he planned to do some backpacking in the mountains. She knew how much he enjoyed such outings, and wished him a safe time.

Before picking up Brenda and the baby, and heading north on Interstate 5, Scott stopped at the apartment he shared with Tori Doolin. They'd been having lovers' spats lately, and he didn't want to leave without saying good-bye. After a hug and a kiss, combined with a promise to send a card as soon as possible, he drove off into the night.

* * *

Four days later, California Highway Patrol Officer Wood Lee Hicks, an eighteen-year veteran of the force, was patrolling the long, straight, gradually inclining grade of I-5 between Bakersfield and the grapevine, where the southbound highway ascends sharply into the Tehachapi mountains toward Los Angeles. At 6:40 A.M., on Tuesday, April 23, not long after sunrise, a dispatcher sent him to the scene of a traffic accident at the intersection of Laval Road and Wheeler Ridge Road, close to a truck stop and a gas station near the Interstate.

Hicks reported, "I found a large semi stopped on Laval Road with some damage to the left side. A pickup, sitting on the south shoulder of the road, had damage to the left side and the windshield." The pickup, a blue-gray color, bore a personalized license plate with the letters, AHOYMTY. According to Hicks, "An Oriental male, in his twenties, admitted that he had been driving the pickup." The man produced a driver's license identifying him as Charles Ng, and said that he'd made an "abrupt" turn to the right and struck the semi truck.

In his recollection of the event, Hicks said he saw a large duffel bag in the bed of the pickup, and a German shepherd which appeared to be with a male bystander. The CHP officer ran the pickup's license plate to check for stolen vehicles, but nothing turned up. He prepared his report and released the driver to continue his trip.

Wednesday morning, Tori Doolin riffled through the incoming mail and found a green envelope from Scott. She laughed at the name he'd printed, "Tori Ann Dueling." The deliberate misspelling was a private joke between them, a tongue-in-cheek reference to their recent arguments. Before she tore it open, Tori noticed the postmark indicating that the letter had been mailed in Wilseyville. She withdrew the greeting card, imprinted with the words, "Fish Got to Swim, Birds Got to Fly." In handwriting she recognized as Scott's, she read:

I know it is D-o-o-l-i-n. Maybe we're mirrored in each picture, never doing it the way anyone else does. I am safe on Monday noon. Take care.

Love,
Scott.

They were the last words from Scott that Tori would ever read or hear. But she didn't know that when her doorbell rang on Wednesday morning.

She looked through the peephole in the entry door, saw a short Asian man, and decided not to answer. A few minutes later, it rang again. With some irritation showing in her voice, Tori asked, "Who is it?"

A male voice responded, "It's Charles. Charles from up north." Tori opened the door and recognized Charles Gunnar from her previous visit to Lonnie and Brenda's cabin. The Asian stood next to him. It struck her as odd that Charles not only failed to introduce his companion, but directed him to wait in the cab of the truck. The next words from the husky man's voice stunned Tori. In a subsequent report, she stated, "He told me that he had found all of them dead in the cabin. That there was blood all over the place. There were clothes all over the place. He said that he had taken the bodies and burnt them. He used a name for it; I don't know what it was. It was putting them on a pyre and burning them Indian style, and that he had then buried the bodies, and that he had cleaned the house."

Recoiling in speechless horror, Tori tried to make sense of the horrifying words. Scott? Brenda? The baby? My God, what could have happened?

Lake, in his role as Charles Gunnar, didn't give her time to voice the questions. Tori recalled, "He stated that he wanted all of Scott's belongings to take back with him to make it look like Scott had moved out so that nobody came looking for him.'' Her mind spinning with mixed emotions and confusion, and moving slowly as if in a nightmare, Tori nodded her consent. ''I gave him Scott's ten-speed bike; I gave him Scott's clothing and miscellaneous items. He wanted the receipt for the gun that Scott had bought from him. And I told him it was locked up in his safe and I didn't know the combination . . . so I couldn't get that for him. He wanted the pink slip to the truck and a Plymouth that was already up there, as well. I did not have those.''

Lake walked Tori out to the truck. Her heart pounded at the sight. It seemed like just yesterday that she'd seen Scott drive away in it. ''He gave me a tour of the damage, and told me the reason he had to bring Scott's truck was because his German shepherd was about to have puppies and it was in the back on a mattress.'' As they spoke, the Asian man remained completely silent. Lake had tried to cover up the deaths at Wilseyville, he said, because it looked like there were illegal guns and drugs in the cabin, and he didn't want the police snooping around.

If Scott was dead, Tori didn't want his name tarnished. Completely overwhelmed by shock, she didn't know what to do.

Continuing with his explanation, Lake told her that he planned to forge a letter to Lonnie Bond's landlord to state that Bond had moved out.

After Gunnar and his pal had loaded Scott Stapley's belongings into the bed of the truck, they promptly left. Tori Doolin had never felt more depressed and confused in her life.

In Michigan the families of Brenda O'Connor and Lonnie Bond couldn't believe it when phone calls and letters from their loved ones suddenly ceased without explanation. They felt the gnawing pain common to any family when a relative goes missing without any hint of what happened.

Several other families had recently felt the same horror when their kin had vanished:

Donald Lake
Charles Gunnar
Maurice Rock
Sheryl Okoro
Randy Jacobson
Harvey Dubs
Deborah Dubs
Sean Dubs
Paul Cosner
Clifford Peranteau
Jeffrey Gerald
Michael Carroll
Kathleen Allen
Lonnie Bond
Brenda O'Connor
Lonnie Bond Jr.

Two babies, four women, and ten men. God knows how many others. All missing. All having been in contact with Leonard Lake, and many having crossed paths with Charles Ng.

Chapter 19

No one could accuse Leonard Lake of being inefficient or of not following up on details. The real estate manager who had rented the house to Lonnie Bond spoke of a call she received from him. "He told me that he thought my tenants skipped out on me and that they had left their car, along with the pink slip because Lonnie owed him some money. And I went out to check that out. I found an empty house. No . . . I found no people in the house." The departed tenants had strangely left many of their possessions including dishes and clothing.

By early May, there had been so many victims that Lake could transfer money from one to the other for his personal use. Using Randy Jacobson's identification, he cashed a check to him that appeared to have been written by Kathleen Allen from her credit union account.

Still busily trying to milk every possible asset from the vanished men and women, Lake drove again to Milpitas. At

the home of Eric Gouveia, the young man who supervised Mike
Carroll at the pizza restaurant, Lake knocked on the door. When
Eric's fourteen-year-old sister answered, Lake gave her a note
bearing the signature "Mike Carroll" and giving his "friend"
permission to take Mike's things. Lake became aggressive and
insisted on entering the house, but Eric directed him to the
garage door. As soon as Eric opened the garage, Lake walked
in and immediately grabbed a box marked with Carroll's name.
He placed it on the floor, and stated that he wanted Mike's .22
caliber rifle and a shotgun.

"Mike doesn't have any guns here," Eric said.

"Yes, he does. And I want them," Lake growled.

"How in hell do you know that?"

"Mike told me, and he said they were his."

"No, they're actually mine, not Mike's. They're in my bedroom," Eric patiently insisted.

"Well, I'm going in and get them, then."

"No, you're not."

As the conversation grew louder, Eric's mother and sister
entered the garage, followed by Joe Sundberg, Eric's stepfather
and owner of the pizza restaurant. A bear of a man, with a
beard and gravelly voice, Sundberg's face made it clear that
he didn't care for Lake's behavior. Sundberg later described
the confrontation. "I didn't like the guy. And I didn't like the
way he looked at my wife's low-cut neckline. I told him to
back out of the garage." Sundberg unequivocally informed
Lake that he wasn't getting any guns. "The guy was sassy,"
said Sundberg. "He looked at my fourteen-year-old daughter
even worse. I thumped him on the chest and sent the women
into the house." Lake scuttled away without any loot.

At last, potential victims had stood up against the schemer.
He'd finally met someone he couldn't charm or threaten. It
marked the beginning of a serious decline in the fortunes of
Leonard Lake.

* * *

Depressed and needing to boost his self-esteem, Lake visited his sister Janet on the first day of June. She would recall that he generally dropped in at her Excelsior district apartment on an average of once each month. He hadn't missed a visit for over eight months since the time his Asian pal had lived there temporarily in September 1984.

He busied himself on that Saturday with home improvement projects.

On Sunday, June 2, 1985, Lake needed some materials, so he and Charles Ng drove to a South San Francisco lumberyard-supply store at the corner of Railroad Avenue and Spruce Street. It wasn't a particularly chilly day, but Ng wore a heavy parka, perfect for concealing shoplifted items.

Leaving the Honda in the store's front parking lot, Lake and Ng strolled inside. Ng stopped to examine a display of table vises, while Lake wandered to another section.

Reserve South San Francisco Police Department officer John Kallas entered the store a few minutes later, and happened to see a short, muscular Asian man walking toward him carrying a large vise. Fully expecting him to turn left toward the sales counter, Kallas was surprised when the Asian passed within two feet, turned right, and marched quickly out the front door. Instantly Kallas approached the salesclerk and asked if he'd sold a vise. The clerk said he hadn't. "Well," replied Kallas, "if no one sold a vise, then you just got ripped off."

Accompanied by another clerk, Kallas sprinted outside to the parking lot, looking left and right for the Asian man. He heard a car door slam, but with his vision obstructed by a pickup truck, he couldn't see the source of the noise. Moving past the truck, he glanced off to his right and spotted the same man standing at the passenger door of a copper-colored Honda Prelude, about seventy-five feet from the entrance.

The Asian, apparently recognizing that he'd been seen,

moved away and walked diagonally toward the intersection of Spruce and Airport. The clerk shouted, "Hey, fella, I'd like to speak to you," but Ng continued walking at a brisk pace until he vanished from sight.

Kallas returned to the Honda, looking for the vise, but could only see a box of wrenches on the backseat. Straining to see inside, he caught a glimpse of something on the floor behind the passenger's backrest, so he circled the car for a better look and saw that it was a work jacket. Another clerk joined him at the parked Honda. Kallas said, "I wonder what he did with the vise." As the trio stepped to the car's rear, Kallas could see that the trunk lid was ajar. A clerk lifted it up, and Kallas said, "There it is." The heavy, blue-gray steel vise sat upright in the rear left corner of the trunk.

Back inside the store, while the clerks stood watch over the Honda, Kallas inquired if anyone had called the police. Remarkably, no one had thought to do it, so he grabbed a phone and dialed the number familiar to him. As he lifted the receiver to his ear, a husky, bearded, bald man approached and started to say something, but Kallas raised his hand for quiet until he completed the call. When he recradled the phone, the bearded man asked if he could pay for the vise. Kallas shook his head. "I'm just a customer," he said, and advised the man to talk to one of the clerks.

Within moments of the call, at 1:15 P.M., Officer Daniel Wright pulled his cruiser to halt near the store entrance. Kallas exited and waved Wright toward the Honda. Wright parked adjacent to it, stepped out, and heard a quick briefing of what had happened. Noting the license number, 838 WFQ, he used his portable radio to "run the plate through our communications." It came back registered to Lonnie Bond, but it should have been on a Buick, not a Honda.

Since the Honda's trunk lid remained open, Wright looked inside and saw the vise, which was still marked with a $75 price tag. He later recalled, "There was a South City Lumber and Supply bag directly next to it, and I looked through that for any type of receipt," but found none. John Kallas wondered aloud if any more stolen property might be in the car, so Wright scanned through the trunk's contents. He later reported, "I found a backpack, lifted it, and it was heavy. Inside it, I found a gun case, which contained a semiautomatic Sturm Ruger .22 caliber handgun and a silencer." Examining the weapon closer, he noted a serial number, 12-70329.

Again using his portable radio, Wright checked the number through a computer system and found that the weapon had been recently purchased by R. Scott Stapley in San Diego.

Wright had just completed logging the information when the bearded man exited the store, approached him, and said that everything was all right. He had taken care of the bill for the vise that his friend had carried out. So there was no reason to pursue the matter.

"Who are you?" Wright asked.

"My name is Stapley," replied the husky, balding man.

"Do you have any identification?"

"Sure do." He reached for his billfold and withdrew a driver's license, in the name of Robin Scott Stapley.

"Do you know who owns this vehicle?"

"Yeah. It belongs to Lonnie Bond."

"Where is Mr. Bond?"

"He's up north."

"Does he know you have his vehicle? Can I get hold of him via telephone to check it out?"

"I don't think he has a telephone."

Wright once again used his radio, this time to check for any warrants on Robin Scott Stapley. Meanwhile, he asked the man who used that name if it was okay to search the Honda.

"Sure. Go ahead. You already have anyway."

Picking up the silencer, Wright told "Stapley" that it was an illegal possession. He placed him under arrest, handcuffed him, and radioed a request for another officer to transport the suspect to the station. Afterward, Wright arranged for the Honda to be towed and impounded for a more thorough search. At his sergeant's order, Wright followed the tow truck to conduct the Honda search himself. Inside it, he found a stun gun. He also discovered nine slide photographs that would turn out to be of Lonnie Bond, Brenda O'Conner, and Lonnie Bond Jr.

Noting the vehicle identification numbers under the windshield on the dashboard, Wright called in for another check. He learned that the vehicle was related to a missing persons report involving Paul Cosner of San Francisco.

The mounting evidence gave the case far more importance than a shoplifted vise and possession of illegal weapons. Wright was ordered to secure the Honda and its contents in an impound cage for the homicide squad to examine. The gun, slide photos, and the other documents were stored safely in an evidence locker.

At the police station, the bearded man calling himself Scott Stapley faced more serious questions. The commander in charge, needing an experienced interrogator, telephoned the on-call investigator for that weekend, Detective Gary Hopper, asking him to get into headquarters as soon as possible.

Meanwhile in an interrogation room, another officer spoke to Stapley, hinting that a landslide of discrepancies made him look awfully suspicious. The Honda belonged to a man named Paul Cosner, who had been missing for nine months. But someone had attached license plates registered to a Buick owned by Lonnie Bond, another missing person. Getting to the point, the officer asked the suspect just what the hell was going on.

Leonard Lake slumped in his chair, his face slack, his eyes turning moist. He asked for a piece of paper and a pen, saying he needed to write a note to his wife. His interrogator courteously removed handcuffs so Lake could write. While Lake scrawled a message, he asked for a glass of water, which the officer brought in a Styrofoam cup. As he slowly caved in to the overwhelming circumstances, Lake started talking. He admitted that his real name was Leonard Thomas Lake, and divulged that he was wanted by the police for outstanding charges in Mendocino County. In a soft, deliberate voice, speaking slowly, he also identified his companion who had stolen the vise as Charles Chitat Ng, adding that Ng had served time in Leavenworth. Then he completed writing the note, on which he scrawled:

> *Dear Lyn,*
> *I love you. I forgive you. Freedom is better than all else. Tell Janet I'm sorry. Mom, Patty, and all. I'm sorry for all the trouble.*
>
> > *Love,*
> > *Leonard*

He folded the paper and stuffed it in his shirt pocket.

Before the handcuffs could be snapped back on his wrists, Leonard Lake reached under his collar, pulled out a cyanide pill, and gulped it down with a quick swallow of water. Moments later, he collapsed on the floor, in convulsions. At that precise moment, Detective Gary Hopper arrived, saw Lake on the floor, and summoned emergency medical help. Still showing a weak pulse, Lake was rushed to a nearby hospital and put on life-support systems.

None of the officers could recall a suspect ever attempting suicide with the use of cyanide. Some of the older hands could recall hearing about a top Nazi named Hermann Göring escaping the noose in 1946 by ingesting cyanide in a Nuremberg prison. What could have motivated this guy Lake to imitate such a notorious and desperate measure? This case had suddenly taken on dark and heavy proportions.

Because several names of missing persons had popped up, the watch commander called the San Francisco PD unit responsible for such investigations.

Inspector Thomas L. Eisenmann heard the phone ring in his

Novato home that Sunday evening, and knew it was going to be a bad day. He answered and heard his colleague Bruce Freidiani, of SFPD Operations, say, "Tom, South San Francisco PD recovered a car belonging to Paul Cosner, missing nine months, and made an arrest. The guy took a cyanide pill. You want to go on the case?"

One of the hardest working cops on the force, Eisenmann seldom turned down the opportunity to grab a case, especially if it hinted of serious challenge. Assigned to child abuse investigations, he sometimes helped the missing persons unit. Born, raised, and educated in San Francisco, Eisenmann joined the Navy not long after graduating from Lowell High School. He served aboard the *USS Duncan* in the Vietnam conflict, and set foot in nearly every Asian port. Just before ending his tour of duty, Tom's police officer brother-in-law suggested he take an upcoming exam to join the force. The ship's captain helped by allowing Eisenmann to take the test while still aboard. In 1968, the SFPD offered him a job, and Eisenmann started walking a beat on "wild and woolly" Fillmore Street, where he encountered a bustling heroin trade, abundant gambling, and an army of scantily dressed hookers flashing skin to throngs of pedestrians and cruising motorists. After he'd worn out more shoes than he could remember, he served a stint in the crime lab, then joined the child abuse/exploitation unit, finding and busting perverts who dealt in child pornography.

Eisenmann had helped Irene Brunn in the missing persons unit when Harvey, Deborah, and little Sean Dubs vanished. Looking forward to working with her again, he called her at home. They agreed to meet at headquarters and drive together down to the South SFPD station. The trip from Novato, about twenty-five miles down Highway 101 and across the Golden Gate Bridge, would normally take less than an hour. But that Sunday night, an overturned chemical truck at San Rafael made traffic a nightmare, so a weary Eisenmann was late meeting

Brunn, who rolled her eyes while making a show of glancing at her watch, a full two hours after his call.

Finally, in the meeting with South San Francisco officers, Eisenmann and Brunn listened to the briefing. The turning point that led to Leonard Lake's capitulation, they learned, took place while the suspect still claimed he was Robin Scott Stapley. An officer, holding the driver's license Lake produced, had asked him his date of birth. Lake couldn't come up with the right answer. So the officer had said, "We know you're not Stapley." At that point, Lake had asked for a drink of water, along with pen and paper.

Brunn and Eisenmann next went to the impound center to examine the Honda, which had been secured inside a wire cage. Because it belonged to Paul Cosner, in an SFPD case, the South San Francisco PD watch commander released the vehicle and the associated evidence to Brunn and Eisenmann to take it back to the city. Eisenmann drove the Honda while Irene followed. During the trip, Eisenmann felt a chill in his spine. The owner, he realized, was undoubtedly dead, so he took great care not to unnecessarily touch anything.

Back at headquarters, before exiting the Honda, Eisenmann found several more documents. He also turned up a Greek fisherman's hat. When Irene saw it, it struck a chord of recognition. She searched her memory, struggling for a hit. All at once, like morning fog rolling back to unveil the Golden Gate Bridge, it came to her. An ATM videotape had recorded someone using a card belonging to Harvey Dubs, one of her missing persons. The video picture had been fuzzy, showing mostly the back of his head, but he wore that same peculiar hat. And, Irene remembered, he had dark, thick, blunt-cut hair, along with other facial characteristics of an Asian man.

The next morning, Monday, Brunn and Eisenmann faced a pompous captain who lectured them about the possibility of a major homicide case, as if they hadn't already figured that out. Brunn rolled her eyes in contempt while he played Sherlock

Holmes solving a whodunit. When he'd finished his imperious speech, they ignored it and went back to work. Irene contacted Sharon Sellitto, Paul Cosner's sister, and obtained her permission to search the Honda. (Sellitto would later angrily complain that she wasn't notified when the Honda was found, and heard about it on a radio news report.)

Both officers watched a criminalist apply Luminol to the Honda's interior. Like a magic potion, the chemical glows in the dark where it touches bloodstains, even old ones or those invisible to the eye. Several blotches of blood showed up inside the car, except on the passenger's seat and sun visor. Close examination indicated that a bullet had creased the chrome strip lining the passenger side of the windshield. A ballistics expert determined that a bullet had pierced the head liner and the passenger-door panel. Searching the interior, they found photographs of Lake and a young bare-breasted woman, a receipt from a travel agency for Charles Gunnar, a First Interstate bank card in the name of Randy Jacobson, and several identification cards in the name of Robin Scott Stapley. Under the seat, they discovered a bill from the Pacific Gas and Electric Company (PG&E) in the name of Claralyn Balazs with a post office box address in Wilseyville. The document showed recent meter readings indicating someone had been using electric power on the property.

"Where in the hell is Wilseyville?" Brunn asked. They checked a detailed California map and found a tiny dot over in Calaveras County, a three-hour drive from the city. Through Department of Motor Vehicle records, they traced Balazs to a residence in San Bruno.

Their initial attempts to raise Balazs by telephone failed. Eisenmann called the San Diego PD missing persons unit and checked the status of the cases on Scott Stapley and Lonnie Bond. Both men, along with Brenda O'Connor and the baby, had moved to Wilseyville. Irene Brunn finally reached Claralyn Balazs on the telephone and learned that she had been married

to Leonard Lake, then divorced him, but had continued a relationship. The woman didn't seem particularly moved by the
fact that Lake lay in a coma at the hospital. Brunn arranged to
meet with Balazs at the home of Janet, Lake's sister. Lake's
mother showed up, as well.

Balazs said her family owned the property at Wilseyville,
but no one was currently living there. Brunn and Eisenmann
exchanged glances, recognizing the contradiction between her
statement and the PG&E bill showing electricity usage.
Claralyn added that she hadn't been up there for some time.
The detectives asked her if she would show them the house
and property. Balazs consented, and said she would meet them
up there at ten o'clock the following morning in Wilseyville's
only store.

Before the day ended, a woman who had sold the car to
Cosner helped by revealing she had burnt a hole in the passenger
seat and scorched the sun visor with cigarettes. It appeared that
Lake had replaced both items.

More details emerged about the gun found in the Honda's
trunk, which had been traced by its serial number. It had been
purchased in San Diego on March 30, at the Accuracy Gun
Shop, by Robin Scott Stapley, and picked up sixteen days later.
Lake had somehow acquired it within the last two weeks.

Eisenmann arranged an official request for permission from
Sheriff Claude Ballard, of Calaveras County, to allow an investigation by SFPD officers in Wilseyville. Ballard agreed, on
the condition that two of his men participate. Eisenmann called
Detective Norm Varain, and said, "We have a case that looks
like the ball will be bouncing in your court." Varain laughed,
and replied he and Detective Steve Matthews would certainly
"play ball." They agreed to meet at eight o'clock, Tuesday
morning, in San Andreas, which would give them time to drive
the twenty-plus miles up to the sole Wilseyville store.

Laughing and joking about a free trip to the mountains, Brunn
and Eisenmann walked by the desk of a man they regarded

as a legend among detectives. Homicide Inspector Napoleon Hendricks, an imposing six four, commanded respect from superiors and peers alike for his brilliant career in narcotics and homicide. He looked up at the pair, and with incredible prescience, said in a deep, booming voice, "Remember the Dubses." Irene would never forget his uncanny prediction.

Chapter 20

Tuesday morning got off to a bad start when Brunn and Eisenmann got lost en route to San Andreas. Somehow, they drove through Sacramento, fifty miles out of the way.

During the long drive, Brunn remarked, "Y'know, there was a Chinese guy using the Dubses's credit card, and we have a Chinese guy that walked away from the lumberyard." She turned to Eisenmann and asked, "What do you think?"

He shrugged, gave her a sidelong glance, and replied, "C'mon, Irene. There are a half-billion Chinese people. What are the chances of any connection?"

"Okay," she conceded. But in the back of her mind, she believed there just might be a real link.

Despite the wayward journey, they arrived just a few minutes late for the meeting with Norm Varain and Steve Matthews at the San Andreas Sheriff's Office. All four drove up to the Wilseyville store to meet Claralyn at the appointed time of ten o'clock. Inside the store, as they talked, Claralyn "Cricket" Balazs walked in. The officers were surprised to see that she brought along Leonard Lake's mother, Gloria. But their surprise turned to anger at her next comment. She told them she had already been to the cabin the night before to remove a few personal things that would embarrass her if the police found them.

Brunn and Eisenmann felt betrayed. Cricket had told them no one lived at the cabin, and now she had taken things out that might relate to the investigation. They asked her why she hadn't played it straight with them, to which she simply repeated her explanation that she didn't want to risk them finding and confiscating pictures, videotapes, or other items too personal to become public.

A short trip from the store took the group to a gated turnoff from Blue Mountain Road, where Cricket produced a key and opened the gate. They drove up the curving dirt road to the cleared space in front of the green house. A few yards away from the entrance, stood a recently constructed concrete-block building that resembled a World War II bunker, in a fissure gouged from the hillside. In the dirt yard, sat a gray-blue pickup truck with personalized license plates, AHOYMTY. Another vehicle, an old blue Plymouth, was parked nearby.

Cricket Balazs preceded Brunn and Eisenmann through the entry door, then conversed alternately with the sheriff's detectives, and Lake's mother. The two San Francisco sleuths glanced around inside the two-bedroom, one-bath house. By force of habit, Eisenmann ran his hand over a door frame. *Bingo!* He found three clear capsules filled with a powder. From his experience as a narcotics investigator, he knew they were not ordinary prescriptions because the capsules had been separated, refilled, and rejoined with clear cellophane tape. They would turn out to contain cyanide.

Both investigators toured the two bedrooms. In the larger one, they noted holes bored in each cornerpost of the bed, and similar holes in the floor. In a drawer they turned up eyebolts that fit into the holes. A scenario filled their minds, in which the eyebolts could be used to bind or handcuff a person in a spread-eagled position on the bed. In another drawer they found a pile of flimsy, see-through lingerie, including a blue baby-doll top with matching panties. They also noticed a guitar case that contained an instrument decorated with odd stickers reading "Shred" and "To be destroyed." On a desk counter, they noted an Olympia typewriter.

In the living room, they observed one wall covered with a mural depicting a forest glowing in autumn colors of red, yellow, and gold. A brown recliner chair sat near the wall. Irene's attention was caught by a bookcase on which sat a Sony video-cassette recorder, along with a sophisticated video duplicator called a Hybrid-8 generator. This time, she didn't have to dredge her memory very long. It hit her almost instantly. "Oh, shit," she muttered. Cricket heard her and said, "You guys have been here long enough. I think it's time you left." Eisenmann reasoned with her and the officers stayed, but decided to contact the district attorney in San Andreas to obtain a search warrant.

Flipping open a notebook, Irene copied the serial number of the cassette player and looked for a number on the duplicator, but could see that it had been obliterated. She asked Norm Varain for permission to use his radio phone to call San Francisco. When she reached Inspector Glenn Pamfiloff at headquarters, she asked him to pull the Dubs file and look up the serial numbers of Harvey's missing video equipment. She scribbled them into her pad, thanked her colleague, then rushed back into the house. *The Sony VCR number matched! My God! The legend, Napoleon Hendricks had been right.*

She whispered to Eisenmann, "Don't say anything. We've got a match on the Dubs video stuff." With this discovery, they had enough evidence to support requesting a full search warrant of the entire house. They secured the premises. Brunn and Steve Matthews departed for San Andreas, leaving Eisenmann and Varain to guard the place and to keep the two women company.

With the help of District Attorney John Martin, of Calaveras County, and Judge Douglas Mewhinney, Brunn and Varain obtained the requested search warrant, then rushed back up the curving two-lane road to the cabin. Meanwhile, Eisenmann and Matthews chatted with Cricket Balazs, occasionally interjecting questions about the structure made of cinder block. She told them it was Leonard's shelter and workshop designed to survive some kind of world emergency. No, she said, she didn't have a key to it, nor could she grant permission to search it.

Changing the subject, the investigators asked about Charles Ng. Cricket said Ng was a friend of Lake's who had lived with them for a time at Philo before both men were arrested. Ng had gone to prison, while Lake made bail, but skipped out. Expecting Cricket to deny having recently seen Ng, the officers were shocked when she admitted driving him to his apartment on Lenox Way the previous day. She volunteered that he might have gone to Chicago. Eisenmann, years later, would characterize Cricket as a woman "who lets you know she has information, then wants you to pull it out of her."

Lake's mother, Gloria, spoke of Leonard's being near death, and how it hurt her when her younger son, Donald, had vanished months ago. She admitted, too, that she and Cricket had "cleaned house the night before."

Cricket grew impatient and irritated with the delays and questions, and finally told Gloria it would be better if they left. Anyway, they needed to visit Lake in the hospital. She drove away in a huff.

With the investigative scope rapidly expanding, Sheriff Ballard released additional officers to follow Brunn and Matthews up to the house where they would join the search team. Detective Larry Copland, thirty-two, would become a key figure. The native Californian, broad-shouldered and solid at a little over six feet, with sandy brown hair, became a cop in 1976 with the Los Angeles Police Department after earning a degree in criminology at Fresno State. He relocated to the Calaveras County Sheriff's Department in 1979 and was promoted to detective three years later. Assigned to the narcotics squad, he met nearly every biker, jailbird, gang-banger, methamphetamine cooker, and marijuana farmer in the region. Easygoing, soft-spoken, and completely honest, Copland earned respect not only from his peers, but also from the outlaws he chased. With his reputation as a tough but fair cop, he established a communication pipeline with gang leaders, as well as informants, creating a system of networking that led to major drug busts on the average of once a month. Continuing with his education, he earned a master's degree at Cal State, Sacramento.

As well as joining in the actual searching of the Balazs property, Copland teamed with Steve Matthews to tag each item found, and to keep meticulous records of descriptions, locations, and dispositions of all evidence collected. In addition, he even videotaped much of the evidence-handling procedures. He would spend a full month on the crime scene.

The locked bunker intrigued Brunn, Eisenmann, and Copland. When they finally stepped inside the combination toolshed/workshop, they saw an array of construction tools, as expected, along with shovels, picks, a wheelbarrow, and other ordinary implements. One wall featured a prominent photo display of scantily clad young women, which made them realize they faced a staggering task of identifying and tracing down each of the models to determine if they had been victimized by Lake. An eerie atmosphere filled the shadowy interior of the structure. Something about it seemed ghostly and uncomfortable. One of the deputies finally commented that the inside seemed so much smaller than the exterior dimensions.

By pacing the perimeter outside, the investigators realized there was considerably more space inside than used by the workshop. Eisenmann later described what happened when they reentered the building. "As we looked around the interior, we saw piano hinges on a plywood wall, and realized there was a hidden door behind some shelves. We waited until the second search warrant arrived, and opened it."

Closer inspection of the hinges caused Eisenmann to frown. They were bent as if someone on the other side had pushed or pounded on the concealed door. When the officers opened it, they found that it led through a narrow passageway to a rectangular chamber. They would label it "the living area." The room contained a bed, a table with a lamp, a desk, a dresser, shelves for food storage, some clothing, and various other supplies. A copy of *The Collector*, by John Fowles, rested on the bookshelf.

At one end of the chamber, a plywood partition divided the space, making yet a third tiny room no more that 3½ feet wide by 6½ feet long. It contained a narrow platform, about two feet wide, on which lay a foam-rubber pad that might be used for a bed. A five-gallon plastic bucket with a roll of toilet paper sat in one dark corner. It soon became evident that the cell had been completely soundproofed. A mirror had been inserted into the wooden wall between the living area and the tiny cell, providing a one-way view into the cramped cubicle.

Few solitary-confinement cells in the world would be more isolated, primitive, or claustrophobic.

A typed sheet of paper was posted on one wall. Eisenmann felt a knot in his stomach when he read the words, all in upper case:

RULES

1) I MUST ALWAYS BE READY TO SERVICE MY MASTER. I MUST BE CLEAN, BRUSHED, AND MADE-UP WITH MY CELL NEAT.

2) I MUST NEVER SPEAK UNLESS SPOKEN TO. UNLESS IN BED, I MUST NEVER LOOK MY MASTER IN THE EYE, BUT MUST KEEP MY EYES DOWNCAST.

3) I MUST NEVER SHOW MY DISRESPECT, EITHER VERBALLY OR SILENT. I MUST NEVER CROSS MY ARMS OR LEGS IN FRONT OF MY BODY, OR CLENCH MY FISTS, AND UNLESS EATING, MUST ALWAYS KEEP MY LIPS PARTED.

4) I MUST BE OBEDIENT COMPLETELY AND IN ALL THINGS. I MUST OBEY IMMEDIATELY AND WIHTHOUT (sic) QUESTION OR COMMENT.

5) I MUST ALWAYS BE QUIET WHEN LOCKED IN MY CELL.

6) I MUST REMEMBER AND OBEY ANY ADDITIONAL RULES TOLD TO ME. I MUST UNDERSTAND THAT ANY DISOBEDIENCE, ANY PAIN, TROUBLE, OR ANNOYANCE CAUSED BY ME TO MY MASTER WILL BE GROUNDS FOR PUNISHMENT.

It became clear what the concrete-block prison had been used for when the search team viewed a videotape found by Eisenmann and Norman Varain. Next to the driveway, Eisenmann had directed workers to dig in a soft spot outside the bunker. They uncovered a white plastic five-gallon paint bucket with a sealed top. According to a report written by Varain, it contained ''several photo albums which depicted different white females in various stages of undress and completely nude.'' Leonard Lake's journal also was found inside the bucket. The final two items, a pair of videotapes, were labeled with the letter ''M,'' but just one was inscribed with the words ''M-Ladies, Kathi/Brenda.''

When the investigators slipped the tape into a VCR and watched the television screen, they saw Kathleen Allen enduring mental torture, being threatened, stripped naked, forced to massage Charles Ng, and posing for lurid photos while Lake directed her every move. When they viewed another segment of the tape, they learned about the imprisonment of a second woman, one who had lived no more than 100 yards from the bunker.

In the opening shots of the taped scene, Brenda O'Connor sits in the same brown chair Kathi Allen had used, with the same backdrop depicting a mural of a forest in fall colors. On a table to Brenda's right, a lamp provides muted light. She is dressed in a long-sleeved tomato-red jersey with a white bodice and blue jeans. Her light brown hair is cut in a pageboy and she is without makeup. Her hands are cuffed behind her.

Leonard Lake's voice breaks the silence, apparently answering her question about what happened to Lonnie Bond and Scott Stapley. "Well, if you must know, I didn't do anything with them."

Brenda asks, apparently for the second time, "What did you do with them?" Her voice is soft but firm.

"I didn't do anything with them." Lake sounds perfectly calm.

"Did you guys kill them?"

"No, we didn't kill them."

"Are you going to let us go soon?" She sounds wistful.

"Probably not."

With a barely perceptible tremble, Brenda asks, "Never? What are you going to do, kill us?"

"That's sort of up to you, Brenda," Lake says.

Brenda's next question reveals that she thinks Lake's name is Charles Gunnar. "Charles, what are you going to do to us? Why are you doing this?"

" 'Cause we hate you," he answers, his voice full of cold malice.

"What did we do to you?"

"Shut up," he commands, and adds, *"What a hairy day."*

Her voice quaking and breaking into a falsetto, Brenda says, *"Gotta get my baby down here."*

Lake speaks cryptically. *"Your baby is sound asleep, like a rock. Brenda, the neighborhood doesn't like you. . . . The neighborhood doesn't like Lonnie, and we haven't liked you since you moved in."*

"So, we'll leave," she offers.

"Oh, you've already left. We've closed you down . . . we got together and we took you away. We took Scott away. Lonnie's going to earn a decent living for the rest of his life, hopefully."

"I know he is."

"Your baby is going to take—to be taken away." Lake seems to be panting, and comments, *"Excuse the heavy breathing."*

Now a trace of panic enters Brenda's voice. *"What do you mean, gonna be taken away?"*

Still speaking in a dispassionate tone, Lake answers, *"There's a family in Fresno that doesn't have a baby."*

Brenda pleads, *"You're not taking my baby away from me."*

Even though Lake is not in the scene, his smirk is obvious. *"They've got one now."*

Charles Ng, clad all in black, appears in the picture. In an alto voice, he says, *"It's better than the baby is dead, right?"*

More spirited, but still sitting, Brenda protests Lake's comment about giving her baby to a Fresno family. *"What do you mean they've got one now? That's my baby."*

Lake's words turn menacing. *"Brenda, you have a choice. We'll give it to you right now."*

"What?" she asks.

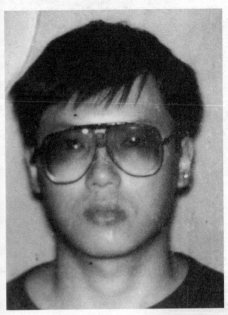

Charles Ng fled to Canada after police discovered his sex slave bunker. (*photo courtesy Orange County, CA Superior Court*)

Leonard Lake committed suicide after being arrested. (*photo courtesy Orange County, CA Superior Court*)

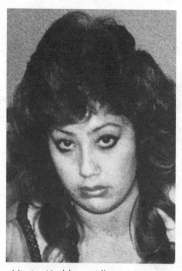

Victim Kathleen Allen, 18.
(*photo courtesy Orange County, CA Superior Court*)

Victim Mike Carroll, 23.
(*photo courtesy Orange County, CA Superior Court*)

Victim Jeffrey Gerald, 25.
(*photo courtesy Orange County, CA Superior Court*)

Victim Charles Gunnar was best man at Lake's wedding.
(*photo courtesy Orange County, CA Superior Court*)

Victim Randy Jacobson, 35.
(*photo courtesy Orange County,
CA Superior Court*)

Victim Paul Cosner, 39.
(*photo courtesy Sharon Sellitto*)

Victim Cliff Peranteau, 24
(*photo courtesy William
Peranteau*)

Victim Robin Scott
Stapley, 26.
(*photo courtesy Dwight
and Lola Stapley*)

Victims Lonnie Bond, 27, and Lonnie Bond Jr., 1. (*photo courtesy Orange County, CA Superior Court*)

Victim Brenda O'Connor, 19, Lonnie Bond Jr.'s mother. (*photo courtesy Orange County, CA Superior Court*)

Victims Harvey and Deborah Dubs with son Sean, 16 months. (*photo courtesy Orange County, CA Superior Court*)

Line on Wilseyville property indicated telephone trench where bodies were found. Bunker is to right of the line. (*photo courtesy Orange County, CA Superior Court*)

Lake's secluded Wilseyville residence was a three hour drive from San Francisco. (*photo courtesy Orange County, CA Superior Court*)

Concrete block survival bunker was built into the hillside by Lake. (*photo courtesy Orange County, CA Superior Court*)

Bunker contained a hidden cell for a sex slave.
(*photo courtesy Orange County, CA Superior Court*)

The secret door to the slave
cell was concealed by shelves.
(*author's collection*)

Brown chair sex slaves
were videotaped in.
(*author's collection*)

Investigators spent several months digging for bodies and
evidence.   (*photo courtesy Orange County, CA Superior Court*)

Partially unearthed body of one of Lake's and Ng's victims.
(*photo courtesy Orange County, CA Superior Court*)

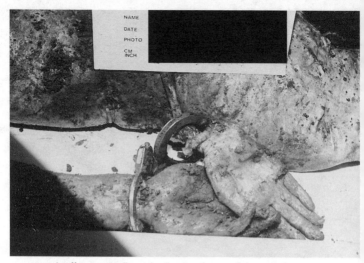

Handcuffs were still on the body of one of the murder victims.
(*photo courtesy Orange County, CA Superior Court*)

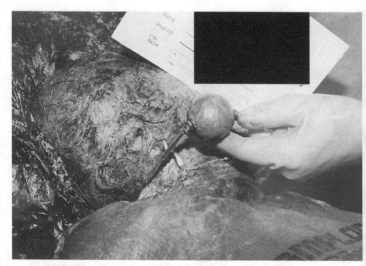

Several victims were found with gags made from red
rubber balls. (*photo courtesy Orange County, CA Superior Court*)

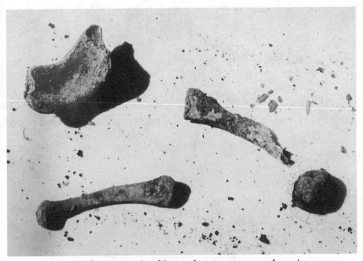

Forty-five pounds of bone fragments were found,
representing about twenty-five additional bodies.
(*photo courtesy Orange County, CA Superior Court*)

Kathleen Allen is seen sitting in the brown chair during
Lake's "M Ladies" videotape.
(*photo courtesy Orange County, CA Superior Court*)

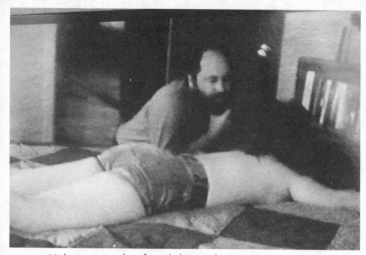

Videotapes police found show Lake taunting a captive,
partially undressed Kathleen Allen.
(*photo courtesy Orange County, CA Superior Court*)

Brenda O'Connor, on videotape, being unshackled by Ng.
(*photo courtesy Orange County, CA Superior Court*)

Lake's "M Ladies" videotape shows O'Connor being
forced to strip while Ng helps.
(*photo courtesy Orange County, CA Superior Court*)

Lake watches closely as a topless O'Connor drinks water.
Ng's hand holding stun gun is on the left.
(*photo courtesy Orange County, CA Superior Court*)

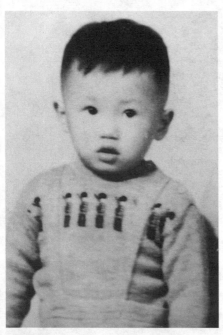

Charles Ng was born in Hong Kong on Christmas Eve 1960. (*photo courtesy Orange County, CA Superior Court*)

As a teenager, Ng had already shown signs of destructive behavior. (*photo courtesy Orange County, CA Superior Court*)

Leonard Lake used Sir Lancelot, a one-horned goat, to lure young women into posing nude for his camera. (*photo courtesy Orange County, CA Superior Court*)

Lake in paramilitary garb with two unidentified women. (*photo courtesy Orange County, CA Superior Court*)

PHILO MOTEL

Dear Lyn,

I love you, I forgive you, Freedom is better than all else Tell Fern I'm sorry Mom, Patty and all, I'm sorry for all the trouble.

Love Leonard

C 12959

Lake's suicide note. (*photo courtesy Orange County, CA Superior Court*)

Vise Ng tried to steal which led to the end of his and Lake's crime spree.
(*author's collection*)

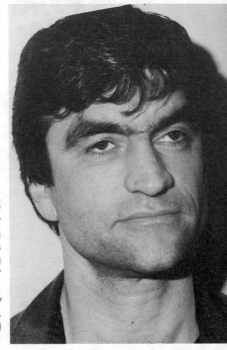

Informant Maurice LaBerge. Now deceased, the gag order preventing his photo from being published is no longer in effect.
(*photo courtesy Orange County, CA Superior Court*)

Ng was hustled onto a plane for the U.S. within minutes of the Canadian court's decision to allow extradition.
(*photo courtesy of the Stapley Family*)

Ng in cage at Calavaras County, CA Court.
(*photo courtesy Orange County, CA Superior Court*)

Inspector Tom Eisenmann of the San Francisco, CA Police Department. (*author's collection*)

On the case for 14 years, Mitch Hrdlika was deputy sheriff, then investigator for the district attorney. (*author's collection*)

Calavaras County, CA district attorney Peter Smith. (*author's collection*)

Defense attorney William Kelley. (*author's collection*)

Resuming his calm demeanor, Lake spells it out. "You can cooperate with us. By cooperating with us, that means you will stay here as our prisoner. You will work for us, you will wash for us, you will fuck for us. Or you can say, 'No, I don't want to do that,' in which case we'll tie you to the bed, we'll rape you, and then we'll take you outside and shoot you. Your choice."

Slumping and subdued, Brenda says, "I'll cooperate."

Ng chimes in again with "That's wise."

Lake, sounding a bit surprised at her capitulation, notes, "That was fast."

Once more, Ng comments, "Very wise."

Brenda makes it clear her concern is less for herself than for little Lonnie Bond Jr. She begs, "Are you really going to take my baby away from me?"

Merciless, Lake says, "Yes, we are. Personally, I don't think you're a fit mother."

"Where's Lonnie?"

Lake tells her, "They've been taken away. There's a place up in the hills where they'll split wood for the rest of their happy lives."

Hope shows in her voice. "You mean you haven't killed them or anything?"

"No, I haven't killed them, although if they die, that's, uh, that's their problem. To be honest, I could care less. They had better cooperate, too. They're getting the same choice you're getting. To be honest, for all I know, maybe they are dead right now." He seems to be teasing with dark, enigmatic hints of Bond's and Stapley's fates.

Brenda asks, "Is that why you invited us over here for dinner?"

"Uh-huh."

Ng interjects, "It's part of the game."

Lake seems to be growing impatient with his fearful captive. "You guys have been such assholes, Brenda. You know, Lonnie hasn't been all that bad. I'll give you that, except for his shooting . . . but you've been an asshole like I can't believe. You have been so damn rude, and for no reason that I can figure."

Perhaps rationalizing, or afraid to admit her true reasons for being rude to Lake, she explains, " 'Cause I can't stand it up here. It's in the middle of nowhere."

"Ah . . . ," says Lake.

They exchange a few comments about letters from Brenda to Lonnie that Lake has read. Brenda asks, "Are you going to keep me up here the rest of my life or something?"

"No," Lake answers. "To be honest with you, I probably won't keep you here for more than a few weeks. But, uh, after that, we'll probably pass you around . . . there's other . . ."

Brenda seems to be distracted and turns her face toward the lamp, muttering, "That light's hot."

Pitiless, Lake responds, "Suffer." Again speaking in obscure riddles, he says, "It's, uh, there's people that are going to want to know that we did our job. There's already some guys that took Lonnie and Scott away."

"Why do you guys do this?"

"We don't like you. Would you like me to put it in writing?"

Ng adds, "It's done. Just take whatever we tell you."

Sounding as if she is close to tears, Brenda chokes, "I can't do this . . ."

"We're going to sit back and enjoy ourselves," Lake taunts. "It's been a hectic day and you are going to learn the true meaning of fuckface."

Standing near the chair, Ng nods. "Uh-huh."

Lake asks Ng, "Where are the manacles?"

The black-clad man responds, "The manacles, yeah . . . ," and produces ankle clamps linked together with a chain.

Brenda twists in her chair and asks, "Can you loosen these?" She is referring to the handcuffs behind her.

"We're going to take them off in a minute," Lake promises.

While Brenda asks again, "You didn't hurt Lonnie, did you?" Ng removes his black shirt. He steps in front of her, reaches for the neckline of her jersey, and says, "Since you say you're hot, I'll take it off for you." He begins ripping the garment open.

"What?" Brenda cries in shock.

Lake, his voice sounding amused, says, "Well, she could actually take it off herself, but . . ."

As Ng rips the jersey open, he answers Lake, "Well, with the cuff(s) on, it's hard."

"Oh," says Lake, "I was going to have you take the cuffs off."

Brenda protests, "I'm not hot."

Ng continues to tear at her shirt, leaving only shreds hanging on her and exposing her bra.

Lake asks Ng, "Where are the manacles, Charlie?"

Ignoring Ng as he strips the shirt from her, Brenda makes another plea. "Would you please just go get my baby? . . . You can't keep my baby away from me for sex."

Lake, disregarding her whimpering, asks again about the manacles. Ng shows them to him, and Lake says, "Oh, put them on her. Then take the handcuffs off." Finally addressing her concerns about her child, Lake adds, "I'm taking your baby because your baby is innocent in this. There's nothing . . ."

While Ng kneels in front of Brenda, and binds her ankles, she says, "But so am I . . . you two are crazy."

"Well," says Lake, "maybe the whole neighborhood is crazy. The point is, you haven't been particularly innocent while you've been here, Brenda. In fact, you've been *something of a first-class asshole. However, we are going to give you an opportunity to, uh, make up for it.'' As Ng wields a knife, and cuts away the remaining shards of her jersey, Lake chides, "You're so crude, Charlie. I actually liked that T-shirt. Okay. . . .''*

Ng interrupts. "It's gone now. Lets see what we're buying.''

"Okay,'' says Lake.

Brenda asks, "What are you going to do? Sell me or something?''

"No, as a matter of fact,'' Lake mutters. "We're not going to sell you at all. We're going to give you away.''

Ng raises the knife again, slips it between her breasts, and slices the bra in two. Too late, Brenda objects. "Don't cut my bra. . . .'' The white undergarment falls away, exposing her breasts.

Ng informs Brenda, "Nothing is yours now. It'll be totally ours.'' He stands, his shadow completely covering her.

"Take her handcuffs off, Charlie. And let her get out of that [chair].''

Ng obeys, leaning over to reach behind Brenda and removes the cuffs. Perhaps seeing tears in her eyes, he says, "Okay. You can cry and stuff like the rest of them, but it won't do you no good. We are pretty, ha, cold-hearted, so to speak.''

(These words, "the rest of them,'' would eventually haunt Charles Ng.)

Lake cuts in. "Frankly, I'm as hot as they come. Did you take the cuffs off of her?''

Ng answers in the affirmative and addresses Brenda. "I'll get my weapon handy in case you try to play stupid.''

Brenda, probably sensing the serious danger she faces, and deciding to play along with the menacing pair of men, says, "I ain't going to play stupid. I don't want to get killed, you know."

Ng chirps, "Yeah, that's [good]."

Lake snaps an order. "Stand up, Brenda." She seems to hesitate, and he loudly repeats, "Stand up."

She complains again about the heat from the lamp and groans that she is feeling sick. Lake growls, "Suffer." Out of camera range, he holds something up, presumably a whip. "See this, Brenda. I'm only going to show it to you once."

"What are you going to do, beat me?"

"It's a very vicious . . . as a matter of fact, I just might. But, if you do exactly as you're told, without any fuss, no. Now what's it going to be, full cooperation? Are you ready for your shower, kid?"

Ng replies, "Yeah."

Probably referring to her jeans and underwear, Lake says, "Take them off and run her in."

In a fearful, birdlike voice, Brenda asks, "I'm going to take a shower?"

"Uh-huh," Lake says.

Ng adds, "Clean you up."

Lake continues, "Actually, you're both going to take a shower."

Ng, his voice more enthused than before, says, "Yep. I always do that. It's luckier."

In a patronizing tone, Lake explains, "See, Charlie owes me one, so, uh, I get you first. But he's got his heart set on taking a shower with you, so who am I to turn him down?"

Ng inquires of Brenda, "You want to take a shower with the leg irons or . . . ?"

Lake commands, "No, take them off."

"Okay." He kneels to remove the ankle chains. She

looks down and covers her face momentarily with her hands, as if hoping to wake up from this nightmare.

"I think she believes us," Lake comments. "You better believe us, Brenda, or you'll be dead."

"Right," Ng agrees.

Harshness grating in his voice, Lake gives Brenda an order, "Take your jeans off. In fact, take your panties off, too, while you're at it."

Eagerly, Ng says to her, "Why don't you do it yourself, while I do mine?"

Lake, menacing again, repeats the command. "Stand up and take your jeans off, Brenda."

She rises unsteadily, looks to her right at a rattan couch with floral-patterned cushions, mostly covered by a blanket striped in muted colors. Heavy dark-green drapery covers a window behind the couch. Brenda pleads, "Can I do it over there? That light is . . ."

"Right there," snaps Lake. Ng echoes him.

"I'm getting dizzy," Brenda appeals.

"I don't care. Do what you're told."

"I'll pass out. I'm afraid. I'm real dizzy."

Ng demands, "If you don't do it, I'll do it for you, so. . . ."

Brenda's voice is shaky. She is possibly stalling for time. "Well, wait till I'm not dizzy anymore."

Ng shows a touch of patience. "Okay. I'll give you a few seconds."

Lake makes an offer. "Actually, Charlie, I can move the camera over to the couch. Move over to the couch, Brenda. That's away from the heat."

She complies, shuffling the few steps to the couch. Ng orders her to sit, and she obeys, saying, "Yeah, I feel shaky and real dizzy." She gulps air and adds, "I'm going to pass out. I guess that light or something. . . ."

Ng tells her, "Well, you can pass out, but we're going to wake you up."

Impatiently, Lake snarls, "Brenda, I have a lot of animosity against you, and I would just as soon start you out with a nice firm whipping right now to make you believe how serious we are."

Ng backs him up. "This thing would hurt, believe me."

Lake asks, "How would you know?" The comment draws a brief chuckle from Ng.

Lake, apparently growing weary of her resistance, orders her to stand. "Slide them down," he orders. "And then sit down."

Brenda rises, and tries again to delay the inevitable. "I'm just—just too dizzy."

"Slide them down. All right. Charlie. . . ."

Lake apparently leaves the camcorder on a tripod and finally appears on the screen, holding a handgun equipped with a silencer. He has a dark, full beard and a bald pate reflecting light. The menacing weapon startles Brenda causing her to raise her hands, palms toward the barrel, and drop into a sitting position.

Ng looks at Brenda. "Yeah, that could be the truth, uh. Yep. Sure. Her lip's turning pale."

Lake's voice is skeptical. "Her lips are pale anyway. You got the, uh. . . . ?"

Ng asks Brenda, "Feeling better? You want some water?" Lake mutters under his breath.

"I'll take something to drink," Brenda says. "I've been sick all day. Real bad." She appears to reach for a cigarette on the table.

Lake warns, "You know, you don't want to smoke that. Did you give up smoking?"

"No."

"You have now," Lake admonishes. As she seems

ready to throw up, Lake warns, "[if] You do it, you clean it up."

Brenda's voice is trembling. "Well—" She groans inaudible words, then whispers, "Dizzy and sweaty. Hot. Shaky." Lake finally agrees that the room is very hot and asks Ng to turn on a different light in the kitchen, while he's in there getting ice water for Brenda. Ng returns carrying a glass, hands it to her, then strips to his undershorts. The microphone picks up the tinkling sound of ice as she drinks. She complains, "God, my ears. I keep hearing 'shhh' . . ."

Lake moves to the couch and plops down on Brenda's left side. He starts to fondle her breasts. In what appears to be a reference to her figure, he asks Ng, "Now tell me, isn't she a little better than Kathi?"

Ng replies, "Sort of. Maybe a little—basically the same."

Lake disagrees, "No, Kathi's was . . ." His voice trails off, then rises. "She just had a baby. She looks okay." (Note: Lake was wrong. Lonnie Bond Jr. was born on April 5, 1984, so it had been one full year since Brenda had given birth.)

Ng speculates that Brenda was probably a little younger than Kathi, but Lake corrected him. "No. She's a year older."

Brenda complains again about her dizziness. "All I can hear is the 'shhh' in the top of my head." Ng asks if she wants some aspirin, but she declines the offer. "I've been feeling like this the last couple of days. I don't know why. Like I'm pregnant or something."

Ng speaks up quickly. "Not the right time for that kind of shit."

"I don't want to have this baby," Brenda says.

Ng steps aside and picks up what appears to be a stun gun.

Investigators watching the tape recalled that a stun gun had been found in Cosner's Honda.

"Well," says Ng, in muddled rhetoric. "We told you what's going to happen to the baby. Just don't ask us or else it'll be history. So I don't want to hear nothing about it. It will be taken care of. . . ."

Brenda's emotions show as she decides to cooperate. "Give my baby to me. I'll do anything you want if you—"

Lake breaks his silence to interrupt her. "You're going to do anything we want anyway, and we don't want to have a dirty house around with the baby."

Choking, Brenda cries, "He can't live without me."

"He's gonna learn," Lake asserts. "Come on, stand up. Jeans off. Panties off and everything else. Shove them down." To Ng, he commands, "Watch that she doesn't fall over in the shower and split her head."

Ng concurs. "Oh yeah, yeah, I won't."

Brenda gives up at last, unzips her jeans, and removes them. With obvious reluctance, she also slides her underpants down, and stands naked before the two men. Feebly protesting once more, she says, "I don't need to take a shower. I just took a shower."

Like a petulant child, Lake retorts, "You do, too."

Ng says, "Both of us are going to make sure you're clean before we fuck you. That's the house rule."

Lake agrees, "Traditional." He takes her hand and leads her out of camera range. Ng walks out, too. Only their voices can be heard.

Ng volunteers, "Let me make sure there's towels and all that other shit."

Lake says, "Give me your hand, Brenda. Give me your hand."

She replies, "I don't—" And her voice fades.

Lake addresses Ng. "Take good care of her, Charlie.

Charlie, see if you can not get her hair wet. Just wash her body . . . Not that you have to worry about it."

Ng says, *"You have to worry about it."*

Brenda's voice can be heard, but her words are unintelligible. Lake says, *"I don't know. Maybe he does, for all I know. I don't care."*

Ng complains, *". . . wrong with this showerhead. It pisses me off."*

Again, Brenda speaks, but her words are garbled.

Ng growls, *"Okay, okay."*

Lake patronizingly says, *"Take care of her now, Charlie . . . make sure she brushes her teeth and uses mouthwash."*

Ng sounds irritated. *"What the fuck's wrong with this shower? Taking a shower . . ."*

The picture ends; the voices terminate; the screen turns snowy.

A hushed group of investigators sat, stunned and sick. They had witnessed two young women enduring a nightmare, and two men playing God with their lives. One by one, the officers filed outside to take a breath of fresh mountain air.

In a San Francisco hospital, Leonard Lake lay in a comatose state, being kept alive by life-support systems. The search for Charles Ng grew in intensity with each passing hour.

* * *

As darkness settled in over Wilseyville, the brass closed operations for the day, posting deputies to keep the Balazs property secure.

Irene Brunn and Tom Eisenmann drove back down to San Andreas to the Black Bart Hotel. They were pleasantly surprised to see that their chief had arranged for bags to be packed at their homes and sent to the inn.

Chapter 21

The long days of June can bring scorching temperatures to Calaveras County. Investigators at the Balazs house near Wilseyville sweated under a boiling sun on Wednesday, June 5, as they split the property into carefully measured sectors. Detective Larry Copland kept meticulously detailed notes recording everything the team picked up, tagged, and bagged.

Tom Eisenmann towed a mobile office from San Andreas to be used as field headquarters. Deputies set up large tables to use for sorting and identifying evidence. Initially, it appeared that the process might take a few days. Instead, it would tediously drag into weeks, and then months.

Along one side of the house, a 160-foot trench that had been dug to bury telephone wire had been freshly covered. A second trench, partially filled in, ran near the bunker. Several other areas showed signs of recent digging. On six different plots of ground, the searchers found blackened soil that signaled the sites of hot fires. The spots had been carefully raked, and all surface debris had been removed. The trenches and burn sites seemed to offer the best potential as locations to start excavating for evidence related to the missing persons.

Sheriff Ballard brought in specially trained search and rescue dogs to take advantage of their extraordinary olfactory sense. Dogs can often sniff out evidence that escape all human abilities. It turned out that one of the canines made the first discovery that set off alarms of multiple murders. During a rest break, the curious dog walked a short distance away and returned carrying a bone between its teeth. Close examination revealed remnants of flesh still clinging to the bone. A pathologist would declare the grisly find to be human remains.

Not far from the bunker and its secret chamber, a sheriff's deputy, who had arrived to help, walked around the property with Tom Eisenmann. The two men spotted a four-foot by eight-foot section of plywood on the ground, partially obscured by a scattering of the iron-rich red dirt common to the region. Both men noticed ants crawling out from under the edge of the wood, carrying what appeared to be tiny pieces of white gravel. The deputy, knowledgeable about all kinds of flora, fauna, and country creatures, said, "You know what we're looking at, don't you? Those little white things are maggot larvae. That means there's dead flesh under there."

By sifting the dirt removed from under the plywood, and various other digging sites, the searchers turned up more bone fragments, including a section of a human spine, and bits of human teeth.

Dr. Boyd Stephens, chief medical examiner for the city and county of San Francisco, joined the task force on Wednesday. He would report that "hundreds" of bone fragments found in the telephone trench had been subjected to cremation. Thus, the reason for six burn sites on the grounds became clear. Eventually "thousands" of bone pieces were gathered from the entire property. A few of them measured from one to two inches in width or length, but most of them were no bigger than a fraction of an inch. Over the next few days, the doctor's toil would escalate into staggering proportions. The work performed by Stephens impressed all of the police personnel, including Irene Brunn. She would one day remark that Stephens had done a wonderful job with his excellent control of the crime scene. She also complimented the Calaveras County cops as "first-class investigators. They didn't miss anything."

On the third day of the search at Wilseyville, the investigators heard the expected news from San Francisco. Leonard Thomas Lake had died from cyanide poisoning. The militaristic survivalist, who had served in the U.S. Marines, who had always linked himself with weapons of war, conducted warlike "operations," and even wore military clothing, had lost his personal war. He had been born a few weeks after the end of WWII, and had died on the anniversary of the most important invasion of that war, the storming ashore of allied troops at Normandy, on D-Day, June 6, 1944. For Lake, the war he waged against innocent people, and his battle with life itself, had ended in a dismal suicide. Like the dictators of WWII, in his wake he left carnage that would reverberate for years.

Lake's death would be the first tally on an appallingly long list. The next two entries came from a grisly discovery by men excavating the telephone trench. They exhumed the first decomposing corpse approximately ninety-two feet from the terminus of the trench at the telephone connection box near the house, and the second one 101 feet away. The first body, probably an African-American man, would never be identified. In addition to the ravages of decay caused by being buried for months, the remains had been damaged by animals that had apparently dug into the shallow grave and torn away the feet. The other victim, also African American, wore a three-piece corduroy suit. The whereabouts of Maurice Rock, the music lover who had vanished from the pink palace, had been discovered at last. His billfold, with identification, turned up at another digging site. Tom Eisenmann admired one of the techniques that finally helped identify Rock. It hadn't been easy, due to the ravages of decomposition and the absence of fingerprints or dental records. Determined specialists obtained a photograph of Rock from his family. Then they took a picture of the deceased man's facial remains, which consisted of not much more than a skull. With special projection equipment, they overlaid the two photos, and found a precise match in bone structure and teeth. Thus, Maurice Rock would not be just another John Doe.

Another occupant of the pink palace, Rock's friend Sheryl Okoro, had also vanished at about the same time. Among the photographs discovered in the bunker, Brunn and Eisenmann recognized a picture of Okoro standing on the deck that projected from the back of the Balazs house. In the photo, Sheryl's wrists were locked in handcuffs. Hope by the searchers that her body would turn up gradually faded. Nothing more than a section of leg bone and a piece of neck vertebrae dug from one of the trenches would eventually be proven, by DNA testing, to be the only remains of Sheryl Okoro. The rest of her body would remain missing, permanently.

Now that the case had unequivocally turned into a homicide investigation, Irene Brunn and Tom Eisenmann's duties as missing persons experts had concluded. Homicide detectives would take over in their places. Eisenmann had spent five days on the gruesome property, while Brunn had stayed a full week. They would both remain irrevocably linked to the case, and would continue to help out in any way they could. Eisenmann drove the unmarked car back to the city, while Brunn found a vacant seat aboard a police helicopter for the return trip.

Days of digging still faced the sweating searchers. Probing the red earth with the caution of archeologists, they turned up more plastic barrels. Several sealed packages contained hundreds of dollars in coins of all denominations. Two Tupperware containers disgorged rolls of silver dollars along with valuable gold pieces, foreign coins, and jewelry. One of the plastic paint tubs, unearthed near a pumphouse, had held Leonard Lake's journal for 1983 and 1984. Word spread that he'd also recorded 1985 events, but the diary never fell into police hands. Several more sealed drums contained drivers' licenses, Social Security cards, bank cards, checkbooks, and other identification documents belonging to Kathi Allen, Mike Carroll, Randy Jacobson, Paul Cosner, and Jeffrey Gerald. Cosner's cards and papers, along with his glasses, turned up in a rectangular plastic box, dug up on adjacent property near the dirt road entrance. The sun visor to his Honda, as well as the license plates, were recovered from the telephone trench. A bullet had pierced the sun visor, which would lead to a theory that Cosner had been shot by someone riding in the backseat of the Honda, possibly Lake or Ng.

The death toll increased with the unearthing of a third decaying male body, exhumed near a chicken coop. He, too, was from the Haight district of San Francisco. Randy Jacobson, the guitar-playing Vietnam veteran, who had sought solace in marijuana, had vanished from the pink palace in June 1984. The medical examiner found that his body ''was totally encased in lime,'' and that he had ingested cyanide, Leonard Lake's poison of choice.

With the knowledge that two babies, Sean Dubs and Lonnie Bond Jr., were among the missing persons, the searchers dreaded finding their tiny bodies. But no verifiable traces of the two were found. A charred piece of a human liver that turned up would create controversial arguments, and would be questioned in considerable detail. The medical examiner concluded that the organ came from a child, but couldn't conclusively establish the victim's age. Eventually, the tissue would be examined by other experts who stated with a reasonable amount of certainty that it came from a child at least three to seven years of age. It raised the chilling specter that more than two children may have perished in the hellish scenario unfolding at Wilseyville.

Another discovery caused a new round of speculation. The diggers found a pair of handcuffs that had been severely scorched by fire. Why, they asked, would anyone burn handcuffs? The only logical explanation, some decided, was that the manacles had been on the wrists of a yet undiscovered victim who was cremated.

Two more videotapes also caused consternation. When Larry Copland popped one of them, labeled "Taboo," into a VCR, it at first appeared to be nothing more than a taped movie. But when he rewound it, a split-second flash of something obviously unrelated to the movie appeared in the first few seconds of the tape. He played it again, but the vision didn't show up. Copland discovered that the image would only appear, very briefly, in the rewind mode. By experimenting, he was able to manipulate the machine, enabling him to eventually capture a still picture of the scene. In it, two stiff bodies partially wrapped in plastic and in sleeping bags, seemingly in full rigor mortis, appear to be on a blue wheelbarrow. Copland had seen a blue wheelbarrow near the bunker.

A plethora of assorted items became part of the gruesome inventory. Diggers in the telephone trench wiped dirt away from a metal nameplate that belonged to a Suzuki motorcycle. They also uncovered a camera, which contained a roll of film. When it was later developed, three photographs of buildings near a San Francisco apartment on O'Farrell Street, where Jeffrey Gerald had once lived, made it obvious who had owned the camera. The guitar in the house had also belonged to Gerald, as did the jacket found in the Honda. A receipt from a video store contained Harvey Dubs's name. Decorative oak-framed mirrors were from Cliff Peranteau's apartment, as were a Buddha figurine, candlestick holders, a pair of ceramic fish, a small personalized Pennsylvania license plate that read "CINDY,"

and a sweater that had belonged to Cliff. The Olympia typewriter would be matched to several letters received by families
and friends of the missing people. Cutoff jeans, exactly like
the ones Kathi Allen wore in a segment of the "M-Ladies"
video, were found in the house. Shirts embroidered with
"Guardian Angels" and "Scott" were found in the trench. One
buried container hid nearly two dozen baggies of marijuana.

Within the first week, three bodies had been found, one
unidentified. Maurice Rock, and Randy Jacobson, along with
a couple of bones that belonged to Sheryl Okoro, confirmed
the deaths of three of the known missing people who had
crossed Leonard Lake's path. Eventually, Calaveras County
DA John Martin would announce that tooth fragments had
been matched by dental records to Kathleen Allen and Brenda
O'Connor.

The bodies or whereabouts of at least ten missing people
who had been in the destructive path of Leonard Lake remained
in question.

Two of them turned up on Monday, July 8, over one month
after the digging had started. Detective Larry Copland, while
patrolling less than a mile from the Balazs house, noticed signs
of freshly turned earth next to Blue Mountain Road near an
intersection with Schaads Road. He and Steve Matthews noticed
shreds of cloth and tufts of other material scattered on the
ground off the road's shoulder. Closer scrutiny revealed several
shards of bone that animals, probably coyotes, had dug out of
the loose red dirt. Copland thought the tufts looked like stuffing
from a sleeping bag. The officers photographed their find,
secured the perimeter with yellow crime-scene tape, and summoned Dr Stephens.

Under the medical examiner's direction, workers painstak-
ingly scooped and brushed away the dirt, and disinterred two
bodies, both encased in sleeping bags, buried one atop the other.
Using extreme care, they lifted the two bundles from their

graves, and laid them out for initial examination. Duct tape had been used to encircle both bags, and to seal the open ends.

Dr. Stephens ordered the grim bundles removed to a lab where the thick shrouds could be removed under clinical conditions. After the bodies had been taken from the sleeping bags, Larry Copland recognized the grim bundles. He was certain he had seen them before in a half-second scene at the beginning of a videotape titled "Taboo." They had been loaded onto a blue wheelbarrow while still in full rigor mortis.

First, Dr Stephens unveiled the body of Lonnie Bond. He had been placed in the charnel bag headfirst, fully clothed except for shoes. A plastic bag had been wrapped around the head. Handcuffs encircled his wrists, and a rope ligature bound the ankles together. A ball gag, made by threading a leather thong through a two-inch red rubber ball, had been jammed into his mouth and securely knotted behind his neck. Dr. Stephens discovered that the cause of death was a bullet wound to the head. The slug had entered the left side of the skull, above and behind the ear, traversed toward the right, in a downward and forward path, and had never exited. "Animal activity," as the doctor said, "had taken some of the tissue and material from the area of the right upper extremity and shoulder." The handcuff on his left wrist encircled only fleshless bone.

Scott Stapley's body, taken from an olive-green sleeping bag, also had been buried fully clothed but barefoot. Plastic trash bags wrapped his upper torso, while a smaller white bag encased his head. Gray duct tape bound his wrists behind the back, and strapped his ankles together. He, too, had been silenced with a ball gag before being shot to death. His killer had fired three bullets into Stapley's body and mouth. One slug had smashed through his upper teeth and destroyed the maxilla bone below his cheek. Pieces of the bullet, along with fragments of his teeth, had been forced down his throat, tearing into the vocal cords. Another bullet had penetrated the right side of his forehead, just above the eyebrow, and remained inside the skull.

The third slug had entered through the clavicle and taken a downward path, fracturing three ribs.

The search continued at Wilseyville, but no more bodies turned up during the sizzling summer. Experts would estimate that the remains discovered in and around the property near Wilseyville, counting the five bodies actually found, the scant remains of Sheryl Okoro, and forty-five pounds of bone fragments, probably represented at least twenty-five dead victims.

Just prior to the discovery of the two bodies that were the remains of Lonnie Bond and Scott Stapley, a news report circulated among the task force, rippling with the ferocity of a summer thunderstorm.

Charles Ng had been apprehended in Calgary, Canada!

Chapter 22

According to Charles Ng's own account of his escape from the lumberyard in San Francisco, he simply walked away to avoid arrest, and contacted Cricket. "I told her what happened, that Leonard might be busted at the south city lumberyard for shoplifting, and asked her to drive me down there to check on him and see if he was okay. We jumped in her car and drove to the lumberyard." Ng said he ducked down in the backseat while Cricket cruised slowly past the store.

In Ng's subsequent account, Cricket could see Lake standing near a police cruiser, drinking from a bottle of soda. She said, "Shit. Leonard got—there's cops." Because police were present, she feared stopping, and drove away. Cricket finally dropped Ng off at a bus station. From there, Ng called his aunt and announced that he planned to take a vacation. Complaining that he hadn't yet received an overdue check from his employer, he asked to borrow some money. His aunt picked him up, gave him $400, and drove him to his apartment on Lenox Way. While she waited outside, he called the owner of Dennis Moving and said that a pal in Hawaii had committed suicide. He needed time off, he said, to visit his late buddy's family in the Islands. After he'd packed a suitcase, his aunt drove him to San Francisco International airport. En route, he mailed a package, which, he acknowledged, "might have" contained guns.

Ng bought a ticket on American Airlines to Chicago. In his account of the events, he couldn't recall whether he had used his own name, or the phony identification he'd been using, Mike Kimoto.

In Chicago, Ng said, he stayed part of the time at a friend's home where he received the package he'd mailed to himself. Later media stories reported that the friend was another former U.S. Marine that Ng had known during his incarceration at Leavenworth. Ng allegedly spent four other nights at the Chateau Hotel in Chicago under the name of Mike Kimoto, until his buddy gave him a ride to Detroit, where Ng crossed the border into Canada. From there, he made his way west to Calgary, where one of his sisters lived.

By the first week of July 1985, Charles Ng had been targeted in an international manhunt by the FBI, Interpol, Scotland Yard, and the Royal Canadian Mounted Police (RCMP). The law enforcement community knew he had relatives in Hong Kong, England, and Canada, so suspicions ran high that he might flee to any of those countries. Even though the dragnet alerted Calgary police to be on the lookout, Ng would have had little difficulty blending into the crowds of that city. There are more than 30,000 Asians among Calgary's population of 600,000. Furthermore, the city swarmed with visitors to the world famous Calgary Stampede, an annual celebration featuring a Wild West rodeo, which happened to be in full swing at the time of Ng's arrival.

Ng's family offered no comment about suggestions that he temporarily used his sister's Calgary home for a hideout. He denied it. Within a few days, he had fashioned a primitive lean-to campsite in Fish Creek Park, situated in a small wooded valley that runs through the southern sector of Calgary. A short walk from his squatter's camp would lead to a public-transportation stop.

One afternoon, fourteen-year-old Ronald Finlaison and his buddy, riding bicycles along the creek and exploring the trees, saw Ng's lean-to and dugout. Curious, they approached it and noticed him lying under the tilted plywood shelter. Ng looked at Finlaison, and muttered, "I am tired," and asked the boys to leave. They scurried away and reported the incident to their parents. Police were summoned, and Finlaison met them at the campsite. But Ng wasn't there.

On Saturday, July 6, Sean Patrick Doyle, a forty-six-year-old high-school teacher and part-time security guard, nudged his partner, George Forster, forty-eight, inside a downtown Hudson Bay Company department store. While on the lookout for shoplifters, Doyle had spotted a short Asian man, wearing a T-shirt, blue jeans, and running shoes, acting suspiciously as he slipped a "tin of salmon" into a shopping bag. Telling Forster to take a post behind a hidden two-way mirror, Doyle watched as the looter bagged a two-liter bottle of Pepsi-Cola, then moved around the store adding canned soup, sugar, and other foodstuffs. He slipped several of the items into a blue knapsack. Just as Doyle had figured, the suspect bypassed the cash register, stepped onto an escalator, and headed toward the exit. Doyle signaled Forster, and the two men followed.

A few steps outside, they stopped the shoplifter, informed him he was under arrest, confiscated the bag, and escorted him back into the store. Forster reached for the knapsack, but the suspect protested, "That's mine." When they asked him for identification, he reached into a fanny pack for his "wallet," and jerked out a .22 caliber handgun.

Forster reported, "As soon as I saw he had a gun, I put a choke hold on him. Sean grabbed for his hand . . . gave him a sort of a shoulder block, and the three of us went to the floor."

In Doyle's account, he said, "I tried to put my hand over the trigger guard . . . he was on his back and I was on top of him. He bit me on the wrist twice, trying to make me let go." The gun fired two times. One shot hit nothing, but the second one caught Doyle in the fingers of his left hand. "I felt like I'd been hit with a hammer. A surge of adrenaline rushed through me. I could actually taste it." The angry teacher, who stood about five seven, and weighed no more than 140 pounds, wrestled the gun from the shooter's grip.

At that moment, the Calgary police arrived and took control of the suspect. George Forster recalled, "I have never been as happy in my life to see a pair of dark-blue pants with a red stripe."

A crowd had gathered around, and started applauding. They evidently assumed the melee was a stunt related to the Calgary Stampede. "They thought it was a hell of a show," said Doyle.

Booked on charges of attempted murder, robbery, and possession of a firearm, Charles Ng was taken to the city jail and strip-searched. The officers grimaced when they realized Ng had lost control of his bowels and soiled his shorts. It was reported that "Ng decided to take his own life. Using his soiled underwear, Ng tried to hang himself, but was stopped by guards who took the shorts from him, leaving the suspect naked in the cell . . . depressed, suicidal, and fearful." As a protective measure against self-harm, Ng was given "baby dolls" to wear, a quilted one-piece coverall garment.

Sergeant Dave Haddon, of the Calgary police, with the help of Sergeant Barry Whistlecraft, who would later become chief of police of the Tsuu T'Ima Nation, an Indian reserve on the southwest corner of Calgary, searched Ng's campsite at Fish Creek Park. Among the numerous items they seized were camping equipment, clothing, boots, food, knives, and cooking gear.

They also listed a towel Ng had used for a headband and a 35mm Ricoh camera, serial number 50225954. A trace would soon reveal that the camera had been picked up by Robin Scott Stapley from a San Diego repair shop the previous April. The towel proved to be part of a set stolen from Clifford Peranteau's San Francisco apartment.

In the early afternoon of the day Ng was arrested, at 2:20 P.M., Whistlecraft and another officer informed the prisoner of his rights under the Canadian Charter to silence and to counsel, similar to the familiar Miranda advice given to suspects in the United States. Ng, dressed in green coveralls, sat at a table in one of three chairs crowded into an eight- by six-foot interview room. When asked if he was the Charles Ng being mentioned in the news, he initially stared in silence at the interrogators. Whistlecraft asked the suspect if he knew Leonard Lake, and Ng quietly answered, "Yes." The brief and monosyllabic answers continued.

"How long have you been in Calgary?"

"A few days."

"Where have you been staying?"

"Nowhere."

"Where is nowhere?"

"The street."

Whistlecraft suggested that Ng wasn't being truthful. "No one sleeps on the street in Canada. You look too clean and you are clean shaven." The detective asked if Ng's sister had been hiding him.

"No."

Hoping to elicit more information, Whistlecraft hinted that it might be necessary to arrest Ng's relatives in order to get the answers he needed. Ng didn't take the bait. The interview ended after only five minutes.

In a cursory medical and psychological examination of Ng

that afternoon, a nurse described his condition as "depressed." She recommended that he remain under constant observation, noting that he could be "highly suicidal," and that he had "vowed never to be taken alive."

In San Francisco and Calaveras County, officials expedited the dispatch of detectives to Calgary, hoping that Ng might provide information helpful in clearing up the horrific mysteries clouding Wilseyville. Just as Norm Varain had been involved from the first day, Ed Erdelatz, of the SFPD, had also been working on the homicide cases since Lake's arrest the previous month.

By Sunday afternoon, the two California detectives faced Ng in the same tiny cubicle and recited the Miranda rights. According to a later defense report, Ng stated that he didn't want to say anything. But a short time later, he spoke to the detectives for nearly four hours. Ng refused permission to record the conversation, so the detectives took handwritten notes.

Both Erdelatz and Varain organized their notes of the interview into categories headed by victims' names. Regarding Paul Cosner, Erdelatz wrote, "Ng initially stated that Lake told him he'd bought the Honda from some guy and had to install new seat covers. At a later point in the interview, he stated that Lake shot Cosner in the Honda." According to Ng, Lake had admitted reaching to the rear seat, grabbing the gun, and firing into the back of the victim's head. Ng claimed that he'd waited on a street corner, and that when Lake arrived to pick him up, Cosner's dead body was in the passenger seat. Lake, as Ng recalled, said the first shot had missed the victim and hit the sun visor. Ng allegedly admitted helping Lake stow the body in the car's trunk.

Lake, Ng reported, then drove to Cosner's apartment, where he stole two guns, but had left abruptly without taking anything else because a ringing phone had "scared him." Following the long drive to Wilseyville, Ng said, they had buried Cosner during a rainstorm at night, in a previously dug hole approximately one mile from the cabin. Lake, he said, spoke of plans to return to the burial site to better conceal it.

Regarding the disappearance of Harvey, Deborah, and little Sean Dubs, Ng claimed that Lake had said, "Don't ask me about what happened to the Dubs family." However, Ng said, Lake admitted that he'd been inside their house before the trio vanished. It was "something about taping a wedding." Ng claimed he had refused to be involved because of the baby. Then, Ng said, Lake divulged that he'd returned to the apartment, pulled a gun, and "handcuffed the father." Lake had forced Harvey Dubs to ingest strong sleeping pills, waited until dark, then herded them into a van, with "the mother" carrying the baby. Lake had misled them into believing they would be released after he'd obtained money with their credit card. But, Ng said, Lake had strangled both the mother and the father and buried them in already dug holes. Ng claimed ignorance about the baby's fate. Soon afterward, he said, they both went to the apartment, and he waited in the car while Lake entered the apartment by using a duplicate key. Lake packed seabags with Dubs's property, and left them by the door. Ng admitted retrieving the bags, after which he and Lake took them to Ng's apartment on Lenox Way. The contents, he said, included videotapes, a VCR, a camera, and clothing.

Later, Ng stated, he, Lake, and Cricket had used the victim's credit card to purchase a meal at Benihana's, with Cricket signing the transaction slip. Another meal, this time of Chinese food, was also paid for with the card.

Ng's comments about Charles Gunnar and Donald Giuletti were extremely brief. He knew nothing of the Giuletti killing, he said. The only thing he'd heard from Lake about Gunnar came on the day Ng returned to California from Leavenworth.

Lake, he stated, had said, "Charles Gunnar is no longer with us. Don't ask."

In the matter of Ng's missing coworkers, Jeff Gerald and Cliff Peranteau, Ng certainly couldn't deny knowing them, but asserted that they had simply failed to show up at work. He admitted a desire to move past both men in seniority on the job, and said that Lake had suggested a way to achieve it. "It should be like 'Nam," Lake had allegedly said. In order to move up on the list, Ng should simply lure both men into the country to be killed. Ng then acknowledged offering opportunities to Gerald and Peranteau to be paid for helping his friend move. When Peranteau came to Wilseyville, Ng said, Lake shot him in the head, burned his body, and put the bones in a bucket to spread around the property. Ng disavowed knowing anything about Jeff Gerald's disappearance.

Regarding Michael Carroll and Kathleen Allen, Ng said that he didn't wish to say when he first saw Kathi, but the last time he'd seen her, she was alive in Wilseyville. Lake, he said, had driven him to the Greyhound bus station. Lake later allegedly told Ng that he'd "taken Kathi for a walk," and had returned alone. Ng acknowledged knowing Mike Carroll in prison, and claimed that Mike had admitted to Lake that he "always cheated on Kathi." Mike and Ng were to meet in San Francisco in February, but, Ng asserted, he had no idea what had happened to him. Once more, Ng refused to comment on Kathi Allen.

Ng said nothing about Brenda O'Connor but made a horrifying assertion about her child, Lonnie Bond Jr. Lake, he said, had strangled the child, and had admitted to "putting the baby's head between his thighs and twisting the upper body." Ng confessed to telling Lake, "If you want to kill the baby, make sure [he] doesn't suffer."

The pink palace, Ng knew, was the home of Randy Jacobson, Maurice Rock, and Sheryl Okoro. Lake had used people from the apartment building as laborers in Wilseyville. Erdelatz wrote, "He thinks that Lake killed them but Lake said that he didn't need Ng's assistance. When talking about killing, Ng told Lake, 'I need a good reason or a lot of money.' '' Lake, Ng stated, talked about killing people by handcuffing them and giving them chloroform. Yes, Ng said, he had opened post office boxes in San Jose and the little town of Pioneer in order to receive Randy Jacobson's checks. He claimed that he had never seen Rock or Okoro, and couldn't recognize photographs of them.

Ng came right to the point regarding Lonnie Bond and Scott Stapley. He stated that Lake shot both men in Bond's cabin while Brenda was out shopping. Ng admitted helping Lake drag the bodies out and hiding them temporarily under Lake's porch. Lake, he said, planned to burn the bodies.

Erdelatz also queried Ng about a young woman who had been shot to death in Hawaii, at a car rental agency on the military base. But Ng denied knowing anything about it. Regarding a rape case in December 1981, Ng said he didn't want to talk about it.

The questioning ended.

Erdelatz and Varain wanted to get Ng's words on tape, so they met with him again while he ate dinner. After repeating the Miranda advice, with a recorder running, Erdelatz said, "Now, when we originally came in here and spoke with you several hours ago ... you indicated that an attorney had come here and suggested to you that you not talk to the police. Is that right?" Ng said it was. Erdelatz did his best to persuade Ng to speak again and allow the conversation to be recorded.

Ng refused. "You might try to be good to me to coerce me," he said.

To make certain no misinterpretation of Ng's comment would occur, Erdelatz said, "Well, let me ask you this. Has anybody ... in any way ... mistreated you?"

"No," Ng said, but added, "I just kind of feel ... I don't want to talk."

Taking one last shot, Erdelatz asked, "Okay, if I were to

read to you the information that we wrote down earlier, if we have something down that is incorrect, would you tell us that it's wrong?''

Ng shook his head. Two lawyers, he said, were on their way to visit him and would arrive shortly. ''I want to have a lawyer before I say anything else.''

Both detectives left, feeling frustrated. They knew that anything they'd heard Ng say would probably never be allowed as evidence in court. Furthermore, Charles Ng hadn't admitted actually killing anyone. Leonard Lake, according to Ng, had conceived and carried out all of the plans that had led to several deaths. The only one who had done any killing, in Ng's version, was Leonard Lake.

Of course, another huge obstacle stood in the way of Charles Ng ever facing trial in the United States. If the detectives had discovered solid evidence pointing to his participation in multiple murders, prosecutors would very likely seek the death penalty. But Canada had abolished capital punishment. In 1976, the United States and Canada had entered into a treaty in which Canada could refuse extradition unless the requesting state pledged not to seek the death penalty.

Ng faced serious charges related to the shoplifting and shooting in the Hudson Bay Company department store, and if convicted, would probably face several years' imprisonment.

But the chances of returning him to California to face trial appeared almost nonexistent.

Chapter 23

The Canada trial of Charles Chitat Ng in the Court of Queen's Bench of Alberta, Calgary, wound down one week before his twenty-fifth birthday. Judge Allen Sulatycky presided. The prosecution and defense had agreed on a trial without jury, in which the judge alone would arrive at a verdict and pronounce the sentence.

Sean Doyle, the teacher-security guard who had suffered a wound to his hand, testified about the scuffle in a Hudson Bay Company department store that culminated in Ng's arrest. A clever job of cross-examination by the defense attorney created the impression that Doyle was not precisely certain of the placement of his hands on Ng's pistol. If the weapon had accidentally discharged as a result of the struggle, then it would be difficult to prove that Ng had intended to shoot or kill anyone.

The defense called no witnesses, and chose not to put the defendant on the stand.

On December 18, 1985, Judge Sulatycky pronounced Ng not guilty of attempted murder. It came as no surprise when the judge said the evidence did not support such charges. But, as Ng stood motionless facing the bench, Judge Sulatycky pronounced him guilty of assault and robbery. The defendant was ordered to spend a minimum of 4½ years behind bars. By early January, he arrived at Edmonton Prison, Alberta Province, nearly 200 miles north of Calgary, and over 300 miles from the U.S. border at Montana.

Officials in the United States optimistically announced the immediate launch of efforts to extradite Ng as soon as possible. California had charged him with kidnapping, false imprisonment, burglary, and unlawful flight. San Francisco and Calaveras County investigators continued probing the cases at Wilseyville to determine the possibility of Ng facing murder charges should Canada ever agree to send him back.

At the Edmonton Prison, corrections personnel placed Ng in protective custody, meaning extremely limited contact with other inmates. However, he did establish a friendship with one man who would become a pivotal figure in his future. Maurice Joseph Laberge occupied the isolation cell adjacent to Ng. The two men also managed brief words in passing during their allotted hour in the exercise yard. Thus, the acquaintance started. Soon, they began exchanging notes by sliding slips of paper under their doors. A gap between the door's bottom and the floor allowed retrieval of the papers by each man.

Laberge soon knew a great deal about Charles Ng. And Ng understood that Laberge was no angel.

Born on February 20, 1952, in Willow Branch, Saskatchewan, Laberge became part of a family that would increase to ten siblings: five boys and five girls. His early medical problems included a bout with rheumatic fever, breathing problems, and an undescended testicle. His parents reportedly provided a loving atmosphere and a normal upbringing, but weren't reluctant to physically punish any of their children who deserved it. Like Ng, Laberge attended a Catholic boarding school, but only for two years. The family moved several times, landing temporarily in Detroit, Michigan, then to Moose Jaw, Saskatchewan Province.

A chronic bed wetter until the age of twelve, Laberge also complained of allergies to dust and smoke. He fared well in school, except for being victimized by bullies. They teased him about his undescended testicle, telling him that he wasn't virile or a complete man. Laberge became so self-conscious about it that he would finally undergo corrective surgery in 1975.

After dropping out of school at eighteen, Laberge drifted from one menial job to another. For a time, he tried door-to-door sales but had little success persuading families to sit for group photographs. He moved on to work as a gas station attendant, gravel truck driver, house plasterer, and laborer.

With his slim, wiry 176 pounds packed on a six-foot frame, Laberge exuded an aura of dangerous power. His dark eyes appeared calm and sleepy under black arched brows. A firm chin, wide mouth held in a self-satisfied smirk, and his quiet self-confidence attracted women who liked to flirt with disaster. He started dating at fifteen and experienced his first heterosexual affair soon afterward. His next girlfriend eventually gave him a daughter, but he married a different woman in 1980. The union lasted a short time.

While still a teenager, Laberge developed a fondness for marijuana and alcohol. He was not a docile drunk. In 1976, after several drinks during a pool game, a dispute erupted and he lost his temper. He swung the pool cue in a wide arc and clubbed one man in the head, nearly severing his ear. Still in a rage, Laberge then grabbed a heavy beer mug by the handle, broke it against the table, and slashed his second adversary's face with the jagged remains, destroying one of the man's eyes. The wild skirmish cost Laberge eighteen months behind bars.

The pattern of misconduct began for Laberge at the age of fourteen when he and a companion broke into Moose Jaw School and smashed a toilet with a sledgehammer. From there, he fell into a habit of illegal activities: assault, breaking and entering, possession of stolen goods, unlawful dwelling in a house, auto theft, and other small-time crimes. A 1968 charge of rape, when he was sixteen, was dropped. Between 1968 and 1981, his rap sheet tallied forty-three convictions for various misdemeanors and felonies. None of these offenses earned Laberge any more than two years in jail. But he pushed the envelope too far in December 1982, in Lethbridge, Alberta Province.

Laberge described what happened. "There was this family, and the father was the manager of a Super Value store. I, along with my accomplice, arrived there on a Saturday afternoon to rob the manager [before] he was going to make a deposit. We arrived a little bit later than we should have, though, because on Saturdays, the money is deposited sooner than on other days. So we followed the manager home when the store closed, [then left] and came back after it got dark to kidnap him, take him back to the store and make him open the safe. My accomplice stayed in the truck. I was dressed in battle fatigues and a balaclava [a knitted woolen cap that covers the head, neck, and top of the shoulders] and got out to make sure the manager was home. It was a very windy night, and a gust blew the gate closed. Two boys ran out of the house. They thought somebody was stealing their garden tools. I confronted them with a revolver, took them to the basement of the house and tied them up with tape. The parents were not at home. One of the boys told me that his mom and dad had went (sic) to the Legion, so I left the fellow who was with me, took the truck, and went to the Legion to see if their car was there. I returned to the house and continued to wait. At about nine o'clock, I carried David [age 15] upstairs to the spare bedroom, pulled his pants down, and sexually assaulted him. I performed fellatio on him, then made him perform fellatio on me. I then left him on the bed with his hands and feet tied. Shortly before eleven P.M., the parents came home. I was waiting in the bedroom. I overpowered them with the revolver, tied them with tape, and took the father out of the house. I put him in the trunk of his car and drove to the Super Value store. I made him open the safe, took the money out, tied him to a candy counter, and left.''

Other reports about the crime revealed additional details. In the course of tying up the two boys, ages nineteen and fifteen, Laberge threatened to shoot them if they refused to cooperate. He overheard them whispering about his physical characteristics, which they were trying to remember so they could later identify him. Again, he threatened to kill them. When he sexually assaulted the younger boy, Laberge also attempted to sodomize him, but failed to make entry. With the boys hog-tied, he waited nearly three hours for the adults to return home, after which he committed the robbery.

After another attempted store heist in Saskatoon, Laberge was arrested. In the trial for the Lethbridge incident, charged with armed robbery, kidnapping, and sexual assault, Laberge took the stand and denied any involvement in the crimes. But the eyewitness testimony of his victims, along with physical evidence, doomed him. He was convicted on November 26, 1982, and sentenced to twenty-five years' imprisonment.

To a thirty-year-old man who had never faced more than a couple of years of confinement, twenty-five years might as well have been a century. He needed a way to ease the hard time, and perhaps shorten it. Laberge decided to become a jailhouse informant.

In January 1986, he met Charles Ng. "Initially, when I arrived at the penitentiary, the only time I saw Charles Ng would be when he was in the exercise yard. I was on one side and he was on the other. We were fairly consistent in going out to the yard even when the weather was cold. . . . About three weeks after we had been exercising this way, I was approached by the head of security. He wanted to know whether or not I would be in favor of being exercised with Mr. Ng. I didn't have a problem with it. It began either the following day or shortly thereafter. It started in March and continued until July of 1986.

"Our cells were side by side, and had adjoining doors which enabled us to reach our arms underneath each other's door if we wanted to. We could pass books back and forth. It was convenient.

"When I first met Charles Ng, he began to tell me bits and pieces about the things that he had done in California . . . a place called Wiseyville (sic). At first, he spoke in very general terms about it. As time went by and we spent more time together, he became very detailed, very candid, and very open about what exactly he had done, and what his role was in those incidents. He began to divulge some of the, what I term, more gruesome aspects of these terrible crimes. When he first started talking to me, I paid no particular attention to what he was saying. I started to keep a record to remember for later on. When we were finished in the exercise yard, I would go upstairs and make notes of what we had talked about."

Laberge learned that Charles Ng possessed a natural talent and skill for drawing. Ng started passing cartoons under the door, many of them relating to the missing and dead victims in the California cases, most of them grossly pornographic. "I would receive cartoon caricatures from Charles, depicting what we had talked about. . . . When I had twelve or fifteen of these pieces of paper, I would seal them in an envelope and send them to my lawyer. I think there were in the neighborhood of maybe one hundred and fifty cartoon caricatures."

According to Laberge, Ng also spoke of the videotaped abuse of two women near Wilseyville, and mentioned being worried about the police seeing it. "I asked him what exactly it was that the police would see on this videotape. It had to do with Kathi Allen and Brenda O'Connor, two girls who Lake and Charles Ng had kept for some time in a cell ... at Lake's acreage. He told me that the tape shows a female complaining that it is too warm and that he had a butterfly knife, he called it, and he flicked it open, and cut her clothes off. ... He told me that he went into the shower—this thing had actually taken quite a bit of time. ... One of the things he did is stopped and made something to eat, made himself some rice and actually came back to eat the rice while Leonard Lake was carrying on with one of those victims ... Kathi Allen."

The relationship between Laberge and Ng even had aspects of offbeat humor. As is customary in prison, men often address one another by colorful nicknames. Laberge said that he had dubbed Ng, "Slant," while Ng referred to him as "Froggy, Uncle, or Grasshopper."

Laberge described three of the graphic cartoons Ng had given him during their comradeship. One, said Laberge, "shows a caricature of a man who is ... Leonard Lake, and he is holding a whip in his right hand and fondling himself with his left hand, saying, 'Oh, I love you Kathy (sic)! I really do!' There is a female, bound hand and foot, on what appears to be a bed or a small table. She is going, 'Oooch!' It shows Charles Ng behind the videotape recorder which is sitting on a tripod, saying, 'Rice is ready! Dinnertime!' "

The second cartoon, said Laberge, "depicts a man who is labeled as Boyd Stevens (sic) who was, I believe, a coroner in California, and a lady ... dressed in mourning, leaving with a small bag with the name Allen on it. She passes underneath a sign that says 'Calaveras County Remains Claiming Station.' Another man ... slightly balding with a mustache ... says, 'And I think this bag is yours.' It's a much larger bag with the name 'Dubs' on it. On the table is another somewhat bigger bag ... and it says 'Bond' on it."

Cartoon number three, picturing the interior of a prison cell, is captioned "San Quentin—Years Later," and is dated July 10, 1986. Laberge said, "This picture depicts a jailhouse mirror, jailhouse toilet, and a spiderweb in a corner. It caricatures a very skinny-looking Slant, or Charles Ng, picking his nose, wearing glasses, and slogans on the wall that say, 'No kill, no thrill'; 'No gun, no fun. . . .' " On the cell wall are childishly crude portraits labeled Carroll, Cosner, Peranteau, Dubs, Gerald, Allen, and Bonds. "We had a talk at length about this, and he had drawn this cartoon, and the purpose was . . . to demonstrate what the future was going to be like for him, once he was extradited to the United States."

Most of the vulgar drawings featured explicit and obscene sexual activities, including rape, bestiality, and a wide range of perverted, deviant carnal behavior.

By the close of July, Laberge said, he began to recognize certain detrimental effects of his relationship with Ng. Having successfully completed a number of correspondence courses while in custody, which drew him close to earning a bachelor of administration degree, Laberge expressed the hope that he might straighten out his life. He'd also reached a goal of becoming computer literate. "In 1983, I started to take a pretty good look at where I was. I was doing a lengthy sentence. Not too many of the things I had tried in life had worked out very well, and I made the decision when I got out that I would be doing other things besides ending up in jail."

These measures, he said, had been recognized by the National Parole Board and had helped him earn an "ironclad" release date in 1989, after which he planned to obtain an advanced degree and enter the business world. The association with Ng, according to Laberge, was not conducive to his goals. "I was applying to be transferred to another institution. There was starting to be what I felt were some negative comments made by staff in relation to me exercising with Mr. Ng." Moreover, he said, "I became very uncomfortable with the fact that Mr.

Ng had told me these things, the gruesome aspects of these horrible crimes. I didn't feel particularly safe being in that exercise yard anymore. So I requested that I be placed back in exercising alone." The association between Laberge and Ng ended, but the far-reaching effects would last a long time.

Soon afterward, Canadian prison authorities transferred Ng to a recently opened prison at Prince Albert in the remote central interior of Saskatchewan Province.

One inmate at Prince Albert formed an impression of Ng distinctly different from that held by Maurice Laberge. Lance Blanchard—a tall, gangling, bearded man, with unusually long arms and huge hands, high cheekbones and a prominent nose—spoke slowly in a rumbling, deep voice. Surprisingly, in contradiction to his rugged, intimidating appearance, Blanchard's words were articulate and reflective of a superior intelligence. His demeanor seemed inconsistent with the violent crimes that brought him to a special segregation unit at the maximum-security prison. Evil, destructive urges had driven him to commit rape and assault with intent to maim, which earned him a sentence of more than thirteen years. Inside the stark walls, Blanchard's inner turbulence erupted again, and he stabbed another prisoner to death during a fight. His sentence was increased to thirty-four years, with the earliest possible parole date pushed out to the year of 2013.

In the same manner that Laberge and Ng had started communicating, so did Ng and Blanchard. They occupied connected cells. Blanchard described it. "I was next door to him. We communicated on the average of eight to ten hours a day. We would write letters back and forth, and also talk." They also passed drawings to one another.

Asked if Ng had affected Blanchard in some particular way, the big convict said, "Very much so. At the start, uh, it was mainly an interest and sharing in martial arts. Over the course of a number of months, we got to talking and he learned more about me and I learned more about him. As a result, he saw what I was looking for. At the time, I explained to him that I was basically filled with a lot of anger and frustration, and I had no way of venting it.'' Blanchard told Ng that before being imprisoned, martial arts had helped him find a measure of internal peace. Ng had the right answers. ''With his life's knowledge,'' Blanchard said, ''he was able to give me a [an interest] in Buddhism, Shinto, and Taoism.'' Ng gave Blanchard a book titled *The Tao Teaching*.

''At first, I just laughed it off.'' But, Blanchard said, he would read verses from the book, and Ng would explain the hidden meanings. ''And, as a result, one of the things he taught me was violence was not the way. He taught me so much about learning to find internal peace. . . . I have no more anger, no more frustration in me. I don't look at people with anger or want to hurt them. I used to just love fighting. Now, I won't fight. I will not harm another human being.''

While attributing his conversion to the teaching of Charles Ng, Blanchard expressed dismay over the treatment he said Ng had endured in prison. ''For example, a number of officers would play around with his food. They would remove portions of his food. Switch it for others. Some days he wouldn't get a shower, or be allowed to clean his cell. Other days, his exercise would be cut short. Or, they would deliberately call him out for an interview five minutes after he got his exercise, and keep him out there, using up his hour.'' In addition to such treatment by guards, said Blanchard, ''we had a number of inmates who would put either urine under his door or excrement. And the guards wouldn't put a stop to it. No other inmate that I know of in the special handling unit in the sixteen years that I was there ever had to endure this. I know that if you take a fraction of what Charles had to endure, any other inmate would've retaliated, either physically or through complaints. And then after a period of time they would've assaulted somebody. Charles refused to do that.''

Blanchard explained Ng's reactions to the treatment involved as "a thing called sitting still and doing nothing. It doesn't mean literally sitting still. What it means is not disrupting the flow of what is around you. That what is gonna happen, happens. You shouldn't intervene. A break in the equilibrium of our surroundings can have catastrophic effects."

Ng, he said, was kept from intermingling with other inmates. Even the interaction with Blanchard took place with the wall between them. But Ng never complained. He just kept quiet, which impressed Blanchard, who wanted to learn how he did it. "I was Canada's longest special handling unit inmate, which was sixteen years." Following the teaching by Ng, Blanchard said, "they saw such remarkable change in my behavior, I was granted permission to come out of the special handling unit. They also said that if I continued on my path that I would be reduced in security quite rapidly. They couldn't believe the change in my behavior." His life had been changed, said Blanchard, and he owed it all to Charles Ng.

Ng did not spend all of his time interacting with Maurice Laberge, Lance Blanchard, and a few other inmates. In the long days, months, and years in the Canadian prison, he spent endless hours studying law, legal cases, methods for filing motions, tactics, and court precedents. He read everything available on the subject. His accumulated knowledge would lead to a series of legal battles that would boggle the minds of attorneys, judges, scholars, and law enforcement personnel.

In October 1988, Ng faced the opening stages of court hearings to determine the issue of his extradition to the United States, where murder charges had been filed against him.

Chapter 24

Royal Canadian Mounted Police constables, dressed in the traditional red coats, black trousers with a yellow stripe, and boots shined to a mirror gloss, guarded Charles Ng in the Court of Queen's Bench, Alberta, in Edmonton. On Monday, October 17, 1988, hearings opened under the watchful eye of Madame Justice Marguerite Trussler to determine if existing evidence supported twenty-five charges against Ng. Trussler's ruling would be a major turning point in the expanding controversy regarding extradition. Already, the case loomed like a nuclear cloud over international borders, and had aroused passionate debate among various activist groups. Amnesty International took an interest, and the United Nations even scrutinized the issues involved. Trussler's ruling would mark the first round in a long fight over the fate of Charles Ng: to extradite him to California where murder charges awaited him, or to keep him in Canada and risk a flood of killers crossing the border to avoid facing death penalty trials.

Among the court spectators sat Sharon Sellitto, forty, and her mother, Virginia Nessley, sixty-eight. It had been nearly four years since Paul Cosner, Sharon's brother, had met someone supposedly interested in buying his bronze-colored Honda Prelude, and had vanished. Sellitto and Nessley had vowed never to stop seeking answers and justice.

The two women had left Calaveras County just a few days earlier, after Sellitto had trekked with a reporter up the dirt driveway where Leonard Lake had lived. Weeds now grew over the filled-in charnel trenches that had concealed plastic buckets full of artifacts belonging to the dead and missing victims. Workmen had long since razed the bunker and its secret cell. Nothing remained but an innocuous scar in the hillside.

Tears misted Sellitto's view. She wanted nothing more than to know what had happened to her brother. Did his body lie buried somewhere under that red earth, within shouting distance of where she stood? She kneeled, picked up a fistful of the iron-rich soil, and tossed it skyward, letting the breeze carry it away.

Before she left Wilseyville, Sharon whispered, "If Paul was up there, I said good-bye."

Sitting in the ornate courtroom, Sellitto and her mother wanted to hear every word, hoping to learn details of what had happened to Paul, but realizing they might be asked to leave at any moment. Justice Trussler had made it clear that significant portions of the hearings might be closed to the public. Virginia Nessley concentrated on trying to catch the eye of Charles Ng, who sat in the prisoner's dock, dressed in drab-green coveralls and tennis shoes. "I'm trying to make him uncomfortable," Nessley explained, "but he won't make eye contact with me. . . . I want him to be made to tell where Paul is buried."

Sellitto, for the first time casting her eyes on the man she vehemently hated, expressed surprise about his benign appearance. She'd expected a monstrous gargoyle. "He's just a creepy little killer. There's nothing special about him." With her feisty knack for turning colorful phrases, and for making her strong emotions clearly evident, Sellitto had already attracted reporters looking for quotes, and would continue to do so for much longer than she or anyone else could anticipate.

In the closed hearings, Justice Trussler heard testimony about the statements Ng had made to SFPD Inspector Ed Erdelatz regarding the dead and missing victims. He'd spoken of Lake's involvement in the crimes, but portrayed himself as nothing more than a bystander whose participation was limited to an appearance in the videotapes and assisting Lake in burying two bodies.

There would be no verdicts by Trussler of guilt or innocence, only a conclusion whether enough evidence existed for Ng to face trial for multiple murders. She would also make a recommendation regarding extradition to Canada's minister of justice who would make the official decision. Ultimately, most experts predicted, the case would be decided by the Canadian Supreme Court, and the process could take several more years. In California, Governor George Deukmejian made an open appeal for Canada to extradite Ng as soon as possible, expressing hope that officials would take into consideration "a decent respect for human rights and for the rights of survivors of Ng's alleged victims."

Two more of those "survivors" traveled from Southern California to Edmonton as the hearing neared conclusion. Lola and Dwight Stapley, the parents of murder victim Robin Scott Stapley, arrived to hear the outcome. They met with representatives of a group calling itself Victims of Violence, a nonprofit organization established in advocacy of crime victims, which had been lobbying for the prompt extradition of Ng. They wanted him out of Canada as much as the Stapleys and Cosner's family wanted him to face trial in California.

Madame Justice Trussler closed the courtroom on November 1 through November 4, and issued a strict gag order applying to everyone participating in the secret hearings. No information could be leaked about a witness who was scheduled to testify, a man who had been put under special protection to guarantee his safety and keep his identity a secret. Maurice Joseph Laberge took the stand to tell all about his encounter with Charles Ng during the time they were in prison together.

Another man in the courtroom witnessed the entire testimony of Laberge, and would later be required to report what he had heard in a different forum. Royal Canadian Mounted Police staff sergeant Raymond Joseph Levesque Munro listened to every word. Nothing he heard surprised him, since he'd been assigned to assist as an investigator for the Canadian government in the extradition proceedings.

Maurice Laberge answered questions with articulate ease. Mr. Bruce McFarlane, the Crown's barrister, first asked Laberge a series of questions about his criminal history. The witness openly acknowledged his habitual pattern of criminal behavior, including the offense for which he was currently imprisoned. Laberge proudly pointed out that he had earned a tentative release date of February 1989, leaving him only a little over two months yet to serve. He didn't know it at the time, but he wouldn't actually be paroled until August 9, 1990.

The next questions led him to describe the details of meeting and befriending Charles Ng in the prison exercise yard, the horrific revelations, and then the approximately 150 cartoons he claimed Ng had drawn. At that point, the barrister asked Laberge to identify Ng. The witness pointed a long finger at the defendant, and said, "Sitting in the blue sweater, in the prisoner's docket, with the glasses on."

In clipped tones, McFarlane said, "Pointing to the accused fugitive for the record, m'lady."

Laberge obligingly described what Ng had told him about the videotaped torture of two young women, and related it to the cartoon depicting Lake flogging a naked, bound female while Ng watches and eats from a bowl of rice. Descriptions of more cartoons followed, with Laberge reciting from memory what Ng had allegedly said about each one.

When Laberge had finished with his testimony, he was hurriedly escorted out through the back way, avoiding curious news-media representatives. His identity would remain a secret for the rest of his life.

Journalist Rick Mofina reported in an article for *Penthouse* magazine that a tightly restricted meeting of eight court principals took place in which Ng offered to plead guilty to all the murder charges in exchange for a life sentence. Each person in attendance signed pledges not to divulge what took place. But, wrote Mofina, California attorney general John Van de Kamp rejected the bargain, saying, "There are some cases that cry out for the death penalty more than others. And from what we know of that case, that certainly looked like the definition of a death penalty case."

On Tuesday, November 29, Justice Trussler announced her decision. Charles Chitat Ng, she said, shall be remanded to the custody of the Canadian penal system until such time as extradition can be carried out. The victims' families listened with mixed emotions. While opening the door to extradition, the justice had ruled that six of the twenty-five charges against Ng were not supported by adequate evidence. One of the dropped counts had charged Ng with being an accessory after the fact in the murder of Paul Cosner.

Sharon Sellitto told reporters, "I'm very happy with the proceedings . . . but the travesty is Paul's murder was not included in the extradition indictments . . . they just threw Paul aside."

While Ng's attorneys announced plans to file an appeal, California officials offered assurances that if Ng was ever returned to face trial, he would be charged with at least twelve counts of murder, including the killing of Paul Cosner.

* * *

The waiting game continued through 1989. In Edmonton, a man who claimed he had known Ng for years contacted newsmedia reporters, and said he'd been silent long enough. Although he wished to keep his identity a secret, he wanted to disclose details of telephone conversations he'd had with Ng before the suspect fled California. Ng had described to him, the informant claimed, how he and Leonard Lake had raped, tortured, and killed several people. Ng, he said, had even asked for advice about the best ways to burn corpses. More chilling yet, Ng had allegedly described how he and Lake had released some of the victims and hunted them down like animals in the mountain forest. In one case, the informant said, "they let him think he was getting away. Ng allegedly laughed and said, 'The dumb bastard walked right into our fucking arms.' He was proud of that. He told me, 'We let him scream and squeal for a while, then we wasted him.' "

Of course, prosecutors took a dim view of the man's statements. Nothing the informant had said could be admitted into a court of law without corroborating evidence.

That same year, another informant stepped forward with an equally jolting story. Ed Popovich, who had been in Leavenworth with Ng, swore in an affidavit that Ng had confessed horrific crimes to him. Popovich said, "After I got out of Leavenworth, Ng would write to me, sometimes twice a week. Then, when he got out, he visited me and showed me a stack of pictures. They were of his friend Leonard Lake, and some kind of a bunker in construction." When Ng went to San Francisco, said Popovich, he "was expecting Lake or Cricket to pick him up at the airport." Ng reportedly called Popovich frequently, referring to his partnership with Lake as the "Brotherhood team," and saying that he and Lake would be selecting targets for money and weapons. "Some time in April, he called me and said he had killed a 'fat cat,' Ng's words for somebody rich. Ng asked me if he could get away with using the guy's credit cards. He said 'they' had transportation now. Ng referred to it as 'we did it,' meaning Lake and himself. He asked me to come to San Francisco and then the team would be complete. Lake, Ng, and I could pull some 'operations.' "

Popovich acknowledged talking with Ng about using lime to dispose of bodies. "We also once discussed the best way to burn bodies.

"I remember him telling me they . . . had snatched a 'boofer,' which is what Ng called a black person. Ng told me he used a Ruger model .22 on him. He told me there was nothing left of the guy. He said Lake had burned the body and that there were just teeth and bones left. He also told me he had done a faggot. That he and Lake had taken the guy to the bunker and wasted him. He said that they tortured his ass."

Once, said Popovich, "Ng told me that he got a 'whore,' meaning a woman, and had taken her up to the bunker and 'wasted her.' He said he had this on videotape, and asked me if I wanted to see it. I never did. He said he had taped a couple of them. Lake had gotten the video equipment from someone that they had wasted, meaning killed. I think he was referring to more than one person. Around this time, Ng stated that he and Lake had roasted a 'sucker.' To Ng, the term 'sucker' meant a baby or child. This is what I understood this term to mean."

Popovich reported that Ng had targeted a coworker. "He referred to [the coworker] as 'slime' and a 'puke,' and he was going to waste him. Ng told me that Lake didn't want to do many of the killings, and that he (Ng) had been doing the majority of the killings." The activities about which Ng spoke, said the informant, were called "operations" by Ng and Lake. "Ng told me that beside burning bodies, they buried some in and around the area of the bunker." Popovich named a fellow Leavenworth inmate who allegedly gave Ng a ride from Chicago to Detroit.

Continuing with his litany of horror, Popovich said, "Ng told me that he had tortured and sexually abused the women they had at the bunker." Popovich stated that Ng had admitted using a knife on one of the female victims, and quoted Ng as saying, "I cut the bitch up, chopped her up." On another victim, "He said he had used a concrete reinforcing rod. I believe that he meant he had beaten her with it. He said he used pliers on one, on her nipples." Popovich thought Ng had videotaped torturing the women. "Ng told me he had anal intercourse with some of the women, as well as sexual intercourse and oral copulation. He said he always 'wasted' them afterward. He said Lake participated with him in this. They were together, and had videotaped some of these activities and would send me a tape."

All of the admissions by Ng, said Popovich, occurred during telephone conversations. "I knew it was Charlie Ng, since I recognized his voice from my past associations with him. Additionally, he would always identify himself by saying, 'Brother, it's me.'

"The last call I received from Ng was in mid-April 1985. This was to ascertain if in fact I was going to come out and join Ng and Lake. I told him I couldn't, although I had vacation time, I didn't have any money. Ng offered to send me money, but never did."

There had been no further contact with Charles Ng, Popovich said.

The remarkable statements by Ed Popovich would never be used as evidence against Charles Ng.

Canadian Minister of Justice Kim Campbell finally signed a warrant for Ng's extradition to the United States to face a murder trial that could result in the death penalty. At last, it seemed that Canada had cracked the barrier preventing such action.

Don MacLeod, Ng's Canadian defense attorney, though, hadn't capitulated. He fought feverishly for months to prevent the extradition, and convinced the Supreme Court of Canada to hear arguments about Campbell's decision.

While the international community watched with deep interest, seven Canadian Supreme Court justices listened to lawyers' presentations, then retired to consider the precedent-setting matter. Dwight and Lola Stapley, sitting near Sharon Sellitto and Virginia Nessley, waited nervously in Ottawa. On September 26, 1991, the justices announced their decision. By a slim 4 to 3 margin they had ruled that Charles Ng could be extradited to California and face trial that might result in a verdict of death.

Within minutes, a phone call came to RCMP officers standing by. They hurried Ng to a waiting aircraft, and hustled him aboard before anyone could change their minds. A few hours later, Charles Ng entered a cell within the cold, foreboding walls of Folsom Prison, a few miles east of California's capital, Sacramento.

Chapter 25

Just two days after his arrival at Folsom prison, armed guards loaded Ng into the back of a van and drove him down the twisting, undulating two-lane Highway 49 to the Calaveras County courthouse in San Andreas. A police vehicle led the way while another one followed. They arrived two hours later at the county seat's government center, a cluster of buildings including the Sheriff's Department and the courthouse. The normally quiet, tranquil center, in preparation for the highly publicized arrival of Ng, resembled a military post prepared for battle. Sharpshooters stood at alert on the courthouse roof, while a battery of sheriff's deputies patrolled the perimeter, complete with guard dogs.

Inside, twelve officers, deputies, and prison guards lined the courtroom walls. Dwight and Lola Stapley, Sharon Sellitto, Virginia Nessley, and Dian Allen, victim Kathleen Allen's sister, waited in the front rows, anxious for the murder arraignment hearings to commence. Allen told a reporter from the *Sacramento Bee,* "I wanted to see what kind of a person would do this."

Sellitto observed, "He's the same cold face I saw up in Edmonton."

Justice Court judge Douglas Mewhinney, tall, slim, and balding, a native of the county, had been the district attorney prior to being appointed to the bench. Months earlier, he had appointed two local attorneys, Thomas Marovich and James Webster, to defend Ng.

The prosecution would be handled jointly by John Martin, Calaveras County District Attorney, and Deputy Attorney General Sharlene Honnaka. The State Attorney General's Office had inherited the duty when Calaveras County petitioned the state to help finance the trial. The number of murder counts would obviously require a protracted trial, which could conceivably bankrupt the tiny, rural county.

District Attorney Martin, originally from Pennsylvania, had followed his father into the law profession. Short, trim, with salt-and-pepper hair, he had earned the respect of his colleagues by an extraordinary command of legal knowledge, and an even-handed approach to its application.

Honnaka, a stocky, solid woman, was recognized as one of the top prosecutors in the Attorney General's Office. Shy and quiet, she dressed conservatively in dark suits, and avoided reporters' incessant questions with the grace of Greta Garbo wishing to be left alone. When a tactless journalist asked Honnaka to reveal her place and date of birth, she smiled and diplomatically replied, "Bette Midler and I were both born in Hawaii before it became a state." Since Hawaii had officially joined the Union as the fiftieth state in August 1959, Honnaka must have passed at least her thirty-second birthday at the time of the arraignment hearings.

* * *

For Charles Ng, the years of studying legal procedures while locked up in Canada had armed him with an arsenal of knowledge he would use to wage an all-out war on the California justice system. A jail guard claimed he'd overheard Ng say, "If you want to delay the system, all you have to do is fire your lawyers." It was a tactic he would use generously. Years earlier, in October 1984, when Ng had been arrested for shoplifting, he'd been represented by San Francisco attorney Garrick Lew. In the early Canadian hearings, Lew and San Francisco deputy public defender Michael Burt had advised Ng, who seemed to like both men.

One of the first issues faced by Judge Mewhinney surfaced when Charles Ng filed a handwritten motion to dismiss court-appointed defense attorneys Marovich and Webster, and replace them with Lew and Burt. Mewhinney denied the motion, but Ng had fired the first salvo in an ongoing battle that would infuriate the tax payers, inflate the staggering court costs, and start a bizarre game of musical chairs that would unseat, reseat, fire, and reinstate a dozen defense attorneys and seven judges. Observers and experts alike would be dumbfounded at Ng's skill in manipulating the system. Over one million felons in the United States sat behind bars in jails and prisons. Many of them had worked every possible angle to find legal loopholes. Yet a thirty-year-old immigrant from Hong Kong would succeed in causing unprecedented delays, disruptions, and legal maneuvers that put all the other jailhouse lawyers to shame.

Several attorneys grimaced when they read newspaper articles in the *Sacramento Bee* and the *Edmonton Journal* reporting that Ng, while imprisoned in Canada, had given a departing inmate a list of seventy-seven people he wanted killed. The inmate, called "Sam," said that many names on the list were law enforcement officials. Ng's motivation, the informant reportedly said, was to delay extradition for three or four years. According to Sam, if the hit list failed, Ng would try to kill a prison guard, which would guarantee twenty-five years in prison, giving him time to plan and implement an escape. The list, the inmate said, was handed to him just before his release. Ng reportedly wanted him to follow the Canadian prosecutor home and kill him. Other names on the list allegedly included informers who had cooperated with officials. According to the information that reporters had dug out, Ng ended his note to Sam with, "Take good care and I'll see you when the time comes. For the meantime, happy hunting."

The already tight security around Ng was cinched up a couple more notches.

Ng also complained about the four-hour ride back and forth between San Andreas and Folsom prison each day. Sitting in a cage enclosed in the back of a van, with no seat belt to prevent his sliding and swaying, he experienced motion sickness during the first few trips and vomited on himself. Also, during breaks in the court sessions, Ng was locked up inside a six- by four- by three-foot steel mesh-wire cage, evoking images of Hannibal Lecter in *The Silence of the Lambs*. Judge Mewhinney understood Ng's complaints, but in view of the circumstances, could find no remedy. The Calaveras courthouse was not equipped with a high-security holding cell for prisoners as notorious as Charles Ng. Folsom had the nearest facilities, so the daily trip, in the judge's opinion, could not be avoided. Nor could the cage. There would have been hell to pay if, after all the uproar to bring Ng back from Canada, careless officials allowed him to escape. It wasn't going to happen on Mewhinney's watch.

The prosecution team, DA John Martin and Deputy AG Sharlene Honnaka, relied on an energetic DA investigator to make certain witnesses were available, to coordinate handling of the evidence, to provide transportation when necessary, and to probe into last-minute questions arising during the proceedings. Mitch Hrdlicka enjoyed every minute of it. He'd been a young sheriff's deputy when the case broke, and had guarded the Wilseyville house several nights. He would always remember the eerie, ghostly feeling around the place.

Hrdlicka and his colleague Larry Copland frequently faced down bikers, dopers, and a variety of thugs. Hrdlicka learned to use his gregarious personality instead of confrontational tactics to calm potentially dangerous suspects. He soon developed a reputation as a decent and fair police officer. DA John Martin tabbed Hrdlicka in 1985 to join his staff as an investigator, and he became embroiled in the Wilseyville case with a host of other detectives. Not only would Hrdlicka be an integral part of the prosecution team, he would also be a source of great comfort to weeping family members of the victims. Lola Stapley soon started calling him, "My big ol' teddy bear."

Each day of the hearings brought new twists and turns, and opportunities for Ng to interact. One of the murder charges against him was for the killing of Donald Giuletti, the gay disc jockey who was shot to death in San Francisco by an Asian man. Giuletti's roommate, who had been wounded in the attack, later identified Charles Ng as the shooter. But the trial in that case would be in San Francisco's jurisdiction, not in Calaveras County. Remarkably, Ng requested to be tried for the Giuletti killing first. Closer scrutiny of his motion made sense. California's capital punishment law requires proof of "special circumstances," one of which is multiple murder. If Ng was convicted of the single killing of Giuletti, it would not result in Ng being sentenced to death. But if Calaveras County convicted him first, then he might be eligible for the death penalty if subsequently found guilty in the San Francisco case.

The issue of Ng selecting the lawyers he wanted slowly wound its way up to the California Supreme Court where, on a 4 to 3 vote, Ng lost his bid for Lew and Burt to defend him. He promptly filed a malpractice suit against his court-appointed defenders, Marovich and Webster. He also forwarded a motion to dismiss the judge, another tactic that escalated to the Supreme Court. Each new action by Ng and his lawyers meant an additional delay. The world waited for the beginning of a preliminary hearing, which determines if enough evidence exists to send the defendant to an actual murder trial. Months rolled by. Frustrated relatives of victims waited—endlessly—spending life savings to attend the interminable court proceedings. To make matters worse, the judge had imposed a gag order, which choked off any sources of information about the case.

A discovery in September 1992 shocked everyone involved in the case. A few of the victims' relatives held out slim hope that the remains of their loved ones would be found and given proper burials. Most other observers had generally assumed that all of the bodies had been located, or that the search had long since been abandoned. More than seven years had passed since the murder spree came to an abrupt end with the suicide of Leonard Lake and the flight to Canada of Charles Ng.

But on September 10, workers at the Wilseyville property removed a concrete slab at the former site of the bunker. When they dug into the earth below, they found skeletal human remains. Dental records matched the bones to Charles Gunnar, Lake's portly friend. Gunnar had been missing since May 1983.

The discovery had no direct effect on the court proceedings related to Charles Ng. At the time Gunnar vanished, Ng was still in prison at Leavenworth so could not be charged with complicity in the victim's death.

The preliminary hearing kicked off on October 6, with Sharlene Honnaka outlining the evidence in each of the twelve charged cases. Defenders Marovich and Webster, despite Ng's malpractice suit against them, argued motions in his favor. They strenuously objected to the continued use of the cage in which Ng was kept during breaks and meals, and appealed the issue to a federal court, but failed to convince the judge.

Sharon Sellitto, Paul Cosner's sister, couldn't repress a feeling of triumph about the preliminary hearing's commencement. "Hallelujah," she announced, beaming at reporters. "We finally get started." About the cage for Ng, she said, "Actually, it may be a little too large and roomy for him."

Lola and Dwight Stapley welcomed the milestone event. Dwight, now retired from his job as a school principal, spoke to the press, saying, "We've got to know. We realize we can't change it, but maybe it will help if we can learn as much as possible. We know it's going to hurt."

Lola added, "To me, not knowing is the worst thing in the world. Maybe what I find out will be just as bad. I have no idea what to expect."

When the videotapes were shown in court, and Judge Mewhinney allowed family members to remain seated in the gallery section, Dian Allen, who was sixteen when her sister Kathi vanished, couldn't watch. "I don't want to see the pain she went through," she stammered, choked by tears. "Hearing about it was bad enough."

On Friday, November 13, 1992, an unlucky day for Charles Ng, Judge Mewhinney, having heard six weeks of evidence presentations, ordered the defendant to stand trial for twelve murders:

Count I	Sean Dubs
Count II	Deborah Dubs
Count III	Harvey Dubs
Count IV	Paul Cosner
Count V	Clifford Peranteau
Count VI	Jeffrey Gerald

Count VII	Michael Carroll
Count VIII	Kathleen Allen
Count IX	Lonnie Bond Sr.
Count X	Robin Scott Stapley
Count XI	Lonnie Bond Jr.
Count XII	Brenda O'Connor

Outside the courtroom, Lola and Dwight held up clenched fists in a symbol of triumph. Said Lola, ''I was thinking, just one step closer to putting him away for my son's murder. It's been eight years.''

Her optimism about being a step closer would soon dim. It would take six more long years of legal wrangling, changing judges, changing defense attorneys, motions, complaints, venue arguments, and other delays before Charles Ng faced a jury that would decide his fate.

Sharon Sellitto called the manifold problems: ''The curse of Ng.''

Chapter 26

The first link in the chain that led Charles Ng's trial to Southern California was forged when retired Orange County Superior Court Judge Donald J. McCartin joined the parade of judges embroiled in the case. McCartin, who had presided over several of the most publicized murder cases in California, reportedly suggested that Orange County's populous contingent of Asian citizens, combined with relatively low media coverage of Ng's case in the southland, might provide a better chance for empaneling an unbiased jury. By April 1994, McCartin had also stepped off the judicial merry-go-round. Judge James Kleaver from Siskiyou County, assigned to select the venue, ruled that the trial would, indeed, be held in Orange County Superior Court.

New defense attorneys were seated, as well. Ng continued to demand that San Franciscans Michael Burt and Garrick Lew represent him, and hoped he had won the issue when James

Webster and Thomas Marovich were bumped from the case. Ng had not only filed a malpractice lawsuit, but had refused to interact with them in preparing a defense over a period of several months. But he failed in his bid to reinstate Burt and Lew. A judge ordered the Public Defender's Office of Orange County to supply three new lawyers. William Kelley would head up the team, supported at the defense table by Lewis Clapp, with James Merwin researching and presenting legal motions. Ng strenuously objected to being assigned lawyers not of his choice, and stated his outrage in a letter to Robert Fitzgerald, the newly assigned Orange County Superior Court judge. Fitzgerald saw merit in the complaint, removed the public defense team in August 1996, and appointed a prestigious local private partnership of lawyers. When Ng changed his mind a week later, and asked for reinstatement of the public defenders, Fitzgerald balked, which generated a new flurry of appeals and motions to higher courts.

Even the attorney general supported Ng's request to put his fate back in the hands of Bill Kelley's public defense team. The 4th District Court of Appeals ruled that Kelley, Clapp and Merwin could take over again, and also ordered the appointment of a new trial judge.

The revolving door of judges finally stopped with Superior Court Judge John J. Ryan firmly applying the brakes. But Ng would soon accuse Kelley, Clapp, and Merwin of failing to properly conduct his defense, and demonstrated his ire by ceasing most of his cooperation with them. He filed several motions, which are called Marsden hearings—from a landmark case— that allowed a defendant to be heard when he wishes to fire his attorney. Marsden became a frequently quoted name in the courtroom of His Honor "Jack" Ryan. The judge even allowed Ng a short-lived attempt to defend himself, but saw the futility and ordered the public defenders to represent him in trial.

Of course, the legal tug-of-war games took huge chunks of time from the calendar. Ryan reluctantly granted delays to resolve the thorny issues, not wishing to give Ng a wedge to upset the ultimate jury verdicts. But a frustrated and restless public, along with victims' relatives, complained bitterly about the abuse of the system. Brent Harrington, administrator for Calaveras County, voiced the disillusionment: "Everyone's disgusted. It just seems a mockery of the process. As a local citizen, we're all appalled how the system seems to work. It's ten years after the crimes, and it doesn't seem we're getting any closer to seeing something happen in court."

Another twist threatened to disrupt the process when Orange County officials declared the local government bankrupt. The state legislature guaranteed financial help with the trial. The case would eventually cost California taxpayers an estimated $20 million.

William Kelley soon realized that he had taken over a monstrosity. His eyes bulged when an overloaded truck delivered the paperwork. The huge vehicle, crammed full of documents, bulging cardboard boxes bursting at the seams, volumes of binders, photographs, transcripts, and investigative reports, carried more than a ton of paper in various states of disorganization and array. Just to sort and file it would take months.

Insiders, who knew anything about the complex case, realized that most of the evidence against Charles Ng was circumstantial. No eyewitnesses, fingerprints, footprints, fibers, smoking guns, or blood evidence directly linked him to any of the known murders, or to the missing victims whose bodies had never been found. The videotapes put him in the same room with Kathi Allen and Brenda O'Connor, and recorded his comments to them, but the tape stopped short of showing any murders. He had worked with Clifford Peranteau and Jeffrey Gerald, but did that prove he helped kill them? By his own admissions, he had assisted Leonard Lake in burying Lonnie Bond and Scott Stapley, but certainly had not confessed to killing them. He'd been in Leavenworth at the same time as Mike Carroll, but the evidentiary link stopped there. A Canadian prison snitch had accused Ng of making self-incriminating statements, but could he be believed? Would a jury be able to say that circumstantial evidence proved beyond a reasonable doubt that Charles Ng was guilty in twelve counts of first-degree murder?

Perhaps, it was suggested in some quarters, that Claralyn "Cricket" Balazs might provide some answers. Leonard Lake's enigmatic journal had broadly hinted of not only Ng's involvement, but that "C" had participated in many of his covert activities. Cricket knew Lake better than anyone, and spent considerable time with him and Ng during the critical months between the time Ng left Leavenworth, and his flight to Canada.

The prosecutors faced a tough choice. Hoping that Balazs could help, they made a crucial and controversial decision that would be discussed endlessly.

In a document signed by Balazs and her attorney, on October 26, 1992, an agreement was reached that the state of California "will expect Witness Balazs to provide full, complete and truthful statements and information, if any, she may have regarding crimes against the victims . . . whenever reasonably requested to do so by the prosecutors and their investigators, and to produce any physical evidence she may have relating to the charges. The State will also expect Witness to provide full, complete and truthful voluntary testimony in any and all court proceedings. . . ."

In return for her cooperation, "the State of California promises full use of immunity, that is, not to use against Witness, any statements, physical evidence, testimony, or evidence derived therefrom . . . even if it relates to crimes other than those for which Witness is granted transactional immunity. In addition, the State of California promises Witness transactional immunity for all crimes . . . including but not limited to murder, conspiracy to commit murder, aiding and abetting murder, theft, and receiving stolen property, relating to the following victims: Sean

Dubs, Deborah Dubs, Harvey Dubs, Paul Cosner, Clifford Peranteau, Jeffrey Gerald, Michael Carroll, Kathleen Allen, Brenda
O'Connor, Lonnie Bond, Lonnie Bond Jr., Charles Gunnar,
Randy Jacobson, Donald Lake, Sheryl Okoro, Maurice Rock,
and Robin Scott Stapley.'' Neither would Balazs be charged
in the murder case of Donald Giuletti.

Another proviso of the agreement stated, ''. . . if Witness
knowingly fails to fulfill any condition, for example if she
provides knowingly untruthful statements or declines to be
polygraphed, or refuses to testify . . . this promise will be null
and void.''

Detective Sergeant Larry Copland, of Calaveras County,
interviewed Cricket extensively in July 1993, with her attorney
sitting beside her. She admitted possessing knowledge of Lake's
plans, but denied any complicity in them. Copland asked about
''Operation Miranda.'' Cricket replied, ''I told him you can't
just steal somebody and hold them like that, and I watched the
movie. . . . This man in the story kidnaps this woman and keeps
her and she eventually dies. Umm, so I told him you just can't
do that. I understood his beliefs about storing away food and
supplies, you know, preparing for Armageddon, but I didn't
go along with having a sex slave.''

About the bunker, Cricket admitted helping finance it by
contributing ''several hundred'' dollars, but said, ''I told him
I didn't like the idea and that I thought he just couldn't snatch
somebody and keep them locked up.'' When Copland inquired
about someone named Debbie, with whom Balazs had argued,
she quickly responded, ''I remember talking with [Lake] once
about snatching Debbie and then having her disappear, and I
think most of the conversation was my—you know—anger
with her and all that.''

''What did you tell Leonard about Debbie? What did he
want done?''

"Something to the effect of—it wouldn't bother me if she were to—to disappear and why didn't he do something."

"That she'd be suitable for the cell?"

"I remember saying something to that effect."

"What happened?"

"I started feeling bad about it, and Debbie started acting nicer toward me to make me—I don't know—regret saying anything about it to Leonard."

"What if she had disappeared?"

"I would have been worried—frightened, concerned, that he actually did something that we had talked about. A lot of times I had conversations with him when we were friendly, to feed his ego or to go along with his fantasies. And even though he was building the bunker, and doing them, I'd never thought he would really carry it out. It was more to me a mental fantasy. I didn't think it would ever happen."

"Back in Philo, you were aware that Ng and Leonard both had a propensity and a fantasy to snatch women and have their way with them? That they poisoned cats up there with cyanide as an experiment?"

Balazs sounded defiant. "So, that doesn't say I murdered anybody."

Another officer in the interrogation room pointed out that they weren't accusing her of murder. "But you're trying to lead us to believe that you didn't know anything about all of this, yet you lay in bed and have—conversations with Leonard. You talk about plans to build this bunker. You talk about little kids at your school. . . ."

"Yeah. So?"

Copland and his partner pressed harder, but Cricket continued her denials. To their reminder of her helping finance the bunker, she snapped, "So, I was stupid. . . . I never thought he would do it, okay?"

"Did that have something to do with your decision to file for divorce?"

"Probably some, yes. I was a fool for staying in contact with him and letting him live on my property. . . . I know that now, but it's a little too late. I was trying to make up for divorcing him and being mean to him and all the fights that we had by letting him live there. I never dreamed that he would turn it into a—a place to hold his captives. And then, as it got further along, I guess it just got out of control."

"Was there a point when you said, 'Wait a minute, I'm in over my head'?"

"Yeah. I remember thinking when he was wanting me to help him solicit people from shopping malls—this is getting out of control. And I thought that I could, by still seeing him and still having sex . . . maybe I could keep him from doing that. . . . But there was nothing I could do, basically."

Asked about her initial statements to a detective about no one living at the Wilseyville property, Balazs said, "In the very beginning . . . I lied and I said I didn't know he was there. That was all to cover my butt so that I was hoping to get out of harboring a fugitive."

With Copland and his partner probing for additional details, Cricket offered tantalizing tidbits, but complained about being unable to sort so much out in her memory. "You have it all on paper, down day by day. And to me, it's all this—this big scramble."

The interview ended without Balazs contributing anything of substantial importance.

Ng's defense attorney Bill Kelley didn't believe that Balazs had been completely candid with the officers. In a formal motion, Kelley wrote, "The defense agrees there was a conspiracy in this case, but that the conspiracy existed between Leonard Lake and his girlfriend, wife, ex-wife/girlfriend, Claralyn Balazs (aka Cricket), not Charles Ng." Kelley offered as proof the statements Lake and Balazs had made in a homemade pornographic videotape.

Even more disturbing, said Kelley, "Cricket knew all about the murder of [Charles] Gunnar. And the circumstantial evidence surrounding his murder clearly implicates her." According to Kelley's motion, Cricket introduced Lake to numerous people as Charles Gunnar, and she had kept Gunnar's possessions, along with property belonging to Sheryl Okoro, which was discovered at her home when the case broke. Noting that Gunnar's body was riddled with bullets from two different guns, Kelley suggested that the victim was probably killed by two shooters.

"After being given immunity, Cricket told the police that she and Lake had conversed on the subject of cutting up Gunnar with a chain saw. She also engaged in forgeries of government checks payable to the children of Charles Gunnar after his murder, and sold stolen items with Lake, posing as Gunnar, at flea markets."

Balazs had turned over her 1985 "Men of USC" calendar to investigators. They were startled to discover that three pages had been torn out: March, April, and May. Several missing victims had vanished during those months. Had there been information on those calendar sheets relating to the victims? No one but Balazs knew the answer, and if she gave any information about the pages, it never became public.

Cricket had helped the police find one of the bodies. Kelley wrote, "Interestingly enough, when the police were searching the Wilseyville property for human remains, Cricket told them to look under the chicken coop. That is where victim Randy Jacobson was found." Ng, Kelley observed, had not been charged with involvement in Jacobson's death.

Kelley concluded the revealing document by noting, "Cricket was deeply involved in sado-masochistic sexual practices, as was Leonard Lake. Her participation in the *Miranda*

Project gave her ready access to the sexual slaves she and Lake intended to capture.''

Cricket Balazs would eventually be subpoenaed to testify at the forthcoming trial. Her appearance would stun observers and the news media.

As a lead defense attorney, Bill Kelley faced battles on two fronts of the judicial war. Most defenders in a capital murder case are able to focus all of their concentration on neutralizing the prosecutors' evidence, with the full, enthusiastic cooperation of their clients. Kelley was besieged not only by the prosecutors, but forced to constantly cope with Ng's recalcitrant behavior, uncooperative attitude, and efforts to fire the defense team.

''That's the first time any of my clients, in seventeen years of practice, have filed a Marsden motion to fire me,'' Kelley lamented. In his career as a public defender, he'd tried more than 100 cases.

Bill Kelley hadn't always wanted to be a lawyer. As a schoolboy in San Diego, where he was born in July 1948, he'd been interested in athletics and art. During his senior year of high school, his family moved to the San Francisco Bay area. Not long after graduating, he decided to join the free-love, flowerpower, transient lifestyle of the 1960s counterculture, and postponed thinking about a career. ''I wasn't ready for college. There was a lot of stuff out there, and I just wanted to find myself. I was a hippie.'' So he walked the streets of the Haight-Ashbury district, crashing at night in an old Victorian house with other soulmates. Thus, years later when Kelley learned of Leonard Lake's sojourn in the district, he had no trouble understanding precisely what Lake was doing, and where he was doing it.

In that wanderlust period, Kelley hitchhiked across the country and through Canada, ''living by my wits'' for nearly three years. ''Then a light went on in my head. I decided I needed a career.'' He enrolled in a fine arts curriculum, at the University of California, San Diego. After obtaining his degree, Kelley barely scraped by as a freelance photographer. A girlfriend suggested he think about a law degree. In an elective law class, he attended a mock trial, and realized that the human drama appealed strongly to him. Kelley dove headfirst into law school at the University of San Diego, and obtained his degree in 1979. He passed the bar exam on his first try.

Following a two-year stint practicing with an indigent services group in Oregon, he moved to Orange County. A short tenure with a private firm left him feeling unfulfilled, so he accepted a position with the Public Defender's Office near the end of 1981. Kelley soon earned a reputation as a tenacious fighter for defendants' rights, and for his willingness to tackle the toughest ''unwinnable'' cases.

Not long after Judge Jack Ryan began presiding over Superior Court trials in 1984, Kelley defended a client in Ryan's court. They became well acquainted professionally, but Kelly's next opportunity to practice before Ryan wouldn't happen until Charles Ng came to trial.

With the passage of time during the interminable delays, personnel in the case changed. Sheriff Claude Ballard of Calaveras County passed away, as did the father of Deborah Dubs. In October 1995, District Attorney John Martin accepted a position as a Superior Court judge in Calaveras County. Peter H. Smith, his successor, worked closely with Sharlene Honnaka to prepare for the eventual trial.

Smith, a native Californian born in February 1961, was two months younger than Charles Ng. His father, the Honorable Jerome A. Smith, practiced law ten years; acted as mayor of Saratoga, a small town west of San Jose; became a state senator; and served sixteen years on the First District Court of Appeals in San Francisco.

In Saratoga High School, Smith was attracted to classmate Sandra Corbett and followed her when she chose to attend San Diego State. He married Sandy in 1985 while attending Santa Clara University. After passing the bar, he entered private practice in San Jose. "I was behind a desk shuffling papers, and it came to me that I wanted to do courtroom work in criminal justice."

Smith toyed with the idea, then approached his father. He asked, "Dad, what do you think?"

The senior Smith offered a suggestion. "If that's what you really want, you'd better get a job in a district attorney's office."

Peter Smith would later say, "I think that was the first time in my life I really followed his advice." District Attorney John Martin, in Calaveras County, needed a deputy, so Smith interviewed for the job and was hired in June 1990.

Calaveras County isn't swarming with murder trials, but one came up the next year for Smith, and it resulted in a conviction. His cases varied widely, from murder to sexual molestation; from felonies to misdemeanors. Then came the appointment to district attorney. In 1996, he tried four big cases, and won all of them. The case of Charles Ng, with its international attention, dwarfed anything Smith had previously experienced. While he looked forward to the big trial, he first faced reelection. In June 1998, the voters demonstrated confidence in their young DA, and extended his job for another four years.

The pending trial in Orange County became even more important when an unfortunate mistake occurred in San Francisco. Authorities there had planned to try Ng for the murder of Donald Guiletti after the southland proceedings. Even though Giuletti's roommate had been wounded by the intruder, he had wavered somewhat on the eyewitness identification. The other primary evidence, bullets collected from the corpse, potentially could be matched with a gun found on Ng. But, in October

1997, embarrassed officials announced that the bullets had been inadvertently destroyed. The district attorney could still take the case to trial after the Orange County verdicts, but the strength of his case had seriously diminished. Victims' families hoped even harder for convictions in the southland.

One of the key elements Peter Smith and Sharlene Honnaka planned to use in Ng's Orange County trial was the in-person testimony of Maurice Laberge, the Canadian prison pal and informant in whom Ng had allegedly confided about the murders, while drawing scores of salacious and damning cartoons. Even though the jury would clearly understand Laberge's background as a jailhouse snitch who might be trading information for favors, the two lawyers felt reasonably confident that his testimony would be accepted as truthful.

It wasn't to be.

On May 19, 1998, a half hour before midnight, Maurice Laberge raced his Cadillac along a dark country road outside Crossfield, a small town north of Calgary. Next to him, on the car seat, he carried $23,800 in cash. The money had been given to him by an administrator of the witness protection program. In the pitch dark, while careening along at high speed, Laberge evidently failed to see a large farm-machinery vehicle ahead of him, lumbering slowly along the narrow road. A catastrophic explosion of steel, rubber, and glass ended in a fiery pile of twisted, bloodstained metal. Maurice Laberge died in a desolate field, his money scattered for yards.

RCMP staff sergeant Raymond Munro, who had worked for years investigating the Charles Ng case, hurried to the scene from over 100 miles away. He arrived in time to see officers complete the task of picking up Laberge's last payment. Considering the dead man's reputation as a prison informant, Munro would probe the crash to determine if perhaps Laberge had been murdered, but he soon rejected the theory. It was nothing more than a bizarre accident.

In Orange County, Charles Ng shed no tears when he heard

that his ex-prison buddy had been killed in a car wreck. He had other things on his mind. Jury selection for the trial was scheduled to begin in just a few months. And Judge Ryan didn't appear to be very amenable to more delays.

Chapter 27

Judge Jack Ryan patiently listened to each new motion presented by Ng and his defense attorneys, but continued to resist further delays. After Ng's aborted attempt to represent himself, Ryan reinstated Bill Kelley and said to the defendant, "You are just trying to obstruct and delay. That is not allowed." Maintaining his calm countenance, the judge asserted that Ng had "played games within games within games" to postpone the trial. The "game," he said, has come to an end.

One alert reporter recalled hearing Ng using the word "game." In the videotaped abuse of Brenda O'Connor, as the victim asked why she was being subjected to such treatment, Ng had callously replied, "It's part of the game." Laura Mecoy, of the *Sacramento Bee,* wondered if the judge might have been letting Ng know that he, too, recalled the cruel comment.

The Bee had been covering the case from the day Ng fled a South San Francisco lumberyard, and assigned Mecoy to attend the trial. Her long, sun-streaked blond hair, friendly blue eyes, and luminous smile would become a fixture in the courtroom gallery, as it had been during the infamous O.J. Simpson trial. Mecoy often scooped other news-media representatives with interviews of key players as the result of her courteous approach and congenial personality. In the Santa Ana courtroom, the victims' families grew to love her.

In one last bid to delay the trial again, Ng's attorneys moved to have their client declared mentally incompetent, thus unable to stand trial. They requested a sanity hearing in which a jury would decide Ng's mental status. But Ng defiantly resisted the tactic, and declared himself perfectly sane. "I feel betrayed by and deceived by . . . Mr. Kelley," he stated. Asking for another postponement, Ng rationalized that Kelley's motion had distressed him. "It has aggravated my mental anxiety and my ability to concentrate."

Judge Ryan denied both requests, explaining to Ng, "I am watching you, and I am listening to you, and there is nothing wrong with your mental abilities."

Ryan's reputation for firm but fair rulings had earned him the respect of fellow jurists, lawyers, and the general public. Observers in his courtroom could feel his powerful presence and the confidence he exuded. Ryan exhibited a remarkable memory for every detail of cases he tried, and an admirable understanding of the law. His staff unanimously lauded his dedication to the profession, but worried that he worked much too hard. They'd observed him staying late into the night, and then taking bundles of paperwork home with him. In his earlier years, Ryan had served twelve years in the U.S. Marine Corps. A powerfully built man, he could be an intimidating figure. On the other hand, his Irish eyes could register a sly sense of humor, as well as indignant anger. After mustering out of the Corps, Ryan earned a law degree, and was appointed to the bench in 1981. He donned the Superior Court robes three years later, and inherited several of the county's most publicized trials. Court observers at the Ng trial speculated that it must have grated on Ryan's sense of pride that both Ng and Leonard Lake had been in the Marine Corps.

At long last, on Monday, September 14, 1998, the first phase of the trial began with a huge crowd of potential jurors jamming the modern, eleven-story building in Santa Ana, the seat of Orange County. A staggering thirteen years, two months, and eight days had elapsed since Ng had been arrested in a Canadian department store. District Attorney Peter Smith and his investigator Mitch Hrdlicka had traveled from Calaveras County and would live in temporary apartments within walking distance of the courthouse for the duration of the trial. Sharlene Honnaka would make the daily commute from Los Angeles.

Anticipating that most jury candidates would not be able to serve the estimated nine to twelve months predicted by attorneys, Judge Ryan had ordered a pool of more than 3,000 Orange County citizens. The first, and largest, cut came after candidates filled out a multipage questionnaire in which they answered questions about personal experiences, social attitudes, and availability to serve.

In the midst of the qualifying process on Thursday, October 8, another motion by the defenders temporarily halted the weeding out of jury candidates. Ng, appearing bloated and pale from his years of being locked up, wearing slacks, a dress shirt, and tennis shoes, his coarse black hair freshly cut, watched through thick glasses. Ordinarily sitting quiet and placid at the defense counsel table, he seemed nervous, fidgeting and grumbling loudly at Kelley and Clapp. Suddenly he turned toward the judge and growled, "I don't want to be in this fucking courtroom." Pushing his chair backward, he continued, "I don't want a fucking trial, fucking judge." Three Orange County marshals, who performed bailiff duties, surrounded him, wielding batons. But Judge Ryan, unruffled, ordered them to remain calm. He maintained the court's dignity with a simple command, ''Mr. Ng, please restrain yourself.''

Ng continued to grumble to his attorneys, but calmed down and lowered his voice. For the remainder of the trial, Ng would wear a stun belt protruding from under the back of his shirt. Deputy Marshal Roger Hilton, assigned to Ryan's court, held the remote-control device, which, if activated, would send a nonlethal but temporarily disabling charge of electricity through Ng's body.

Jury selection plodded forward in the eleventh-floor courtroom. While candidates sat in the gallery, some staring out large picture windows toward beach cities eight miles away, prosecution and defense attorneys asked panelists seated in the jury box to discuss their lives, experiences, and especially their attitudes about the death penalty.

One candidate, telephone company employee Nancy McEwan, cringed when she heard the charges against Ng, and wondered if she really wanted to serve on such a long and gory case. But she had a premonition that she would be selected, and wound up on the panel.

Candidate Karen Barrett, a soft-spoken woman with a lilting English accent, couldn't understand why she was picked, but would later have reason to believe that Ng himself may have helped select her.

Mauricio Velarde, a Marine Corps reservist, still wearing the buzz haircut, took seat number one in the jury box, and felt disgust when he learned that the defendant had been in the Marines.

Lawyers on both sides used their allotment of peremptory challenges until—at last—eight women and four men remained as the primary jury, with six alternates. The panel ranged in ages from twenty-seven to sixty-seven. Among them were postal workers, telephone company employees, county and school district personnel, and a locomotive engineer. They would be addressed by three digit numbers worn on their chests, rather than by names, to protect their identities.

On Monday, October 26, Judge Ryan's courtroom buzzed in eager anticipation of opening statements. Since yellow tape blocked off the first row for security reasons, Dwight and Lola Stapley, along with Cosner's mother and stepfather, Virginia and Dave Nessley, and Sharon Sellitto, had staked out the second row of the 123 seats. A neatly dressed woman sat close by, ready to provide emotional support to the victims' families if needed. Carol Waxman, whose soft-spoken compassion had helped hundreds of men and women endure the rigors of reliving unspeakable horrors, worked for a community-supported Victim/Witness Assistance Program. Waxman often accompanied distraught relatives to the witness stand or lectern, and physically supported them as they spoke.

Reporters, many of them from Canada, jockeyed for position to see and hear, while photographers and a pool of video cameras crowded into a designated space on the left side of the room, near the jury box. A huge television mounted on a cabinet separated jurors from the jostling photographers.

Shortly after 9 A.M. Deputy Attorney General Sharlene Honnaka stood, greeted the jurors, and explained that opening statements give the attorneys for both sides the opportunity to explain what they expect the evidence to show. "This case," Honnaka said with careful articulation of each word, "is going to show that this defendant, with Leonard Lake, planned and committed the twelve charged murders." She pointed to a chart listing the victims' names and the dates, approximate in some cases, when they vanished. "The evidence will show that . . . from July 1984 until April 1985 these twelve victims disappeared off the face of the earth, and this trial will tell you the story of what happened to them." One by one, Honnaka tolled off the names, and highlighted the tragic circumstances that ended their lives.

Following a description of Lake's suicide and Ng's flight, the prosecutor took jurors on a verbal tour of the Wilseyville property, the house, and the bunker as seen by investigators. "They found buried in the ground, in a plastic container, a videotape. And on this videotape there are four scenes involving victims Kathleen Allen and Brenda O'Connor. . . . We are going to play the entire videotape for you at trial . . . but for purposes of this opening segment, we're going to play a few segments."

With the courtroom lights dimmed, two large-screen television sets, one at either end of the jury box, lit up. The jurors watched as Kathleen Allen sat in the brown chair, terrified, listening to the threats and verbal torture made by Leonard Lake. One juror covered her mouth in horror when Lake told Kathi that she would have to cook, clean, and fuck for them, or die. Silent spectators in the gallery watched in rapt attention until the segment ended. Juror Bonnie Reinhardt felt her throat swelling and her eyes stinging with tears.

Honnaka spoke again, explaining that evidence undeniably placed the taping session inside the Wilseyville house. The second scene established that a bedspread shown in the tape had been discovered in the house. When the screen flickered to life the third time, viewers saw Charles Ng cutting away O'Connor's shirt and bra while she feebly protested. The crowded courtroom remained in hushed silence even after the lights brightened again.

During the video segment showing Ng mistreating Brenda O'Connor, the defendant shifted uncomfortably in his chair as he watched the chilling scene on a smaller set mounted directly in front of him atop the defense counsel table.

Switching to the cases of Lonnie Bond and Robin Stapley, Honnaka mentioned evidence that would place the victims in Wilseyville in early April 1985, and described how investigators later found their bound, bullet-riddled, gagged bodies buried in sleeping bags. "There will be other evidence presented to show the long-standing plan between this defendant and

Leonard Lake. . . .'' Observers wondered just how she would link Ng to the actual murders of Bond and Stapley.

On to the Dubs family, Honnaka spoke slowly. "They disappeared off the face of the earth July twenty-fifth 1984. This defendant was seen walking out of their San Francisco flat." Some property that had belonged to the Dubs family, Honnaka said, was found in the defendant's residence, along with a San Francisco map on which someone had circled the Yukon Street address of Harvey, Deborah, and Sean. Other items belonging to them, she asserted, turned up in searches of the Wilseyville property.

When Honnaka spoke of Paul Cosner, reporters listened carefully, wondering if she could produce more evidence of Ng's involvement than Canadian prosecutors did when Madame Justice Marguerite Trussler ruled the Cosner case excluded from the counts for which Ng should be tried. It was common knowledge that Ng and Lake had been using Cosner's Honda, but what other evidence had turned up to prove the defendant had helped Lake either kidnap or kill him?

Honnaka, pacing back and forth in front of the jurors, informed them that a bullet hole had been found in the Honda headliner. The passenger sun visor, which covered the hole, had been replaced. What appeared to be the original sun visor was found buried near Lake's bunker. A bullet hole in it lined up perfectly with the headliner hole. "And you will hear evidence that the trajectory of the bullet is consistent with having been fired from behind the passenger seat of that car." The prosecutor's words created a visual image of someone driving the Honda, with Cosner in the passenger seat, while an accomplice in the back possibly raised a handgun and shot Cosner. But was there enough evidence to prove that Ng had been in the car?

Other evidence related to Cosner, said Honnaka, was found in a plastic bucket, including his driver's license, additional identification cards, and a handgun, which "could have been" the weapon that caused the bullet holes. The bucket also contained a clip of twelve bullets stamped with a symbol indicating they were "Chinese made," and "a similar brand of Chinese bullets were found in this defendant's apartment. . . ." The Honda license plate also turned up at Wilseyville, Honnaka said, before leaving the subject of Paul Cosner. The victim's mother and sister sat in the gallery, tears welling in their eyes.

Clifford Peranteau, Honnaka pointed out, had worked with Ng at Dennis Moving Company. After he vanished, someone "cleaned out" his apartment, and a Cross brand pen and pencil set engraved with his initials was found in the defendant's apartment.

"Jeffrey Gerald was, likewise, a coworker" at Dennis Moving, said Honnaka. Before he vanished, he told his roommate he was going to help someone move, someone named Charles. Gerald promised to return that evening, but was never seen again.

"With respect to Michael Carroll and Kathleen Allen," Honnaka said, the plan Kathi was forced to hear while being videotaped "actually came to pass." And, "You will hear evidence that this defendant delivered car keys and instructions to a family who had been asked by Leonard Lake to fix Michael Carroll's car and ultimately sell it."

Scott Stapley had owned a camera, which was found in the possession of Ng when he was arrested, said Honnaka. And a bank card in Lonnie Bond's name turned up in the defendant's residence, along with two videotapes containing "scenes relevant to this case." Elaborating, Honnaka explained, "The first was a scene which appears to be identical to the one we played for you." On a second videotape, a short scene which "appears to depict a wheelbarrow with two bodies consistent with the manner in which . . . Lonnie Bond and Scott Stapley were found."

Pausing, as if to be certain she hadn't omitted anything crucial, Honnaka took a breath and said, "Ladies and gentlemen, that is what the people believe the evidence will show in this case. It provides you with an overview of all the different things we will be showing to you. There will be additional evidence in the forms of defendant's own writings that he made. But it is our belief that after you consider all of this evidence, you will find the verdict of guilty is warranted. Thank you very much for your attention.''

She had spoken just forty-five minutes.

At the break, Lola Stapley expressed horrified shock at what she had seen on the tapes. ''I still want to throw up,'' she said.

Sharon Sellitto observed, ''It was like they weren't even talking to human beings.''

Twenty minutes later, Bill Kelley, in a dark-blue pin-striped suit, his middle-parted dark hair curling just below the collar line, stood and spoke. ''May it please the court, counsel, ladies and gentlemen. How are you? Good morning. I am going to talk to you for—probably until lunchtime. Needless to say, I have butterflies, but I will settle in as we talk for a few minutes.

''Last night I was thinking about a movie I saw, a pretty famous movie. You have probably all seen it. It is called *Dances With Wolves.*'' Kelley briefly summarized the plot, and quoted a line he thought memorable, spoken by a medicine man to Kevin Costner: ''We have come a long way, you and I.''

Keeping strong eye contact with the jurors, Kelley said, ''And we are going to go a long way here in this case. We're going to travel and take a long trip. It's going to take a long time, as you know.'' He expressed confidence in their ability to listen and give due consideration to the evidence, and hoped they would, ''abide by your promise . . . to let the presumption of innocence live in your hearts until this case is over.''

Because the case took place in Northern California, Kelley spent a few moments familiarizing the jurors with ''the gold country,'' then zeroed in on his objective. ''The defense in this case is really simple. That is, Leonard Lake had a motive for murder, and that motive was grounded in a deep-seated hatred of women, which began in his early childhood and manifested itself through his life. Leonard Lake also had a plan for murder. And that plan was reflected in something he called the Miranda project. . . . He had an intent to commit murder, and that is manifested in a diary, in a journal that he wrote . . . and even more strongly in a videotape that he made of himself in 1983.''

It appeared that Kelley planned to put a dead man on trial. If he could persuade the jury that Leonard Lake had planned and carried out the murders, they might find that Charles Ng had been nothing more than a pawn under the control of a psychopathic killer.

Kelley spoke of Lake's several attempts to build a bunker before he actually constructed one in Wilseyville. The plan, he said, also included an intent to kill men to ''gain their property and their identities.'' Lake had the knowledge and the ''where-withal'' for the project, said Kelley. ''Leonard Lake's misogyny—we all know that misogyny is a deep-seated hatred for women. He had a hatred for his mother . . . which manifested itself throughout his life and came to a final culmination when he . . . executed the Miranda project.''

Following a concise description of the childhood events that set ''the foundation for his hatred,'' Kelley said that Lake never trusted women again. He quoted Lake telling his family, ''If I ever die, I want to come back as a beautiful blonde because they have all the power.''

Lake's diary, said Kelley, made reference to a fantasy about *The Collector,* a novel in which a ''nondescript little clerk, who is not getting anywhere with women . . . dreams up this plan to capture a woman and hide her. This woman in the book is Miranda.'' In the diary, Kelley pointed out, Lake revealed that he'd been dreaming of the fantasy for twenty years, or since 1963. ''In 1963, Charles Ng was a three-year-old toddler in Hong Kong.''

In the Marine Corps, said Kelley, Lake learned skills that would help him carry out his murderous plans, such as fire control, which could relate to the burned human remains. Also, during his time in the military, Lake's wife "was unfaithful to him, and that intensified the anger toward women."

Once again, the courtroom lights were dimmed and all eyes focused on television screens to watch the image of Lake as he explained his philosophy and fantasy. Kelley drove home the point that Ng was in prison at the time Lake made the tape.

"Lake was an opportunist," said Kelley. "If you were a person who received government-assistance checks, you were a target for him because he wanted your checks. If you were a person who had photographic equipment, you were an 'op' or operation . . . it sounds like a military term to me. Everybody was an 'op' for him."

Reading periodically from Lake's journal, Kelley laid out the story of his life as a fugitive. Donald, Lake's brother, became a victim, after which Lake assumed his identity to join an "escort" club, and forged signatures on his Social Security checks.

"There is another person we need to talk about," said Kelley. "Her name is Claralyn Balazs, nicknamed Cricket. You will hear a lot about her in this case." As Kelley spoke, a technician, sitting between the prosecution and defense tables, slipped a photo onto a projector, which transmitted the image to the television screens. Kelley told jurors the photo was of Balazs, dressed in military garb, holding a pistol, standing with Lake and another woman. He explained her role as Lake's wife/ex-wife/girlfriend. She "knew about his diary, knew about the Miranda project, and assisted Lake by recruiting potential female victims to be photographed."

Glancing toward the clock, Kelley continued. Leonard and Cricket, he said, had made a video of themselves in which they looked at a photo album of young women, and talked about some of the women disappearing. "They joked about the Miranda project on that videotape. . . ." At that time, he asserted, Charles Ng was not even in the state of California.

In the matter of Charles Gunnar, Kelley said, the evidence showed that two different guns had been used to fire seven bullets. "Three .22s to the head and four .380 calibers to the torso, strongly suggesting two shooters. . . . [Gunnar] disappeared in 1983, when Charles Ng was not in the state of California." Observers, noting that Ng wasn't charged in the Gunnar case, recognized that Kelley's strategy was to build an image of Lake perpetrating a series of murders, and hope the momentum would carry jurors into believing that Lake, without Ng's help, had killed all of the victims.

Lake and Cricket, Kelley said, posed for a homemade pornographic movie in which she identified herself as Sheryl Okoro. "She [Okoro] was a person . . . that Charles Ng is not charged with killing because he did not kill her. . . ." Sharlene Honnaka interrupted the soliloquy with the trial's first objection.

"Your Honor, he is making an argument."

"Sustained."

Kelley shifted back to Cricket, revealing that three pages were missing from a calendar she had turned over to investigators. "The police asked her to explain that, and she couldn't explain it. She had no explanation for it." When a female friend visited Lake in Wilseyville, said Kelley, Cricket wrote notes to herself saying, "We are all going to get in trouble if she finds out?"

"Again," Kelley reminded the attentive jurors, "Charles Ng was not in the state of California, folks." Cricket, he said, was given full immunity.

Finally getting around to speaking about his client, Kelley sketched a verbal outline of Ng's childhood, his tour of duty in the Marine Corps, the period of living with Lake and Cricket in Philo, his absence from California (without mentioning prison), and his return in July 1984.

Pouncing again on Lake, Kelley said that the fugitive lived by stealing property and selling it at flea markets. The defender spoke of people living at the pink palace in San Francisco:

Maurice Rock, Sheryl Okoro, and Randy Jacobson, all of whom vanished after meeting Lake. Rock's body, some remains of Okoro, and an unidentified body, Kelley said, were found near Wilseyville. "You won't see any evidence linking Charles Ng to those homicides."

"You are going to learn that Charles Ng had his own apartment when he was working a full-time job with the Dennis Moving Company in San Francisco . . . paying rent, living and working in that area. And you are also going to learn that he never owned a car. . . . It is about a three-hour drive from San Francisco to Wilseyville. Charles Ng didn't drive."

Another major figure in the case came under Kelley's spoken scorn. "His name is Maurice Laberge . . . to call him a career criminal would be an understatement." Calling Laberge the "big gun" of the prosecution's case, Kelley explained that the informant had been killed in a car accident the previous May, but had previously testified in Canada. "Some of his testimony is going to be presented by the prosecution in the case." In addition to being a habitual criminal, Kelley said, "He was also an accomplished liar and a pathological perjurer to whom an oath meant nothing."

Slowing down as he reached the end of his talk, Kelley said, "So, what you are going to learn, folks, is . . . the prosecution's case is built on circumstantial evidence. There is not going to be anybody who says, 'I saw Charles Ng kill somebody.' "

Reporters furiously scribbled on pads as Kelley stated, "I am not saying Charles Ng is an angel here, folks, because he is not. That is pretty apparent. But he is charged with murder, remember, ending people's lives, not cutting off people's clothes, as offensive as that was.

"And I know you will remember that, and abide by your promises as we move through this case. So let's travel down the road.

"Thanks for your attention. Thanks."

* * *

The courtroom emptied for the lunch break. Sharlene Honnaka and Peter Smith bypassed throngs of reporters and cameras in the hallway. In a little over an hour, they would begin questioning witnesses in the biggest case of their lives.

Chapter 28

Prosecutors often like to present their cases in reasonably chronological order to make it easy for jurors to follow. Of course, logistics occasionally interfere with those plans due to witnesses being unavailable at certain times. The first few days of the trial, though, are usually trouble free.

Sharlene Honnaka and Peter Smith chose to open with the shoplifting incident at a South San Francisco lumberyard and store. John Kallas, who had been a reserve police officer in 1985, took the stand on Monday afternoon, and Smith asked the questions. Kallas told of seeing a short Asian man walk out the store's front door carrying a vise on June 2, thirteen years ago. The witness identified a photograph of the bronze-colored Honda in which the thief had deposited the loot, and another photo of "a bearded man" who, while introducing himself as Robin Scott Stapley, had offered to pay for the vise. A photographic lineup had been shown to Kallas soon after the incident, and he had pointed to a picture of Charles Ng as the individual who had stolen the vise.

Officer Daniel Wright testified next, and said he had responded to a report of shoplifting at the lumberyard, checked the Honda license plates, and found they were registered to a Buick belonging to Lonnie Bond. He had also discovered a handgun in the car's trunk and traced the serial number to Robin Scott Stapley.

During cross-examination, Bill Kelley stated, "We're willing to stipulate that the bearded man was Leonard Lake, Your Honor, so I don't have to call him the bearded man anymore."

Detective Gary Hopper, now retired, recalled being summoned to work that day, and seeing Leonard Lake in convulsions shortly after he had ingested cyanide. Another stipulation by the defense informed the jury that Lake had died a few days later. Among items found on Lake were a driver's license and other cards belonging to Stapley, a bank card in the name of Randy Jacobson, and a travel agency receipt made out to Charles Gunnar. The Honda, Hopper said, had been turned over to Tom Eisenmann and Irene Brunn of the SFPD.

Day one of the trial ended smoothly, but on Tuesday, the entire day was lost due to the absence of a sick juror.

On Wednesday, Judge Ryan had no choice but to release two of the jurors. One of the men had fallen ill, and a female juror's husband had died during the previous night. Two women out of the six alternates replaced them, changing the jury's makeup to nine women and three men. The attrition rate certainly could not continue at that pace. With a smile, Ryan faced the panel, and said, "I would like to order all of you to stay healthy."

Inspector Irene Brunn walked briskly to the stand on Wednesday morning. Now a twenty-five-year veteran of the SFPD, she recalled taking missing persons reports on Deborah, Harvey, and little Sean Dubs, and on Paul Cosner. While investigating the Dubs case, Brunn had listed missing video equipment and tapes. Harvey's Volkswagen Rabbit had been found at the San Francisco International airport nearly a month after the family had vanished. Cosner's Honda had been recovered on the day of Lake's arrest and suicide. Inside it, Brunn had found a PG&E bill for property in Wilseyville in the name of Claralyn Balazs. That piece of paper, said Brunn, had led her and Tom Eisenmann to Claralyn's Bay area home where, with a search warrant, they had located a letter addressed to Sheryl Okoro. Brunn testified that Balazs, known as Cricket, had agreed to meet them at the Wilseyville house, but raced up there ahead of the police and removed personal items. Later that same morning, inside the house, Brunn had found video equipment belonging to Harvey Dubs.

Sergeant Larry Copland, Calaveras County Sheriff's Department, replaced Brunn on the stand and described how he and other searchers had discovered the bodies of Maurice Rock, Randy Jacobson, and an unidentified African-American male, all buried in a telephone trench. Several years later, Copland said, the body of Charles Gunnar had also turned up. Jurors' faces turned grim when the witness spoke of burned bone fragments unearthed on the property. Copland also described the concrete bunker and the discovery of a secret cell inside it. Next, he told of the digging up of a plastic container that held a videotape labeled "M Ladies, Kathi, Brenda."

Before Honnaka played the tape, jurors were given copies of the transcript so they could follow along as Leonard Lake and Charles Ng verbally tortured two captive women and stripped them naked. This time, the entire tape ran, giving horrified jurors and observers a glimpse into Kathleen Allen's and Brenda O'Connor's last days of life.

In the second row of seats, Dian Allen, Kathi's sister, trembled and sobbed in silence, tears streaking down her cheeks. During the lunch break she spoke to reporter Laura Mecoy. "I felt like it was me . . . I could tell that [Kathi] wasn't going to say anything because she was scared. She was trying to save her life.'' About Leonard Lake's oily charm, she said, ''I would expect to see this slick, mean monster, and he tries to come off as a nice guy. . . . I can see why she probably would have trusted him.''

That afternoon, Copland resumed his testimony, identifying items seized at the Wilseyville house. In all criminal trials, defense lawyers always raise at least one objection on the basis that a piece of evidence is more prejudicial than probative. Lewis Clapp interrupted the proceedings by objecting to a freeze-frame photo from the videotape in which Kathi Allen is shown massaging Charles Ng. The prosecution wanted it admitted in order for Copland to testify that the bedspread depicted in the photo had been found inside the house. Clapp argued that showing the massage was prejudicial. The photo could be trimmed just to show the bedspread. ''Overruled,'' said Ryan, ''I don't find it to be prejudicial. It's probative.'' Clapp thanked the judge and sat down.

Sharlene Honnaka asked a series of questions that allowed Copland to identify a long list of exhibits, most of which were personal belongings of the victims; items recovered from the house or from sealed, buried containers. The revealing blue garment Kathi Allen had worn in the video became Exhibit 28. Her cutoff jeans and a gold chain with a ''floating heart'' pendant she had worn were also numbered and offered into evidence. So were the bent latches taken from the cell door, driver's licenses, bank cards, Social Security cards, as well as checkbooks belonging to Kathi Allen, Mike Carroll, and Scott Stapley.

Copland verified that he'd found shirts of Stapley's, and snapped photos of his pickup truck with the AHOYMTY license plates. A miniature Pennsylvania license plate with the name CINDY was marked as evidence, along with a nameplate from a Suzuki motorcycle that Cliff Peranteau had owned. His candlestick holders, a Buddha statuette, and ceramic goldfish that had been stolen from Peranteau's apartment received exhibit numbers. So did Jeff Gerald's metal Social Security card, his guitar and case, a video receipt with Harvey Dubs's name on it, and Paul Cosner's glasses. The numbering of evidence continued with Cosner's driver's license and various cards he'd carried in his billfold.

Nods of understanding rippled through the gallery when Copland examined the Honda sun visor and agreed that it had been pierced with a bullet hole. It became Exhibit 59. And when Honnaka asked him about the discovery of two more bodies—Stapley and Bond—a palpable sadness filled the courtroom while Dwight and Lola Stapley embraced each other, trying not to cry aloud. Copland described how he and two other officers had noticed tufts of padding from a sleeping bag scattered on the ground where coyotes had been digging. Closer investigation uncovered two wrapped corpses, one on top of the other.

While examining evidence seized from Ng's San Francisco apartment, Copland said, he had accidentally glimpsed a scene at the beginning of a videotaped movie titled *Vice Squad*. The split-second image of Kathi Allen could be seen only by running the VCR in the rewind mode. Judge Ryan voiced concern: "You know, there's a problem with introducing a tape and you're only wanting a portion of it to go into evidence. So what you're going to have to do is copy that portion you want in—"

Sharlene Honnaka interjected, "Well, we have a still photo to substitute."

His tongue-in-cheek grin barely showing, Ryan said, "We don't want the jury back there watching *Vice Squad*, whatever that is."

The segment became Exhibit 77. Another tape, labeled "Taboo," flashed a glimpse of two wrapped bodies lying on a blue wheelbarrow. The still photo of that segment was marked Exhibit 78.

With the introduction of one more videotape, which showed

Lake delivering a monologue about his fantasies, the long court day came to an end. Larry Copland stepped down but remained on call, and would be seated in the witness chair eight more times before the prosecution would rest its case.

On Thursday, a darkly clad woman sat in the back row of the courtroom, peering from under the brim of a black felt hat, obscuring her face with her hands, and avoiding contact with reporters. But one of them, Laura Mecoy, recognized the mystery women as Claralyn Balazs who sat with her attorney, hoping not to be called as a witness.

Most of the day was consumed with testimony from coworkers of Cliff Peranteau, Jeff Gerald, and Kathleen Allen, reporting how each of the victims had suddenly left their jobs and never returned. A close friend of Allen's described his last telephone conversation with Kathi after she'd left work at a Safeway supermarket. The last time he talked to Kathi, he said, was when she called him from her motel room to say she was going to see Mike.

Mike Carroll's stepbrother, who also knew Kathi, read aloud a typed letter that appeared to be from her. It stated that she and Mike were staying in Tahoe, had no phone, and their car was disabled. Asked if the signature appeared to be Kathi's writing, the witness answered, "I know it's not."

Larry Copland testified again, and told the jury that several notes and letters to the victim's coworkers, relatives, or acquaintances had been typed on the Olympia typewriter found in Lake's bedroom at Wilseyville.

Since Judge Ryan reserved Fridays for other court business, such as sentencing, hearings for separate cases, and a host of tasks not associated with the major trial, the Ng proceedings would be on Mondays through Thursdays. When the court day concluded on Thursday, Cricket Balazs hurried out with her attorney, relieved at not being summoned to the stand.

* * *

Monday, November 2, began with the Safeway manager describing a telephone call from Kathi Allen in which she requested time off because she wanted to be with her boyfriend, who had found a job in the Tahoe area. Later, he said, a letter from her stated that she planned to stay in her new location. It bore a Wilseyville postmark.

The prosecutor next called witnesses who spoke of the Dubs family. Harvey's boss lauded the employee's reliability. Karen Tuck, Deborah's best friend, spoke of the last phone call between them, which ended abruptly. Tuck said, "Deb was expecting someone to come over to talk to Harvey or see his video equipment . . . the doorbell rang or someone knocked . . . so we terminated the conversation." Tuck's husband, George, testified that he went to the Dubses' apartment the next day, and found it deserted, with Harvey's video equipment missing.

The next witness, Dorice Murphy, a tiny, bespectacled, older woman, had lived in her apartment forty-five years, located across narrow Yukon Street from the Dubs family dwelling. One of the jurors scribbled a note to herself describing Murphy as "a spunky senior." On July 25, 1984, at about 5:45 P.M., said Murphy, she had observed an Asian man straining to carry a suitcase out the front door of the Dubses' apartment. A Volkswagen Rabbit belonging to Harvey had backed up the narrow, uphill street, and the Asian man placed the object he carried in the trunk. The car, driven by someone other than Dubs, sped away. When Murphy later spoke to the police, she had identified Ng from a photo lineup.

Bill Kelley's cross-examination, during which he often peered over the top of his half spectacles, elicited from Murphy that she hadn't been wearing her glasses when she saw the Volkswagen. Some of her answers to Kelley seemed unrelated to his questions, forcing him to repeat many of them. Sharlene Honnaka, on redirect, established that Murphy had actually put on her glasses after her husband had noticed that the Dubses were not in their car, which enabled her to see the Asian man clearly.

After Dorice Murphy spryly marched out of the courtroom, Barbara Speaker, who had lived in the apartment below Harvey and Debbie Dubs, took the stand. She, too, had seen an Asian man carrying bundles from the apartment, two days after Murphy's observations. In addition to selecting Ng's photo from a group of pictures, Speaker had taken an extra step. Sharlene Honnaka introduced into evidence a yellow 8½- by 11-inch sheet of paper upon which Speaker had drawn a picture of the Asian man she'd seen. It resembled Charles Ng.

Once again, Larry Copland settled into the witness chair. He revealed that an automobile rental receipt had been found, which showed that Claralyn Balazs had rented a Toyota pickup on January 19, 1985, from a San Francisco agency, and returned it on January 21. She, or someone, had driven the vehicle 347 miles in two days. In answer to a question about the mileage from San Francisco to Wilseyville, Copland said it was approximately 165 miles. The pickup had been rented on the same day that Cliff Peranteau vanished.

Although Ng had not been charged in the death of Sheryl Okoro, Lewis Clapp asked Copland to identify a photo of her, in which she wore a shirt emblazoned with a leopard's face. The shirt had been among evidence collected from Cricket Balazs, and the photo had been taken in the master bedroom of the Wilseyville house. Clapp read into the record a stipulation: "Prosecution experts formed the opinion from DNA testing that certain remains found at Wilseyville . . . were those of Sheryl Okoro." The defense seemingly wanted to keep the jury focused on Lake and Cricket, and to suggest his culpability by highlighting victims directly traceable to him, thus blurring the image of Ng's involvement.

On Tuesday, day five of the prosecution's case, jurors heard George "Wes" Blank and his daughter testify to events that might tie Ng to victim Michael Carroll's presumed death. Blank, the man who had taken custody of Charles Gunnar's daughters, had previously known Leonard Lake. Lake had called him, Blank said, and requested that he take possession of Mike Carroll's yellow Capri, which had been left by Kathi Allen in the Safeway parking lot. "Charles" would deliver the keys. Ng kept the appointment at a bus station, where Blank's daughter met him to pick up the keys. Later, according to Blank, Leonard Lake had instructed him to sell the car.

During the lunch break, Juror Nancy McEwan saw a woman sitting in one of the chairs lining the south wall of the eleventh-floor hallway, and noticed her features resembled Kathi Allen's. The woman was Dian Allen, who was only sixteen when eighteen-year-old Kathi vanished. Dian took the stand at 1:30 P.M.

Peter Smith reached into a paper bag and removed a floating heart pendant affixed to a gold chain. Dian choked back a sob and dabbed at her moist eyes. "It's a necklace Kathi used to wear all the time," Dian said, her voice throbbing. Smith mercifully kept the questioning brief. After Dian emotionally spoke of her last meeting with Kathi, Smith thanked her and sat down. Bill Kelley wisely declined cross-examination.

The defense spent the afternoon questioning Larry Copland again. They established that Lake and Cricket, who was posing as Sheryl Okoro, had made a porno tape and sent it to a man named Hal, who collected erotica. After taking Copland through a series of questions that seemed to have no discernable connection with Charles Ng's guilt or innocence, Clapp wound up the day by asking, "Were you present when Dr. Boyd Stephens recovered what he believed to be a piece of liver in the Wilseyville area?"

Copland replied, "I was on the property, yes," and agreed that Stephens had shown it to him.

"Was it burned, or charred?"

"Yes, sir," answered Copland, and pointed out on a chart where the liver tissue had been discovered in a trench.

Clapp ended the day by leaving jurors and observers in suspense. Was the liver from a human being? Clapp indicated that the medical examiner would eventually have the opportunity to testify about it.

On Wednesday, by grilling the owner of Dennis Moving Company, Sharlene Honnaka informed the jury that Ng had worked there from September 28, 1984, until he left for Canada in June 1985. It was an important point, since it connected Ng to the two victims who had also been employed at the firm, Cliff Peranteau and Jeffrey Gerald. Dennis Goza, the owner, read aloud a letter purportedly from Peranteau, which asked that his last check be forwarded to a post office box in Mokelumne Hill, a little more than ten miles from Wilseyville. Honnaka put the spotlight on the various times Ng had been absent from work, establishing that the defendant hadn't worked on Sunday, April 14, Monday, April 15, or Tuesday, April 16, 1985. Jurors quickly jotted reminders in their notebooks, recognizing that Kathi Allen had vanished on Sunday, April 14. Ng had worked on Wednesday through Saturday that week, but took another few days off afterward. Said Goza, "He was off the twenty-second through April twenty-seventh, 1985."

"Did you receive a phone call from Mr. Ng explaining why he wanted that time off?"

"Yes, I did. His mom and dad were in a car accident in

Southern California. Neither one spoke good English, and he asked for the time off to go down there to be with them just to help them through the accident. . . ."

Jurors would eventually piece together the facts of the case, and recognize that no such accident had occurred.

On June 3, 1985, prior to his departure for Canada, Ng had called Goza again, and stated that he had just stepped off the plane in Honolulu. The witness recalled that Ng said, "A close friend of his had committed suicide; that he was going to—he had to leave town to be with his friend's family, and that he would probably be back to work. . . ." At least, observers whispered, the suicide part was true.

Goza established that Ng had returned to work three days after Kathi Allen vanished, then had taken a full week off. The prosecutor probed back in time, to January, and demonstrated that Ng had worked on Cliff Peranteau's last day at the firm, a Saturday, then had taken Sunday off, but had been on the job the following five days. On cross, the defense had tried to suggest that Ng's work schedule had prevented his participation in Kathi Allen's murder, but made little headway. One juror noted, "The dates weren't real clear to me and it seems, not clear to the defense, either."

The real Michael Kimoto, whose identity Ng had frequently used, stepped forward to testify that his wallet, containing identification documents, had been stolen while he was surfing south of San Francisco in 1983. Charles Ng had used the driver's license and cards in 1984 and 1985. A bit of quick math made it clear, though, that Ng hadn't been the thief, since he was in Leavenworth at the time. But Leonard Lake had frequently visited the region where Kimoto surfed. A juror asked herself, "Why did Ng need fake identification if he wasn't involved in any crimes?"

The jurors next heard from the woman who had sold the Honda to Paul Cosner. She described its pristine condition other than cigarette burns in the passenger seat and on a sun visor.

When she'd later examined the car, as requested by the police, the seat and sun visor had been replaced.

With Larry Copland taking another turn on the stand, Lewis Clapp played the videotape featuring Cricket as Sheryl Okoro, the one that had been sent to a collector of erotica. Copland had seized it from the recipient. Fortunately for spectators, he played only the first five minutes of it, and omitted the segment in which Cricket masturbated while Lake zoomed in to capture every detail. Clapp's purpose for showing the tape was unclear to several jurors and to most spectators.

When Sharlene Honnaka questioned Copland, she handed him a camera that had been unearthed from the telephone trench. He testified that film inside it had been developed. The photos proved to be of buildings outside an apartment where Jeffrey Gerald had lived. The inference, of course, was that the camera had been stolen from Gerald, who had worked side by side with Charles Ng. Jurors noted that Lake had no connection with Gerald or Peranteau, other than through Ng.

Another employee of Dennis Moving quoted chants Charles Ng used at work, such as "No gun, no fun"; "No kill, no thrill"; and "Daddy die, mommy cry, baby fry." The witness disgustedly said, "They were rather sick," but an objection caused his opinion to be stricken from the record and the jury ordered to disregard it. Peter Smith asked if Ng ever brought weapons to work. Yes, he had, said the witness, and described one. "It was a butterfly knife . . . when you open the double handles, the blade can cut from both sides." He also told of the Super Bowl pool in which the employees, including Cliff Peranteau, had participated.

Cynthia "Cindy" Tanner, Peranteau's longtime girlfriend, informed the jury that she had entered his apartment after he vanished, and noticed several items missing, including oak framed mirrors, candlesticks, ceramic fish, a miniature license plate with her nickname on it, a small Buddha figure, and a distinctive towel. Jurors' pencils flew over their notepads. She also stated that the signature on a letter supposedly from Peranteau, requesting his Super Bowl winnings, was a forgery.

That letter had been written to Richard Doedens, a dispatcher at Dennis Moving, who testified next. He said that he had organized the Super Bowl pool that Cliff Peranteau won in absentia.

The final witness for the day was Kenneth King, retired SFPD officer. One juror thought he resembled Colonel Sanders of fried-chicken fame. King, as part of a three-man team, had conducted a search of Ng's apartment on Lenox Way, and seized, among other things, a Cross pen and pencil set engraved with the initials CRP, which would turn out to be Clifford R. Peranteau. The searchers had also turned up a map on which someone had circled Yukon Street, where the Dubs family had lived.

Chapter 29

On Thursday morning, while jurors waited in the hall, Bill Kelley argued that two General Electric videotape recorders found in Ng's Lenox Way apartment should not be admitted into evidence because they would be prejudicial. "They've never been linked to the Dubses, except by pure speculation," said Kelley. The serial number of one machine had been filed off, and the other could not be traced, but a machine taken from the Dubs residence was a General Electric brand. Judge Ryan commented, "It is unusual to have a serial number removed unless it has been stolen. . . . They [the prosecution] want to argue to the jury that it was taken from the Dubses, so there is relevance. I don't see that it is prejudicial. Your objection is overruled."

Kelley raised another objection, hoping to prevent a Dennis Moving Company employee from testifying that Ng had invited him to spend a weekend at Wilseyville for some target practice.

Peter Smith explained, "Your Honor, the witness will testify along the lines that Charles Ng invited him up to a property that a friend of his owned . . . two or three hours away from San Francisco; that they could leave on a Friday night and return the following day. I think it is highly relevant because it shows an issue about luring people away from San Francisco to the country. It is also important because Mr. Kelley is trying to establish that, if Mr. Ng didn't drive, and Wilseyville is three hours away—how is he getting back and forth from Wilseyville to San Francisco? This not only infers the ability to make the trip in a short period of time, but also shows a comfort level with going to a piece of property, which I think the jury can reasonably infer is Leonard Lake's."

Judge Ryan, observing that Kelley had already made "a great effort" to show difficulty for Ng to easily commute to Wilseyville, started to say, "It has to be admissible—"

Charles Ng spoke up. "Before you rule on it, can I be heard?"

Ryan, unperturbed, replied, "Talk to your attorney."

Ng, using broken syntax, ignored the advice and argued, "There is a Marsden issue here. I never make this statement to these people. He's essentially admitting without talking to me that I make these statements. There is . . . reports from past thirteen years that never reflect these guys make these statements. . . ." Ng called the allegation "absurd" that he'd invited coworkers to Wilseyville, and suggested someone was making up stories. The witnesses, said Ng, hold ". . . hostility and anger toward me." Kelley, he contended, "doesn't even make that suggestion of unreliability, Your Honor. What kind of a lawyer is this?"

Kelley, his face darkening, said, "I have explained to Mr. Ng that if you rule it admissible, it would be taken up on cross. . . . He seems to think I am conceding [a witness] made the statement. I think he doesn't understand the nature of this objection."

Patiently Ryan explained to Ng that witness statements were subject to cross-examination, allowing the attorney to cast doubt on the testimony, but Ng continued his remonstration. "Basically, I complain about his lack of preparedness. . . . He doesn't even familiarize himself with the facts and information that is in his domain . . . he doesn't want to tell the judge that he is unprepared. He doesn't remember the facts of the people and why these people would want to make statements against me. . . . These [coworker] guys essentially so biased [and] evidence is highly incredible to begin with. They have already expressed strong view and prejudice against me. They want me dead. The whole thing is gang up and say, to make sure we pay back on this guy for what—for Peranteau and Gerald because they believe I did the crime." A few spectators wondered if Ng had almost made a crucial slip of the tongue. About the defense lawyers, Ng said, "I just sit, seeing them bungling along. I can't stand it today because I try to convey my concern and he just ignore it."

Judge Ryan tolerantly allowed Ng to wind down his diatribe, then advised, "Mr. Ng, you have an attorney. You ought to talk to him because—"

Bill Kelley interrupted, frustration quaking in his voice. "If we are going to continue this, I have to ask for the prosection to [step outside]. I mean this is—Mr. Ng is going to get into areas here that he is going to shoot himself in the foot, Judge, and I am not going to let it happen."

"I told him to talk to you," said Ryan. "I didn't invite him to talk."

"I am not suggesting you did," Kelley replied. "I am advising Mr. Ng, on the record, to be quiet . . . if he continues on with this in front of the prosecutors, he is going to do something that is harmful to himself. . . ."

Ryan's patience had worn thin as he addressed the defendant. "The problem, Mr. Ng, is the record belies any suggestion that Mr. Kelley is less than prepared. Just watch him cross-examine these witnesses. He, and Mr. Clapp, are getting, I think, everything they can out of these witnesses. Now, where the case goes, that is up to the jury, not up to the court. But you are telling me he is not prepared. He is every bit prepared. He is as prepared as anybody could be on this case as complex as it is, as many reports as there are. He knows where he is going. He and Mr. Clapp have a plan in mind. And if you sit back and watch, you can see it. Whether it is successful or not, that is a different issue. But they are playing the game right, Mr. Ng.''

Smarting at the rebuke, Ng spoke again. ''I just want to make my motion—''

''You just made it,'' snapped Ryan.

Ng forged ahead. ''. . . These witnesses all can testify on the stand and . . . reflect these states of mind that they are clearly hostile against me. . . .''

''Your motion is denied, Mr. Ng. Anything else?'' Judge Ryan sounded like *Sergeant* Ryan, USMC.

Sharlene Honnaka quickly spoke up to raise a separate issue before Ng could voice another objection. Her action seemed to diffuse the angry tension in the air. Ryan rejected her request and ordered Deputy Marshal Roger Hilton to bring the jury in.

Retired SFPD inspector Kenneth King, who had testified the previous day, resumed his place in the witness chair. The defense, wishing to show that Ng's involvement with the victims—if any—had been orchestrated by Leonard Lake, formed questions to suggest that Lake had stayed overnight with Ng at the Lenox Way apartment. Lewis Clapp approached the witness, carrying a stack of photos King had snapped inside Ng's apartment. He asked about a picture of a table in the kitchen, implying that it had been set for two people. King didn't agree. A juror watched disdainfully and thought, ''That's nothing but a card table, and there's only one chair. Nice try!''

In another photo, Clapp inquired about a toothbrush holder, noting that it held four toothbrushes. The same juror noted, "I live alone and have four toothbrushes. I'm not buying it. The defense is clearly reaching. Personally, I think in most cases they should say, 'No questions, Your Honor.' "

The two employees of Dennis Moving that Ng had fought to keep off the stand, Hector Salcedo and Lawrence Boen, testified about their association with Cliff Peranteau and Ng's use of chants at work. Both men recalled hearing him say: "No kill, no thrill''; No gun, no fun''; "Daddy dies, momma cries, baby fries.'' Salcedo recalled having beer at Peranteau's residence one night when Ng showed up unexpectedly. Ng, he stated, had shown them some marijuana and had invited both men to help harvest his friend's crop "a couple of hours away in the hills.'' Bill Kelley's cross-exam exposed several inconsistencies in their statements, but Smith repaired the damage by having Salcedo reaffirm his testimony.

Boen said that Ng had invited him to a shooting session at a friend's property. "He mentioned, you know, we could go up on a Friday night and the next day we could go shooting and then we could come back . . . it was just a couple of hours away. I never made it, never went.'' Kelley asked Boen about an incident in which someone at Dennis Moving had posted a drawing of a Chinese man, under which was written "No kill, no thrill,'' which became a "running joke'' among employees. But the witness could only recall having heard coworkers talk about it; he had not personally seen the caricature or caption.

It took only a few minutes, just prior to the lunch break, for another witness to report that he'd bought a blue Suzuki motorcycle from Leonard Lake, complete with ownership papers, on April 10, 1985. Lake had explained that "his buddy'' Cliff Peranteau, over in San Francisco, had asked him to sell it. An ex-police officer, the witness commented that he'd felt uneasy with Lake, and wouldn't let his wife and kids get out of the car during the sales transaction.

In the afternoon session, Paul Cosner's girlfriend, Marilyn Namba, told jurors of Paul's stated intention to show his Honda to a potential buyer on November 2, 1984, and of their plans to watch television together later that night. She had never seen him again.

The next witness, Jeff Gerald's platonic female roommate, recalled that on February 24, 1985, he had told her he was going to meet Charlie Ng at a bus station to do a "side job" of helping someone move. "Jeff said he would be back by suppertime, and bring Chinese food for dinner . . . I never saw Jeff again." The witness asserted that she had answered the phone on a dozen previous occasions and had spoken to Charlie Ng. Three days after Gerald vanished, the woman said, she came home from work and noticed some of his things had been taken, including a guitar.

Juror Nancy McEwan admired Gerald's roommate as the day's final witness, and noted that she "was definitely a no-nonsense person."

Spectators filed out, convinced that Ng had invited some of his coworkers to Wilseyville, but wondered if the prosecution had presented enough evidence to support the charges that Ng had helped kill them.

Nearly every morning of the trial, before jurors were admitted into the courtroom, defense lawyers presented motions regarding the prosecution's forthcoming witnesses. Monday morning, November 9, 1998, was no different. James Merwin, Bill Kelley's appeals expert, stood and vehemently objected to Peter Smith's intent to ask another Dennis Moving employee about alleged comments Ng had made to him. In a brief about the matter, Smith had written, "Ng told Perry McFarland that he had killed 12 people, but refused to give details other than some were blacks and some were homosexual." After detailed discussion and evaluation of the issues, Judge Ryan ruled for the defense, saying, "I am going to exclude that for now." Such testimony might have represented an iceberg to Ng's *Titanic*.

Brenda O'Connor's mother, Sharron, settled into the witness chair and identified photos of her daughter, her "son-in-law," Lonnie Bond, and her grandchild, Lonnie Bond Jr. Brenda's sister sat in the gallery, and juror Nancy McEwan noticed a strong resemblance to the photos of Brenda. The juror had also figured out, by this time, the identities of family members occupying the second row: Scott Stapley's parents and Paul Cosner's relatives.

Jeff Gerald's father stepped forward to identify a photo of his son and confirm that he hadn't heard from Jeff since February 1985.

The witness that lawyers had discussed in the early-morning motions, Perry McFarland, was the first coworker to acknowledge that he had been a friend of the defendant. Ng, McFarland said, had brought a bald, stocky man named "Tom" to help remodel McFarland's house. When the media later gave extensive coverage to the horrendous murders, McFarland realized that Tom was actually Leonard Lake. The witness recalled that Lake had left a duffel bag overnight at his house. Curious, McFarland and his wife had looked inside and found it contained a woman's negligee, videotapes, and a book on bondage. Upon completion of the job, McFarland had given Lake a ride to Wilseyville. Subsequently, when he discovered that photos of his wife were missing, McFarland had contacted Ng, who promptly retrieved them from the thief, Leonard Lake.

Gallery observers thought that McFarland had perhaps not

realized how fortunate he'd been as a result of being courteous to Charles Ng.

Before stepping down, McFarland repeated the chants he'd heard Ng using at work: "No gun, no fun"; "No kill no thrill"; and "Daddy dies, momma cries, baby fries."

Ray Houghton, Jeff Gerald's junior high-school pal and member of his band, verified to the jury that photos developed from Jeff's recovered camera had been taken at the apartment they had once shared. He also identified Jeff's guitar that had been found in Wilseyville.

Jeff's longtime girlfriend, with whom he had spoken during an hour-long telephone call to her New Jersey home, recounted his statement that he was going to earn $100 for helping a friend move.

A ballistics expert verified the existence of two bullet holes in the passenger side of the Honda, one in the door panel and one in the headliner, which had been made when a slug passed through the original sun visor. Both .22 bullets had been fired from the backseat. He also declared that bullets of the same caliber, seized from Ng's apartment, strongly resembled ammunition taken from a cartridge found at Wilseyville. The testimony seemed to suggest a thread, albeit tenuous, linking Ng to the crimes.

Dr. Boyd Stephens, San Francisco medical examiner, was sworn in to tell jurors gruesome details about the bodies. Observers' eyes turned toward the families in the second row. Would they be able to endure the grim testimony? During the expert's two hours on the stand, Honnaka introduced ghastly pictures, close-ups showing the decomposing bodies of Scott Stapley and Lonnie Bond. Several observers turned pale. The victims had been bound, handcuffed, ball-gagged, wrapped in sleeping bags, and buried. Lola Stapley bowed her head, removed her glasses, and wept softly while Dwight gently held his right arm tightly around her shoulders. Dwight would tell reporter Laura Mecoy, "I think it's important for the jury to see how personal it is. It's damned personal when it's your son, and you see his legs wrapped up and his hands bound."

A female juror hid the emotions roiling inside her. About the testimony, she later said that she found Dr. Stephens a "very honest, credible man."

On Tuesday, Tori Doolin Lewis, who had been Scott Stapley's girlfriend, gave jurors her version of Leonard Lake's sudden arrival in San Diego a few days after Scott left. At the time, she had known Lake as Charles Gunnar. Lake and Ng had arrived in Stapley's damaged pickup, said Lewis. The stunning announcement by Lake that he'd found "all of them dead in the cabin and burned the bodies" had disoriented Lewis. Lake and Ng, she testified, had departed with many of Scott's personal belongings.

During the remainder of the day, and on Thursday (the jurors took Wednesday off to celebrate Veterans' Day), several witnesses corroborated previous evidence, and tidied up a few loose ends.

On November 16, a chilly, gray Monday morning, the prosecution's list of witnesses had dwindled to nine. Two of them, retired Calgary police officers David Haddon and Barry Whistlecraft, who had searched Charles Ng's campsite in Fish Creek Park in July 1985, listed evidence they'd found. It included Scott Stapley's camera, a towel from Cliff Peranteau's apartment, a Ruger .22 handgun, and identification in the name of Mike Kimoto. The lad who had discovered the lean-to camp, now an adult, described the incident and how he had realized from a newspaper photo that the camper was Charles Ng.

A forensic anthropologist testified that the bone fragments

found on the Wilseyville property represented at least four adults, one child, and an infant, and perhaps more. The defense grilled him extensively, questioning the accuracy of his conclusions.

Next came the highway patrolman who responded to the scene of a pickup accident near Bakersfield, California. Charles Ng, he said, was the driver.

The day concluded with the testimony of a fingerprint expert who positively identified the remains of Scott Stapley and Lonnie Bond. Only three witness for the prosecution remained.

Sharlene Honnaka and Peter Smith brought out the big guns on Tuesday morning, after having Sergeant Larry Copland verify that a few documents had been found in the telephone trench.

Next, Honnaka questioned Sergeant Raymond Joseph Levesque Munro, RCMP. As the witness spoke of the Canadian court hearings in which he had testified, he referred to the judge as "m'lord," and mentioned that the opposing counsel referred to one another as "my friend."

Honnaka, getting to the point, asked Munro, "During the time that you served as an investigator in the extradition proceedings, did you have occasion to come into contact with a person by the name of Joseph Maurice Laberge?"

"Yes, I did."

"And did Laberge testify at that hearing?" Munro said he did. "During his testimony," Honnaka asked, "did the subject of drawings, which he had received from the defendant, arise?"

Reporters stirred. At last, the notorious cartoons, about which they had heard through cracks in the gag orders, were going to be exposed.

One by one, Honnaka introduced a series of crude, obscene pencil-and-ink drawings, most of them on lined 8½- by 11-inch sheets of paper. She'd prepared enlargements, and mounted them on an easel. People's Exhibit 224, captioned "Calavaras (sic) County Remains Claiming Station," depicted a figure, identified as Boyd Stevens (sic), handing out small bags, ostensibly containing human remains, labeled "Dubs" and "Allen." The macabre graphic sent shudders through observers. Another drawing showed Lake beating a nude female, Kathleen Allen, with Ng observing while eating rice.

A third drawing, like a sequential comic strip arranged diagonally on the paper, in a four-frame rendering of two figures, gave their names as "Lake" and "Slant." It depicted them carrying a stretcher, on which lies a sleeping person. Suddenly, they dump the victim into a fire. In the last frame, the burning victim screams, "Ah! You mother fuckers," while one of the bearers laughs, "Hoo! Ha ha!"

The final cartoon, captioned "San Quentin—Years later," featured a bespectacled figure lying in a prison cell. Ng's chants are printed on one wall, while seven drawings of eleven victims are taped to a second wall. Each picture is labeled with a name: "Carroll, Cosner, Peranteau, Gerald, and Allen." The two largest pictures, imprinted with " Dubs' and Bonds,"each portrays families of three figures, a man, a woman, and a baby. Only one of the twelve victims for which Ng faced murder charges was not included: Scott Stapley.

In the jury box, Nancy McEwan felt revolted. Later, she wrote to herself, "The cartoons, drawings, or whatever, made me sick. I fought back tears. I didn't even go to lunch with my new friends. I wanted to be alone."

Since Maurice Laberge had been killed in a car accident, the court allowed his testimony from the Canadian hearings to be read into the record. After eliciting from Sergeant Munro that Laberge had an "extensive criminal history," Honnaka handed the RCMP officer a sheaf of paper and asked him to read Laberge's words aloud. In the first segment, Laberge openly admitted years of criminal conduct resulting in repeated jail terms. He spoke freely of the robbery and sexual assault that landed him in prison, sentenced to twenty-five years. "I met Charles Ng in early 1986," Laberge had testified, and told of the relationship in which Ng had given him the drawings and had spoken of the crimes in Wilseyville, including the video-taped sessions with Kathi Allen and Brenda O'Connor.

Honnaka asked Munro to read a segment of Laberge's testimony about the taping session. "He told me that the videotape shows a female complaining that it is too warm, and he had a butterfly knife he called it, and he flicked it open and cut her clothes off."

Observers easily recognized the sequence in which Ng had stripped away Brenda O'Connor's blouse and bra. Munro read on, shifting to Laberge's testimony about another taped sequence. "He said that he stopped, and made himself some rice and had come back and was eating rice when Leonard Lake was carrying on with one of these victims. At this point in time the victim he was talking about was Kathi Allen."

Immediately, Honnaka reached for the cartoon in which Ng depicted himself eating rice while watching Lake flog Kathi Allen as she crouched nude and bound on a bed. At Honnaka's request, Munro described the picture, making an unmistakable relationship to the video.

Munro's voice captivated onlookers, as he read Laberge's description of the "Calaveras County Remains Claiming Section" cartoon and the drawing in which stretcher bearers Lake and "Slant" dump a victim into a fire. About the latter item, Laberge had explained, "Well, this particular cartoon came as a result of the discussions we had [about] Leonard Lake and Charles Ng taking these people and killing them and then burning them."

Regarding the "San Quentin—Years Later" drawing, Laberge had testified, "I received this cartoon . . . very near the end of the lengthy discussions we had in reference to all these various people that Charles Ng had killed. . . . He had drawn this cartoon and the purpose was . . . to demonstrate what the future was going to be like for him once he was extradited to the United States.''

To prevent the defense from surprising jurors by revealing more about Laberge's history, Honnaka drew from Munro information about Laberge being paid $36,000, Canadian currency, as part of a witness protection program into which he was placed after release from prison. She also read a stipulation into the record giving more details of his crimes from the words of the boy he sexually assaulted, and Laberge's changing stories about that event.

Bill Kelley wanted the jury to understand every aspect of Laberge's criminal history and to focus attention on cash payments given to the ex-convict. He cross-examined Munro extensively, and asked about the fatal car wreck at which over $20,000 in cash had been found. The witness brushed away any suggestion of possible assassination or mystery. It was nothing but an accident, he said. In Kelley's questions, he made certain the particulars of Laberge's sex crime was graphically clear. The grilling was interrupted by the lunch break, and continued into the afternoon.

When Munro finally stepped down, Judge Ryan couldn't resist a little humorous commentary about the formal expressions used in Canadian jurisprudence. ''I think we should adopt some of the Canadian language,'' Ryan quipped. ''I'd be 'm'lord', and Mr. Kelley would be Ms. Honnaka's 'friend.' '' His words and grin brought laughter from the jury box.

The prosecution's final witness, Lloyd Cunningham, a forensic document examiner, explained how he had verified that several typewritten letters and notes, purportedly from the victims, had been prepared with the Olympia typewriter found in Lake's bedroom.

When questioned about a check bearing Kathleen Allen's signature, the witness told of comparing it to other examples of her writing, and concluded that she had not signed the check that was written on May 2, 1985, after she had vanished.

Labels on videotapes allegedly stolen from Harvey Dubs were, according to Cunningham, printed by Dubs. And several signatures of the name Michael Kimoto had been made by Charles Ng.

Regarding the obscene cartoons Maurice Laberge had attributed to Ng, Cunningham testified than Ng had done all of the printing. On cross-examination, Bill Kelley asked who had drawn the figures, and Cunningham could only say, "I don't know." The issue would play heavily in the upcoming defense segment of the trial.

The final prosecution witness stepped down, and Peter Smith announced, "The people rest at this time."

Charles Ng had been charged in the murders of seven men, three women, and two babies. Had Honnaka and Smith presented enough evidence, through sixty-two witnesses and 238 exhibits, to convict Ng? Had they convinced all twelve jurors that Charles Ng was guilty, beyond a reasonable doubt, in the murder of twelve victims? Could Bill Kelley and Lewis Clapp undermine the prosecution's salient points?

Sharon Sellitto and her mother, along with Lola and Dwight Stapley, in their quest for answers and for justice, had prayed for answers. But great gaps in the available information still tore at their hearts and minds. Other victims' relatives also hoped for resolution, mostly in the conviction of Charles Ng. He had flaunted cruelty in the face of a helpless woman, saying it was part of the game.

The "game" would continue after the Thanksgiving Holiday, on Monday, November 30.

Chapter 30

Bill Kelley announced to the reassembled court on Monday, November 30, 1998, that he would make no opening statement. He would present his case for the defense and rely on the jury's judgment.

It soon became apparent that Kelley's case, or at least his strategy, was simple. He would continue to put the late Leonard Lake on trial. From the defense point of view, Lake did it all, and Charles Ng was nothing but a puppet who followed his master into the depths of Hell by trying to please him.

Kelley's parade of witnesses began with eight people who provided an abbreviated biography of Lake's childhood and early adult years. One of Lake's sisters, Sylvia, painted a verbal picture of the lonely boy left at a train station by his mother, and his resentful teen years growing up in the San Francisco home of his grandparents. A male cousin filled in a few more details of Lake's youth, explaining the fractious relationship between Lake and his younger brother, Donald.

Lake's first wife, Karen, livened up the testimony with her recollections of his two tours in the U.S. Marine Corps, involving action in Vietnam, and his bizarre sexual needs. He'd been cruel and excessively controlling, she said. She also mentioned his obsession with *The Collector* and "Operation Miranda." His peculiar tastes, she stated, led to divorce in 1979.

A chunky, nervous woman, about forty, identified only as "Ms. L," seemed on the verge of tears as she testified next. She accused Lake of photographing her in the nude, tied, and spread-eagled on the bed, when she was only sixteen, and of having no memory of how it had happened. "Maybe he drugged me," she suggested. Afterward, he blackmailed her into more provocative poses, she claimed, by threatening to tell her mother: "He was very persuasive and controlling." During one modeling session, the witness stated, "He raped me of my virginity."

One of the women on Lake's long list of female conquests during his years around Ukiah, in Northern California, spoke of his slick charm that lured her into an "intimate" relationship, but without sex. Lake had teased her about being a virgin, and tried to convince her that he could tell if she truly was chaste by having her sit on his lap. He wanted, she said, to be her first lover, but she held him off because his odd fantasies frightened her. Lake had mentioned his "blood brother" named Charles Gunnar, with whom he had a pact, said the witness. Whoever married Lake would be required to sleep with Gunnar because Lake had slept with Gunnar's wife. Another fantasy, she recalled, was to have a complete harem serving all his needs. Lake also told her that he believed in human sacrifice. Once, the woman disclosed, Lake had pinned her down on a bed and asked, "Are you playing games with me, trying to make me rape you?"

When she refused a marriage proposal, Lake left for the final time. Her house was burglarized the next night, and a neighbor described the intruder as resembling Lake.

Jennifer Gordon swore to tell the whole truth, and spoke of her relationship with Lake that started in October 1972. His initial "sweetness," she said, turned to an aberrant obsession with sex, including swinging and bondage, that eventually led to her trying to please him by resorting to prostitution. She'd posed for "volumes" of lurid photos for him, but he frightened her by fantasizing about snuff films. They'd parted in 1973. Gordon was the third witness who said that Lake spoke of keeping cyanide available so he would never face life in prison.

Soon after splitting with Gordon, Lake moved to "The Ranch," in partnership with Venus Salem. The diminutive woman, wearing oversized horn-rimmed glasses, and letting her long, straight, gray hair hang past her shoulders, testified about being exploited by Lake, and finally selling her half of the property to him.

With each of the first eight witnesses, cross-examination by Smith or Honnaka consisted of a few questions directing attention back to the defendant. Did you ever meet or have any contact with Charles Ng? Each witness answered no.

The tactics of diversion and refocus were easily recognized by jurors. One of them later summarized it: "It was odd hearing about these 'old hippies' and their 'back then' sex lives. A little bondage here, and little bondage there. Okay, so Leonard Lake was weird!!" The juror grew anxious to hear evidence relating directly to the defendant, Charles Ng.

More tales of bizarre behavior and sexual antics entertained the jury and observers the remainder of that week. They laughed when a man, who'd been a teenager at the time, told of working with Lake and described the excitement of being around naked women when he joined denizens of The Ranch in celebrating the summer solstice. Another witness spoke of living with Lake, and hearing of the older man's obsession with survivalism and sex. Gina Travers, only nineteen at the time she stayed with Lake, corroborated other testimony about his strange desires.

Charles Gunnar's former wife, Vicky, still attractive, with light-brown hair twisted into a bun, wore a blue-checked suit and spoke softly as she described her three-year marriage and her contacts with Lake. After she'd left Gunnar, and after his disappearance, she said, Lake had told her, "Charles is not coming back." Lake had occupied Gunnar's house and used his yellow VW van, Vicky recalled. She thought it very odd when, one day in mid-1984, she left work and found the van parked at the curb with keys in the ignition. Lake never explained why he had returned it to her. No, the witness said, she had never met Charles Ng.

Jurors sighed and appeared bored. If the defense was trying to show that Lake's deviant behavior demonstrated hatred for all women, they were failing. Several members of the jury remembered that Lake's sister Sylvia had testified about his maintaining a "pretty friendly" relationship with his mother, the woman who had allegedly deserted him and planted the seed of resentment. Some of them impatiently wondered when the trial of Ng would start again.

The Unicorn named Sir Lancelot came into the spotlight with the testimony of "Otter," who had surgically altered the little white goat, and saw the manipulative side of Lake in his use of the animal to lure young women into posing for him.

Several more women, who had been teenagers in the late seventies and early eighties, testified about Lake's quirky sexual attitudes and persistent efforts to photograph them in the nude. Male residents of The Ranch sketched a different view of Lake as a boastful misfit and a troublesome nuisance whom they suspected of commiting a rash of burlaries and thefts on The Ranch and in Ukiah.

They spoke of being relieved when he finally gave up his place on The Ranch and moved away.

In the jury box, Nancy McEwan observed, "Maybe they're trying to prove a 'Charlie Manson' thing where he controlled his people. That doesn't make the 'controlled' people innocent! . . . What's going on? Is Leonard Lake on trial or Charles Ng? The defense is going on and on about Lake. We all know (I hope) that he was a very bad person; in fact a murderer. But what about Charles Ng? No wonder this case is supposed to last so long!"

Kelley and Clapp called several more women to the stand in the first week of December to relate how they had been seduced and manipulated by Lake. A few of the witnesses also spoke of Cricket Balazs. The owner of an escort service in San Francisco revealed that Leonard became a member as "Donald Lake." It soon became apparent that Lake had probably killed his own brother. Additional testimony informed jurors that he also used Charles Gunnar's identity.

A balding, graying, bespectacled man, speaking softly from the witness chair, admitted that he'd placed an ad in a San Francisco paper in which he offered to have sex with men. He'd given himself a pseudonym, "Phil." The ad was answered by a man calling himself Tom Meyers. After they'd engaged in sex, the witness said, Meyers invited him to spend a weekend at a mountain cabin, but he'd refused. Afterward, Meyers pestered Phil about getting together again, and became angry when the offers were declined. Examining a photo of Leonard Lake, the witness thought it resembled Meyers, but couldn't be positive. Phil said that his analyst had recommended that he continue to see Meyers and bond with him. Laughter rippled through the room when the witness said, "I stopped seeing the analyst."

On December 8, an alternate juror fell ill, and was excused from duty, reducing the pool to only three.

Next, a female neighbor of Paul Cosner's recalled seeing a man who wore a red-and-black-checked "lumberjack" shirt outside the apartment, talking with Cosner. The witness positively identified him as Leonard Lake. Surely, thought observers, the jury could easily convict Lake of murdering Cosner, if he'd survived to stand trial. But was there enough evidence that Charles Ng had participated?

Finally, Ng's name was mentioned by a defense witness. Ernie Pardini, the Philo resident who helped Lake, Balazs, and Ng move to Indian Creek Ranch, recalled seeing the short, quiet Asian man not long before a police raid in which both Lake and Ng were arrested. Pardini noted that Lake appeared to be verbally abusive of Ng. At least one juror thought the comment painted a picture of Ng as a friendless loner with low self-esteem.

A long line of witnesses placed Lake and Cricket at Wilseyville and testified to seeing Lake around the pink palace in San Francisco. Juror Nancy McEwan noted to herself, "I think I finally get it. The defense is showing us that a lot of people thought Lake was weird and creepy. They seem to be finished with the 'old hippies' and are introducing a 'newer' bunch from Wilseyville and the Bay area. And they are proving that very few people ever saw Charles Ng at Wilseyville. . . . He was clearly there, though (to me, at least), as seen in the video." Ng's videotaped behavior at the cabin, to McEwan, held sinister implications. "At least," she noted, "I know I don't go to my friend's houses and run around in my underwear waiting to shower with people."

The juror also found it frustrating when objections prevented witnesses from completing something they'd started to say. "That's what's wrong with our system. We don't hear enough. I want to know everything. What's wrong with the whole truth?" The repetition of information also irritated McEwan.

"I could be wrong, but I get the feeling that all the attorneys think we (the jurors) are stupid or something. I guess that's their job, but some things are told to us over and over. For example, how many witnesses do we need to prove that Leonard liked to take photos? It was obvious to me way back when Larry Copland presented the evidence seized in Wilseyville, lots of photo albums, pictures on the bunker wall, et cetera."

Sometimes, witness testimony can backfire on the lawyers. Kelley called to the stand a woman who had known Cricket Balazs for more than twenty years. She acknowledged having met Ng in Philo. When the case broke in June 1985, the woman said, Cricket came to her house, crying and carrying a stuffed pillowcase and said, "I need to store this someplace." When Balazs later picked it up, she reportedly said it contained papers belonging to Leonard Lake.

During Kelley's questioning regarding an investigator's report of previous statements the witness had made, she blurted out that Cricket had said, "I don't think Leonard Lake could have done this. I think it was all Charles Ng."

Kelley's attempts at damage control were marginally successful. The lunch hour mercifully ended the testimony. Because no more defense witnesses were available, the day ended early.

After several people testified on Monday, December 14, giving evidence that seemed inconsequential, Lake's female cousin, sixteen years his junior, told of visiting him at Wilseyville. She'd stayed ten days in May 1985, and left just one week before the case broke. One night, she said, Lake had cooked a whole rabbit for dinner, but only a few pieces were consumed. The next morning, feeling hungry, she went to the refrigerator, only to find that all the rabbit was gone. Lake told her he'd eaten it, but she found it hard to believe, since there had been eight or nine pieces remaining. The implication dawned on observers. Had Lake taken the leftovers out to the bunker to feed a sex slave prisoner?

The witness admitted that she had posed partially nude for Lake, and had engaged in "intimate" relations with him. Kelley asked if she had ever seen or met Charles Ng, and seemed openly satisfied when she replied in the negative.

Disturbing evidence came from a forensic dentist who testified that tooth fragments found at Wilseyville suggested that the remains were from "more than one child," and that the children's ages could be from six months to seven years. The probability of more than two child victims was confirmed when Lewis Clapp read a stipulation about DNA testing of a portion of a child's liver unearthed at Wilseyville. The organ did not come from Sean Dubs or Lonnie Bond Jr.!

John Kohn, a screenwriter who had helped to prepare the script for a 1965 motion-picture version of John Fowles's book *The Collector,* testified, solely for the purpose of giving the jury a synopsis of the story. No one in the jury box seemed impressed.

Judge Ryan kept a sharp eye on the next witness, a tough-looking fellow who carried a cane with him. He'd been a longtime friend of Brenda O'Connor's and had heard her express fear of a neighbor who kept pestering her to pose nude. After the witness stepped down, Ryan commented that he'd seen him glaring at Ng, and the defendant had dropped his eyes. "I was very concerned," said the judge, "about this man who had star tattoos on him and a leg stick in his hand."

As Thursday, December 17, 1998, came to a close, the judge

announced that the proceedings would be suspended until January 4, 1999. He wished the jurors happy holidays.

On Monday, January 4, 1999, three forensic experts spoke of bones, teeth, and fingerprints. Only one print belonging to Charles Ng had been found at Wilseyville, on a wine bottle. Jurors didn't give the evidence much weight, since only two prints from Cricket were found, despite her frequent presence there.

Ng's aunt Alice told jurors, through an interpreter, that she had given her nephew $400 to go on a vacation in early June 1985. Nancy McEwan, in her notes, observed, "Does the defense actually believe we're going to think he was going on vacation? After all, it was the same day he and Lake were caught shoplifting [and] driving a stolen car from a missing man [that was] loaded with a gun and a silencer. Charles Ng escapes and Lake takes a cyanide pill. Give me a break!"

Mark Novak, who'd been a soldier in Hawaii, revealed after visiting Lake at The Ranch that he had given Lake's telephone number and address to Ng. "At last," wrote McEwan, "we find out how Leonard Lake and Charles Ng met." A bearded auto mechanic, wearing a red plaid shirt, red suspenders, and carrying a leather hat, testified about conversations he had with Lake—who was posing as Charles Gunnar—regarding repairs to the bronze-colored Honda's interior and upholstery.

Frigid weather chilled Orange County to the bone in January, but the atmosphere inside Judge Ryan's court heated up on Wednesday morning. The jury had been given the day off so that lawyers could present a series of motions. The defense wanted to use parts of Lake's detailed journal, but exclude other parts. After a spirited debate by Kelley, Ryan spoke up. "Jury trials in this country are supposed to be searches for the truth. . . . I believe the court should prevent the use of misleading evidence. This edited diary could do that if it's intended to show that Leonard Lake killed all twelve of the victims without the help of Charles Ng.'' He added, ''I believe the diary should be excluded. A lot of it is just pure junk.''

Kelley protested. ''But the diary shows that Lake was thinking of the fantasy for twenty years.''

Ryan shook his head and spoke with a touch of impatience. ''How many witnesses have testified to the building of that bunker? The jury knows what Lake planned.'' The judge ruled the diary would not be admitted.

Another expert on bones led off the proceedings on Wednesday, followed by a forensic anthropologist and a handwriting expert. In the early afternoon, television cameras and a jostling herd of reporters gathered. The word had gone out that Claralyn ''Cricket'' Balazs would be called to the stand.

The courtroom filled up quickly, with observers anxiously anticipating what could be the most explosive testimony of the whole trial.

An attorney for Balzs approached the bench and asked to be heard. He spoke of the immunity agreement, saying it related to testimony about specific victims, and if lawyers questioned his client about any other victims, she would invoke the Fifth Amendment. Judge Ryan said the attorney would be welcome to object if any questions were asked that he thought inappropriate.

With all eyes on her, Cricket Balazs walked up the aisle, wearing black slacks, a dark blouse, and gold-rimmed glasses. Her dark hair had been cut short. She swore to tell the whole truth, and eased into the witness chair. Bill Kelley read the major elements of the immunity agreement, listed the names of the twelve victims, paused, and said in clear tones, ''No questions.''

The surprising decision by Kelley appeared incongruous. But his strategy was actually well thought out. By reading the immunity statement into the record, Kelley might have created

an appearance to the jury that Balazs had something to hide.
If the defender had asked questions, he risked the exposure of
something that Ng had allegedly told her. Court records indicated that Ng had confessed to Cricket his involvement in
killing Donald Giuletti, a San Francisco disc jockey. He had
also allegedly spoken to her about killing a black cabdriver
and a woman in Hawaii.

By not asking questions of Balazs in open court, Kelley had
avoided potentially catastrophic statements about his client.

Since she had not spoken on the stand, the prosecution had no
issues on which they could conduct cross-examination. Balazs
departed, leaving jurors, spectators, and families sorely disappointed.

Five witnesses testified on Thursday, January 7, including
Inspector Ed Erdelatz, of the SFPD, who had been involved in
the case for nearly fourteen years. Most of the questions put
to them were designed to tidy up loose details.

The most interesting event of the day was the playing of
Leonard Lake's self-recorded videotape in which he sat in the
brown recliner and spoke candidly of his philosophy and plan
to carry out Operation Miranda. For the defense, it was one
more plank in their platform of pointing to Lake as the person
who planned and executed each of the murders.

Sad news spread through the court on Monday morning,
January 11. Bill Kelley's father had passed away over the
weekend. Kelley, of course, needed a few days off. Judge Ryan
announced that the trial would resume on Tuesday, January
19.

A sense of excitement buzzed through the courtroom on the
first day back after eight days' delay. While jurors waited in
the hallway, wondering what was going on, the defense team

announced to Judge Ryan that Charles Ng wanted to testify, but only about charges relating to the Dubs family, plus Peranteau and Gerald. So, Kelley said, cross-examination should be limited to those five counts. Outraged, Honnaka and Smith voiced strong protests. If Ng takes the stand, Honnaka insisted, he's subject to interrogation on all twelve counts of murder. The argument lasted the entire morning. Ryan listened, asked several questions, and finally ruled that a broader cross-examination would be allowed.

After a huddle with the other lawyers, at 11:40 A.M., Kelley announced that Ng would not testify, and then surprised everyone in the courtroom by reporting, "The defense rests."

In most murder trials, when the defense has completed its case, the prosecution calls a few witnesses to rebut evidence and testimony presented on behalf of the defendant, and to reaffirm the case against him. But Peter Smith stunned gallery observers when he stood and announced that he and Honnaka would call no rebuttal witnesses. It appeared that the only remaining step, in the guilt phase of the trial, would be closing arguments by each side.

But nothing involving Charles Ng ever stayed within the bounds of expectation.

Chapter 31

On Monday, January 25, defense attorney Lewis Clapp rose to read a new motion by Charles Ng demanding to fire his attorneys, the familiar Marsden procedure. He added a request for the judge to throw out everything that had transpired before, and declare a mistrial. Ng's reasoning centered on his "long-standing disputes" with the defense team, and his claim that he'd been forcibly prevented from testifying in his own behalf.

With admirable patience, Judge Ryan listened, clarified a few points, told Ng, "You're not being forced to do anything," and ruled "the motion and request for substitute counsel is denied."

Sharlene Honnaka and Peter Smith had agreed to split the final argument duties between them. Honnaka would summarize the prosecution's evidence in the cases of Deborah and

Harvey Dubs, the baby Sean Dubs, Paul Cosner, Clifford Peranteau, and Jeffrey Gerald. Smith would handle the speaking
chores for the remaining six: Kathleen Allen, Michael Carroll,
Scott Stapley, Lonnie Bond, Brenda O'Connor, and their baby,
Lonnie Bond Jr.

The trial had started with the homemade videotape of Kathleen Allen and Brenda O'Connor. Fittingly, Honnaka opened
the final arguments with the same tape. While the jurors watched
intently, Honnaka replayed sections of it to emphasize crucial
statements by Lake. She repeated his frequent use of the term
"we" in his threats to the frightened, bound victims.

In the tape, Ng had said to O'Connor, "You can cry like
the rest of them. . . ." Honnaka paused the presentation at that
moment, to let the implication sink in. "The rest of them"
implied multiple victims.

Juror Bonnie Reinhardt jotted down an observation that the
baby was probably already dead at the time Lake and Ng taunted
Brenda, because it would have been extremely doubtful that
they would have arranged for someone to care for the child
while they tortured the mother. Reinhardt also couldn't erase
from her mind an exhibit shown to the jury. It was a photo of
Brenda, standing nude on the deck outside Lake's cabin. The
juror noted, "Her eyes were red and swollen, and there was a
look of fear and hopelessness in her eyes." Reinhardt would
later say, "I'll never get that picture out of my mind."

Honnaka, using her hands in broad gestures, reached toward
jurors with palms up, fingers spread to symbolize openness and
honesty. She reminded them of horrific cartoons that seemed
to corroborate threats made in the videos. Pointing to the drawing in which two stretcher bearers, labeled "Lake" and "Slant,"
dump a human figure into flames, Honnaka said, "This tells
you that he and Lake were involved in killing people and
burning them." Holding up exhibits that had been introduced
into evidence, Honnaka walked slowly in front of the jurors to
give each one a close look. Bill Kelley, now and then chewing

on the temples of his glasses, put them down to rapidly scribble notes.

After lunch, Honnaka spoke of the Dubs family, carefully outlining the chronology that placed Ng within a time frame that allowed his participation in the crimes. Observers noticed that when making reference to Ng's confinement in federal prison, Honnaka spoke simply of him being in "Fort Leavenworth." Officially, the jurors hadn't yet heard about his theft of weapons in Hawaii, or his plea bargain that put him behind bars.

Moving on to Paul Cosner, Honnaka again made certain that jurors understood the dates involved, pointing out that Ng was in the area during November 1984, when the victim vanished. Regarding Peranteau and Gerald, she reminded jurors that Lake would never have known either man if Ng hadn't provided the link.

The defense had gone to great lengths to show that Lake had committed murders prior to the arrival of Ng. Honnaka waved that logic away with the contention, "It doesn't matter if Leonard Lake did a thousand crimes before he met up with this defendant. This evidence clearly shows [Ng] was involved in these murders."

Speaking slowly, Honnaka said, "If you find that he knew about these murders and intended for these victims to die, he is guilty! He is as guilty as the person who pulled the trigger." California penal code 187 provides the legal basis for her assertion.

Honnaka thanked the jury and mentioned that Mr. Smith would speak to them on Tuesday.

Peter Smith, earnest and soft-spoken, moved with graceful ease in front of the jury box on Tuesday morning. Wearing a dark suit with a conservative maroon tie, he put the jurors at ease with a gentle smile. He, too, used the videotape liberally, to demonstrate Ng's active participation in tormenting Kathi Allen and Brenda O'Connor. When Brenda cried out, "That's my baby," Smith stopped the tape to point out, "Not only do you hear the words, but you can *feel* the terror and desperation." As he spoke, Smith clasped his hands behind his back, and paced slowly back and forth.

At the videotaped point where Ng remarks, "Surprisingly cooperative," in describing Brenda's capitulation, Smith repeated the cruel words. Each time he stopped the tape, Smith looked into jurors' eyes and asked, "Remember that?" They responded with nods of agreement.

While Smith spoke, and during the tape playing, Ng remained stoic, silent, hunched over the table, reading a document.

Smith, in discussing evidence related to Lonnie Bond, O'Connor, and the baby, showed slide photographs of them, and a driver's license of Scott Stapley. He repeated Ng's words, "It's part of the game," and asked, "What chance did they have?"

To illustrate the point, Smith showed a portion of the tape in which Lake said, "You have a choice . . . we'll shoot you."

The tape segment ended with Ng, on his own volition, cutting away Brenda's bra. After speaking for nearly an hour, Smith expressed confidence the jurors would find Ng guilty in twelve counts of first-degree murder.

Judge Ryan recessed the proceedings until Wednesday morning, expecting the defense to make their final arguments.

Juror Nancy McEwan pondered the day's events at her home on Tuesday night. "Mr. Smith gave an excellent closing argument. Very compelling. He had us take a very good look at the videos while pointing out the importance of listening to them. I really had to hold back the tears.

"You listen to all of these witnesses all these months, and try to put the puzzle together. It's been thirteen years since the crimes, and of course witnesses forget, and get confused. But, as Mr. Smith pointed out, the videos were taken back then and they are real. What kind of idiots actually tape themselves committing a crime? I suspect only evil, crazy ones. Very sick. Did they make those tapes for themselves, to watch some boring Saturday night?

"I kept glancing at Mr. Ng during the videos. He just sits there like he's writing a letter or something. Maybe he's making more gross cartoons. Does he think it's funny? Of course, I'm still open to the defense argument. That will be tomorrow."

Anyone expecting to hear Bill Kelley and Lewis Clapp summarize their case were to be astonished at Wednesday's events.

The day opened with reporters quickly filling the gallery, and chatting about a huge graphic Kelley's team had erected. A poster stood on tripods in front of the jury box, stretching its entire length, upon which targetlike red circles represented Lake's many crimes, with his portrait occupying dead center of the display.

But Charles Ng was having none of it. He demanded to be heard. Sharlene Honnaka strenuously objected. While jurors waited outside, a full gallery waited inside, and lawyers waited at counsel table. Judge Ryan gave Ng nearly an hour to hand-write his motion in which he insisted on testifying. In whispers, reporters speculated that it wouldn't be allowed, since the prosecution had already presented closing arguments. It would be like seeing your opponent's hole card in a blackjack game, then making your bet. Unheard of!

In Nancy McEwan's recollection of the day, she said, "Around eleven in the morning, a bunch of media people came running out of the courtroom and got on their cell phones or lined up at the two pay phones. What's going on? Something

big! I thought they had probably come to a plea-bargain
agreement in exchange for life in prison. I was disappointed.
I wanted my vote and my say in deliberations. They finally
called us into a very crowded courtroom. I immediately noticed
Mr. Ng's chair was empty. I figured I was right about the plea
bargain, and that the extra bailiffs we saw go in were there to
take him away. Then, I was shocked to see him sitting in the
witness chair!''

Ng sat calmly, wearing tan slacks and a light-pink dress
shirt, but with the usual bulge missing. The stun belt had been
removed. His face appeared bloated as he peered from behind
the thick spectacles.

Lewis Clapp stood to do the questioning. Reporters wondered
if Ng had made the choice to testify out of hatred for Kelley.
Earlier that morning, in line at a coffee vendor, Kelley had said
to a journalist, ''Fours years of work down the toilet!''

After swearing to tell the truth, the whole truth, and nothing
but the truth, Charles Ng began answering questions. In the
voice of an adolescent, he used a remarkably sophisticated
vocabulary, reflecting a high level of intelligence and an extraordinary memory. [*Editor's Note: Ng's syntax errors are not
corrected.*]

First, through Ng's answers, Clapp built the chronology of Ng
meeting Lake. ''How did you view him?'' asked the attorney.

''I viewed him as a veteran, as a person that was in Vietnam,
in the Marine Corps. He told me he was a staff sergeant when
he was retired, so I look at him as a person that have, like,
senior to me. . . . I view him as a patriot because he had fought
for the country, and I view him as a person who was very
knowledgeable about different things like homesteading . . .
history, and geography . . . And also, things of common interest
in the Marine Corps that . . . we usually talk about.'' He added
that he felt loyalty to Lake, ''. . . so my tendency is to follow
his advice and respect his judgment.''

About the chants attributed by coworkers to Ng, such as

"No kill, no thrill," and the other violent slogans, the defendant attributed them to his experience in the Marine Corps, calling them "traditional," like "a war cry," and indicating that formations of Marines shouted them in cadence while running. He'd used them at work, he said, in the spirit of "jocular type of locker-room talk."

Zeroing in on work records, Clapp asked Ng if he had worked on Saturday, January 19, 1985, the first day Cliff Peranteau had failed to show up. Ng answered yes.

Clapp asked, "On the second day that Cliff Peranteau didn't show up, where were you?"

Ng said, "I was at work." Several jurors made notes, and reporters in the gallery glanced at one another. It was an ambiguous question. If Clapp meant the second consecutive day, which was a Sunday, Ng had not worked then according to his boss's testimony.

Clapp made it technically correct by asking, "How many hours did you work that day on the twenty-first?"

Ng quickly answered, "Seven and a quarter hours."

Speaking rapidly, Clapp moved on. "The third day that Cliff Peranteau did not show up for work, where were you?" Ng said he was at work. Unless listeners were looking at a calender of January 1985, the questions and testimony sounded like Ng had been on the job several consecutive days, including the weekend Peranteau vanished. It could give the impression that he was much too busy to be involved in the victim's fate. Careful listeners, though, realized that he'd been off on Friday night, when Peranteau was last seen leaving the Dennis Moving Company workplace, Saturday night, Sunday, and hadn't reported back to work until Monday morning.

Transportation had been a problem, Ng said, and his trips to Wilseyville were usually by Greyhound bus from San Francisco to Stockton, where Lake picked him up and drove him the remaining fifty miles. Clapp wanted jurors to understand that an overnight or weekend trip required three or four hours of travel each way.

Lake sometimes stayed overnight at Ng's San Francisco apartment, he acknowledged, and the extra Oral B toothbrush did, indeed, belong to Lake. Several items seized during the police search had been left there by Lake, said Ng, including a Cross pen and pencil set engraved with Cliff Peranteau's initials.

Regarding the bunker, Ng testified that Lake had mentioned a secret cell inside it, but had said it was his "domain" and ordered Ng not to "intrude on it."

The gruesome cartoons, said Ng, were drawn to relieve boredom in solitary confinement. "It came about as a way to kill time, and as a result of information that [Laberge] had supposedly read about me or heard about me . . . it result in a jocular activity between me and him . . . . He would draw part of the cartoon and slide it over to me, and I would embellish it and send it back. That is kind of humor thing between him and me." Jurists failed to see the humor. Ng added, "Originally, the cartoons are not related to any aspect of the case at all." Laberge, he said, had obtained newspaper accounts, police reports, and other documents, and had constantly inquired about details of Ng's case, thus gaining "an amalgamation" of information he later traded for favors. According to Ng, Laberge had prompted and coaxed him into putting gory details in the cartoons. The drawings, he insisted, were not an admission of guilt.

Asked about the use of Mike Kimoto as an alias, Ng replied that Lake had admitted stealing the wallet at a beach, and had given the ID cards to Ng and had "instructed" him to open a post office box in that name.

Knowing full well that the prosecution might bring up in cross-examination the prison sentence in Leavenworth, which had not yet been openly revealed to the jury, Clapp asked Ng if he'd been convicted of a burglary and sentenced to a prison term. "Yes," said Ng. "I received a three-year sentence at Fort Leavenworth, a military prison. . . . Most of the people there were first-time offenders from various branches of the services." He said he fully expected to be deported when released.

Moving on to the case of Jeff Gerald, Clapp asked if Ng had called the victim's residence and arranged to meet Gerald at a bus station. He denied having made such a call.

Up to this point in the trial, the jury had heard incomplete details about the information Maurice Laberge had allegedly given to authorities regarding Ng's "confessions" to him. Lewis Clapp, in his next series of revealing questions, stunned observers.

"Did you tell Maurice Laberge that it was a big-time mistake in killing Harvey and Deborah Dubs because certain video equipment had been kept?"

"No."

"Did you tell Maurice Laberge that after you killed the Dubs family, you buried them away from the rest?"

"No."

"Did you tell Maurice Laberge—did you ever make this statement: 'Deborah Dubs was good to my dick. She could control her hole muscles'?"

"Oh no, never. I never talked to him about my—in terms of these victims, what I knew about or what I didn't know about." Another near slip of the tongue?

After probing Ng's knowledge about Laberge's criminal history, Clapp continued with the remarkable questioning. "Did you tell Maurice Laberge that they could prove that you were responsible for the Dubs kidnapping because they found Dubs's property at your apartment?''

''No.''

''Did you ever tell Maurice Laberge that Leonard killed Harvey Dubs—''

''Right.''

''—and that you killed Deborah and Sean Dubs?''

''No.''

''Did you tell Maurice Laberge that it was hard to kill the baby, but 'the hole' was a piece of cake?''

''No.''

''Did you tell Maurice Laberge that you didn't care about killing Deborah Dubs, but killing the baby was strange; Lake told you it would be good training experience, like the [Nazi] SS when they were given a puppy at the beginning of their training and forced to kill the puppy when they graduated?''

''No.''

''Did you tell Maurice Laberge, 'At first, I felt funny about wasting the baby, but then I figured it was better that way than having no parents'?''

''No.''

After a pause to inquire about Ng's knowledge regarding Lake's journal, Clapp pursued the tough direct questions again. ''Did you tell Maurice Laberge that you told Debbie Dubs she would have to decide fast whether she wanted your dick or her baby because her baby was already dead?''

''No.''

''Did you tell Maurice Laberge that you rammed a .45 into her cunt and then put it in your mouth?''

''No.''

''Did you tell Maurice Laberge that killing Debbie Dubs was the first time and pulling the trigger made your dick hard?''

''No. Never.''

''Did you tell Maurice Laberge that hearing her beg just before the kill was the best part?''

"No."

"Did you tell Maurice Laberge, 'They won't find Peranteau or Gerald because I burned then after we killed them'?"

"No."

"Did you tell Maurice Laberge that you killed Peranteau by shooting him in the head, 'No gun, no fun; No kill, no thrill'?"

"No, but this is example of how he morphed the information from the police report into these so-called direct quote from me."

"Did you tell Maurice Laberge that you tried the asshole death grip on Deborah Dubs?"

"No."

"Did you tell Maurice Laberge that the asshole death grip is to strangle a girl with her panty hose and twist it as you are fucking her ass?"

"No."

"Did you tell Maurice Laberge that with regard to Debbie Dubs, 'The kill was sweet, the kill was good, it made my dick hard'?"

"No."

"Did you tell Maurice Laberge that killing Sean Dubs was not easy, but it was just business, part of the operation?"

"No."

"Did you tell Maurice Laberge with regard to the Dubs baby, 'I didn't torture the baby. I just killed it. It was a quick and painless kill'?"

"No."

"Did you tell Maurice Laberge that 'the hole's—Deborah's—hair was really dark, kind of brownish black [and] . . . at the time my dick was king. What am I supposed to do? After I have sex with her, and her husband and the baby is dead, am I supposed to let her go?' " Ng said he had not.

While reporters, observers, and the jury sat in astonished silence, wondering why the defense would question Ng in such explicit and shocking terms, Clapp doggedly persisted. He asked Ng if he told Maurice Laberge that it had been a mistake to keep Peranteau's pen set after killing him; if he and Lake had returned after killing the Dubs family to burglarize their apartment; and that the Dubses were "fucking honkies." The defendant repeatedly answered, "No."

While denying that he'd helped kidnap the Dubs family, or that he'd told Laberge anything about it, Ng admitted returning to the Dubs apartment to take property. "Leonard came to me and basically told me to help him out with a job. He drove me to this place, gave me a key, and told me to go in the apartment . . . there should be a suit bag and a flight bag right next to the doorway . . . to come down and put it in the trunk. Basically, that's his instruction to me, that there should be nobody in the house. . . ."

A map with the Dubses' Yukon Street address circled had been seized from Ng's apartment. "Where did that map come from?" inquired Clapp.

"I have no idea. I know that map. It's an additional map that looked like it was mine. But the one the prosecution used against me, it did not belong to me."

Easing the tension with inquiries about videos, cars, mail, and evidence found buried at Wilseyville, Clapp led up to the shoplifting incident at the lumberyard. Ng testified that he had taken the vise, "Because Leonard told me he need a new vise for his workshop up in Wilseyville and he didn't want to pay for it. . . . We went there to get some supply . . . because he working on Cricket's house, if I remember correctly."

Clapp, pacing, moving nervously, asked, "Well, when Lake would ask you to steal a vise, why didn't you just tell him no?"

"Well, I just think because that's one of the thing he do. He always called that the freebies, meaning if you could pay—if you could steal it, why pay for it? That type attitude."

To several observers, the next question from Clapp seemed to symbolize the heart of the defense case. "Would it be accurate to say that just about anything Leonard Lake told you to do, you would do?''

"No."

"Can you give us an example of something that you wouldn't do if he told you to do it?"

Ng stumbled with his answer. "Well, there's a line that I won't cross is basically, you know, like something that—either hurting, killing somebody, something serious, I won't do it."

Growing hoarse, Clapp asked for the afternoon recess. With the jurors out of the room, he explained to Judge Ryan that he needed some time to evaluate the scope of his questioning strategy, so he wondered if the session could end early. Ryan appeared impatient at the defense for opening the Pandora's box of alleged statements by Maurice Laberge. Noting that the prosecution probably would not have probed it in such graphic detail, Ryan commented, "The jury never heard those statements from Mr. Laberge." Clapp replied that he had anticipated use of the statements by the prosecution to impeach Ng's testimony. Ryan shook his head, as if in disagreement, but diplomatically allowed the issue to drop. "If you need more time, Mr. Clapp, I'll give it to you."

With the jury reseated, Ng denied knowing anything about bullet holes in the Honda upholstery, or the killing of Paul Cosner.

If he hadn't committed any serious crimes, why had he fled to Canada? "Fear," Ng explained. He might be arrested and deported. He'd also been found in possession of a firearm when arrested in Canada. Lake had sold it to him, he said. After getting a litany of answers about conditions in the Canadian prison, Clapp asked Ng if he'd ever met Lonnie Bond. He said he hadn't.

"All right. The first time you ever saw Lonnie Bond, was he alive or dead?"

"He was dead." A rumble of surprise resonated through the gallery.

Ng refuted the suggestion that he'd "shot Lonnie Bond full of holes," by commenting that Bond had been shot once through the head. He'd also seen Scott Stapley's body.

Clapp asked, "When you saw him already deceased, did Lake ask you to take some action regarding . . . the body?"

"Yes, he did—to make it look like they died while they were tied up and bound, like biker style." Ng inferred that Lake wanted the victims to appear as if they'd been killed by ". . . biker-type people . . . he told me to find some sleeping bags and put him inside. And also, you know, use some string to tie up his legs and tape to tie up his arms. I don't remember. He got some cheap handcuff that he used for bondage with Cricket that he asked me to put on him, I believe." Ng admitted also putting a ball gag in Lonnie Bond's mouth.

"At some point, did you take part in burying the body of Lonnie Bond?"

"Yes." Jurors' eyes widened. At last—they had heard an affirmative answer.

"When you saw Lonnie Bond and he was already dead, where was he?"

"He was under the porch of Leonard Lake's house, in the back."

"Did you bury him that same day?"

"Yes."

At least two reporters, thinking like amateur detectives, hoped that Sharlene Honnaka or Peter Smith had noted a question to ask Ng. In the glimpse of the bodies on a wheelbarrow, seen in the rewind mode of a videotape, they appeared stiff, as if in full rigor mortis. That might indicate they had been killed within twelve hours of the pictures. The wanna-be sleuths hoped the prosecution, in cross-exam, would ask Ng if the bodies were stiff when he helped bury them. If he answered yes, could it be an indicator that he lied about not being present when Bond and Stapley were killed?

The long day ended. On Thursday, Ng would continue his dramatic testimony, with a full house of reporters analyzing every word.

Chapter 32

Lewis Clapp opened Thursday morning by asking Charles Ng about the "M Ladies" videotape. Ng said he knew the camera was running while Lake taunted each woman, and thought it occurred at night. He had assisted Lake, "to gain the compliance and cooperation of Kathi Allen ... because Leonard Lake wanted to keep her for—as a prisoner."

"As a sex slave?"

"He didn't use that term, but he basically said that 'M Ladies,' the term he used, is basically somebody he is going to keep for a while to fulfill his fantasy." Ng denied knowing of any plans to kill the women. He couched his recollection in stilted language. "I had some idea that he just want to kind of behavioral modify her to gain compliance to just kind of, like become his willing sex partner."

In reference to allegations by Maurice Laberge, Clapp asked, "Did anything of this nature take place with Debbie Dubs?"

"No. I never involved in Debbie Dubs's or Harvey Dubs's or Sean Dubs's disappearance."

Many people had wondered, for years, if Ng actually was innocent of complicity in the crimes, why he didn't tell Lake he wanted no part of the videotape sessions, especially when Lake used the collective "we" in threatening the women. Clapp asked the question.

Ng explained, "I won't confront Lake like that." Haltingly, and jumbling his words, he claimed he couldn't challenge Lake, and that he didn't think the threats were real, so he just "went along with it."

Lake had threatened Kathi with the words, "We will bury you where we buried Mike." Clapp asked if Ng had assisted in burying Mike Carroll.

"No."

The last time Ng had seen Kathi Allen, he said, "Leonard took her for a walk outside, and then he came back . . . he drove me back to the bus stop. . . ."

Reverting to his earlier technique of firing questions laced with obscenities, Clapp unleashed a new barrage of inquiries prefaced with, "Did you tell Maurice Laberge. . . ." In gutter language, Clapp asked if Ng had told his prison pal about oral-sex episodes with Kathleen Allen while holding a gun to her head; about penetrating her sexually with the weapon; about raping her while she was bound in shackles; about sodomizing her; and about frightening her with a knife while raping her. Ng replied with a simple "No" to each question.

As the pinnacle of his horror-filled interrogation, Clapp asked, "Did you tell Maurice Laberge, with regard to Brenda O'Connor and Kathi Allen, that you shot them in the head while they were handcuffed and blindfolded?"

"No."

"Did you tell Maurice Laberge that you put their bodies on a pile of wood and ignited it with gasoline?"

"No."

To questions about Mike Carroll, Ng added more denials, and disavowed any knowledge of burying the Dubs family. Reporters had speculated about the methods used to spirit Harvey, Deborah, and the baby away. Some suggested that the abductors had held a gun to little Sean's head to assure obedient compliance from the parents. Others wondered if the victims had been drugged. Clapp asked, "Did you tell Maurice Laberge, 'We gave them sleeping pills so we could drive them to Calaveras,' and 'We came back the next day and took their stuff'?"

"No."

Laberge had testified for several days at the extradition hearings, and had made allegations that Ng had described the death of Clifford Peranteau. Clapp asked, "Do you recall a statement at the hearings that, 'Peranteau had called me a Chink, so when I killed him, I made him say Chink over and over again'?"

"No."

"Did you tell Maurice Laberge that you shot Peranteau with a .357?"

"No."

The defense had been suggesting that Ng was subservient to Lake, and afraid to challenge him. But they hadn't yet explained the incident during which Lake had stolen a photograph of Ng's coworker while remodeling the man's home, and Ng had immediately recovered the picture. Clapp asked about it, and Ng explained how he had used diplomacy. He claimed he'd told Lake the man was furious and might bring his brother to Calaveras and cause trouble. Instead of risking a confrontation, Ng said, it was better to make him see how to avoid serious problems.

Clapp circled back to the burial of two bodies in sleeping bags, and verified the second victim was Scott Stapley. Lake, Ng said, had prepared the body of Stapley for burial.

In a prolonged interrogation about the exchange of information between Ng and Laberge, Clapp asked, "Do you recall . . . saying that you had put a gun in Stapley's mouth and shot him?" Ng acknowledged hearing Laberge use those words in his testimony, but denied that it ever really happened. Clapp pushed further. "Did you tell Maurice Laberge that you put a gun in his mouth and broke out his tooth?" Ng said that he had not.

In the second row, Lola Stapley trembled trying not to cry, while Dwight held his right arm tightly around her and patted her hands.

Another rapid-fire barrage of "Did you tell Maurice Laberge . . ." questions followed. They included allegations that Ng had spoken of killing two families of three, that Brenda had been forced to perform oral sex on Ng while Lonnie Bond watched, and that Brenda had been kept for "some time" after Bond had been killed.

The same format alleged that Ng had confided details about Paul Cosner, saying that he'd put a bullet in the back of Cosner's head, that the victim had been emasculated with a chain saw, that Ng had hammered nails into Cosner's hands, and that Cosner had been a "hard operation" because he wouldn't cooperate.

Ng had participated in the videotaped taunts of Brenda O'Connor, he said, and had helped imprison her, but had not intended to hurt or kill her. He explained his aggressiveness, as shown in the tape, by saying that Lake had "set the tone" due to his hatred of O'Connor. According to Ng, O'Connor had offended Lake by trying to borrow money from him in exchange for sex. So, Ng said, he helped Lake establish "obedience, dominance, and control."

During Ng's denials of participating in any of the killings, Clapp reminded him that Brenda O'Connor, on the tape, had begged, "You are not taking my baby away from me," to which Ng had replied, "It is better than the baby is dead. . . ." Clapp asked Ng why he'd said that.

"I don't know why I say that. It is just in the heat of the moment. Some of these comments and remarks I make, I didn't even know I make until I saw the transcript." Squeaking chairs and soft groans in the gallery made it clear that some spectators and family members thought the answer shallow and evasive.

"Why did you say, 'It is part of the game'?"

"Just to show the solidarity with Lake during the comment he make. I just kind of like dovetail it to make it look like he and me is on this thing together." Yet Ng adamantly denied knowing the victims would die, or participating in killing them.

"Why did you cut her shirt and bra off?"

"I thought that was something that erotically Leonard Lake would get turned on by that type of activities."

At one point in the tape, Ng had said to Brenda, about taking a shower with her, "I always do that. It is luckier." To Clapp's query about his reasoning, Ng replied, "I don't know the semantics why I say this. I don't really know why I say 'always' and the lucky part. It is just one of those comments that come out without thinking about it." This produced more soft groans from some spectators.

The last time he'd seen Brenda, Ng claimed, she was in Lake's bedroom. "He was about to take her outside, to—I don't know—to the bunker I believe."

Asked about the knife he'd used to cut her clothing away, Ng exclaimed it was a Swiss Army knife, not a butterfly knife, as had been alleged by Laberge.

One last staccato of "Did you tell Maurice Laberge . . ." questions filled the courtroom. No, Ng said, he had not made comments to the informant about specific aberrant sexual acts with Brenda, nor about liking to see her model for Lake, nor that she was more passive than Kathi Allen, nor that Lake had wanted him to "kill the bitches' babies."

At last approaching conclusion of his direct examination,

Clapp asked Ng if he'd intended to kill, agreed to kill, or killed any of the victims in the twelve murder charges.

"No," said the defendant.

After the lunch break, Sharlene Honnaka briskly approached the defendant, who sat erect in the witness chair. Dressed in her usual conservative, dark-colored suit, Honnaka clasped her hands behind her back, and leaned forward in an aggressive stance. Her voice carried through the courtroom, a sharp edge to her words. The relationship between Ng and Maurice Laberge occupied the first few minutes of Honnaka's cross-exam. She asked Ng why he chose to give the informant documents and information about his own case.

The defendant explained, "Some of these rumors [about me] are so outraged that I want to dispel it. And sometimes that's when I correct him with factual information . . . to show that's not true."

Honnaka carefully laid a trap by having Ng admit that he'd never possessed or given to Laberge an actual copy of the "M Ladies" videotape. Then, before springing it, she asked, "You never personally told him anything about your own involvement, face-to-face, your words to him, about whether or not you were involved in killing any of the twelve victims in this case; is that right?"

"Right," Ng replied. "None of these quotes that he attributed to me had been made face-to-face."

"Were you present at the extradition hearings when Mr. Laberge testified that you told him on the video you could hear the handcuffs clicking?"

"I remember that statement he made."

"Now, how would Mr. Laberge know that there were the sounds of handcuffs clicking? That's not on the [printed] transcript, right?"

Backtracking rapidly, Ng rattled out a long explanation, ending with a recollection that his lawyer had brought a copy of the tape, showed it to Ng, after which Ng had met with Laberge and mentioned the sound of handcuffs. "I think he probably make a note of that."

Honnaka raised her voice indignantly. "So . . . you *were* talking to him personally, not from police reports, not from Lake's diary, not from the transcript. You personally are talking to him about hearing handcuffs on the videotape, correct?"

Ng said he believed that's how Laberge had "garnered" the information, or perhaps from speculation, since handcuff noise is well-known to most felons.

"Did you hear Mr. Laberge testify at the hearing that you told him the victims' hands were behind their backs?"

Ng, perhaps trying to avoid falling deeper in the trap, said he didn't remember. But Honnaka helped his memory by producing a transcript of the hearings in which Laberge testified that Ng had spoken of the victims' hands being behind their backs. It was nothing but another lie, said Ng.

Observers tried to hide smiles of understanding. If Laberge hadn't seen the tape, yet could describe visual scenes that were not included in the transcript, the inference was that Ng had lied about his verbal input to the informant.

Honnaka had another example. "Now, Mr. Laberge also testified that . . . you told him when Kathi Allen was in the house, she was dressed only in panty hose with a slit cut in the crotch area. That's not on the transcript, right?"

Ng denied any recollection of the panty hose. So Honnaka had the segment played again on the big-screen television sets, showing Kathi Allen massaging Ng. Viewers could easily see a tear or cut in the crotch of her panty hose. Ng said, "It looks like a rip."

"That information is not contained on the transcript, is it?"

"No," Ng answered, but maintained that Laberge had lied

when he said Ng had informed him of the slit in the undergarment.

Honnaka riposted with a comment from Laberge about Brenda O'Connor being "skinny," and asked, "Nowhere on the transcript does it mention the size of Brenda O'Connor, right?"

Dejectedly Ng replied, "Not that I know of."

As Honnaka asked a series of questions about the timing of Ng's presence in Wilseyville during the first few days of Kathi Allen's imprisonment, his memory seemed to grow vague. He thought he had remained at the cabin while Lake drove to Milpitas and picked her up at the Safeway store, a trip which took about six hours. The prosecutor asked, "What were you doing while Lake was . . . picking up Kathi Allen?"

"I don't remember . . . watching TV maybe." But he did recall Lake explaining the purpose of his trip. "He's going to pick up somebody to bring to Wilseyville . . . it was some woman that he going to put on videotape."

By correlating phone bills and work records, Honnaka established that Ng had been present in Wilseyville within the time frame of Maurice Laberge's allegation that Ng had allegedly said he put a gun into her private parts and forced her to call Safeway to ask for time off. But Ng denied his presence during the phone call.

Using questions to reconstruct the relationship between Ng and Lake, from its beginning in Philo to Ng's confinement in Leavenworth, Honnaka asked if the defendant had received gift packages while in prison. "No," said Ng. Shaking her head, Honnaka produced a letter Ng had written to Cricket Balazs in which he had mentioned "care" packages from her and Lake. Another slight failure of memory? Ng did acknowledge receiving photos of the bunker in its construction phases, but denied any knowledge of a secret cell inside it.

The next questions caught the intense interest of juror number one, Mauricio Velarde, a U.S. Marine veteran and active reservist. Honnaka asked if Ng had claimed to be a U.S. citizen when he enlisted. He had, and he declared that his birthplace was Bloomington, Indiana.

"Didn't you produce a certified copy of a birth certificate in your name from Bloomington?" Ng raised hackles on the Marine juror when he said that the recruiting sergeant had volunteered to use an altered birth certificate. Velarde would later say he found it incredible that a Marine would risk his career, and possible imprisonment, just to sign up a noncitizen.

In the late afternoon, Honnaka closed her questioning by inquiring about Ng's reunion with Lake and Balazs after leaving Leavenworth.

Judge Ryan excused the jurors for the weekend.

With the court in session again on Monday, February 1, 1999, Honnaka resumed her no-nonsense, firm interrogation of Charles Ng. Noting that Kathi Allen had called her boss the next morning from Wilseyville, Honnaka asked Ng what he was doing at that moment.

"Could be many things," he snorted. "Sometimes Leonard had me chop firewood, sometime taking Wubon for a walk, things of that nature. Sometime, I take hike for myself."

Her voice hard, Honnaka bored in on the videotaping of Kathi Allen, which Ng said probably took place shortly after her arrival late Sunday night, April 14. Ng had already said that was the first time he'd ever seen Kathleen. Honnaka asked, "So is the memory pretty clear in your mind about the first time you saw her?"

"No," Ng replied, sounding as if the event was nothing more than a casual meeting. "It wasn't something—I would try to remember."

Indignance seething from Honnaka, she asked why. Ng said, "It didn't occur to me to try to remember, specifically because it wasn't something that stick out in my mind."

What appeared to be an attempt by Ng to trivialize the treatment of Kathi Allen not only angered Honnaka, but also sent blood pressures aloft in the gallery. Honnaka incredulously asked, "It didn't stick out in your mind that you had a kidnapped woman that you were helping to terrorize?"

Speaking more rapidly than before, Ng protested, "No, that is not what I meant. It is not something that I just happen to remember specifically. When it occurred, it just one of these things that happen. I try to forget about it." His words did nothing to quell a sense of indignation among spectators.

Honnaka directed him to the garment worn by Kathi Allen in the massage scene. Ng described the underwear as something between panty hose and panties. "It is like a mixture of both . . . according to what I saw on the 'M Ladies' tape."

Wrinkling her brow, Honnaka asked, "You were there, Mr. Ng, weren't you?" Yes, he said, he just didn't know what to call the "lingerie" she wore.

"How did that hole get there?"

"I have no idea . . . I didn't cause the hole."

Jumping back to the previous taped segment, Honnaka asked, "You took her to the shower, right?"

Ng's response did nothing to repair his sinking credibility. He asked, "Did I or did Leonard Lake?"

In a flat, disbelieving voice, Honnaka said, "I wasn't there, Mr. Ng."

The defendant seemed to scramble for words, mumbling something about not being clear regarding the taped sequence. Honnaka seized his implausible comments to further discredit his testimony. When she got his admission that he had, indeed, joined Kathi Allen in the shower, Honnaka asked, "Did any sexual acts occur in that shower?"

"No." Disbelief clouded the courtroom.

"Why did you get in the shower with her, Mr. Ng?"

"That is one of those—I think Leonard want to have someone keep an eye on her at all times so she won't do anything like hurting herself type of thing.''

The prosecutor let him wiggle on the hook a little longer before asking what happened next. Ng stated that the massage scene had followed after the shower. No, he said, he had not engaged in any type of sex with Kathi Allen, even though he was nude in the massage sequence. ''I couldn't make myself do it. Initially I was thinking of doing it, but I feel sorry for her so I couldn't do it.''

''Did you tell Maurice Laberge about any of these events?''

''No.''

''Did you ever tell him that Kathi Allen was whipped?'' Reporters knew that Honnaka was leading up to a drawing that depicted Lake flogging the victim as Ng watches while eating rice.

So did Ng. He quickly replied, ''Oh, no. I remember he try to talk about that cartoon. No, those things never occurred . . . you want to show me the cartoon?''

''Sure, Mr. Ng,'' Honnaka said, with no attempt to hide her patronizing tone. ''Let's take a look at the cartoon.''

Examining the drawing, Ng admitted that he had given it to Laberge, and said that, ''It was something funny. . . .'' Ng's convoluted explanation seemed to indicate that the drawing was an attempt to find humor in Lake's erotic fantasy of whipping a nude woman. ''The background where I was standing with a bowl of rice, that is a joke because in the transcript, Lake was talking about how 'you will fuck for us, work for us, and cook for us,' when, in fact, you know, none of the 'M' ladies have ever cooked for us or washed for us.'' It did not go unnoticed that Ng omitted the sexual allusion. Ng continued, ''And I was the one actually doing most of the cooking when I am up there. So that was why I put that as like essentially the satire of the whole unrealistic situation placed on those transcript.''

As Honnaka pursued the subject, Ng repeatedly used the term ''satire'' to describe the obscene, violence-ridden cartoons.

The humorous aspect of torturing Kathi Allen, or anyone else, escaped the packed gallery.

Attempting to learn more about what had happened to Allen between the time she arrived, probably after 10 P.M. on Sunday, and when Ng left on Tuesday to deliver keys to Mike Carroll's car in Milpitas, Honnaka asked the defendant for details. But he claimed a memory lapse that made him unable to recall anything between Sunday night and Tuesday morning.

Lewis Clapp's long litany of questions, each beginning with, "Did you tell Maurice Laberge . . ." had appalled observers and many of the jurors. Sharlene Honnaka repeated several of the expletive-filled queries, the reciting of which was no less disgusting. Ng held the position that he hadn't told Laberge any of the incriminating stories.

The prosecutor directed Ng's attention to a particularly lewd drawing of a black man, sexually assaulting a woman from behind while holding a taut ligature, possibly panty hose, around her neck, and saying, "Ima give you master Ng's asshole death grip, bitch." Laberge had once quoted Ng as defining the death grip as strangling a woman with panty hose while having anal intercourse with her. Ng denied drawing it, but acknowledged printing the words. She asked if the ligature appeared to be panty hose, but he disagreed, saying it resembled "some kind of a fabric, like a rope-type thing." He explained his motivation for printing the obscene words. Laberge, he said, might have seen a police report alleging that Ng had used the "death grip" phrase. "Laberge kind of pulled my leg . . . and I end up making the writing . . . as kind of a satire to show that this is how ludicrous this kind of saying is."

The word "ludicrous" resounded through the courtroom, but not in the context used by Charles Ng.

Additional cartoons depicting the death and cooking of babies were spotlighted. Ng admitted drawing several of the "satirical" works, and in long, convoluted explanations, he said he had been "goaded" into it by Laberge.

* * *

The day seemed to pass quickly as Honnaka peppered the defendant with questions about his involvement with Lake over a period of months. Both denials and claims of ignorance about criminal activities filled his testimony.

More of Laberge's allegations popped up. With regards to victim Cliff Peranteau, the informant had quoted Ng saying, "When I was loading the gun, he was so scared he pissed himself. I put it behind his left ear and cocked it slow so he could hear every click. . . . Peranteau kept saying, 'Please, please, Charlie.' " According to Laberge's statements, Lake had ordered Ng to "kill the pig." Ng had allegedly said, "Good-bye, Clifford," and pulled the trigger. According to Laberge, Ng said, "His head jerked and blood flew out of his mouth. No kill, no thrill. No gun, no fun." Further, Ng had allegedly told the informant that he'd shot Peranteau with a .357, put him on a pile to burn, and left handcuffs on him by mistake, so they burned, too.

To Honnaka's questions about the veracity of these allegations, Ng denied all of it. She brought up the evidence of burned handcuffs found on the Wilseyville property, but he claimed no knowledge of them. Laberge had accused Ng of saying that Peranteau and Jeff Gerald would never be found because their bodies had been cremated. Ng refuted all of the alleged statements.

Honnaka asked Ng where he was on Sunday, February 24, 1985, the day Gerald vanished. Ng said he couldn't remember. He stated it wasn't particularly noticeable when Dennis Moving employees suddenly left without explanation, since it wasn't a career job and workers sometimes just dropped out with no explanation.

Trying to pin down the April 1985 chronology of events at Wilseyville, Honnaka asked Ng when the videotapes of Brenda O'Connor were made. His best recollection, he said, put it on

April 22. And the burial of Lonnie Bond, and Scott Stapley, occurred on April 24. She wanted to know if Ng had noticed the dead bodies under Lake's porch before April 24. No, Ng said, he hadn't. Honnaka pointed out that in the videotape, reference had been made to Bond and Stapley having been "taken away," implying they had been killed on or prior to April 22. But Ng insisted that he hadn't seen them, and during the time between the two dates, he had taken the dog for walks, chopped firewood, and hiked in the woods.

"Where was Brenda O'Connor on the days before you noticed the two bodies?"

Ng wasn't certain. He could only recall that he'd taken the week off from his job because Lake had said they needed to go to San Diego to tie up some loose ends. No, he said, he hadn't noticed a pickup with AHOYMTY plates, sitting near the house. But it "suddenly showed up."

Before they left for San Diego, Ng said, he thought that Lake had locked Brenda O'Connor up in the bunker. Early in the morning of the 23rd, they'd been in the accident in Kern County, then, according to Ng, had gone on to San Diego where they loaded some things into the pickup, and headed back to Wilseyville.

Honnaka wanted to know what time of day, on the 24th, Ng had seen the two bodies under the porch. Ng recalled that it was "real late" on the night they had returned from San Diego. Observers recalled the video glimpse depicting two bodies, covered by sleeping bags, on a blue wheelbarrow. The tape had been made in bright daylight.

In Ng's account, they had arrived at night, and Lake had recruited him to help bury two bodies. "He took me to the porch in the back of his house, and there it is, the two bodies lying down there."

Wanna-be sleuths in the gallery had hoped that Honnaka would ask if the bodies were stiff, which might indicate they'd been killed within the last twelve hours, since rigor mortis ordinarily begins to relax after that period of time. Ng saved her the trouble of introducing the topic by bringing it up in his testimony about putting a ball gag in one of the dead men's mouths. "I try to touch the body as minimally as possible because, you know, it's like, they look like they been dead for days and they pretty stiff."

The comment suggested serious inaccuracies in Ng's story. As he added details about the gruesome work, Honnaka asked, "And the limbs are really stiff while this is going on, right?"

Perhaps Ng detected the trap. He answered, "Not stiff enough that I can't get the job done, if that's what you meant." Honnaka dropped the issue. Ng told of wrapping the bodies, taping the bags, and placing them in the pickup bed, then driving in the dark approximately a half mile to bury them in a previously dug hole. He said he had no idea who had dug it.

Playing segments of the videotapes again, Honnaka questioned Ng in detail about his involvement, and Lake's use of "we" in threatening the women. His answer to a question about why he showered with them, shook listeners with its strange reasoning. "Leonard wanted me to. Both of these [women] are smokers, and he doesn't want to smell cigarette, nicotine breath." Perhaps realizing how lame he sounded, he added, "And I don't know why. There's no specific reason he wanted to run them in the shower . . . I don't know. I can't explain. Maybe at that time is just heat of the moment thing." Furthermore, he said, he wasn't even sure he had entered the shower with Brenda O'Connor.

If Ng's credibility had been eroded, more cracks in it appeared when Honnaka brought up another comment he'd made in the videotape of Kathi Allen. "You told Leonard, at one point, that 'the piece' was on the table, right?"

"Yeah, I remember saying something like that."

"What did you mean when you said, 'the piece'?"

"Oh, I just want to let him know that his gun is on the table, so in case Kathi run for—Kathi might grab the gun and shoot him or something like that."

"Now, she's sitting there handcuffed, right?"

"Yes."

"And she's got leg manacles on?"

"Yes, I believe so."

"And there's two of you and one of her, right?"

"Yes."

"And the reason you told Leonard about the gun on the table is that you were afraid Kathi might pick up the gun and shoot him?"

Ng could manage only another, "Something like that."

Regarding the sequence featuring Brenda O'Connor, Honnaka reconfirmed Ng's statements that prior to the filming, he had never seen any dead bodies, had never seen the baby, and had never met O'Connor. He agreed, and described his version of first seeing her. "I remember it was late, dark, it was after dinner. Leonard . . . set the camera up and tell me to get ready for 'M Ladies II'; I think that's what he call it. And that's when Brenda—he went outside to the bunker area and then he came back with Brenda handcuffed, huffing and puffing." Ng added that he thought the baby was in the bunker during the videotaping.

Jurors watched carefully as Honnaka played segments of the tape again, stopping it now and then to ask Ng about his taunting of O'Connor. He rationalized each of his recorded comments: He didn't think Lake was serious about killing her; he didn't know who Scott and Lonnie were at the time; his acts were made in the "heat of the moment"; and he didn't believe she was really sick or pregnant.

The prosecutor asked, "You didn't have any sexual pleasure out of doing the acts . . . against this victim?"

"I actually feel pretty regret about this. It's just, you know, one point in time in my life I surrender my independent judgment and get involved in things I really feel . . . disturbed about afterward. This is why I don't want to have anything to do with it anymore." Asked about cutting Brenda's clothing from her, Ng explained, "There was a movie called *Death Wish III* or *IV.* There was a scene that some thugs went into a house, Charles Bronson house, and cut off her—basically subdued a woman and did this scene. I remember that Leonard Lake remark he enjoyed that scene and got turned on by it. When I did that, it was with that thought in mind, that this might turn him on."

"So you just decided all on your own to cut her clothes off, right?" Honnaka knew that her question would undermine one possible defense strategy, that all of Ng's actions had been carried out Lake's orders.

Ng gave her the answer she sought. "Yes."

She set his response in stone. "Without any instructions from Leonard Lake?"

Ng concurred, and sank deeper into the mire of his reasoning when Honnaka asked about his disrobing to shower with Brenda. He knew in advance she would shower, he said, because the previous "M Lady," Kathi Allen, had showered. Ng added, "He just want to clean her up before any activities in the bedroom."

During the taping session, Ng had kneeled to adjust Brenda's manacles, and had commented, "It's totally ours." These words, he rationalized to Honnaka, were an attempt to "act macho." He explained, "I don't want to act like a wimp."

Echoing his dubious words, Honnaka asked, "You don't want to act like a wimp with a woman who is asking for her baby and her husband and her friend; is that your testimony?"

Denying any knowledge of the people Brenda mentioned, Ng said, "I was focusing on getting her compliance." Perhaps attempting to downplay the callousness, he said that when he finally believed Brenda's complaints about feeling sick, he'd rushed to get her some ice water and aspirin.

Honnaka played another portion of the tape and asked, "After your offer of water and aspirin, you told her to be quiet about the baby; you didn't want to hear any more about it?"

"Yes," said Ng, ". . . it was disturbing me. I wanted to get that subject off my head."

"Oh, so you were disturbed about the fact that she was worried about her baby, so you told her to be quiet about it, or else it would be history? Is that right?" Ng could do nothing but agree.

Toward the end of the taping session, Ng had wielded a weapon. He told Honnaka that it was a stun gun, which he had taken to Canada with him.

In a particularly dramatic segment of the tape, Lake had said to Brenda, "You better believe us or you'll be dead." And Ng had said, "Right." Ng told Honnaka, "That's again to demonstrate solidarity, the projection of solidarity. Whatever he said, I kinda chime in and say yes."

One last taped comment by Ng was played for the jury. In it, he implied the existence of multiple victims by saying, "Cry like the rest of them." Honnaka wanted an explanation. Ng said, "There's no rest of them. I try to project seriousness, make her feel like . . . this is not the first time, so she might take our words more seriously."

A cold, harsh tone sounded in Honnaka's voice. She pointed out that a tape had already been made of Kathi Allen, in which victim Mike Carroll had been mentioned. In the video of Brenda, ". . . there's mention of Lonnie and Scott being taken away, and about her baby sleeping like a rock . . . and that's not what you meant when you said, 'Cry like the rest of them.'?"

Ng seemed rattled. "No, because none of them have cried in my presence—I mean in terms of Kathi Allen or—well, that's the only one I knew of."

After a final barrage of questions taking Ng through the

lumberyard incident and his flight to Canada, Honnaka announced, at four o'clock Monday afternoon, "The people have no more questions at this time."

Lewis Clapp used the remaining hour with inquiries to Ng about his relationships with Laberge and Lake. Damage repair would start on Tuesday morning.

Beginning the day by showing Ng photographs of the overhanging deck under which he had seen the bodies of Stapley and Bond, Lewis Clapp asked court clerk Terri Walsh to assign the photo an exhibit number. It turned out to be Defense Exhibit 666.

Clapp jumped from topic to topic, starting with inconsistencies in the testimony of Maurice Laberge during the Canadian extradition hearings. Laberge had referred to the garment Kathi Allen wore during the massage episode, as panty hose, but Ng claimed he had always referred to the underwear as "panties." Clapp spent several minutes showing the jury that Ng regarded Lake and Cricket Balazs as his family with whom he could relate openly, unlike his true family. Lake was like a big brother, said Ng, who helped him forget his low self-esteem.

Even though Ng wasn't charged with the murders of Cheryl Okoro, Randy Jacobson, or Maurice Rock, Clapp asked questions to assure the jury that the defendant had no connection to those victims. Reverting back to Laberge, Clapp introduced more of the obscene cartoons, some of which demonstrated how Laberge and Ng exchanged papers by sliding them under their adjacent cell doors. The drawings purportedly demonstrated the prison conditions, as well. According to Ng, they were attempts at "lighthearted" humor between the two men, and were a catharsis in coping with the years of confinement.

Another one of Clapp's probes may have produced an unintentional result. Ng stated that, as a general rule, when he gave Laberge documents, the informer had only about ten minutes to review the papers before the men were returned to their cells. Jurors' hands flew to their notebooks. A remarkable ability for memorizing lengthy details from printed reports had already been attributed to the informant, and it would have been miraculous if he'd been able to read and absorb the material in such a short time. Ng tried to recover by speculating that someone was making photocopies of the papers for Laberge. Some observers wondered why the prosecution didn't object to testimony that was pure guesswork.

Ng's work records in San Francisco came under Clapp's questioning again. They showed that the defendant had worked regularly several days following his return to San Francisco on May 25, after helping bury two bodies. He claimed that he had hurried back to the city in order to distance himself from Lake, traumatized by the taping episode with Brenda O'Connor and the horror of burying Stapley and Bond. In the gallery, whispers were exchanged. If Ng worked so hard for several days to keep away from Lake, what was he doing with him in a South San Francisco lumberyard a week after he'd left Wilseyville?

Reaching the end of his redirect, Clapp elicited from Ng an outpouring of denials about killing anyone, about intending that anyone be killed, or about helping Leonard Lake carry out any murders.

Acknowledging that he'd done "horrendous things" as seen on the videotapes, Ng said, "I certainly regret it. It was when I was young and adventurous and surrendered my independent judgment. That, I always going to regret."

Lewis Clapp thanked the jury and sat down. Judge Ryan declared a break at 10:30 A.M. After the jury had filed out, Bill Kelley lodged a complaint to the judge about Sharon Sellitto, sister of victim Paul Cosner. From her seat in the gallery, Kelley said, she could be heard sighing loudly during the defendant's testimony. The judge tactfully repeated his hope that all observers in the audience would refrain from any noise or gestures.

When court session resumed, Honnaka and Smith made another surprising announcement. They would conduct no further cross-examination, nor would they offer any rebuttal testimony. Smith respectfully asked Judge Ryan if they could simply begin again with the closing arguments since Ng's testimony had introduced new facts to be summarized. Ryan agreed. In the early afternoon, Sharlene Honnaka stood to address the jury once more.

Chapter 33

Pointing out to jurors that the "best evidence" could be seen in the videotape, Sharlene Honnaka directed a staff assistant to play it again. At its conclusion, she spoke again of the horrific conduct pointing to twelve murders. She pointed to contradictions and discrepancies in Ng's testimony, and suggested that even though Maurice Laberge had a long criminal record, his reports about Ng's confessions contained believable details. At one point, she dramatically held up the Ruger .22 handgun, complete with silencer, that had been found in the Honda. Paul Cosner, she said, had been killed on November 2, 1984, a day that Ng had been absent from work. Sharon Sellitto and her mother wept softly as Honnaka spoke. The prosecutor ended the day by holding up a sweater that had belonged to victim Cliff Peranteau.

A few of the reporters, in hallway discussions, wondered if Honnaka's presentation had been powerful enough. It seemed to be functional, but without the visceral drama or indignation that is often utilized by prosecutors in the vital summation process. Some of the news writers had also noticed a gift-wrapped package lying on a table near the jury box, and speculated about its contents.

On Wednesday, February 3, Honnaka addressed the jury again. For the first time in the trial, she wore a brown-and-yellow-plaid suit, instead of the usual dark colors. She hit highlights of Ng's testimony and pointed out, "It's never Ng's fault. He always lays the blame on someone else. . . . He was not under the control of Leonard Lake. He was his own person. He was making his own independent choices and the things he wanted to do." The tapes, she said, "speak louder than any of his words from the stand." The deputy attorney general spoke for only twenty minutes before giving way to Peter Smith.

District Attorney Smith's style contrasted sharply with Honnaka's. She had delivered her speech in a stylized, orderly manner, often asking the question, "How do we know . . . ," and then answering it. Jurors would later describe her as the "tougher" of the two prosecutors, while saying that Smith seemed like "the nice guy." He smiled often, spoke softly, moved in a slow, measured pace, and kept close eye contact with the jurors.

The videotapes filled television screens again while Smith pointed out what appeared to be voluntary involvement by Charles Ng. He took the jurors through evidence relating to Mike Carroll, Kathleen Allen, Lonnie Bond and his infant son, Robin Stapley, and Brenda O'Connor. After speaking no more than forty-five minutes, the dignified district attorney asked jurors to find Ng guilty in twelve counts of first-degree murder.

Just before the jurors took their morning break, Bill Kelley made one of his usual motions, and in summarizing his point, slipped and said, "We know why Ng killed . . ." Everyone knew he meant to say Lake, but had erred. Someone hurriedly pointed out his mistake, and he corrected himself.

Standing in front of his ten-foot-long posters that looked like red targets, with a photo of Lake in the center, Bill Kelley addressed jurors to argue for the defense. "You can't like Charles Ng, folks," said Kelley, "that's just not possible. But you have to put that aside and ask yourself, 'Did the government prove he killed them?'" The thrust of his speech heaped all the guilt on Leonard Lake.

The bulk of the prosecution's case, said Kelley, came from an unreliable informant who traded his lies for favors. Referring to Maurice Laberge as a pedophile, a perjurer, and a snake, Kelley told jurors that stories made up by Laberge were nothing but inflammatory lies presented for their emotional appeal. "When you have a history of crimes that involve deceit, lies, violence, and drugs ... you can't believe a word that person says," Kelley said.

Interrupted after one hour by the lunch break, Kelley spoke again in the afternoon. He took jurors once more through Ng's work records, emphasizing the distance between his city apartment and Wilseyville, ostensibly minimizing Ng's presence at the crime scene. Admitting that Mike Carroll and Ng had been in Leavenworth at the same time, Kelley suggested there was little chance they had met there.

Just as Honnaka had held a gun aloft during her talk, Kelley strapped a rifle on his shoulder and wielded the silencer-equipped handgun. "You know what I'm doing," he said, and acknowledged the drama of his performance. "It's not proof, but it's the same kind of drama you saw on those videotapes." Affirming the repugnancy of Ng's behavior on the tapes, Kelley hammered home the point that the defendant's actions did not prove that he'd killed anyone. "No matter how many times you see that tape,'' Kelley said, ''there's one thing you never see, and that's anybody being murdered.''

Lewis Clapp replaced Kelley in the late afternoon. He spoke earnestly and passionately, appealing to the jury's ''better angels,'' and their logic, asking them to ''utilize the law'' in deliberating the case. He even demonstrated a sense of humor in apologizing for raising his voice, and slyly noting that he'd done it ''so the reporters can hear me.''

One of the major points Clapp highlighted lay in jury instructions the judge would read before the jury retired for deliberations. He pointed out that trials utilize two kinds of evidence: direct and circumstantial. Direct evidence, if found to be true, establishes a fact. Circumstantial evidence, if found to be true, proves a fact from which an inference can be drawn. Speaking slowly and with careful articulation, Clapp explained that a finding of guilt may *not* be based on circumstantial evidence unless the proved circumstances cannot be reconciled with any other rationale conclusion. If the circumstantial evidence is susceptible to two reasonable interpretations, one of which points to guilt and the other to innocence, the jury must adopt the interpretation that points to innocence. It is a fine point of law, but a critical one.

The evidence presented by the prosecution, said Clapp, had been entirely circumstantial.

Jurors went home Wednesday night with the explanation weighing heavily on their minds.

Thursday morning, February 4, Clapp took the floor again, after being reminded by Judge Ryan of a promise to conclude by noon. Ryan had assured the jury he would release them at midday. Clapp nodded and began an attack on evidence the prosecution had presented about bone fragments. He sharply criticized investigators for not using anthropological techniques in collecting the human remains. The district attorney's investigator Mitch Hrdlicka, sitting next to a journalist, seethed with indignance, whispering that every possible precaution had been taken. Dwight Stapley, angry about the tactics, whispered to his wife, "Next time Clapp looks at me, I'm gonna yawn." He didn't, though.

After an hour of rather dry argument, Clapp spoke of Ng's testimony. Following the morning break, he attacked Cricket Balazs and the missing three pages of her "Men of USC" calendar, and suggested that if she'd spoken, she might have harmed the case against Ng. "Why didn't the prosecution ask her even one question?" Clapp complained. Observers wondered why the defense had also dismissed her with no questions.

Next, Maurice Laberge's "inaccuracies" fell under the wrath of Clapp, followed by detailed references to Lake's taped soliloquy about his plan to build a bunker.

Several people glanced anxiously at the wall clock. Clapp showed still photos of a nude Brenda O'Connor, taken on the outdoor deck, in broad daylight. The tape, according to Ng, had been made at night. The inference, in Clapp's view, suggested that Ng had nothing to do with her death. Observers scratched their heads. The clock ticked past 12:00, 12:15, and reached 12:30. Judge Ryan, who had been coughing and sneezing with symptoms of a cold, seemed displeased at the defender for not finishing on schedule, and dismissed the jury until Monday. He also ordered Kelley to dismantle the huge "target" display board, which had been blocking the judge's view of the jurors.

It took Clapp another hour on the morning of February 8 to complete his five-hour argument. "Things are not always what they appear," he asserted. "I beseech you not to be sucked in by your emotion." When he finally completed his speech, he reached for the mysterious gift-wrapped package that had been lying on a table for days. Tearing away the decorative paper, he revealed a copy of *The Collector,* by John Fowles.

The prosecution, bearing the burden of proof, is entitled to present a final round of argument to the jury. Sharlene Honnaka, dressed all in black again, gave the jurors one more look at the videotape, calling it "the single most incriminating piece of evidence in this case." Frequently stopping the tape, she spoke of Ng's aggressiveness: "The defendant's motive is sexual thrill." Point by point, Honnaka hammered away at Ng's culpability in the twelve murders. After one hour before the jury, she asked for guilty verdicts, thanked them, and sat down.

The trial had lasted from October 26 to February 8, nearly 3½ months. Now, it would be placed in the hands of twelve jurors to determine the guilt or innocence of Charles Chitat Ng.

Reporters huddled, speculating about a possible hung jury, wondering if enough evidence had been presented to convince all twelve of them, beyond a reasonable doubt, that Ng had killed a dozen victims. A few of the news-media representatives hung around in the hallway, hoping for a quick verdict. But they slowly drifted away as clouds gathered on the horizon, threatening rain.

On a dark, rainy Tuesday, reporters and victims' relatives read newspapers, sipped coffee, and chatted quietly in the courtroom. Twice that day, jurors sent a note to the judge asking for clarification and for transcripts to be read. The pattern would be repeated as the days passed; Wednesday, Thursday, and into the following week. Another week slipped by. It seemed the jury must certainly be having serious problems. Please, family members prayed, please let them come to a verdict. It would be horrible to go through another entire trial. By Tuesday, February 23, 1999, hope had dimmed. Then, an announcement heated up telephone circuits as reporters, families, and a network of courtroom spectators called one another. The jury had reached a decision. Would it be a verdict, or a dismal note to the judge that they could not unanimously agree on a verdict?

The hallway buzzed with crowded activity on Wednesday morning as photographers, television-camera operators, reporters, and spectators waited near the double doors. Deputy Marshal Roger Hilton unlocked them a few minutes before 9 A.M., and seats filled quickly.

When the twelve grim-faced jurors filed into the box, and settled into their chairs, a hush fell over the assembly. Judge Ryan asked if they had reached a decision.

Hearts fell when the jury foreman, Mauricio Velarde, the Marine reservist, stood and announced they were deadlocked. But smiles and sighs of relief bloomed when he told the judge the deadlock applied to only one count. They had reached verdicts on the other eleven.

Suspense hung heavy as lawyers discussed with the judge what to do about the one deadlocked count. Bill Kelley advised Ng that he could be retried on that single count, no matter what happened on the other eleven.

Judge Ryan read a note from the jurors, then asked the foreman about the deadlocked count. "If you continue to deliberate, is there any probability that you could arrive at a verdict?" Velarde thought it was possible. In a poll of each panelist, nine members agreed with him, but two said it would be impossible. The judge pondered the issue for a few moments, then asked if the jury had reached verdicts on the other eleven counts. Velarde said they had. Ryan declared a mistrial on the one count. Dwight and Lola Stapley, along with Sharon Sellitto and her mother, Virginia Nessley, held their breaths. They had sought justice for so long, and desperately longed for the completion of the horror. The crowd rumbled in nervous anticipation.

A hush fell as the court clerk, Terri Walsh, cleared her throat to read the verdicts aloud. "We, the jury in the above entitled case, find the defendant, Charles Chitat Ng, guilty of the murder of Sean Dubs as charged in Count I. We further find the murder to be of the first degree.''

The crowd sat motionless, but a palpable tension tightened expressions throughout the room.

Walsh spoke again. ''We, the jury in the above entitled case, find the defendant, Charles Chitat Ng, guilty of the murder of Deborah Dubs as charged in Count II . . . in the first degree.''

Her voice steady, Walsh continued to read:

Harvey Dubs—guilty
Clifford Peranteau—guilty
Jeffrey Gerald—guilty
Michael Carroll—guilty
Kathleen Allen—guilty
Lonnie Bond Sr.—guilty
Robin Scott Stapley—guilty
Lonnie Bond Jr.—guilty
Brenda O'Connor—guilty

Sharon Sellitto ran from the room. Virginia Nessley sat in stunned silence, tears running down her cheeks. The terrible irony raised goose bumps all through the gallery. The jury had hung, seven not guilty votes to five guilty votes in the Paul Cosner charge. It had been Cosner's Honda in which Ng had placed the stolen vise, the incident that had broken the case. It had been Cosner's sister and mother who had pushed investigators early on. It had been Sharon Sellitto and Virginia Nessley attending every court hearing in seven years, in a quest for answers and for justice. Now, only Paul Cosner's murder remained open to question.

Still, a sense of triumph reigned among those already convinced of Ng's guilt. Some reporters expressed surprise at the eleven guilty counts, having predicted a split of six to six.

Peter Smith said there was a strong possibility that he would seek a new trial to resolve the Cosner issue, but reporters doubted it. The state had already spent multimillions of dollars to reach verdicts on eleven counts. And, since the jury had also found the special circumstance of multiple murder true, a penalty phase of the trial still faced the lawyers, the judge, and the jury to determine if Ng would receive life in prison without parole, or the death sentence.

The likelihood of ever reaching a conclusion in the matter of Paul Cosner seemed infinitely small.

In the hallway, among a clamor of television cameras and reporters, a distraught Sharon Sellitto said, "I cannot believe this is the way it is going to end. This is the legal system. It sure as hell isn't the justice system. . . . If it wasn't for my brother, they wouldn't even have had a damn trial."

Dwight and Lola Stapley, while sympathetic with Cosner's family, beamed and hugged one another. They'd heard the verdict for which they had fervently hoped during nearly fourteen years of agony. Lola said, "I could feel Scott's hand on my shoulder, saying, 'Okay, Mama Jo, we made it. I told you it was gonna be okay.' I could honestly feel it. He was here, and now maybe his soul will rest."

Commencement of the penalty trial was scheduled one month hence, on the eighth day of March.

In the interim, Charles Ng filed a malpractice suit against his lawyers and tried to fire them again. At a hearing on Thursday, March 4, Bill Kelley announced his refusal to step down, despite the litigation. The action evidently infuriated Ng, who stood up, ignored the possibility of being stopped by activation of the stun belt he wore, and marched angrily toward the door leading to his holding cell. Judge Ryan ordered the bailiffs to shackle him and bring him back. "I thought," said the judge, "the threat of fifty thousand volts would keep him quiet, but

I don't think that threat will keep him quiet today . . . he's very upset. He's very mad."

After being forced back to his chair, Ng called Bill Kelley a "liar" and accused him of misrepresenting his wishes. Addressing Judge Ryan, Ng said, "You told me before that it was my choice. I don't want this sham of a show trial."

Maintaining his remarkable patience, Ryan advised Ng that the defense lawyers "are doing the best they can. You should cooperate with them the best you can."

Ryan ruled against several defense motions to squelch evidence prosecutors planned to present during the upcoming penalty phase.

In addition to the Stapleys, members of other victims' families helped fill the courtroom on March 8. Brenda O'Connor's mother, Sharron, her brother Richard, and three sisters, Sandra, Sherry, and Debbie sat in the fourth row. They chatted with Cliff Peranteau's brother William, and half brother Robert McCourt. Kathleen Allen's sister, Dian, sat in the rear, dreading her turn to speak. Jeffrey Nourse, a cousin of Deborah Dubs's, and the victim's best friend, Karen Tuck, took seats nearby. Jeffrey Gerald's father, Roger, and sister, Denise, showed up, as well.

Sharon Sellitto and her mother were noticeably absent.

Peter Smith addressed the jury, telling them, "Based on the evidence we present in the penalty phase, and on the circumstances of the crime, we will ask you to return a penalty of death." He explained that their duty would be to weigh and balance the mitigating versus the aggravating circumstances. They could use evidence from any part of the trial, and consider the details of the crimes, the presence or absence of other criminal conduct by the defendant, and even prior felony convictions. The burden of proof beyond a reasonable doubt would not be applicable in this phase.

The defense reserved the option to present opening statements later.

Sean Patrick Doyle took the stand first, and described in detail how he had helped subdue Ng in a Hudson Bay Company department store on July 6, 1985, and had sustained a gunshot wound to his fingers. Sergeant Donald Bishop, Calgary PD, filled in more information of the struggle and capture, as did Paul Vanderstoot, a detective for the Calgary PD.

The emotional part of the proceedings, in which the law allows victims or their families to tell how the crimes impacted them, began with Sharron O'Connor. Peter Smith gently questioned her. While a photo of Brenda, holding little Lonnie Bond Jr., appeared on the TV screens, Brenda's mother recalled her daughter's and grandson's many visits to Michigan. The witness described little Lonnie as "so sweet." Choked by tears, she said, "He used to follow his grandfather around, crawling all over the house." The murders had torn the whole family apart, said Sharron, but they'd since reestablished their unity. She recalled how Brenda, as a child, had climbed aboard a motorized lawn mower and started it in motion. But couldn't shut it off, and screamed as she drove it into the street. Brenda was a great cook, said Sharron, but had once called her mom from San Diego for instructions in roasting a turkey. "She'd left the package of giblets inside." Gentle laughter escaped aching throats in the gallery.

Because no identifiable remains had been found, there had been no funeral nor any grave site to visit. "We held a family memorial in our backyard." A rose bush helped them remember Brenda. "She loved pink roses."

Sandra Bond replaced her mother on the stand, and explained that she had married Lonnie Bond's brother. "This is double indemnity," she sobbed. "I'm getting grief from both sides." She and Brenda had been pregnant at the same time, and had anticipated their children growing up together. Not only did she lose her nephew, but also her beloved Brenda. "I don't have a little sister anymore. I've lost my identity." She'd seen the horrifying tape for the first time, and wished she hadn't.

A young man in his late twenties, with the physique and looks of a movie star, next answered Smith's questions. Robert McCourt's voice trembled as he spoke about his half brother, Cliff Peranteau, and described their troubled childhood in foster homes. They'd been abused and separated, but Cliff risked punishment to visit each of his eleven siblings. McCourt tried mightily to hold back the tears, but his torn emotions took over, and the masculine-looking youth cried openly as he told of the ruinous toll Cliff's loss had on their mother. "She refuses to admit that he's dead" and she wouldn't even allow a photo of Cliff to be brought to the trial so "Ng wouldn't have the satisfaction of seeing him again."

As the words choked in his throat, McCourt said that he doesn't allow himself to accept Cliff's death. "I just prefer to think of him as traveling the country."

Several jurors dabbed at their eyes, and sniffles could be heard throughout the room.

Detective Steve Satterwhite ended the day by telling jurors how he had arrested Charles Ng at Philo on April 29, 1982, clearing up in the jurors' minds events that had sent the defendant to Leavenworth.

On Tuesday morning, Smith called Jeffrey Nourse to the stand, and asked him about his cousin Debbie Dubs. "She was like a sister to me," he said. She had once received last rights during a serious illness, but with her "enthusiasm for life," had fully recovered. "She was a joy to be around," and an accomplished cartoonist. Nourse had known and liked Harvey Dubs, too, calling him a "quiet, loving, caring human being." Speaking softly, he said, "Not a day goes by, I don't think about Deb, Harvey, and Sean, and our wonderful friendship.

Every year, at Thanksgiving, we pray for them, and it still hasn't sunk in that they are gone.''

The woman whose phone conversation with Deborah Dubs had been interrupted by someone arriving to see about the video equipment spoke next. Karen Tuck had grown up with Debbie, she said, and Sean was her godson. Deborah, in return, was godmother to Tuck's oldest son. ''She was such a warm person, with so much to give,'' her friend lamented. ''And the little guy had such a great smile. I wish so much that I could have watched him grow. . . . I've been distraught. She was my best friend ever.''

Jeff Gerald's father described his son as ''loving, the great humorist of his time, and so nonviolent . . . he was born on Father's Day. I'll never forget it.'' Trying to describe the impact, he said, ''You go through anger at first, and then the big question is simply, 'Why?' You seek professional help, but there is no answer.''

Denise Gerald said her brother ''was the finest person I've ever been with. He was funny, passive, and warm. He loved music. His goal was to play and entertain.'' She spoke of the debilitating effect on her family. ''Mom is alive, but part of her died. I lost the father I knew. Our world changed . . . the void is great. The void is forever,'' she cried.

Dian Allen, who'd seen Kathleen's suffering on the video-tapes, recalled typical sibling rivalries, but said that Kathi always came to her rescue when problems arose. ''She could always make me laugh. She was a caretaker and wanted to be everyone's friend.'' The loss of Kathi, Dian said, ''destroyed my family. It killed my mother. She drank herself to death because she couldn't handle the tragedy of losing her daughter and waiting so long for Ng to be returned from Canada.'' Tears flooded her face as Dian's throat tightened. She managed to squeeze out the words, "I miss her strength. You just can't replace a family member you love. She never got to get married, or see me do it. It's not fair! It destroyed my life. She was such a good person. . . ." Dian's voice failed, and she stepped down.

Dwight Stapley, courageously trying to smile, took the long walk up to the stand, and told of his son's athletic prowess in school, the happy memories of sailing with him, and the horrible shock of losing him. "I expected to lose my mother, my dad, my brother, my sister, and maybe even a spouse, but never a child." He described the stunning effect when they found out that Scott was a victim in the breaking news shortly after Lake killed himself. "Lola got a telephone message from a news anchor at a San Francisco television station. He wanted to talk about our son, and the death in Calaveras County." In a state of shock, they didn't even know if the caller had meant that Scott had been killed, or had accidentally killed someone. The trembling father told jurors that he and Lola had spent their life savings—$65,000—to attend all of the hearings in Canada and California. The tragedy had been extremely hard to bear, especially for Scott's siblings. If there was any positive effect, Dwight said, it was in learning never to argue with loved ones.

Lola Stapley settled into the witness chair, holding a large photograph of Scott. Expressing her love as tears streaked her face, Lola said, "He nicknamed me 'Mama Jo,' " but she had never known why. She'd been undergoing counseling for three years to deal with her grief. "All I could do is cry." A majority of jurors cried along with her. Scott's sister was pregnant when he died, Lola said, and the family had worried that she might lose the baby. "But he's a teenager now, and he's named after Scott." Lola faced the jury as she said her grandson had recently written a school essay on the theme of wishing he had met his uncle Scott. She recalled family dinners with Scott in attendance. "Each of the four men had their own recipes for spaghetti." They'd gather in the kitchen for the complicated ritual of preparing it. After an hour or so, Lola's daughter would say, "Mom, are they ever going to stop arguing and start cooking?" Now, said Lola, "we know that Scott is still there when we make spaghetti at our family dinners."

The morning session of sadness and tears lasted only two hours.

Judge Ryan had promised jurors, during the selection process over four months earlier, that he would give them at least three weeks off for family commitments during spring break. He announced, "Court is in recess until April 12."

Bill Kelley and Lewis Clapp, despite facing a malpractice lawsuit and the defendant's wish to fire them, would work intensively during the hiatus to save the life of Charles Ng.

Chapter 34

Reporters and journalists crowded the courtroom once again on Monday, April 12. Among them was Craig Lockwood, who had attended the entire trial and written a piece about Ng for *Orange County* magazine. Another veteran of the U.S. Marine Corps, Lockwood had worked as a correspondent during the Vietnam conflict. In the humid jungles of Southeast Asia, he'd learned to use waterproof notepads, and still used them.

At the morning gathering in the hallway, Lockwood shared a bit of information he'd gleaned during the hiatus. In his research of the case, he'd traveled to Philo, in Northern California, and met with a local resident who had known Lake and Ng during their stay in the hamlet. Lake, the resident had said, once rented a truck from a neighbor to haul an old freezer to a landfill. Nothing unusual about that, except that the freezer door had been welded shut! Had Lake disposed of a body that early? Could the killings have started much sooner than anyone even guessed? It would be one of the many mysteries never solved.

Bill Kelley stood before the jury to deliver an opening statement. "We know that Mr. Ng is going to die in prison," he said, "but you have to decide when and where." The comment wasn't entirely accurate. In California, a jury ends the penalty phase with a simple verdict: life without the possibility of parole, or death. But technically, it is a recommendation. The judge can reduce a verdict of death to life without parole if he believes circumstances warrant it. And certainly, a jury has no input regarding where an inmate is to be incarcerated, or when the condemned prisoner is to be executed. San Quentin prison, near San Francisco, houses the state's only execution chamber, and most of the men on death row are kept there. Kelley's statement was no doubt meant as a metaphorical suggestion about the decision jurors faced.

Leonard Lake, said Kelley, was the "main guy" who "had his own agenda," and who had killed people unconnected to the case against Mr. Ng. Cricket Balazs, Kelley argued, had been granted immunity, allowing her to "walk on eighteen murders."

Pacing in front of the jury box, Kelley said that his client suffered from a mitigating mental illness. "I'm not saying he didn't know what he was doing, but we need to understand the engine that drove his needs." Looking over the top of his glasses, the defender noted, "We are products of our lives and our childhood . . . and Charles Ng experienced harsh treatment from his father." In Hong Kong, Ng was "tied and beaten by his father with a cane," yet he felt compelled to remain loyal, like a dog that is beaten but dependent on its owner for food. So, said Kelley, Ng fit the medical definition of "dependent personality disorder."

From then on, according to Kelley, Ng needed someone on

whom he could rely for direction. He tried to find it in the U.S. Marine Corps, but wasn't accepted by his peers. He dreamed up this "nutty" idea of breaking into the armory in order to impress his fellow Marines. "I'm not saying he didn't know it was wrong, but he was driven by his background." Later, Ng attached himself to Leonard Lake, who "took him in" and acted as his "anchor."

After being arrested in Canada, Kelley explained, Ng developed an "incredibly" close relationship with attorney Michael Burt. "From time to time, Ng and I have had trouble," Kelley admitted, and attributed it, in part, to Ng's need for Burt as an "anchor."

Another factor the jury could consider, Kelley said, was the exemplary behavior shown by Ng in prison, where he'd been kept almost all of his adult life, and where he had sponsored Korean orphans and "rescued" another inmate from antisocial behavior.

Ng had not been treated well in prison, said Kelley. He was subjected to unnecessary isolation, treated like a convict while being held in custody to face trial, held in a cage at the Calaveras County court, and forced into uncomfortable rides in a van that made him physically ill. Yet, he had never reacted negatively. Instead, he "made origami art," to express himself peacefully.

"Life without parole is severe punishment," Kelley told jurors. "But that's what I'm asking you for." Expressing confidence that they would think about the things he'd said, Kelley thanked the jury, and called his first witness.

Dr. Stuart Grassian, psychiatrist, had studied Ng's prison records, and noted that the defendant had never been involved in any violence or escape attempts, despite what appeared to be harsh treatment. But, according to Grassian, it depressed him and impaired his ability to help with his defense. Observers wondered, then, just who had engineered all of the delays.

In the Marine Corps, said the doctor, Ng had liked the "semper fi" concept, meaning "always faithful," but had not been accepted by men around him, which made him feel "debased and valueless." The dependent personality disorder afflicting Ng, Grassian observed, had started during his childhood in Hong Kong. The armory break-in, according to Grassian, stemmed from Ng's failure to achieve any success and to be accepted. "He had to do something glorious in his mind, and this caper was it."

In cross-examination, Sharlene Honnaka revealed that the doctor had not bothered to view the "M Ladies" tape, so he couldn't comment on Ng's aggressive treatment of the two female victims. A few observers wondered how this defendant, if suffering from "dependent personality disorder," could have asserted himself so strongly during the armory raid. And when Lake had stolen photos of the wife of Ng's pal, how had Ng so forcefully recovered them?

Ng's aunt testified in her native Chinese language, which required an interpreter, and told of beatings Charles had endured as a child. Later, as a youth in San Francisco, Ng had backed her car into a neighbor's vehicle, and had immediately contacted the owner. Kelley wanted the jury to see that the defendant honestly accepted responsibility for the accident.

Peter Smith asked her if Ng's father had worked long hours and had put high value on education. Yes, she said.

On Tuesday, April 13, three guards at Folsom Prison, two males and one female, described Ng's docile behavior while in custody there. He had always acted with courtesy, never swore or attempted any violence, and had avoided any trouble. A fourth officer, who had been part of the team transporting him from Folsom to San Andreas for court hearings, spoke of his trouble-free conduct. The arduous round-trip, he said, was exhausting and uncomfortable, but Ng had remained courteous and compliant.

A Department of Corrections counselor who was in frequent

contact with the prisoner added to the accolades regarding Ng's behavior while incarcerated.

Two of the prison personnel witnesses were built like professional football linebackers. In back row whispers, a couple of reporters agreed that they would damn well behave, too, under the control of those guys.

At 11:25 that morning, an earthquake rumbled across the southland. In the eleventh-floor courtroom, the shaking could easily be felt. With his usual aplomb, Judge Ryan said to the crowd, "Don't worry. If the building collapses, at least we'll be on top of everyone else."

More testimony about Ng's excellent comportment as a prisoner came from a Department of Corrections employee who worked in a prison library, and from two sheriff's deputies who manned the local jail.

A former Marine who'd known Ng at Camp Pendleton near San Diego spoke of the defendant's quiet conduct that never included smoking, drinking, drugs, or violence. Peter Smith drew from the witness that Ng had often practiced martial arts and wanted to imitate actor Bruce Lee.

Three more Marine veterans testified and spoke of Ng as "above average" in his military conduct, a quiet loner, a Marine "of the best order," and an "outstanding weapons handler." All of the witnesses had been surprised when they heard of Ng's involvement in the armory break-in.

Ng had made several friends since being jailed in Orange County, by mail correspondence and by phone. One man had contacted him regarding a mutual interest in origami, and had developed a fondness for Ng. According to the witness, he'd lost his father, and Ng had provided comfort through "genuine concern." He considered Ng a true friend. "His convictions for murder do not affect me one bit," the witness declared.

Another origami buff had seen Ng on television and written

to him. "Now, we speak on the phone three or four times a week. If Ng is taken out of my life, I would feel a sense of loss."

Sally Jean Pyle, the woman who had corresponded with Ng in Leavenworth, and had eventually spent a conjugal hour with him in an Oklahoma motel, candidly told her story to the jury. She concluded by saying, "I cared a great deal for him, and I still do."

On Wednesday, April 14, most of the morning was used in hearings to determine if a juror had inappropriately spoken about the case with someone outside the courtroom. She denied any wrongdoing, but Judge Ryan replaced her with an alternate to avoid any appeals issue on the matter.

Two male cousins of the defendant testified in the afternoon, recalling happy boyhood memories, and saying that his family still loved him. Dr. Paul Leung, another psychiatrist, gave an analysis of Asian family dynamics in Hong Kong, showing how dependent personality disorder could have developed.

Kelley's parade of witnesses extended into Thursday with a "social cultural development" officer from the Saskatchewan penitentiary under whom Ng had performed as editor and type-setter of the prison newspaper. The witness said Ng's perfor-mance was excellent. "It was a pleasure to have an employee of his caliber."

Ng had reportedly helped convert a violent, antisocial inmate at the Edmonton prison into a well-behaved model prisoner. Lewis Clapp had traveled north to interview Lance Blanchard, the large, ungainly convict, and videotaped the meeting. Kelley played the tape so that jurors could hear Blanchard's own words, which were highly complimentary of Ng.

An expert in prison behaviorism, who'd worked twenty-three

years for the California Department of Corrections, told jurors he had analyzed Ng's history of confinement from reports, and found that he had adjusted well to the prison environment.

On Monday, April 19, Kelley introduced his twenty-fourth witness in the penalty phase, Dr. Abraham Nievod, an expert in clinical psychology. He spoke for most of two days, attempting to mitigate Ng's behavior in the videotaped torture of Kathi Allen and Brenda O'Connor and the defendant's participation in drawing the obscene cartoons in concert with Maurice Laberge. The doctor supported previous diagnoses of dependent personality disorder. The strongest portion of his exhaustive testimony came when he played the "M Lady" tape, frequently stopping it to explain in detail his opinion of causative factors driving Ng to participate in the threats, taunts, and stripping of the women. The doctor also threw in analysis of Lake's behavior, as well. Generally, according to Nievod, Ng was trying to "mirror" and please Leonard Lake.

The prosecution had emphasized Lake's use of the word "we" as he spoke to the two enslaved women. Use of the plural pronoun, they insisted, was evidence that Ng had fully participated in the previous crimes and would continue to do so. Kelley put a question to Dr. Nievod suggesting that, in the old days, when a king or monarch used the word "we," he was using the term as a "royal we," meaning he spoke for the country or for his subjects. The doctor concurred with Kelley's view that Lake used the "royal we," as a sign of authority. "He really wants the person he is talking to, to think there are more people behind him" and that the victim is totally alone. "It reinforces the manipulation."

In regard to Ng ripping and cutting off Brenda O'Connor's blouse and bra, Nievod wavered somewhat in his rationalization of the actions. "I think Charles goes overboard here, and it is pretty awful because she becomes immediately afraid once he starts using the knife to cut her blouse. But he is still taking his orders from Lake . . . and to please Lake."

At 3:45 on the afternoon of April 20, one of the most touching witnesses of all was called by Bill Kelley. Kenneth Ng, the father who had been pitilessly criticized for beating his son, walked slowly forward, stood stoop-shouldered while taking the oath, and seemed to be swallowed by the witness chair. A small, well-dressed man, wearing a gray pin-striped suit with a maroon tie, Kenneth Ng's face appeared clouded with sadness. Bags under his eyes suggested years of worry and hard work, and the nearly total absence of a chin made him appear meek and humble, certainly not the child-beating monster that had been portrayed. He agreed to testify in English, without an interpreter. Within a few minutes, though, he apologized, saying, "I am sorry because maybe my English is not very good. So it is hard for you people to understand. But I will try to explain."

Judge Ryan, clearly sympathetic to the man, answered, "You are doing very well with your English, Mr. Ng."

"Well, I didn't go to school much," the witness confessed. "It is only about one or two year. But I learned English when I try to—I learn it from English Army actually."

The senior Ng described his own tragic, poverty-stricken childhood during WWII, and how it made him understand the importance of a good education for his own son. "So, you know, at that time schooling in Hong Kong was quite tough because good school is hard to get in. But I tried so hard." He said he had virtually begged Catholic school headmasters to admit his children, and had convinced them despite not being Catholic, and in face of competition from wealthy professionals in Hong Kong. "I am working class," he explained, "sometimes working seven days a week."

It was necessary for his son to achieve good grades to stay in the school, he said. "I mean if your study is no good, they just kick you out."

The media coverage of his son's activities had deeply embarrassed and saddened the family, Ng said. Tears welled in the eyes of observers when he said, "Our family, we feel very sad, too, and we feel sorry about—so I keep asking myself, why we try to give them the best and try to teach them good if it come out like this. I don't understand." He added, "And also, I feel for all involved . . . I also feel very sorry for those people, the family who involved in this case.

"I want to tell you decent people, because I come up in a family like this . . . you need a good education. So I try to give my children good education, try to bring them up good. And I don't know how to say, I don't know Charles was involved in these things. I just don't know how to say to you good people." It was one of the most profound apologies ever heard in a courtroom.

Asked if he had punished Charles when the boy hadn't done his homework, Ng nodded his head. "Yes, of course. I am very angry. I beat him with a stick. It is really hard . . . but I didn't know. And now they are teaching . . . is different way than the old way we do." Admitting that his wife had unsuccessfully tried to intercede, Ng said, "Now I look back, well, maybe this not the way to teaching the children, I know. If I can pull back twenty or thirty years backward, the way teaching children may be different." Trying not to show his own emotions, the little man said, "I punish him—because I love him—I love him. I want my children to be good."

Ng had tried to discourage his boy's interest in martial arts, he said, because he wanted him to concentrate on academics.

Several times during his testimony, Kenneth Ng looked toward his son, but the defendant gazed steadfastly at the table in front of him.

In reference to his profession as a salesman, Ng made a confession that won him a place in the hearts of observers and jurors, plus a high measure of credibility. "My family is Christian, but unfortunately I am bad Christian because, you know, I feel when you are doing sales, you are a liar. Your are a bigger liar because you try to sell stuff, and you don't have honest word anyhow.''

Speaking of his own military experience, he once again apologized for his language usage. ''I pick up English in Army, and self-learned. So maybe I am speaking wrong, so please excuse me.'' He wondered if Charles had tried to emulate the military experience by joining the U.S. Marines.

After Kenneth Ng answered questions about the difficulty of visiting his son in prison, Lewis Clapp asked, ''Would you like to have Charles be in your life alive so you can still have contact with him?''

''Yes, of course. I know after this thing I do hope I still having him either in the jail instead of death. Because after all, he is our only son. And the foolish way he did, we didn't know and try to—we got no chance to teach him and to stop him. I am very regrets. I am very sorry about the people who involves it, the family, I do feel very sorry for them.''

Lola Stapley, in the second row, whispered, ''Oh, what a nice man!'' Human emotions in a trial are immeasurable.

Peter Smith's gentle cross-exam reinforced many of Kenneth Ng's earlier statements. There was no attempt to impeach or humiliate him.

The defense had made some headway in creating the picture of Charles Ng as an abused child. But the reversal in strategy, by putting Kenneth Ng on the stand to appeal to the jury's sympathy, appeared to be far more effective. One reporter said, ''He just saved his son's life.''

The last witness in a long, convoluted, exhausting trial took the stand on Wednesday, April 21, 1999. Charles Ng's mother, Oi Ping, testified through an interpreter. She spoke of crowded living conditions and overprotectiveness in Hong Kong. She recalled her son's pets: a chicken that was killed and cooked, a turtle that was "too smelly" to keep, and a dog she feared, which she had forced Charles to release in a park. Their son was beaten by his father, Oi Ping said, in an effort to motivate the boy to complete his schoolwork. After Charles had been sent to England to live with an uncle while attending school, Oi Ping personally brought him home, because she didn't like the relative's treatment of her son. News stories had hurt her deeply, she said, because they "describe Charles as a devil . . . we were very shameful."

During visits to her son in prison, said Oi Ping, "he doesn't say anything to me. I felt very, very hurt, because I came from so far away." A relative had explained to her, she stated, that "he felt that he was all chained up, his feet and his hands are bound, he doesn't really want us to see him, so he doesn't like us to visit him."

Lewis Clapp asked, "If he is executed, how would it affect you?"

"I will be very sad, of course."

Peter Smith's cross-exam lasted two minutes, after which he thanked her and said, "I have no other questions."

Bill Kelley announced, "The defense rests."

Now, only the final act remained: final arguments by both sides.

Chapter 35

"Good morning ladies and gentlemen ...," began Peter Smith on Thursday, April 22, as he stood in front of twelve attentive jurors and two alternates. He appeared relaxed, hands behind his back, right fingers grasping his left thumb.

"I would like to begin by asking you to consider two numbers that I am going to write on this board." He picked up a broad-tipped marking pen, printed the numbers "11" and "10" on white easel paper, and asked jurors "to consider them as they relate to this case."

"Those two numbers stand for eleven murders in ten months. Eleven murders you found this defendant, Charles Ng, guilty of in the first degree." Smith pointed an accusing finger at Ng, who stared blankly forward through his thick lenses.

"The people are asking that you return a verdict of death. That is obvious." Smith lingered a few minutes on reminding the jurors of their duty to weigh mitigating versus aggravating factors, and provided a brief definition of the terms. Sitting momentarily on the end of a table, he fell silent as in deep thought, then asked, "What is fair in this case? Think about it, ladies and gentlemen . . . how do you get around the significance of eleven human lives? How does any evidence the defense presented mitigate the murder of eleven human beings?"

Using an enlarged photo of the Wilseyville house, Smith commented on the horror that had taken place there.

The surviving families were victims, as well, Smith said. "I ask that you have sympathy for them." Kenneth Ng and his wife had also suffered, he declared, but asked the jurors not to allow that to mitigate the crimes of Charles Ng. "He doesn't deserve it . . . he has victimized not only these eleven people and their families, but he has victimized his family, as well."

Naming each of the missing and murdered people, posting photographs, and recalling personal facts about each of their lives, Smith asked that they not be forgotten. When he spoke of Kathleen Allen, the district attorney played segments of the tape once more.

Using photographs of Lonnie Bond, happily smiling while holding his baby boy, Smith switched into a jarring contrast with a recollection of Bond's body as it was discovered buried inside a sleeping bag.

Playing the tape segment of Brenda O'Connor, Smith asked, "Did you hear the terror in her voice crying out for her baby?" Each of the jurors watched soberly, a few of them close to tears. Several observers in the gallery wondered if the often repeated use of the tapes would reduce the power of them or have a desensitizing effect on the jurors. But Viola Najar, juror number four, would later refute that idea. "The first time I saw the tapes," she said, "they really didn't bother me much at all. But each time they played them, I saw something new; more of what had happened to those two women. The repetition had a cumulative effect of horror. I think it was a good strategy by the prosecutors.''

When Peter Smith began to speak of Scott Stapley's death, his mother sobbed, as did Sharon Sellitto sitting near her. Their heartbreak seemed to affect three jurors, whose tears also began to spill. Sellitto had returned for the ending phase, but had left her mother at home in Ohio.

Smith commented on the defense tactics of seeking sympathy for Ng due to his difficult childhood, his prison behavior, his ''alleged mental disorders,'' and his origami art. The ''abusive childhood,'' said Smith, didn't ring true. Ng had lived in relative comfort in a crowded society. The punishment from his father was consistent with standards of the time and the culture. Smith commented on Charles Ng's upbringing as compared to the impoverished, tragic background of the father, Kenneth Ng. To observers, the inference was clear; Kenneth Ng had suffered as a child, too, but certainly hadn't murdered anyone. He had only tried to make a good life for his children and provide them with a quality education. ''Charles Ng would go on picnics, had swimming lessons. His family had a car, which was rare in Hong Kong at that time. He led a privileged life.''

Ng's isolation in a Canadian prison, said Smith, was ''tough,'' but was it as tough as the defense implied? ''He took a number of correspondence courses . . . and he was the only inmate who had a hot plate in his cell where he cooked rice.'' Smith noted that another prisoner, Lance Blanchard, had testified about Ng becoming his mentor, and that they had conversed eight to ten hours a day. Ng not only had a computer in his cell, he also had worked on a newspaper staff. Smith asked, ''How is this consistent with dependent personality disorder?''

At Folsom, Smith said, the defendant had an upper bunk full of books, a phone, visiting privileges, and extensive library usage. Smith admitted that the cage in Calaveras County looked ''pretty inhumane,'' but explained that it was used only as a temporary holding cell for two-way protection. ''If you have any problems with that cell," Smith remarked, "I ask that you think of Kathleen Allen and the time she spent in the bunker cell." In the Orange County jail, Smith said, Ng had established relationships with people on the outside. "So, was his life really that tough, as the defense wants you to believe? Maybe not." Smith added a reminder that Ng had fled from custody in Hawaii, driving home the point that he might attempt escape if given the opportunity.

Smith scoffed at the proposition that Ng's skill at origami should be considered as a mitigating factor to save his life. The defendant's other artistic skill, noted Smith, had been used to "satirize" murder and other horrific acts. "Satire? What is funny about that?"

The defense had praised Ng's sponsorship of orphans while in prison. Smith, in answer to Ng's alleged patronage and concern for children, indignantly said, "I have two names for you when you consider this—think of Sean Dubs and Lonnie Bond Jr."

Moving on to the issue of mental disorders, Smith pointed out that protracted testimony from psychiatrists stemmed from their evaluations *after* Ng had committed the crimes. Furthermore, said Smith, the defendant had taken psychology courses before he was evaluated and examined. "Most importantly," Ng had refused to submit himself to a court-ordered psychiatric exam arranged by the prosecution. "And remember what two doctors said: In their opinions, Mr Ng has this dependent personality disorder, but he is not void of free will, choice, or knowing right from wrong." Challenging the diagnosis of dependent personality disorder, Smith reminded jurors that Ng had depended on no one other than himself in making decisions to join the Marines, breaking into a military armory, and running to Canada after being caught shoplifting.

"So, at what point does Mr. Ng realize that what he is doing with Leonard Lake is wrong? After the first murder? Probably. After the second murder? More than likely. After the third murder? Certainly. Why does he keep coming back?. . . . He is living in San Francisco by himself. He has a job. He is functioning as an independent person . . . but he keeps coming back to Calaveras County, keeps getting himself involved in these murders—eleven murders. And why does he do that, ladies and gentlemen of the jury? The people suggest that he is doing so because he likes to kill.''

Summarizing the life and crimes of Ng, Smith said, ''It is not his father's responsibility. It is not his mother's. It is not his culture. It is not Hong Kong. It is not the Marine Corps. It is not Leavenworth. It is not the prisons in Canada. It is not the prisons here in California. It is Charles Ng's responsibility. He is responsible for eleven lives.''

For the last time, Smith directed the jury's attention to television screens to view the torture and taunting of Kathi Allen and Brenda O'Connor. He spoke in an earnest appeal. ''That is Charles Ng's legacy, ladies and gentlemen of the jury. That, and the fact that he has been found guilty of eleven murders. He has earned the death penalty, and the people of the state of California ask that you give it to him. Thank you very much.''

Peter Smith had spoken for forty-five minutes.

Judge Ryan had agreed that the defense could deliver their final arguments on Monday.

Lewis Clapp worked the entire weekend preparing his presentation. Wearing a dark gray suit with subtle blue pinstripes, he waited nervously on Monday morning for his colleague James Merwin to complete a few last-minute motions. Clapp couldn't help but think of advice he'd once received during his membership in a choir. The director had singled him out and said, ''Lewis, you must put more heart into your singing.'' Facing one of the most crucial trial duties in his career, Clapp hoped he would be able to put enough heart into the final phase of the proceedings.

He stood at 9:50 A.M. and greeted the jury. "It's been a long trial and it's taken a toll on you, and on me," he said, his voice surprisingly steady and strong. "I want to thank you for your honest effort to reach just verdicts."

Clapp took issue with the prosecutor's use of "the people" as a collective representation of their side. "There are many people," said the defender, "who do not want the death of Charles Ng."

This case, Clapp argued, "is not about whether the victims' lives had value. It's not about grief felt by victims' families. It's not about killing the defendant to find closure. It's about doing justice within the framework of the law."

Using a poster-board chart, he spent a few minutes defining mitigating versus aggravating factors, and suggested, "I am trying to help you."

Offering considerations for weighing the evidence the jury had seen and heard, Clapp noted that "many of the documents were forged by Lake or Cricket," and that "almost all property of significant value was in the possession or turned over by Cricket."

One of the major factors in the case, Clapp declared, "was how involved Cricket was."

Just as Peter Smith had posted two numbers for the jury to consider, Clapp posted an eighteen and a zero on his chart. Eighteen, he said, represented the number of murders Cricket had been given immunity for. Zero, said Clapp, was the number of days she had spent in custody.

Turning from his opinions about Balazs, Clapp directed his fury toward Leonard Lake. "He was a killer, no question about that, before Charles Ng ever came along."

About the families seeking closure, Clapp wondered if it could really happen. "Closure is not a legal term and it's not used in court. Closure is a term popular in the nineties as a finality to something tragic. But what it really means is a license for revenge." Spectators shifted in their seats, frowns on their faces. "Our system is not about revenge," said Clapp to the jury. "You are not a tool for revenge. You are not anyone's personal executioner. I'm asking you not to allow closure, which is really nothing but revenge."

In a quick review of Ng's crimes, other than homicide, Clapp said his client had been caught shoplifting in Canada because he needed food, and that the armory break-in was committed by Ng as a brash youth looking for approval from fellow Marines. "If you think about Ng's life, there was not a single act of violence unassociated with Leonard Lake."

Ng's childhood, the defender said, had been characterized by beatings and loneliness. He was forced to submit to authority. These abuses had provided the roots for his mental illness. "We gave you five doctors' opinions that he has dependent personality disorder, and the prosecution didn't refute that." Ng's illness allowed Lake to dominate him, said Clapp. As the defender spoke, Sharon Sellitto rose and marched out of the courtroom, but returned within a few minutes. She and several observers wondered how Ng could be so subservient to a criminal, yet so resistant to the authority of the law, lawyers, and judges.

Clapp asserted, "If Ng hadn't met Leonard Lake, the psychopathic killer, we wouldn't be here today."

Juror Karen Barrett noticed something about the defendant that gave her an odd feeling. The attractive, young woman, who spoke with a charming English accent, at first thought she imagined it, but it soon became apparent that her mind was not playing tricks. Charles Ng appeared to be making an attempt to establish eye contact with her. Barrett averted her gaze each time, embarrassed and uncomfortable.

* * *

Emotionally charged words are often used by lawyers in the all-important final arguments. Clapp used them liberally. He made an allusion to the jury "deciding to order Ng's execution." Juries, of course, do not order anything. They arrive at a verdict.

In a departure from such firm declarations, Clapp appeared humble when he said, "Here's where I'm on shaky ground, because I don't know what you were thinking when you found him guilty of eleven murders." He rhetorically asked, "Did you decide he was the actual killer?" Pacing nervously, Clapp explained, "Ng does not have to be the triggerman to be guilty under the conspiracy theory. There is no strong evidence that he was the actual killer. So the question remains, what was Mr. Ng's level of participation?"

Having established the central question, Clapp inquired further. "I offer this," he said.

"What if Mr. Ng was part of a conspiracy to help Lake obtain property?

"What if Mr. Ng was part of a conspiracy to control Kathi Allen and Brenda O'Connor?

"What if Mr. Ng knew about the murders but didn't stop them?

"What if Mr. Ng chose not to break away from Leonard Lake?

"What if Mr. Ng rationalized in his own mind that the crimes were Lake's problem?"

Letting the list of questions hang in the air for a moment, Clapp asked, "How certain are you that wasn't the attitude he had? Perhaps he didn't do the actual killing. If so, is he as deserving of death as someone who is the actual killer?"

Again reverting to emotional language, Clapp said, "If you are going to kill a man, you should have no doubt he was the actual killer."

Jurors, he said, can give weight to factors of sympathy in considering the death penalty. For Ng, Clapp explained, such factors could include his upbringing, mental illness, his shy personality, his service as a Marine, and his adjustment to prison despite terrible conditions. The prison behavior, Clapp pointed out, demonstrates that life without parole might be a better alternative.

Even his kind treatment of the Oklahoma woman with whom he corresponded in Leavenworth, and later met, showed Ng's value as a person, said Clapp, adding that the sexual encounter "was a shame because it kind of cheapened what happened."

"Charles Ng is not a monster," Clapp reiterated. "People want to pigeonhole him as such. But he has a value to other human beings."

Holding up photos of Korean orphans Ng had sponsored, and of his family, Clapp said, "You know his family loves him. Don't say he should be killed because he brought pain to them." The defender opened a folder, and read aloud messages from a sister who was unable to attend the hearings, begging for his life to be saved.

Life in prison without the possibility of parole, said Clapp, is a "horrendous penalty. . . . You are controlled and ordered around at every point of daily life. You are owned by the state. There is no contact with loved ones. There is emptiness, overwhelming despair, and a daily longing for what you can't have. The rest of your miserable life is nothing but pain and sadness. That is enough for a man like Charles Ng."

Informing the jurors that they were not required to vote for death, Clapp closed his argument by suggesting four considerations the jurors could entertain. "You may exercise mercy while giving justice. You may decline doing another senseless, needless killing. You may decline bringing grief to Ng's loved ones. And you may decline ordering this execution, because it is not necessary."

Taking a deep breath and pausing as if to be certain he hadn't forgotten anything, Lewis Clapp said, "Thank you for your attention and for your hard work. I leave the life of Charles Ng in your hands." He had spoken for 2½ hours.

Judge Ryan read the required formal instructions to the jury. Court clerk Terri Walsh administered the swearing in of bailiff Roger Hilton to accept responsibility for the jury's welfare. The nine women and three men filed into the deliberations room to consider a matter of life and death, literally.

It took them three days of discussions, tears, sleepless nights, nightmares, tension, more discussions, emotional trauma, and finally, a resolution. On Wednesday, they decided to take the first vote. It came out eleven for the death penalty, and one undecided. The one juror asked for more time to think it over. The individual's ruminations took several days.

Juror Karen Barrett waited at home on Friday while the reluctant juror pondered the tough decision. Her phone rang. Expecting a call, she answered with her customary cheery "Hello."

A male voice asked, "Is this Karen Barrett?"

Puzzled, she asked in turn, "Well, who is this?"

Without identifying himself, the caller said, "I need to know if this is the Karen Barrett I know."

Now growing alarmed by the odd behavior, Barrett repeated, "Who is this?"

"This is Charles," he said.

Momentarily she wondered if it was her ex-husband, but the voice wasn't quite right. Nervous but curious, she inquired, "Charles who?"

Once more the caller insisted, "I need to know if this is the Karen I know on the jury."

In a flash, it dawned on Barrett. She later commented, "The voice recognition kicked in." Incredulously she asked, "Is this Charles Ng?"

The caller answered cryptically, "Oh, I'm sorry. I just wanted to tell you I think you are very nice."

Stunned, confused, and wondering if it was really the defendant, Barrett said, "Well, I can't— You know, how did you get my number? How did you get a hold of me?"

"I had a friend help me."

Barrett wanted no more of this crazy contact. Indignantly she said, "You can't talk to me," and slammed the receiver down. She felt her cheeks turn hot, and tears forming in her eyes. Without even thinking, she telephoned Deputy Marshal Roger Hilton in Judge Ryan's courtroom. Hilton calmed her and reported the incident to Ryan.

On Monday, the jurors assembled in the deliberations room, and made the verdict unanimous. But before it could be announced, Judge Ryan held a hearing, closed to the public and press, to evaluate the impact of Barrett's mysterious caller. On the witness stand, the bewildered juror testified that she could not positively identify the voice as Charles Ng. No, she said, the call would have no effect on her ability to arrive at a fair verdict. Ryan asked her not to divulge the incident to anyone, not even the other jurors.

Information about Ng's use of telephones in jail revealed that no restrictions had been placed on his telephone privileges. The jurors' identities had never been made public, much less their phone numbers or addresses. No one admitted knowing how Ng had obtained the name and number of Karen Barrett. Ng had nothing to say about the matter, but Barrett's number was later found in his cell.

Shortly after noon on Monday, the jurors filed out of their room, faces grim, and took their seats in the jury box. Each of the twelve would never forget the moment.

Bonnie Reinhardt fought off a terrible urge to run from the room.

Norm Schickedanz felt the weight of the decision, but endured it with a sense of pride. Later, quoting Thomas Jefferson's observation that jury service was equal to service in war, Shickedanz said, "This wasn't our duty, this was an honor. It's what makes our system work."

Karen Barrett trembled with a case of nerves after the strange phone call, but knew that she had voted according to the evidence, her heart, and her conscience.

Viola Najar's thoughts focused on the "monumental" decision in which she had participated. Despite the stress she'd endured, she was convinced she'd made the right choice.

Diana Ribaudo, a first-time juror, thought of the victims' families and the tears she had shed during their testimony.

Denise Coon realized it was a moment in her life that would remain with her forever.

Terrie Macias, remembering the two murdered babies, felt a profound sadness, offset by the joy of her own pregnancy.

Kelli Maynard reflected on how tough it had been to make the decision, but accepted in her heart and mind that it was the only correct one.

Paul Williams felt a giant sense of relief, and confidence that all twelve jurors had given the defendant every possible consideration for leniency, but could find no sympathy for him.

Heidi Falcon could feel herself trembling, and pondered the huge responsibility of delivering such an important verdict. But, in a flash of clarity, she knew they had done the right thing.

Nancy McEwan felt a great sense of emotion, but also a clear conscience about the responsible way the jury had weighed the evidence.

The remaining two alternates, even though they had not joined the other twelve in deliberations, had similiar thoughts and emotions. Patty McSwain wondered, "Who died and made us God?'' But with a mental picture of Brenda O'Connor's mother smiling through tears as she spoke of her dead daughter and grandson, McSwain knew she would have voted for death. The other alternate, Renee Oran, had thought, philosophically, ''Even that SOB deserved a fair trial.''

The foreman, Mauricio Velarde, a U.S. Marine Corps reservist, wondered, ''Who am I to make a decision of life and death?'' But, in his heart, he knew he had done his duty. He delivered the verdict form to Judge Ryan, who read it and handed it to clerk Terri Walsh.

The packed courtroom fell silent.

Walsh read aloud from the signed paper, then came to the climactic announcement that resounded with a single word: ''Death.''

In California, Superior Court judges must review voluminous documentation before formally passing sentence. Judge Ryan set June 30 as the date he would make the verdict formal.

It had been the costliest trial in California history, using an estimated 20 million dollars of taxpayers' money.

It came as no surprise to the crowd in a standing-room-only courtroom on Wednesday, June 30, that Ng's lawyers needed to argue several motions before sentencing could take place. Judge Ryan limped to his elevated desk, still suffering from surgery to his leg a week earlier. News spread that Ng, on the day Ryan underwent the surgery, had filed a motion to disqualify the judge, and thus cause more postponements.

Eight of the jurors and two alternates sat in a section reserved for them near the bailiff's desk, hoping for catharsis from the final act.

Moments after Ryan opened the proceedings by ordering bailiffs to remove the convicted killer's shackles, defender Lewis Clapp rose to plea for a delay. His client, Clapp said, had been awake all night because jailers had packed all of his material, and strip-searched him, in preparation for the anticipated move to San Quentin's death row. Ng sat at the end of counsel table with his eyes closed. Just a short time earlier, he had also completed hand printing another motion.

Judge Ryan asked a couple of questions about the previous night's events, and said, "I've read his motion. It was obviously written by someone with his faculties intact." He denied the request for a delay.

Regarding the effort to disqualify him, Ryan stated that no legal grounds supported the move. "Motion denied."

Defender James Merwin spent several minutes reading and discussing a motion about the the juror who had allegedly received a telephone call from Ng. Sharlene Honnaka protested. "It's ludicrous," she said, "to ask for relief in a trial based on a telephone call by the defendant to a juror."

Before Ryan could inquire further, Lewis Clapp rose again. "Your Honor, Mr. Ng is so weary, he's dozing off."

Remaining calm, Ryan asked Ng how he felt. The defendant slurred his words. "Not able to concentrate. No sleep. Up all night working on motion."

Ryan asked, "If your boxes were packed, how did you do that?" Ng mumbled something else, and the judge snapped, "He's alert. Let's proceed. He is not falling asleep; that is clear to the court." The no-nonsense judge won a new level of admiration from disgusted spectators.

Honnaka, addressing again the mistrial motion based on the defendant's telephone call to a juror, said, "This action is based on his own misconduct, so Mr. Ng is not entitled to any relief."

Ryan, sounding tired and impatient, listened to the arguments, and made his ruling: "Denied. Next issue."

Clapp stood again to appeal for a sentence of life without parole, citing the opinion that Leonard Lake was the actual killer and that evidence had never shown Ng as the triggerman.

Ryan explained how the law required him, as the judge, to weigh mitigating versus aggravating circumstances in order to make a ruling. He summarized the evidence related to all eleven counts for which Ng had been convicted. As he spoke, Ng sat with his eyes closed, as if asleep. The judge pointed out that Leonard Lake had probably commited murder prior to Ng's arrival, but had never killed multiple victims, such as the Dubs family, before Ng joined him. Regarding murders of Ng's coworkers, "he certainly was the connection," said Ryan. And Ng had no doubt established the link to Mike Carroll, which led to Kathi Allen. Regarding Allen and O'Connor, the judge said, "The tape speaks for itself." In the other counts, Ng had confessed helping bury two bodies. Ryan explained, "If one person could do the killings, one person could have done the burying." The inference was clear—Ng had been Lake's partner in both activities.

Yes, said Ryan, there was some mitigation in the fact that Lake apparently exerted some domination over Ng. "The bunker was completed before Ng left Leavenworth, Lake knew how to make bodies disappear, and he had killed his brother and his best friend. . . . Also, the murders of Kathleen Allen and Brenda O'Connor were the culmination of Lake's fantasy and his project. These are mitigating factors."

Several people in the packed gallery began to squirm and wonder if Ryan would, indeed, exercise his power to overturn the jury verdict, and send Ng to prison for life.

The issue seemed in even greater jeopardy when Ryan recalled that psychiatrists had diagnosed Ng with various personality disorders, which probably led to Ng's subordination to Lake. But Ryan calmed some fears when he noted that the psychiatric testimony, in the court's opinion, was weak. "One would wonder how an individual with such disorders could teach Taoism to a violent criminal, or burglarize a military armory, or escape from the [Hawaiian] Islands, then flee from California to Canada." Ng had also "taken on" every trial

judge he had faced, observed Ryan, who quickly stated he
wouldn't use that issue in his consideration. "And how about
his demeanor in court?" asked Ryan. He instantly added, "Nah,
I'll strike that." But, he said, he didn't think the psychiatrist
testimony deserved much weight.

An important element of the trial had been the statements
from the late Maurice Laberge, jailhouse informant, regarding
Ng's alleged confessions. Said Ryan, "Even if some of Laberge's charges were false, he had too many details to disregard
what he said."

The defense had emphasized mistreatment by Ng's father.
Ryan agreed that such abuse is not acceptable, but noted that
"we also heard good things the father did." It would have
carried more weight, said the judge, if the treatment had been
entirely cruel.

Other factors he had examined, said Ryan, included Ng's
behavior in prison and adjustment to confinement despite harsh
treatment, plus Ng's artistic skills, and his sponsorship of
Korean orphans.

The tension had built among observers, but Ryan relieved
it when he said, "This court finds that the aggravating factors
are so substantial . . . and outweigh the mitigating circumstances. The motion is denied to strike the special circumstances. So is the motion to modify the jury's verdict."

Peter Smith asked the judge to allow victims' families to
speak. But Bill Kelley objected, citing the irrelevance of such
speeches, which would not be considered by the judge in passing sentence. Ryan overruled him.

As a relative of victim Clifford Peranteau stepped forward,
Lewis Clapp rose again to announce two more motions. A loud
sigh passed through the audience. The defender wanted the
judge to first consider yet another Marsden hearing in which
Ng wished to fire his defense attorneys, and to hear Ng's request
to absent himself during statements from victims' families. At
10:15 A.M., Ryan cleared the courtroom to hear the Marsden

issue. One hour and forty-five minutes later, the crowd filed back in and took their seats.

Judge Ryan, speaking for the record, said that during the closed hearing, Ng had been awake and alert. If he'd lost sleep the night before, it had been his own choosing. He had rejected the Marsden motion.

Seven relatives of murdered victims wished to speak. William Peranteau, Clifford's brother, led off by stating that the loss had changed many lives in his family. "Some of us have become stronger, some weaker. Most of all, we, too, are victims." Through the years, none of them had ever seen any signs of remorse by Ng. It had been impossible, said Peranteau, for his mother and siblings to accept Clifford's death. The family hoped that Ng would be executed. When the speaker addressed Ng directly, demanding that he stop "acting like a coward" and accept the punishment of death, Kelley objected. Peranteau read the last greeting card Cliff had sent to his mother, which he had ended by writing, "Mom, I love you and my family. Write soon. Your son, Cliff."

"That is all we have," said the distraught brother.

Kathleen Allen's younger sister sobbed as she appealed for Judge Ryan to give Ng a sentence of death. Jeffrey Nourse, cousin of Deborah Dubs, said, "They were just starting their lives together. Nothing can bring them back . . . we support the jury's decision."

Lonnie Bond's brother David choked as he said, "This is too much for anyone to bear. The only penalty for Charles Ng is death. The sooner the better."

During the emotional appeals, Charles Ng sat motionless, staring at nothing, his expression an inscrutable mask.

Sharron O'Connor, Brenda's mother, said, "May God forgive me, but I want Charles Ng dead!" She read aloud several notes from her offspring. One of them expressed the desire for Ng to suffer. "I want him to be afraid to die. I want to see the terror in his eyes as he is about to die." Another said her pain was so deep she'd thought, at times, about ending her own life. The mother lamented that it had almost ruined their very existence. The death verdict, she said, had appropriately been delivered on Brenda's birthday.

Dwight J. Stapley Jr., brother of Scott Stapley, with the help of his family, had written some comments that directly addressed Charles Ng. But he and his parents had been advised that it would be better to speak about Ng, not to him, so Stapley modified his delivery. Speaking first for himself, he recalled happier days, fifteen years earlier, when he and his brother had truly grown to know each other. "Now, that's all we have left." Bowing his head to the notes he held, Stapley read the words of his father, Dwight, stating that Ng had "devastated their lives." His voice breaking, Stapley said, "Fourteen years, two months, and eight days ago, after having shot Scott in his leg and his shoulder, Charles Ng or Leonard Lake shoved a gun into my son's mouth, shattering his teeth and breaking his jaw, making it impossible to identify Scott from dental records. Ng or Lake then pulled the trigger. If Scott was not already dead, it killed him instantly. I scream thinking of the terror Scott must have felt waiting for the final killing shots . . . I have cried. I have lived in grief . . . Charles Ng has deprived me of a part of my life." If anything good had come out of the tragedy, said Stapley, it was in learning that they need each other more than ever.

Lola Stapley spoke for five minutes. "My son will never get to live out his dreams . . . we will be scarred emotionally for the rest of our lives." She reminded everyone listening that Scott had been accepted into a master's degree program to obtain a teaching credential, and was only twenty-six when his life ended. Lola said that she felt compassion for Ng's parents, too. "But at least they will be able to visit their son . . . and speak to him on the telephone." Pausing to control her emotions, Lola said, "Never again will we see Scott's sweet face or hear his voice, his laugh or receive his teddy bear hugs." She would always miss the special greeting from Scott when he said, "Hi, Mamma Jo. What's up?"

Lola paused again, then unfolded a written statement by her daughter, Mary Dee Stapley The mother, in delivering the words, changed them from directly addressing Ng. The statement chastised Ng for the losses he had caused.

Lola then thanked everyone who had supported them over a period of fourteen years, and said, "We could never have survived without you."

Soft sobs and sniffles were the only sounds as she walked back to her chair next to Dwight, who held back his tears and smiled bravely at her.

While Ng sat slump-shouldered, a blank expression on his face, Judge Jack Ryan cleared his throat, and said in a resounding, strong voice, "Charles Chitat Ng, it is the judgment and sentence of this court . . . for eleven counts of murder for which the jury found you guilty, and the finding of 'true' in the special circumstance of multiple murder, and the jury's verdict of death, it is the order of the court that you be punished by death within the walls of San Quentin Prison at a time to be set by this court . . . in the manner prescribed by law."

A scattering of applause and cheers resounded through the gallery.

Peter Smith, in announcing that the state would request dismissal of murder charges against Charles Ng in the matter of Paul Cosner, asked that one last speaker be allowed. Sharon Sellitto, sister of Paul Cosner, rose from her chair, leaving her weeping mother in the second row, and walked to the lectern while Bill Kelley objected. Ryan ruled that she would be allowed to speak.

Sellitto began, "My mother at one time had two children . . .

but one of them vanished in November 1984." She summarized the traumatic search for Paul, the hiring of private detectives, the empty horror of never finding him, and the fourteen years of seeking justice. "When Ng confessed in Canada," Sellitto said, she had hoped he would eventually be convicted of Paul's murder. Closure eluded them, though. "It was stunning and breathtaking," Sellitto said. Having spoken many times in court and on television, she had usually kept her composure, but at this last opportunity to express her frustration and sadness, she began to tremble and cry. Carol Waxman, the pillar of strength from the Victim/Witness Program, stood beside Sellitto, a steadying arm around her shoulder, and gave her the strength to continue. "When I searched for my brother, there was television coverage. Ng was living in the same area, and saw me, but did nothing." Her voice filled with daggers. "Ng has shown nothing but contempt for life and the law. There is no remorse in him. He must be put to death. My mother and I have been his prisoner for too long." One by one, Sellitto listed each of the eleven victims, capped by her brother's name, and said, "They deserved to live. Charles Ng deserves to die. Only then will we be free."

A local attorney who had earlier been asked about the irony of a hung jury in the Paul Cosner issue suggested a silver lining to the dark cloud. He said that it demonstrated extreme and exhaustive deliberation by the jury, and showed that they had not simply given a knee-jerk reaction by lumping the cases all together. Moreover, said the lawyer, such care by the jury could very well impress appeals court justices that the deliberations had, indeed, been meticulous and sound.

Within three hours after Judge Jack Ryan declared the court recessed, Charles Chitat Ng had started the journey to San Quentin Prison, north of the Golden Gate Bridge, to join 540 other men on death row.

Several of them had been there for at least twenty years. Fewer than half had begun the automatic appeals that apply to capital punishment.

From the time of California's reinstatement of the death penalty in 1978, to the moment of Ng's sentence, the state had executed seven men. Several years earlier, lethal injection had replaced the old gas chamber as the method of execution.

Charles Ng is a master at filing legal motions. No one will be surprised when he fills the jurisprudence pipeline with an avalanche of writs and appeals. Unless Ng can find a way to force a new trial, and be exonerated, his life will eventually end just a few miles from the sites where several of his victims vanished.

The victims' families, and the majority of California's population, according to two general elections held to affirm the death penalty law, want the killer to be executed.

Oscar Wilde wrote, "For he who lives more lives than one/More deaths than one must die." There are many who think a single word should be substituted in that ballad. "For he who *takes* more lives than one/More deaths than one must die."

If Charles Ng is to be executed, is it for the people, for the victims' families, for justice, or for retribution? For whom should he die?

Among soft breezes rustling through the pines near Wilseyville, a visitor might hear any one of eleven muted voices whispering, "Die for me."

ACKNOWLEDGMENTS

As usual, my hat is off to Paul Dinas, Editor-in-Chief, Kensington Publishing Company, for his astute selection of this chronicle, and to Karen Haas for her nurture during the process of researching and writing it.

To assemble all the facts and to manage a project with the enormity of the Charles Ng–Leonard Lake story can be overwhelming. The trial extended from October 1998 to June 30, 1999. A staggering volume of court documents, transcripts, photos, videotapes, and other evidence consumed hundreds of hours to read, copy (many with handwritten notes), sort, and digest. Most of the documentary research for a true crime book is a solo task involving a great deal of time and several bottles of aspirin.

But examining documents is only half of the battle. Without interviews and discussions, it is impossible to flesh out the story properly. And that segment of the research requires boundless cooperation from victims' families, investigators, lawyers, reporters, and other knowledgeable insiders. I was extremely fortunate to receive abundant help from a long list of terrific people.

Mitch Hrdlicka, DA investigator for Calaveras County, is in every sense a gentleman who truly likes his fellow human beings. And, on top of that, he's a helluva good cop. His assistance was invaluable. So was the generous and thoughtful response given to me by Hrdlicka's boss, District Attorney Peter Smith. I can see why he won reelection to his post, and will probably win any election he seeks. Detective Sergeant Larry Copland joined Hrdlicka and me for lunch and conversation, making my trip to Calaveras County a real ''gold strike.''

Smith's opposite number in the case, Bill Kelley, patiently sat for interviews, and provided helpful insight into the defense case for Charles Ng. His colleague Lewis Clapp is a gentle man who always speaks with a courteous smile. One of their investigators, Kathy Sakoguchi writes remarkably comprehensive and literate reports, many of which land in the court records and provide journalists with extraordinary details.

Among the legions of journalists who sat through all or parts of the trial, and who shared insights with me, *Sacramento Bee* reporter Laura Mecoy tops the list. She not only assisted me in obtaining archived articles, but also helped crystallize concepts with her remarkable perception of events. It was quite helpful, as well, to chat with John McDonald from the *Orange County Register,* Daniel Yi of the *Los Angeles Times,* Bill Wallace of the *San Francisco Chronicle,* Linda Deutch of Associated Press, and Canadian journalists Jim Holt, Simon Avery, and Alan Cairns. Freelancer Craig Lockwood and psychologist Dr. Patrick Callahan also entered into spirited discussions with me during the trial.

In Southern California, nearly everyone recognizes KNBC

television reporter Vicky Vargas, and KCBS reporter Dave Lopez, both of whom exchanged information with me frequently.

My visit to San Francisco was enriched by two of the finest police investigators one could ever meet. Inspector Irene Brunn, who also attended segments of the trial, and Inspector Tom Eisenmann richly deserve the accolades I heard about them.

During the trial, I sat behind Dwight and Lola Stapley, and near Sharon Sellitto and her mother, Virginia Nessley. It's the most difficult part of researching a true crime book: feeling the pain victims' families endure while reliving the horrors. I admire their courage and deeply appreciate the help they gave me.

Other bereaved relatives who spoke to me include William Peranteau, Robert McCourt, Dian Allen, plus Sharron O'Connor and her daughters.

My neighbor Robert Schuller aided me in understanding the weapons mentioned, and two trial observers, Franco and Franca Sdringola, helped lighten up depressing days in the courtroom. My niece Kim Forsythe dug some material from the Internet for me. Bill Cook and Geoff Christison, keepers of the exhibits room in Orange County Superior Court, offered me their usual cheerful, courteous, and efficient help.

Judge John J. Ryan, of course, does not discuss the case outside of court. But I did appreciate his courteous greetings and congenial comments during the long months. I hold in very high regard his professional conduct, dignity, humor, and fairness. His reporter, Cheri Violette and clerk, Terri Walsh, provided gracious assistance and welcome smiles. Deputy Marshal Roger Hilton cracked wise when laughter was most needed.

I am extremely grateful to the jurors who gave me an exclusive group interview immediately after the trial. Bonnie Reinhardt coordinated a posttrial restaurant dinner, at which all twelve members, plus two alternates, spoke with me. Nancy McEwan later hosted a barbeque for them, and provided me with additional understanding of the process they endured. My sincere respect and admiration is extended to Bonnie, Nancy, foreman Mauricio Velarde, Denise Coon, Diana Ribaudo, Heidi Falcon, Karen Barrett, Kelli Maynard, Norm Schickedanz, Paul Williams, Terrie Macias, Viola Najar, Patty McSwain, Renee Oran, and Lynne Glenn. They suffered through months of trauma and personal sacrifice that left some of them emotionally wounded. Jury duty is sometimes the butt of jokes, but for these fine people, it was no joke. They served, did their duty, and deserve the heartfelt admiration of each and every one of us.

On a solemn Saturday afternoon, October 23, 1999, relatives of the murder victims gathered in San Andreas at the invitation of District Attorney Peter Smith. On a sun-splashed hillside, more than fifty mourners stood in silence near a new granite crypt that held many of the mortal remains. Smith's soothing voice paid tribute to both the living and the dead. "The purpose of this memorial," he said, "is to give everybody who was involved in this tragedy a chance to put some closure to it."

Afterward, when tears had dried and spirits had lifted, the relatives accepted Smith's invitation to join him in a final luncheon together and to "celebrate life." At last, they were able to laugh and share memories of their loved ones in a new light. The words engraved on the crypt would remain with them forever.

A few weeks earlier, when Mitch Hrdlicka made arrangements for the memorial vault, he suggested to his girlfriend, Jan Hamaker, that some special tribute should be engraved into the granite. Within a couple of hours, Jan handed to Mitch a few words she had written. He thought they were perfect.

The relatives took solace when they read the beautiful inscription.

In Wilseyville We Found You
Our Lost Ones
Though Taken In Darkness
You Will Forever Live In Light
Rest In Peace

Victims Of The 1984–85
Wilseyville Mass Murder

—Don Lasseter

MORE BONE-CHILLING STORIES FROM PINNACLE TRUE CRIME

From the Files of
True Detective
Magazine

HORRIFYING TRUE CRIME
FROM PINNACLE BOOKS